I0335491

Notes from the Second Dimension

Books by Christine Kromm Henrie and David Henrie

Published by Access Soul Knowledge

The Spiritual Design: Channeled Teachings, Wave 1

The Spiritual Design: Channeled Teachings, Wave 2

Notes from the Second Dimension; Volume 1

Helig Design: Kanaliserade Budskap; Första Vågen (Svenska Derivat)

Helig Design: Kanaliserade Budskap, Andra Vågen (Svenska Derivat)

Notes from the Second Dimension; Volume 2

Memoarer från Andra Dimensionen; Del 1 (Svenska)

Books Scheduled for Publication in 2022 - 2024

The Spiritual Design, Wave 3

Notes from the Second Dimension; Volume 3

The Spiritual Design, Wave 4

We wish to thank and acknowledge the many spirits who have contributed to the *Spiritual Design* books, who share their wisdom and love week after week without fail. We consider them our spiritual family, and are honored to present their words to you. Our deepest gratitude is given to the true authors of these books: Ophelia, Bob, Jeshua, Isaac, Zachariah, Ari, Eli, Ia, Tosh, Jeb, the Elahim Council, the Council of Nine, Gergen, Ole, and the multitude of other entities who are silent partners in this collaboration to make the Earth a better home.

~ Christine and David

Notes
From the
Second Dimension

Volume 1

Christine Kromm Henrie

&

David Henrie, Sp.D.

Access Soul Knowledge
Stockholm, Sweden

The Library of Congress has cataloged the hardcover edition as follows

Names: Henrie, Christine Kromm | Henrie, David

Title: Notes from the second dimension: volume 1 /

By Christine Kromm Henrie and David Henrie

Description: 490 pages ; 23 cm. | Access Soul Knowledge, 2019

Identifiers: LCCN 2019905902 | ISBN 9780998987071

Subjects: 1. Spirituality. 2. Channeling (Spiritualism). 3. Reincarnation.

Classification: •BF1275.D2 H-- 2019 | DDC 133.9'01'35—dc22

LC record available at https://lccn.loc.gov/2019905902

Other Formats Available

ISBN 9780998987064 (Paperback Edition)

ISBN 9780998987088 (Kindle e-book Edition)

ISBN 9780998987088 (EPUB e-book Edition)

ISBN 9781951879082 (Swedish Language Paperback Edition)

ISBN 9781951879099 (Swedish Language Kindle e-book Edition)

ISBN 9781951879105 (Swedish Language EPUB e-book Edition)

Cover Photo Art: ID 6702029 © Ldambies | Dreamstime.com

Printed in the United States of America

First Edition

First Printing, June 2019

Revised Format February 2022

Print Date August 2022

Access Soul Knowledge

Stockholm, Sweden & Williamstown, WV, USA

Publisher information at www.AccesSoulKnowledge.com

Contents

184 Cores of Stars and Planets (Jan 15, 2017)
190 Cause and Effect (Apr 23, 2017)
201 Moons are Different (Mar 5, 2017)
209 Isaac, the Gravity King (Mar 12, 2017)
214 Side Effects in the Drawer (Mar 30, 2017)
219 Atmosphere is Operating Correctly (May 7, 2017)
224 Bob is shown my First Project (May 7, 2017)
227 Solar System as Chakras (May 11, 2017)
233 Why were there Three in a Row? (June 19, 2017)
236 A Division of Labor (June 19, 2017)
244 Uranus in Resonance with Sun (Dec 3, 2017)
250 Bob Gets to Choose a Location (June 25, 2017)
254 Bubble Training Begins (July 16, 2017)
260 Spin Like a Dryer? (Sept 24, 2017)
265 Into the Oven (Dec 3, 2017)
267 Bob Travels to View His Solar System (Apr 15, 2018)
273 Ophelia's Special Plant (Apr 29, 2018)
276 The Sun is a Jukebox (May 13, 2018)
280 Bob gets a Suitcase of Elements (May 19, 2018)
284 Alone with the Suitcase (May 19, 2018)
289 Playing the Master Mind (May 28, 2018)
292 The Melody in the Boxes (June 3, 2018)
294 A Healthy Sleep, or Dead? (June 21, 2018)
300 The Moon People (Oct 30, 2018)
305 More Self–Study in Lab (Dec 16, 2018)
307 Moons Resonate with Water (Dec 23, 2018)
311 Let's go Visit the Evolution Group (Feb 3, 2019)
316 Advancements and Rewards
316 Siah's Planet, Etena (Nov 5, 2017)
324 Jungle Bob (Oct 7, 2018)
329 Advanced Bubble Training (Dec 10, 2018)
332 Shrink–Fitting the Bubble (Dec 16, 2018)
337 Jeshua Lectures on Traveling (Jan 6, 2019)
341 Traveling to Siah's World (Jan 8, 2019)
347 Return to Siah (Feb 12, 2019)
353 Bob Joins the Council (Feb 10, 2018)
361 Ole, the Wise Listener (Apr 29, 2018)
368 Training for Earth
369 Guiding and Guarding the Soul (Jan 8, 2017)
372 Gloriously Colorful (Apr 16, 2017)
376 Shooting off Balls of Knowledge (June 3, 2018)

381 Working with Fossils (July 8, 2018)
384 What is the End Result? (Nov 6, 2018)
391 Gergen Makes Himself Known (Dec 10, 2018)
397 Ia Tells Secrets about the Planet (Dec 23, 2018)
404 Bob Brings a Bag of Notes (Dec 31, 2018)
413 Bob Becomes Tom's Mentor (Jan 6, 2019)
415 Gergen says to Appreciate the Small Things (Jan 8, 2019)
418 Three Small Elahims Looking In (Jan 13, 2019)
428 Let the Interviews Begin (Jan 28, 2019)
435 Training Camp for Guides (Feb 3, 2019)
440 Bob Brings a Catalogue to Zachariah (Feb 8, 2019)
449 Where Did They Go? (Feb 12, 2019)
460 Training Camp is a Great Success (Feb 12, 2019)
464 King Henry VIII Rides Again (Apr 14, 2019)
473 Robin Hood Teaches the Rich (May 11, 2019)

482 *About the Authors*

February 2022 Revised Format:

This revised format version is released under the original ISBNs. Variations from original format include the addition of dates when the channeling sessions were held. Subheadings were then reorganized by date, and some additional commentary was added in certain sections for clarity. The original transcriptions of the messages from the spirits are essentially identical, except where changes in punctuation were made to improve readability.

Creation of New Souls

I still remember quite clearly the first day, the first moment actually, when Bob made an appearance in our lives. Christine and I had gone for a hike up to one of the imposingly beautiful peaks that exist along the Front Range of the Colorado Rockies. It was a place we affectionately named Chipmunk Mountain, due to the abundance of these small creatures we had discovered living among the rocky outcrops near the top. It was a sunny, warm day in early October 2016. I had put some nuts and seeds out on a ledge as a gift to the little furry and feathered friends who live upon this mountain, when Christine suddenly said, "There's someone here!", meaning a spirit. She had a clear vision of a rather smallish figure approaching her, and then heard him say quite loudly, "Have you been taking notes?" Without waiting for a reply, he then said, "I have!" before turning and wobbling away, wearing what appeared to be a brown robe and sandals. Since that first encounter, we have been blessed by his reappearance at nearly every trance session we have conducted; blessed not only because of his endearing personality, but for the massive volume of information he has given us over the past few years. It became rather obvious after we published *Wave 1* that we would need to dedicate a series of books to the wondrous tales of adventure and learning he has shared. His incredible insights into the ongoing workings of the spirit world reveal knowledge that has never before been known to man. We presented some portions of his talks in our previous books, *Wave 1* and *Wave 2*, hoping to capture the main ideas, but much of the supporting details had to be omitted to keep the content more manageable. This series, *Notes from the Second Dimension*, should be viewed as complementary teachings related to the *Spiritual Design* concepts. We were only able to publish some six hundred pages of transcripts in *Wave 1* and *Wave 2*, leaving almost two thousand pages of talks sitting unused in the files. This series is an attempt to present some of the entertaining and informative observations delivered by Bob, Ia, and Gergen—

all specialists who reside (in spirit) on the second dimension—that did not fit into the other books either due to space limitations, or they were topics not connected to the main body of teachings.

The spirits who are presented in this book, as well as how these spirits speak through Christine, were all detailed in our previous books, so we will only give a brief reminder of our relationships. There are many spirits who have delivered messages, but only Ophelia, Isaac, and Zachariah have incarnated on Earth, and that was long ago. The other spirits have knowledge of, and are involved with, this plane from the level of the councils who administer activity on this planet. The main contributor to this book is **Bob**, a master designer and, by his own admission, a great traveler. He was created as a sparkle on the second dimension, and developed to a point where he became interested in traveling to other dimensions to study and learn. It was at that stage of his education that **Gergen**, his mentor, consulted with **Jeshua**, my mentor, and decided to match Bob and I up as a friend couple who would help each other to progress in different ways. Bob was selected to be a guide for me when I "walk upon the soil of the Earth," and in return, Bob would come and study with me on the sixth dimension to learn more about form. And so, as Bob would say, the plan was set in motion. Before this project started, I had no idea that Bob was my closest spirit guide and has been with me during every life on Earth, going back about five hundred thousand years. Much of the material in this book is Bob's personal recounting of what he observed as he went from place to place in the spirit world; a first–hand look at how a spirit perceives—in essence, his diary or journal. Another spirit who figures prominently in Bob's life, and therefore in this book, is **Ia** ("EE–ya"), his closest companion on his home dimension. Ia and Bob were created together simultaneously, in a process we will discuss in the first chapter, and even though they have different duties and interests, they are considered a pair couple who will always support and learn from each other. Both Ia and Bob are mentored by Gergen, who in turn was mentored by **Ole**, an elder member of a council on the second dimension. This council oversees the creation and upkeep of all forms of life on Earth, including the human body. **Ophelia**, as you know from The Spiritual Design series, is one of the principal organizers of this project and is present at every session. She monitors everything that Bob says through Christine, and will often give information to him to pass along. A new spirit that Bob talks about frequently is a young spirit whom he calls **Tom**. Ia is one of the teachers involved in the nursery and early education of spirits on the second, and Tom was a student in one of Ia's big groups. Bob often goes to Ia's class to give lectures to the little ones, and he felt a great affinity for Tom. As we will describe in this book, Bob eventually was assigned to mentor Tom, and we were given a glimpse into how Tom was educated and assisted along his way to becoming an independent spirit, one of the many who are working to help the Earth.

In our previous books, we lightly touched on the activities of the spirits on the second dimension who are so closely involved with the workings of nature on this planet. Cultural mythology, from all parts of the planet, is filled with stories of elves, fairies, nature spirits, gnomes, trolls, leprechauns, and other mystical creatures. Even though the modern human has been cut off from much of the spiritual awareness that our ancient ancestors possessed, some individuals are still sensitive enough to detect these entities. Unfortunately, many descriptions are fictitious and sometimes suggest that nature spirits can display negative or unfriendly qualities. All spirits from the second dimension are pure light beings, without malice or negative intentions. From the extensive talks we have had with Bob and Ia, we know there are several types of nature spirits, based on the work they do on Earth. Some work with aquatic life, others with plants or animals, and yet another group is involved in DNA modification. All these spirits are of a similar size, being over a meter tall when fully grown, although they can shrink their size down to a very small ball of light when they are traveling on Earth. Then there are the really tiny spirits called light bearers, who can be the size of a finger or even a fingernail. These are part of a group awareness and many thousands may make up one spiritual being, although they operate independently in nature. These little light bearers are assisted in their work by the myriad of physically manifested insects, bugs, bees, worms, microbes, and other creations, which are all designed by the second dimension to perform specific tasks to maintain the health and balance of the planet. The seas, the animals on land, and the atmosphere above all have visible and invisible groups of spiritual entities working to preserve life and balance in nature. When humans witlessly destroy the bases of the ecological pyramids, it demonstrates our profound spiritual ignorance to the councils that monitor our actions; the same councils that worked to create, through eons of effort, the life forms we are imperiling. It is little wonder they are now expressing their concerns and speaking directly to us (through Christine), hoping to correct the many ways we misunderstand reality. The biggest hurdle we face is our lack of awareness about the true spiritual design behind all creation.

There are several very important philosophies that the spirits want to convey about their narratives. As humans, we have a very difficult time imagining angels or the Creator because we envision them to be "up there", unreachable and untouchable. The spirits tell us that every organism, from the smallest amoeba to the largest whale, a blade of grass, each tree in a forest, an ant—every living thing around us contains an awareness from the **Master Mind**, the part of the Creator that goes out into the **fish tanks** (the various universes, ours being only one of twelve) to have experiences within the worlds of form. All living things (except humans) are occupied by this type of spiritual energy. Plants have emotions, trees have an awareness, and animals can think and feel, because they all contain a little bit of consciousness from the Creator. In addition to the static consciousness in living things, there are innumerable spirits from the second dimension who move silently and invisibly around in nature, tending to all the plants, animals, birds, microorganisms, fish, waters, and even the atmosphere above us. If we learn only one lesson from everything the spirits tell us, it should be that there is a divinity and sacredness present in all of creation. If we take that as a pillar of truth, it would force us to turn a critical eye towards ourselves and examine how we, on a very personal level, treat and interact with those aspects of the Creator. If that single lesson was embraced by society, we would treat animals with respect, and commercialized animal cruelty would vanish. We would cease clear-cutting forests. We would stop spraying crops with poison. There would be no plastic or radiation in the oceans. We would outlaw genetic modification. The planes spreading toxic chemtrails across the skies would be grounded forever. And we would cease and desist the reckless destruction of the protective web around Earth that is caused by microwave radiation. But without waiting for all these big changes, maybe we can become more spiritual within our own minds and hearts—that much we can do all by ourselves.

The second bit of philosophical advice the spirits told us to pass along has to do with your mind-set, the way in which you view the world. A child is aware they don't know everything. There is room in their life for wonder and curiosity; they are open to the possibility there may be a Santa Claus or a tooth fairy, or perhaps an angel hovering over their bed at night. However, all too soon they are sent off for institutional schooling, where they are spoon-fed textbook answers for everything. The mysteries of the unknown are gradually replaced with cynicism and passivity, and any hope to see the world in a spiritual way vanishes under those dark clouds of materialism. Speaking for those of us who spent a lot of time wandering alone in the woods as a youngster, I often felt the presence of energetic beings, or something otherworldly, moving nearby through the forest like a breeze—nearly undetectable, except for the heat wave like distortion in the air as it passed by. The logical mind dismisses these sensations as mere imagination, but yet—is it? To truly understand what is being said by the spirits, we need to embrace a sense of wonderment and give ourselves permission to live in a world that contains mysteries and energies we do not understand. All the conversations with the spirits contain ideas or messages that can seem almost too incredible to believe, yet if you keep an open mind, you may discover the revelations make much more sense than what either science or religion promote as reality. As Socrates said, "I know that I am intelligent, because I know that I know nothing," and that is the appropriate mind-set we need to have when we approach these teachings.

When we talk about the vibrational dimensions, it is based on how the spirits describe the Creator and all the various manifested spiritual and form-based realities that exist. Large portions of our previous books were dedicated to explaining these concepts, so we hope the reader is familiar with this information because it is somewhat critical to following the storyline of Bob's travels to different places. We have included, on page 7, a little diagram showing the home dimensions of the spirits mentioned in this book, as well as the main function of the spirits who occupy those dimensions. Throughout the book, if we refer to "sixth" or "second", for example, it should be understood as the sixth dimension or second dimension.

As a high-level overview, the fifth through tenth dimensions are directly responsible for creating the form we see in our Universe and in the other fish tanks, based on instructions transmitted down from the Creator through the eleventh and twelfth dimensions (the highest councils). The Creator sends a cloud of awareness out into the fish tanks, and a little piece of that Master Mind energy occupies all the life forms, except for those occupied by souls from the various dimensions. On Earth, humans are the only creature that do not have Master Mind awareness within, animating the form. The data collected by the Master Mind is sent back to the center pole, the Creator, and new spirits and new designs are envisioned to bring balance to locations that need assistance. The corrections can be as small as a DNA modification for an insect, or as large as re-locating sheets of galaxies. New spirits are made with a blueprint that contains the intended path or purpose of that spirit, and are fabricated as a small energy bundle containing strands of awareness from the Creator. After the spirit has completed its mission, it returns to the Creator, bearing the accumulated gifts of knowledge it acquired from its independent activities.

The image of the Wheel of Creation was presented in *Wave 2*, but we are including it as a reminder. It is a way to imagine the bands of vibrational frequency that define the dimensions. The Creator, shown as the center pole in the diagram, is the source of energy for everything that exists, including individual spirits. The wheel is divided into three main parts; the Creator, the spiritual dimensions, and the twelve different universes ("fish tanks"), each containing the first through fourth dimensions. Each fish tank is home to unique building blocks, which are used to create various forms, so there are universes of sound, universes of half energy-half matter, universes of energy, universes of light, and some universes of elemental matter. In our Universe, we interpret the first dimension as hydrogen, helium, carbon, gravity, x-rays, gamma waves, et cetera, but the building blocks are different in each of the twelve fish tanks. Even though the fifth through the ninth are spiritual dimensions, they are also realms of form. Only the Creator lacks form.

The process of creation has been explained as a joint effort between the spiritual dimensions and the Creator. The Creator sends ideas out into the spiritual dimensions, where different councils come up with plans on how to execute them. The higher councils send the general intention down to the lower councils, who add more refinement. Eventually, it reaches those on the second through eighth, which are the working dimensions. These are the spirits who manipulate energy to create structures or living entities, using the first dimensional building blocks in each fish tank. The Creator sends parts of its awareness out into the dimensions of form to monitor everything that occurs. This is called the Master Mind, and it reports back to the Creator from all levels and realities. As imbalances occur, the Creator initiates changes by sending out new ideas, but also by creating new souls that are patterned to execute certain tasks. The older spirits on each dimension then have to nurture those new souls and help them fulfill their destiny. The entire system acts like a single organism, although an extremely complex one.

On the next page is a simplistic diagram to show how the dimensions are organized. Each dimension has both a spiritual side and a manifested side. When Bob (or any spirit) goes to other dimensions to study, he can only visit the manifested side. The Library and the vaults on the fifth dimension, for example, are manifested locations on the fifth. The spiritual side can only be accessed by those who were born (or created) on that dimension. But the spiritual area is also sectored by area and purpose. On the second, Bob, Ia, Gergen, and Ole were all created to assist Earth, so their primary area is with other Earth related spirits. Ole, who has been around a long time, has advanced and has access to most of the areas on the second, I would assume. On the diagram, we listed the basic function of the dimensions along with the names of those spirits who are representing the dimension. Spirits do progress into other dimensions. Ari, Eli, and Jeshua were born on the sixth into a group called the Elahim. They will always be Elahim, even though they are now operating in councils on the ninth or tenth.

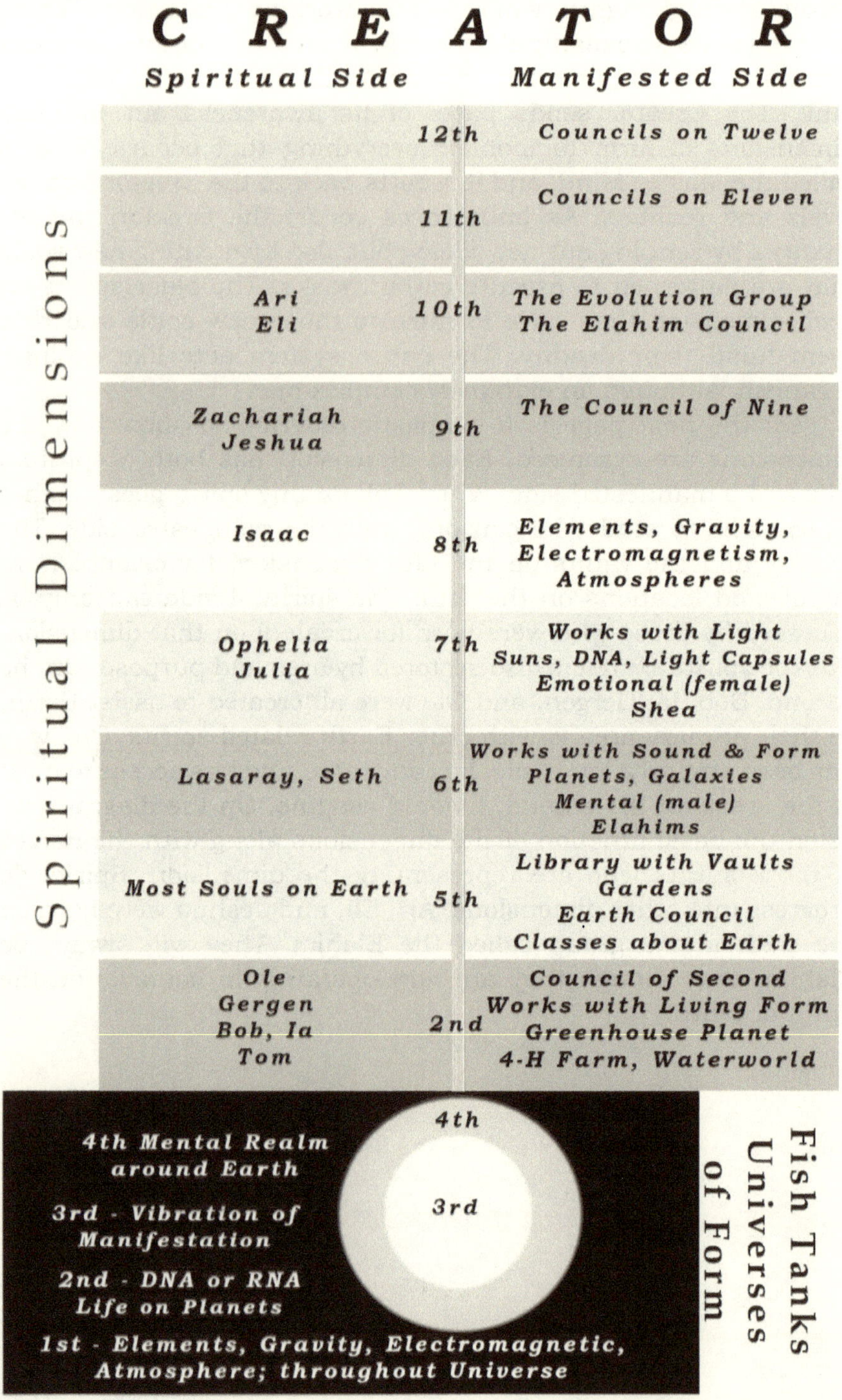
CREATOR
Spiritual Side
Manifested Side
12th
Councils on Twelve
11th
Councils on Eleven
Ari
Eli
10th
The Evolution Group
The Elahim Council
Zachariah
Jeshua
9th
The Council of Nine
Isaac
8th
Elements, Gravity,
Electromagnetism,
Atmospheres
Ophelia
Julia
7th
Works with Light
Suns, DNA, Light Capsules
Emotional (female)
Shea
Lasaray, Seth
6th
Works with Sound & Form
Planets, Galaxies
Mental (male)
Elahims
Most Souls on Earth
5th
Library with Vaults
Gardens
Earth Council
Classes about Earth
Ole
Gergen
Bob, Ia
Tom
2nd
Council of Second
Works with Living Form
Greenhouse Planet
4-H Farm, Waterworld
Spiritual Dimensions
4th
3rd
4th Mental Realm
around Earth
3rd - Vibration of
Manifestation
2nd - DNA or RNA
Life on Planets
1st - Elements, Gravity, Electromagnetic,
Atmosphere; throughout Universe
Fish Tanks
Universes
of Form

To avoid putting information in Christine's conscious mind that may inadvertently influence future readings, she does not listen to or read any of the lectures given by spirits from the higher dimensions until we begin to edit the books. I compile the books and write in the first person, but Christine and I pour over each book for several months after the first draft is prepared. However, our spiritual friends are the ones who dictate the bulk of the content, and our job is to keep their messages as clear and organized as we can. Once the talks have been transcribed, only very minor alterations are made to tidy up sentences that may be confusing. Our goal is always to maintain the purity of the messages they deliver, and all original recordings are stored in multiple locations for future reference and documentation, should a comment ever be called into question. We also have several audio files available on our website, so the reader can get a feel for the way each spirit communicates.

When Christine began channeling the spirits we have come to know so well, during the first few months, Ophelia, Zachariah, Jeshua, and Isaac were the only spirits who communicated. They gave general information about the spirit world, along with instructions on diet and practices we should do in preparation for higher energies to come in. Eventually, they began discussing the various activities in the spirit realms, so we will begin this book with the first mention of the second dimension, when Zachariah introduces Bob.

Z. Bob has been taking notes. He really wants to be a part of this and he has been taking notes. Regardless of what anyone says, he is prepared and has been taking notes for a little while. And he is not someone who just came on a whim. He has prepared and has learned about you and how you communicate with spirit. So, he has been observing how to engage with you in the best possible way. But he really wants to be involved and he wants to be recognized as a person involved in this work. And don't be fooled by his appearance. He is still a valuable source if you choose to work with him. There's something he could actually help you work with when it comes to your own personality, not just for the book. He brings light energy and warmth into stagnation. He actually has healing capacity, this little individual, so don't discard him as a funny elf. He's a healer.

D. What's his name, or what should we call him?

Z. You can call him Bob. He doesn't mind. His spiritual name is—(*Out of respect for his wishes, we will not reveal his name. In our sessions, we converse with him by another name.*) But in physical, he wants to be known as "Bob". Bob makes it more accessible for people because of his personality, it makes it more amusing for the audience if you present him as Bob. Bob comes with a lot of healing capacity. He is wiser than he appears, belonging in a kingdom related to this world. Like deep inside the Earth.

D. What dimension does he come from?

Z. The second. He's from within the Earth. He's familiar with creatures within and on the planet. Not so far in, not like the core. Maybe up to one kilometer down. It's like a realm with helpers of the planet, cleaners.

D. It must be non-physical then, an energetic level?

Z. Yes, it's stabilizing the Earth mass, making sure the water is clean. These are great nature spirits if you like. I do see them, I don't want to say like ants, but small. He is very involved with this realm. He is also here to help you with your development, to allow yourself to fully blossom into the person that you are. And it's very much your own core that needs to be accepted. Your past and some experiences need to be understood they are not a part of who you are as a person, they are simply lessons. They haven't formed you, per se, they are merely experiences. He is here to remind you to continue to laugh and to be more open with who you are. People will find you more attractive if you show both sides; both the vulnerable side, because people need to understand the path you have walked, but also when they see how you have transformed into lighter energies.

It was the following week that our friend from the second dimension entered our life. We also had no idea how much we would come to treasure his joyful presence and somewhat unique way of delivering ideas, or notes, as he often calls the topics he has picked for the day. All the spirits have a specific way of speaking, including word choice, speed, sentence structure, and tempo. Bob, oddly, has a lisp and cannot say "S" very well, which makes his dialogues amusing to listen to, even when he is being quite serious. About a year ago, I told him of our decision to present some of the teachings from his dimension in a separate series of books, -which made him quite happy. In *Wave 2*, Bob described how progress in the spiritual realms is rewarded with additional knowledge or experiences, that he likened to gifts under a Christmas tree. So when he says, "under the tree", that is what he means.

D. I was going to tell you, I've decided to combine much of the information the second dimension has provided into a book, so you will have your own compilation of knowledge. So anything you, or Ia, or Gergen tells me, I'm going to put it all together in one place.

B. Umm! Ole might wanna come too! Huhuhuh, that's a treat!

D. It will be your description of how you see your life and your reality.

B. That's a treat! Ophelia comes in now with her finger! (*His way of saying she was warning him.*) She comes in and she said, "You're not supposed to be sharing left and right," because she knows I get excited about things. Ophelia comes in and she says, "We're going talk about this." But she knows I get excited to share, so she said we're gonna talk about this.

D. She can tell us what we can release to the public.

B. Because if I'm in charge, all sorts of things can be released, and that's what she's concerned about, she says. Ah, but she's happy about that, she's happy about that. Oh, that is one of my gifts, she said, under my tree. It is to be able to just...she said she knew this, she said that you told her. No one told me.

D. It just came upon me, a week or so ago, that I needed to put all your teachings together, because there are so many things you have said that are really funny or really wise.

B. Ophelia says you two talked about this. It's one of my gifts, she said, under the tree. But she said we are all gonna participate, we're all gonna be able to share. And Ia's gonna be able to share more. Because Ia has in her possession all the knowledge of how to bring someone up from scratch, so to speak, and to make it blossom. She said that there are so many people here that are not given the opportunity to blossom, because they are not nurtured in the way that they're supposed to be from the beginning, and that creates, in some way, disharmony. But also, she said some souls put themselves in those situations to see if they can still blossom, even though one has not been given the best foundations from the beginning. So those who do that, they actually take that on as somewhat of a reporting mission, if you like, on how growth becomes, and how one can become a flower, regardless if it's created from a very loving foundation, or not.

How New Spirits are Created (Jan 21, 2018)

On the second dimension, the spirits are created in groups and delivered to a nursery environment in a large bundle of energy, which Bob calls an egg. On other dimensions, it may be that spirits are created individually, but it seems that all spirits are created as part of a group of spirits who share a common objective or purpose. On the second dimension, Ia is one of those who works with the newly patterned spirits. Because she is a partner with Bob, we have been given a unique insight into the way these little ones are taken care of and how they develop and are taught, in accordance with the intention given to them by the Creator. Bob said the newly created bundle of spirits is compact when it is delivered into the nursery from the Mother Energy. But as the individual spirits are separated and moved into their own space, they expand and grow a bit. Ia is only one of the specialists on the second dimension who oversee the process of awakening the energetic egg and then deciphering the Creator's intention for that group. After each spirit has been separated from the bundle, then begins the long process of nurturing and awakening their patterns. Ia and others teach and train the little ones while they grow into sparkles (young spirits).

Zachariah also teaches, but his students are a bit older. He said, –and this may be confusing to you–, that he splits his energy and is able to teach many different levels and classes simultaneously. Ia probably has the same abilities, so she can tend to many ages and groups of little ones at the same "time". Bob has frequently said that Ia is really good at solving puzzles, both in reference to her work with DNA, but also her skills at nurturing and detecting the very faint indications of patterns given to each spirit that comes through her nursery.

B. So, Ia is here, and she has been starting to decipher the first puzzle in the new egg.

D. And how is that going?

B. It's a lot of work. She says there are plenty working on this. She says, "Long hours!" That's what she said. They decipher, it's almost like a cocoon, and it's put in a cradle, a big cradle, but its size is somewhat smaller, but when it's dividing, it expands. Otherwise, they will have to have such a big room to work with!

But they are still sleeping in the egg, all of them, so they are deciphering. The first thing they do is try to detect the rhythm, the heart rhythm, because that is the first sign of what sort of group it's going to be. The heart rhythm is like a song; she says it creates a melody, and there are those who are very skilled at detecting it. They are chanting, in some way—the teachers around it—and they try to listen to the heartbeat in this big egg. They have different expertise around it. Ia is not the expert of that specific part of analyzing the egg, but she's telling that there are those who are really able to tune in on that heartbeat. They are chanting, if you like, to mirror that, so they become in a resonance with the egg. And eventually that (*the chanting*) is the thing that will open it up, that will make it come alive and wake up. But they're chanting with it, it's almost like moving into a trance, to give you a picture, and they are doing so as they connect with this heartbeat. Ia comes much later, and she deciphers the different colors. She says it's like dissecting a frog, you look at different things and you take it out and you analyze it. But it's also like a welcoming ceremony for the egg, because the egg itself responds to the chanting, and that's how they come alive and wake up.

D. They become aware of the sound?

B. Indeed. The sound and light are the foundations of everything. They all come from light, but they wake up by the sound. But the Creator puts in a little melody, if you like, which is the group heartbeat.

D. When you say heartbeat, is it like a light pulse through their energetic body?

B. It's like a vibrating pulse in this egg. It is the same pattern in the whole group, so even though they are later going to be divided into individuals, they will still recall each other because they have the same heartbeat, so they will never be misplaced. They will never become lost and they will always come back to their friends, because they have the same heartbeat, the same vibration. That's how a soul can find its way home, because they know exactly where their friends are, because they follow that rhythm, that heartbeat. It's easier to give it to you in a way of a heartbeat, even though it is the whole being that is in rhythm. It's not a physical organ like a heart, but it is a way to locate your group, and to locate your home. So regardless of where these little souls are gonna go, they are gonna recall and they are gonna be able to communicate. Even if they are sent to other fish tanks (*one of the twelve universes, as detailed in Wave 1 and Wave 2*), they are still gonna be able to communicate with that. And that is also how souls communicate. You two, you communicated with that, that's how you found each other, because you communicated in that heartbeat and in that rhythm.

D. So it's the same for spirits in any dimension?

B. Indeed, indeed. That's why you are never lost, and that's why you never have to be afraid that you are not gonna find your way back home, or find your friends. Because even if some friends are in your spiritual home, and some might be, let's say, incarnated or even in different fish tanks, then it's still that connecting pulse between the two of you, or between you and your whole group as well. So you will always be able to tap into that. But if you are a human, you are so locked in the container that you struggle to hear that signal, it is a struggle to hear their home vibration within their own being. So it's like not hearing your heartbeat.

D. So when humans don't hear their heartbeat, are they more likely to make mistakes in their selection of friends and partners?

B. Indeed, because they only make choices from the container and the mind. They don't make choices from the center core and the heartbeat. And the heartbeat is actually, —I say heartbeat, but it's not an organ, it's not the heart, it's the center point that is the pulse, that's where the pulse is. But it's close enough so it can be known as a heartbeat, so that's why we say that, because it's too confusing to think that there is a pulse in this center point in the solar plexus area. It's easier to think of the heart, because man can sense the heartbeat, but you cannot sense, necessarily always, the pulse in your center point.

D. So when you were talking about recognizing your heartbeat, you were talking about recognizing your pulse?

B. Indeed. That pulse is what connects you to where you are supposed to be, and to your friends. And that pulse was the thing that made the two of you, here, recognize each other. So you send out the pulse to the other one, who has the ability to receive that pulse. But another one who doesn't have the same receiver as you, because you are not coming from the same place, then the pulse, it just goes out into the space, because there is no receiver at the other end, so to speak. So this is how you can recall your spiritual group, your soul group, if you like. BUT you have groups that you incarnate with and they send out different pulses, but it's not as strong. So, it's a way to find each other, because no one likes to be lost. But the pulse just comes out differently. The purest pulse that comes from your center point, it is completely identified and similar to the ones that belong in your circle. So it doesn't matter where you are located, you will always hear it because that pulse has no limits of where it can travel. So at this point, they are trying to make this general pulse in the egg to be established within its memory, if you like, so that everyone will recognize this pulse. It's gonna be on a subconscious level, but it is always noticeable once you have been given it. And that is what this chanting is for, they are trying to make this memory of this pulse, specifically designed for this egg, to be recognized and to be remembered within them. That's the first thing you do.

D. That's really fascinating.

B. Ah, well, Ia told me this.

D. I would like to ask, is the pulse similar to a heartbeat in its frequency, or is it faster or slower?

B. It begins kind of slow, and that chanting makes it go faster, but it's not necessarily like boom...boom...boom, it can be different. So, each egg, each group, has a different melody, and here, you think that the heartbeat is the same, but it's not really, it's all uniquely designed for each of you. But Ia says it begins a little bit slow, and what you do is, you have to warm it up in some way, combined with the chanting. The chanting is so they detect this teeny, tiny little pulse, and they increase it by chanting, and they increase it by providing warmth to this little egg. It's not that small...

D. Compared to you?

B. Oh, compared to me it would be like maybe ten of me.

D. You mean the original egg?

B. The original egg. BUT it's because you have to be able to work with it. But inside it when it starts to divide it can be like hundreds of little sparkles. But at this point, because Ia and her friends, who are also teachers, there are like eight or ten, they have to be able to manage this, so it's smaller as it comes (*the energy bundle is more dense, and then as the individual spirits are separated, they expand in size*), otherwise it would be huge, if it was like hundreds of my size.

D. They would need a really big ladder.

B. Ah, need to be outside to operate that big egg. But it's actually smaller, it's somewhat constricted and then it expands.

D. So, you've been watching them work?

B. Huhuh. Ah, I've been with Ia, of course, because I've been studying the new egg. Ia said that I could come and I could look at her work, but I'm simply observing, I'm watching her work, and she said that if I'm silent and don't ask questions I could observe, because the first phase is actually conducted in complete silence. This egg is extremely sensitive to all influences, so she said, "You don't want the first word they hear to be like a curse, or something." It's similar like that, so she said, "This is the first level, so you are welcome." It's like I'm sitting on a little chair, and I can read what they're doing. It's like opening a cocoon, if you like, and I see how they are deciphering; it's almost like surgery. They take away each and every one, and it almost looks like a lab because they dissect the whole thing, and they put them in different units, based on their patterns. And there are several like Ia. Ia's not doing this by herself, there are like twenty, at least, around this, and they are deciphering and organizing based on patterns. So, they are dividing and—

D. When they first come out, they probably don't interact with them much, do they?

B. They put them in a silent space. Every time you go into a new environment, you have to go into that hibernation phase in some way, so they are doing that. When you do that later on, it could simply be that you do like a meditation, or you go into your light capsule. But here, because this is the first visit they have, then they will be in a light capsule, but they will be sleeping, if you like. It's like having a nap, once they have been dissected and diverted from this group, so to speak. But they are all put in a nursery, they have to be asleep a little bit. It is to awaken and to create that light capsule. They come in one big light capsule, but now they have to be in an individual light capsule, so they are given one. But once you are given a light capsule, then you have to somewhat learn how to be in stillness and to let it become you; and that is what they do in the nursery. So once they are in that big capsule, they are safe, but then they have to get an individual capsule as well. So that is what I see now, they put them almost like in a nursery, they put them in, not a bucket, but we can call it a bucket. It's see-through, so I see it.

D. Like a little incubation chamber.

B. Indeed, I see that, and they are given a light capsule in this bucket and they become it, and they are sleeping in it. It's like planting that seed and eventually they will all wake up. But they will wake up differently, similar like you do here, not awake at the same time. It's the same thing here. But this is what I've been observing, from a distance, because I'm not supposed to interact and engage.

D. Now you can see what Ia's been up to, while you've been out roaming the universe.

B. Roaming around in the universe, hehe, I have indeed.

D. Will Ia eventually follow this group as they develop, maybe go places outside the second with them?

B. Ia's not going to go, Ia gets a new big group.

D. So she starts over?

B. She starts over. I asked her about that, I said, "Don't you want to continue?" and she said, "No, my place is here, I like to give them the best possible option and foundation for them to become the flowers. And for me, it's that joy of being able to give them that first level of comfort and knowledge, but also, to make them aware of their unique capacity, that first step."

D. Yes, because they are just fresh from the Creator, aren't they?

B. Just new.

D. So Ia discovers what their potential is?

B. Yes, and she finds great joy in that, to find that out, and she says, "That's how I grow, because no one is the same." Even though you feel like, "Okay, here is a brand-new little group, and they're brand new from the Creator, but they are still brand new because you never know what the Creator has manifested and created from its little factory; so it's not continuous, the same thing. But she finds great pride and joy in identifying what the Creator has intended for the next level of groups.

D. So she works mostly with the Earth-type sparkles?

B. Ah.

D. There must be a lot of other teachers that have different realities and planets?

B. Ah, ah. I understand that because she is almost the closest to the Creator, so she sees the first thing that comes. So she sees what the new intention is from the Creator, and what she has to work with. So all groups that come, which can be over a hundred individuals, then she says, "When they come, I try to figure out over time what the new intention the Creator has. Because the conditions in different fish tanks and realities changes, and the Creator responds to that." She sees the first sign or key from the Creator of what the new intention is. She says that that is her greatest joy, when she gets a new class, because she says, "OK, I wonder what is here to develop, and what is the intention of this new group of helpers that's going to go eventually and teach and learn different things?"

D. That would be rewarding. (*The Creator is described as the center hub on the Wheel, and the center axis or pole within the sphere of creation; see Wave 2.*)

B. So in some way, she is CLOSER to the pole than I am! Huhuh. Ah, that was different, that was a trick! I'm so focused on being over in the old council, but she's sees the first preview of the Creator's intention and thought. Huhuhuh. Maybe I'll go and sniff around! Huhuh. Oh, she laughs about that! (*He looked to the left, where she was standing.*) She says, "I told you this, but you were never interested." But I am now! I am now! Huhuhuh.

D. That's a different way to look at it, indeed.

B. It's like when you get a baby here, it's the same thing. It's a brand–new thing, and you don't know what the intention is for the new soul coming in, because it is an extension from the Creator. So if you treat the baby well, then it has the potential to fully become the intention both the Creator and the soul had. But if the conditions are not right, or if certain things are placed upon the baby, it might not become what the Creator intended it to be.

D. People see babies as a blank canvass they need to paint in their own image.

B. Ah, but it's not to create in your own image, it's to—like Ia, she's not there to create them in her image. She's there to identify what their true nature and mission and intention and idea is. And if you do that with a baby, you're not trying to make a mirror of yourself. You can just stand in front of a mirror if that's what you want. But you should try to identify what the true potential, and what that mission is from that individual. Not place your own intentions, like, "Oh, I'm the doctor, this one must be a doctor," because you don't know if that is the intention that the Creator and the spirit realm asked of this specific soul to do. So you don't want to hinder that. You want the baby to be able to fully become its unique pattern and person, so it follows the intention. Because it's not just the soul's intention here, it's also what the Creator asked that specific soul to come down and do. So you don't want to put your own intention on the little one, saying, "Oh, I played football. This one must play the football," so it's like that. I can see that, that Ia is closer to the source. She might just have a looksee like this (*bends forward and looks to the left, showing how he wanted to catch a glimpse of the Creator*), when the door opens and they all started pouring in, and she can just look in. She said it doesn't work like that, but I asked, "How do they get there?" And she said it's like a light coming into the nursery, it's like a big ball of light and then it just dissolves and becomes all these little lights, that's a new group coming in. She said it's like a mother, it's like an egg almost, like a light egg. And when it comes down to her, it just opens up and dissolves into a bunch of little lights.

D. So it comes in as a big light and breaks down into a bunch of little lights?

B. Indeed. And she said, "It's the greatest joy when this comes because you know that there is just this purest intention in all of them, both collectively and individually. And as they come, they create the greatest joy. (*Bob's voice suddenly softened as Ia stepped close, and it sounded as if she was the one talking.*) And they become a part of a great chain of change. And as I teach them, they will unfold their unique patterns and light within them, and they will transcend and transform and radiate this light on the plane they are supposed to go to. They are little light bearers, and they can be detected in birds, or just in the wind. But as they come, they are completely pure. I take great joy in understanding how they are best to operate, because all of them are unique. But they are pure, sent from the Source."

D. That's really a beautiful description.

B. Huhuh. (*Bob came back in.*)

D. I'm glad that Ia is getting a chance to have her ideas known, to share the spotlight. She'll end up with a little star on her chest. I'm sure she deserves it.

B. Ahahaha. Umm. Indeed. I'm gonna go and hang with her. I'm gonna go and look at the door! (*He laughs.*) If another egg comes, I'm gonna try to peek in here! (*Laughing.*)

D. To see the blinding light.

B. The blinding light! She said it's not like eggs come every day! I said, "Next time the egg comes, I'm gonna be there. And when the door opens, it might be that the door is a portal to the Master Mind!" But she said it's like an elevator almost, but I'm not sure, so I'm gonna go. I said, "Next time, let me know, and I'm gonna be there when this package arrives."

D. You might want to hang out with the sparkles?

B. Ah, interesting. She says, "They don't really know, so it's my job to figure it out. It's not like I can, when all these little lights start to unfold, that I can just ask, 'What is your business here?' because they're not gonna know!" It's a practice, she said, and she carries that practice and that knowledge to detect the different patterns. It's like a puzzle, she said. She detects the different patterns in these little sparkles that comes—but they don't know. She said, "I can't ask them, 'What is your mission? What is your purpose? How was it up at the Creator? Where did you come from?'". She said I can't ask them because they don't know! But her level of learning is to understand. And she will because she detects different patterns and the way they are patched up. That's how she can read what the intention is of the current group and the intention of the mission that they are going to go on, and what the intention basically is, from the Creator.

D. It seems almost like a DNA pattern?

B. Indeed. They have a little inner map, like a blueprint, and she said that you can recognize the group differently, the collective group and their pattern, because in some way they carry the same pattern. However, when you break it down, you see the different patterns within them, and she said, "That's how I know and I can read," and based on her level of education that she can understand and try to decipher what the intention from the Creator is.

D. Wow. That's quite an honor.

B. Ah. HIGHLY skilled, she is. This is what she's been doing when I have been out traveling! She's been learning about this in her books. Huhuh. I thought she was just...

D. Being a kindergarten teacher, reading stories?

B. Reading stories! No, she's not. She trying to, she said, identify the different patterns within them, based on how they are structured, like a DNA map almost. But it's different colors. It's a color code, color map, within them. And she said, "That's how I know what the Creator wants me to lift forward in that group, as well."

D. That's a very evolved skill that she has developed.

B. Oh, I've just been traveling. Hmm.

D. All spirits learn in their own way, along their own path. You weren't patterned to do that.

B. Ah, she learned a lot there. I'm very proud of her, I'm extremely proud of her!

D. I'm sure she's proud of you too.

B. Ah, she said that she is.

D. Mutual respect then, that's one of the spiritual laws.

B. That's why she's been sitting with Gergen, reading up on all those lights and teeny, tiny details we talked about before. (*Bob said Ia studies the energetic patterns we see as DNA strings.*) This is—this is the details! If I had paid attention to the details, I would have done this too. But I'm keeping busy elsewhere, so I'm doing other things.

D. It's not too late to learn.

B. Nay, you have to be in the capacity that you are doing your best. Like this group, for instance, that just graduated, the first group, they have just been divided, their mission has been deciphered from Ia and her friends and other councils. So they know how to somewhat portion them out on different levels where they're needed to be. Like at this point, for instance, there is a lot going to the Water World, she said, because waters are in need of attention. So there is a lot (*of other sparkles*) with Tom that goes to the Water World, and that is the intention that the Creator had with that specific group.

D. The Earth is three–fourths covered with water, so there is a lot of life in the oceans.

B. When I went, there was a majority that went to the Greenhouse Planet, but I went to the 4–H Farm. Who knows where these (*the spirits in the new egg*) are gonna go. But the current group that just graduated, there is a majority that was sent off to the Water World to learn about upgrading and maintaining and accessing light and oxygen. They're gonna be water engineers.

D. They're not going to be playing with guinea pigs at the 4–H Farm?

B. There's not the same need there. So, this is the details that she's been working on. Anyway, okay, I think I'm gonna go and look at this because if there is an egg coming, –oh, she says it's not, it just came one! Why didn't you call me? (H*e turns and spoke to her, standing to the left.*)

D. She should just give you a little invite, next time.

B. I might just look at them and see lights, I might not be able to decipher their little map, their color map, because I don't have that training, and she said I don't really have the patience either! Huhuh. Because it's not like you look one time and say, "OK, got this," it's a lot of work, it's not like a ready picture. You have to learn how to decipher both the collective group and the individual. It's the same way with humans here. There is a group consciousness as well as the individual, so you have to decipher that. Anyway, okay, okay, I'm gonna go now.

D. Alright, my friend, I look forward to talking with you soon.

B. Ah, okay, bye bye.

A few weeks later, Bob continued his discussion about the progress being made in the nursery on the second, as Ia and the other spirits continue to analyze and nurture the little sparkles who were still bundled together in the big, energetic egg.

B. So, Ia has been working with her puzzle, you know, with the little ones.

D. How's that coming? Do you still watch?

B. I sometimes watch, but it's so quiet. It's like working in silence, and I try to ask, and they say, "Shh," and I say, "What are you doing?" And she says, "Shh", and then I said, "Okay." And then I go around and I try to talk to someone else, and I said, "So, what are you doing, what did you find?" I'm mainly interested, I must say, in what they find, not what they are doing so much, but what they find. So I said, "What do you find over here?" and they say, "Shh". So it seems like a quiet activity of sorts. So after a while, I'm not as amused. They're really friendly. It's not like they are kicking me out or anything. They just say, "Shh". And then I try to go to someone else and say, "What are you finding over here?", and they say, "Shh." Then I thought, maybe if I wait and ask afterwards when this little session is over, "What did they find?" What was the find of the day, so to speak. But they say, "We're still trying to establish that. We're working with that group." So, at this point, they are dissecting this big egg, based on expertise. So one is dissecting the energy of purpose, for instance. It's too complex to tell too much about this, but it is to identify both the purpose vibration, and the location of their future mission via the group consciousness versus the individual one, which comes later. But you have to identify the core of their nature, and how they...it's hard to put into words—mainly because they don't talk too much to me either—but it is to identify the unique pattern and nature in a variety of different aspects. To make it easy, if we take human words, for instance, is it an empathic egg? Is it a scientific egg? Is it an egg that is gonna be working as a teacher? Is it an egg that is gonna work on technology? So, that sort of thing.

D. So, at this point, it is still all together?

B. It's together, like a lump. And each specific expertise here, –and Ia is one–, is trying to identify the intention and the purpose of this specific group that is about to later dissolve into individuals. So, is it a technological group? Are they gonna work on Earth, or are they gonna work somewhere else? What is the expertise here?

D. From your perspective, can you see through it? Is it like a ball of energy?

B. Ah, it's like an egg, but it's more see–through. It's like a shell, but it's not hard as an egg. So it's like a vibrating field and inside there is a pulse, –it's like an organ inside. So in some way it looks like an egg. But they identify the patterns of it.

D. The cosmic egg.

B. The cosmic egg indeed. So, that's what I've been doing, looking around at different things.

The previous session was from January 2018. Bob didn't address Ia's egg again until May 2018, which is in the following exchange. During the intervening months, he had several other topics he was presenting. How spirits are created and educated is an important topic for humans to understand, so Bob circled back to the discussion, picking up right where he left off several months earlier.

D. So are you still traveling as much, or are you mostly working with these things?

B. Ah, I'm home as well, I'm with Ia. I'm curious about this egg. It's changed colors, meaning it has changed its cycle of its creation, so to speak. It came in and it was just white, and now it starts to become light blue. It's going to go through several color changes before it starts to dissolve, and the color changes represent specific learnings, teachings; well, not teachings, necessarily, but it is experiencing certain things that just come to life. So it goes through all sort of colors from the rainbow before they start to dissolve. And now it's in the phase of light blue, that's where they are at.

D. Does this process kind of bind all those spirits into a common purpose?

B. Indeed. It's also, –once it starts to dissolve, in the end, when it has traveled through all these colors of experience and manifestation of its original being and makeup, that's when it starts to split up, and that's when you can see which color is over–represented within that group. In the group that went to the Water World, the color represented, mainly, in that group, was dark blue. The gardeners, for instance, had a lot of green and orange. That's when they know, okay, this specific egg is mainly to be helpful, let's say, like in gardens (*nature*), or in waters.

D. What was your color?

B. My color was red.

D. And that's related to the 4–H Farm?

B. Nay. The 4–H Farm is like a yellow kind of color. But my specific color, my own, had a lot of red.

D. Is that a traveling color?

B. Indeed. I like red. I like all colors, but it represents different levels of understanding and awareness, as well as different aspects of one's personality and specific makeup in order for one to become the pattern. So, within each soul there is a color pattern, whether you come from an egg, –you might come from an egg as well, and I don't know what color you have–, but it represents your mission, personality, if you like, because even as a soul you have a personality.

D. Well, when you told me a year ago to visualize a rainbow when I called for you to come help with something, you said the color was either green or brown.

B. Well, the green and brownish are overrepresented in the second dimension because of the fact that we are taking care of nature and animal life. BUT MY individual color, that would be considered, let's say, like in my center point. It's not necessarily that I am going around like a reddish person, but I have established within me a center of red. You can see it like that, that the center is your core color, and in my case, that one is red. However, in general, where we exist, there is a lot of green and brown. BUT, let's say, like Tom and his friends, who will have this dark blue, their center would be a spot of dark blue. It's just to give you a picture, but it's not like we go around like a color map. Once you practice to expand your own light capsule, then the color that will be strongest visualized will be the center point, and in my case, when I expand and practice my light capsule, then it is actually that my center point, my red point, will be bigger.

D. Huh. Is that why Gergen told you not to put on a red robe when you went to the council?

B. Indeed, indeed. Because he said it is too much.

D. Because everyone would know then that you are a traveler?

B. Exactly! Exactly, so then I would blow my cover (*snorts a happy laugh*) HUHUH. Oh, he knew that! But I wanted to make them see that I was a traveler, but he said, "No, we're gonna have that in disguise, a little bit." Oh, that's true, so I took on another color outside myself. So, it's just to give you a picture, kinda.

D. Well, I follow that.

B. Ah. So, Ia is working with the egg, which has now turned light blue, and they're practicing in a way that detects if they are receptive. So, when they communicate with this big egg, the light blue, they want to see if their frequencies are coming back, and they send in different frequencies.

D. So they are bouncing frequencies into the egg, like radar signals?

B. Indeed. And they want to see whatever comes back. Because this is the first level of communication, and this is the signal that they have to see whether this joined egg receives and returns, and what is it that they return.

D. So they are probing to see what kind of patterns it has?

B. Indeed. And what sort of communication skills it has. All are, of course, in telepathic communication. BUT, let's say that this egg will communicate in pictures more, like the gravity group. (*He is referring to a group of souls on the eighth, who he works with in our lab on the sixth. They are very good at sending him pictures.*) The way they respond to the signals that Ia and her friends are sending in will come back in a frequency that they will interpret or analyze to see what sort of communication skill this specific group has.

D. Huh, that's a really complicated process.

B. Indeed. But everything is like that, you know. When you get a baby here, you have to teach it a language. It's the same thing, there's all sorts of things it has to learn; it has to learn how to walk, and communicate and talk. So, it's the same thing.

An Army of Light Bearers (July 1, 2018)

As mentioned earlier, there are many types of spirits who exist on the second dimension, and they move back and forth between their home and the various planets that host life forms. Some of the spirits are what we can call collective, meaning the larger spirit can fragment itself into innumerable smaller light particles in order to execute certain tasks. The smaller particles are still under the control of the larger spirit's awareness. This is what Bob is referring to when he talks about the cloud or the fog from the Creator. Because the spirit world is separate from the manifested realities that exist in our fish tank, our universe, no spirits actually have a permanent home on our planet. Just as you and I come and go, so do all other spirits, including the particles of the Master Mind that inhabit the living life forms, and the second dimension spirits who tend to these creations.

D. So, what else has been going on with you?

B. I've been dancing.

D. Oh? With yourself?

B. With Ia.

D. Why has Ia taken up dancing?

B. Because I asked her.

D. What kind of dancing?

B. It's spinning. She's going a little bit faster now. She's happy, though, that she's been able to talk (*through Christine*) as well, so she feels in that celebration mode, so we've been spinning a little bit. And I have actually been with her to look at the egg, which now is starting to dissolve. I can see a lot of color green. This specific egg is heading for Earth, and it is a group of gardeners.

D. That's good. The Earth could use some help in that regard.

B. There's gonna be, my feeling is, that they're gonna kickstart certain plants that were beneficial for the climate and environment at a specific time that was indeed similar like the current climate. As the climate and atmosphere shifts occurs and changes, then we respond. So this egg is actually a response from the Master Mind on how to meet the shift and change within the atmosphere on this plane. So they're gonna work on creating, not only new physical plants, but they're gonna actually work a lot with the living entities within the soil. Not only the earthworms, but like the star particles that are invisible to the naked eye, they're gonna shift and change, we need to upgrade them a little bit. These are like, they're living entities, but they are more like biological dots.

D. Are they visible to a human?

B. No, not to the naked eye, but they are visible in like a lab. If you think of the light bearers, but they are even smaller, they're very small, they're not like individuals in that sense. A part of this egg, not all of them, but a group here is designed in a molecule, like a little bit of an atom, so if you think of a regular sparkle group, and they are like 80, then this specific unit that is gonna be moving into the soil, they are like millions. So you can see the difference, if you want to talk size.

D. So they would be like tiny little energetic fireflies?

B. Indeed, in the soil.

D. That will help with all the man-made seeds?

B. Indeed, they are gonna be installed to operate silently, in soil. They are not reporting back to a mentor, like Tom does, but a big part from this egg is like a direct extension of the Master Mind. Everything, of course, is a direct offspring from the Master Mind and the Creator. But this is like the Creator moving silently, like a silent mass, like a little army, –but army in a good way, not army in a bad way. It's like he's moving in, I say he, but it's, you know, the Creator, he–she–it, moves in like a silent big fog through the land—if I compare it to a wind—but in the soil. (*He is describing a mass of light particles that cleans the soils and creatures in the soil.*)

D. So it would have a lot of intelligence that comes in with it, more than you could put in an earthworm or a bug?

B. Indeed, indeed. It's like a silent cloud, or a wind, that can move independently and with no limitations through the soil, and go underneath mountains, if needed, to other regions. They are dots—you know how you see those fish, the big groups of fish, how they just move all at once? It's similar like that, to give you a picture.

D. Nice. Are all the spirits from the second dimension created in an energetic bundle, like the ones Ia tends to? Or are there ways that other groups come in, such as the little energetic beings by the rivers you had mentioned before?

B. Well, everyone here comes from the egg. But in this case, this egg has not only this cloud, they have also regular sparkles, if you like. But everyone comes in as an egg.

D. So all the gardeners and travelers come in like that?

B. Me and Ia came in, probably in the same egg, but we were on two different sides of the egg, perhaps. But we came in with the same cycle of learning and destination. And there are other eggs that comes in that belongs in energetic realities where there is no physical manifestation. But in that egg, it comes in and it's like opening a big box, a big present, and it's like putting all your Christmas presents in one big box. So there is the fire truck, there is a doll, there is the chocolate—it's the same thing, that's how the egg comes in. But it is still addressed to the same destination and the same purpose, in general. So in this case, when Tom came in, there was a huge intention, and it emphasized a lot on the waters. So that group is moving in to assist waters.

D. That's fascinating.

B. So, I don't know if there is another, like a "twin flame", that is out traveling like I do, that came from my egg, my class of education.

D. A backup Bob!

B. A backup, if I go out of function! They bring in the other one.

D. I don't think so. Everything is designed perfectly, so there is no need for a backup.

B. But, the egg is different in size as well. Like, the water egg was in one size. But this egg, Ia said, is much bigger. Maybe my egg was just me! Huhuhuh.

D. Well, you are unique. You are special.

B. Maybe I came in a bubble, like my space bubble.(*The bubble he travels in through the fish tanks.*) I do like to be acknowledged, I do indeed.

D. I think everybody really likes you. Everyone appreciates the knowledge given by each of the spirits, but people respond well to you.

B. Ah, I want them to because I want to make myself heard, and I want to be helpful. And I want to see, you know, if they can hear it, I'm sure that they will change certain things, and also to deliver further, to tell others. Since I cannot be everywhere, what I want to do is plant seeds, to make others tell the story and make changes move like a wind over the Earth. That's what I want, that's what the whole thing is about. But I–I do that.

D. You're doing your part, because everyone likes to listen to you. Maybe we can get you on TV someday.

B. OH, I'm game. Ophelia, she laughs about that. Anyway, okay, Ophelia says we're saving energy because the energy is a little bit low within the vehicle. It is a little bit of a struggle because the energies are little bit slower, and I'm trying to bump it up a little. So that's what I've been doing, you know. I've also been singing a little bit with Ia and the egg. I have joined the kumbaya. (*He then started singing.*) Kum–bye–ya, kum–bye–ya...

D. That's not really what you sing to the egg, is it?

B. Nay. But they have divided, so there is a little group here, like brand–new sparkles; I sing to them, and I can sense happiness in this little cluster.

D. That's nice. You make a good grandpa.

B. Oh, Ia said that I can sing to them, so I don't create harm to the big egg! (*Laughing.*) So she gave me this little cluster group and she said, "You can sing whatever you like, as long as it's uplifting," so that's why I sing kumbaya. She said I can do whatever I want with this little cluster group, but I'm not allowed to come in and sing to the egg because I don't have that training.

D. So some have broken off, and some are remaining?

B. Ah, indeed. Little-by-little it's dissolving. And I got this little cluster.

D. How many sparkles in total are there, aside from the tiny ones that are going out into the Earth?

B. I don't know how many are in the egg, but this little group that I was allowed to sing to, they are like forty to sixty little sparkles. They're kinda small.

D. That's a whole classroom full. Maybe they're going to give them to you to teach.

B. Oh, maybe I should sing like traveling songs to them. I'm trying to identify here, but it's really hard to see. I don't have the training, I can't identify if someone in this cluster is like a new Tom for me, a new student.

D. That might take a while to identify.

B. They're happy, but at the moment they're sleeping, it seems. It's not like they're mine, but Ia said that I could guard them a little bit. I guess there's no harm in that.

D. Maybe she's learning to do a little bit of what you do, talking through this one, and traveling, and now you're learning a little bit about what she does, to round out your skill set.

B. I'm babysitting. It's a great responsibility though. If they wake up, you want to be there. I'm sure that's important. They still keep singing over there (*to the rest of the egg*), so it's a great responsibility to raise this.

Because Bob is telling the story of his life in chronological order, as we would see it, all these sessions are sequential. He may occasionally jump backwards to make a remark about something he had previously discussed, but the notes he brings to each session are very well organized. Ia, Gergen, Ole, and the council on the second are always present when Bob is talking through Christine. So, in this next session, Ia picks up where Bob had previously left off. Eli had been talking and stepped out. Normally, Ophelia will come in briefly to clean the energies for Bob, who sometimes struggles to blend. Based on the facial expressions, I thought Bob had moved in to speak.

D. Didn't need a street sweeper? (*I realized it wasn't Bob when Ia began to laugh.*) You tricked me!

Ia. Tricked you! Ah! Bob said you couldn't be tricked last time, so we're trying something different.

D. You imitated him very well, so I just assumed it was him! So how are you?

Ia. Doing well, thank you.

D. I'm glad you're coming to visit. What's on your mind these days?

Ia. Oh, we are indeed proceeding with the development of our new class.

D. The egg?

Ia. Yes, the egg has dissolved, and we are deciphering. However, not collectively now. They have been given each an older student to work with the teachers. So, they are operating in three groups. There is the little sparkle, there is an older sparkle that would be considered like a ten–year–old or a twelve–year–old in your way of thinking, combined with a teacher. So there is a trinity of communication and growth, where everyone takes part in the progress of learning and teaching.

D. So you teach them right away to look after the younger ones?

Ia. To become teachers, yes.

D. So this is after they have gone to the Water World or the Greenhouse Planet?

Ia. Indeed, they have returned.

D. Does Tom have someone?

Ia. Oh, Tom, indeed, he has a sparkle. He tries to play with his sparkle apprentice, having a memory of being very playful himself. So indeed, we have given him to someone who is very inquisitive, and as well, very active.

D. The chain continues! (*Both Bob and Tom are very active, so it is not surprising that Tom would be given a personality that matches.*)

Ia. The chain continues, indeed. So, there is a need for the comfort of the little ones, as this is the first step of becoming teachers—which is a highly rewarded treat for the twelve–year olds, if we take it as an age. The older teacher simply supervises, combined with creating warmth for both of them as they grow.

D. By the time they become teenagers, are they still in the classrooms, or are they more independent?

Ia. They are always participating in classes. However, the size of the class can change over time. The twelve–year olds, at this point, have started to move into smaller cluster groups, around ten or so. And they will remain like that till they reach about the age of sixteen, compared to a human lifespan. Sixteen is when you are considered an adult, when you are considered to move into your own expertise. Bob, at that point, as we know, went earlier. He went into the beyond, the fantasy land where he felt he was drawn to. His sparkle within created a faster path for him. But normally we tend to go our own individual path when we reach the age of sixteen.

D. Relatively speaking, how old was he? I know he was pulled out of some sparkle classes early.

Ia. Eleven.

D. That's when he first went to the beyond?

Ia. That's when he went with our teacher, Gergen, to the beyond, indeed. He came back, of course, but from that point he was, I would not call it a special school, because it was not, he was simply put in different study areas to trigger his path to come.

D. But he still has a little group he worked with, because he talked about being in the lab with them?

Ia. Indeed. And he has also a group at this particular point, a group of six or seven students that he still cares for. So from all levels, we still take care of those who have been our students. Gergen will always be present for us, for instance, so it is similar like that. The little sparkles in this egg, the newborns, so to speak, they have come to learn to create energy waves. They are here to work with soil and to work with plant life and animals, mainly plants, even on the seabed.

D. Trying to fix some of the damage done by humans?

Ia. They're working to establish higher frequencies of light. Energy levels need to go up around plants and the environment, in order for them to function at all. They will be placed for longer periods of time, even though there is no time, but they will be placed more stationary, this group, than others. So they will move in on certain areas and regions of need. Differently than other sparkle groups who move in and then leave and can enter living entities and even rocks. These are designed to remain. Bob would not have liked to be in that egg! Hehehe.

D. That's not how you travel!

Ia. That's not how you travel, indeed. So, there you go. I just wanted to pop by and give you a little bit of a surprise.

D. Well, you did, because you totally tricked me.
Ia. That was the whole idea, Bob said, he had a secret.
D. Thank you so much for coming, Ia. Talk soon.
Ia. Oh, you are welcome. Bye bye.

Tending to the Sparkles (Dec 16, 2018)

Christine is able to stay in a trance state for about an hour, and we have a routine of sitting once a week on Sunday morning. Ophelia and Bob come to each and every session, and Bob expects that he will be given an opportunity to deliver the notes he has brought for the day. There is usually time for two or three of our spirit team to deliver messages, and the first to speak is the one present from the highest dimension. We have about a dozen who rotate through, including Ari, Eli, Jeshua, someone from the Elahim Council, the Council of Nine, Isaac, Ophelia, Zachariah, Tosh, Gergen, Ia, and several others. Although it rarely happens, sometimes there is not enough time left for Bob to speak. So we have an understanding that we will hold a separate session during the upcoming week if he ever gets bumped. This is not entirely satisfactory to him because he seldom gets to speak first, so he feels less important than the others. Not so long ago, there wasn't time for him during our Sunday session, so we sat again a few days later. The first thing he said when he came in was, "Separate session, my stage! Separate session, my stage!" which shows how strongly he feels about getting a turn to speak. The truth is, he gets about forty percent of the trance time, leaving all the other spirits to share the remainder. Perhaps he has earned this right, since he has been my (David's) closest spiritual guide and companion during every incarnation on Earth, and this is the very first time he has been able to talk directly to me. He does feel strongly about being part of the normal Sunday sessions, because there are untold hundreds of spirits who gather around and observe. The very next Sunday after his "separate session", he showed up and gave Ophelia a note, which appeared to have come from Gergen or the council on the second. The note basically said that the council expected Bob to speak today. Ophelia then asked where he got the note. He told her it was in his office, so he thought he should pass it along. But failed to mention it was he who had written it and placed it on his desk. Ophelia, or course, knew who created the note, as nothing is hidden in the spirit world, but it did make her laugh. He clearly had made his feelings known.

The topic about the creation and care of new souls, which Ia was addressing in the previous talk, had not been picked up again for several months, but when it was, they began right where they had left off.

B. I was not, I was NOT going to miss this opportunity because who knows if another window is gonna come! Someone says, "Ohh, we will put a separate session," but what if a separate doesn't come? So I'm not taking my chances this time.

D. Who wrote that note?

B. I did.

D. I think Ophelia suspected that.

B. I did write it in a way that I know Gergen does; "Bob is excused from council study, to come and visit with the original group and communicate this afternoon," even if it's morning here, but that's what it said on the note. But Ophelia said, "Who wrote this note?" And I said, "Oh, it was on my desk, in my study, and I thought, ohh, maybe I should give this to Ophelia." It didn't have like, "To someone," on it anywhere.

D. No signatures, just a note. I don't think she was entirely fooled.

B. Nay, Gergen's gonna know about this. But we do have a little bit of a break in council meetings, so it wasn't a full lie, but I thought it might look better. But if I'm caught with my hand in the cookie jar, so to speak, then it is absolutely not better. But she tends to know exactly what I'm up to. I did want to come forward a little bit and talk about, -because this mirrors the upbringing and kind of development that exists in ALL spiritual realities, so even if I'm talking about the second, it's not like it's very different in other sparkle kindergartens. After you have deciphered the egg and they start to break up, that's normally when I get to meet them, because I'm not allowed to interfere too much with the egg, you know, sniff around it. It's not like I have a flu or that I will get them sick or anything, but Ia said one time that if I'm too close while they are trying to decipher the melody that radiates from the egg, it can create a confusion. They have a distance as well so that there is no confusion about their energy and their melody, so the egg remains completely pure. But because I have not the training on how to fully detach my melody in the presence of another being, my melody is shown wherever I go. I can't turn my melody down, so to speak, just because I'm deciphering a new melody. So she said that even if I'm there and stand way in the back, because I don't have the ability to transform and make myself quiet, then the egg might be interfered, and their job might be that they are deciphering ME, because they hear my melody!

D. They would think they were all little travelers.

B. Oh, all these travelers. Then Ia would say, "You get all of these, and they're gonna follow you." So, I'm not sure I really want that. When I say that I can't really make my melody quiet in the second dimension to decipher an egg, that is different than when you move across different barriers. Then you actually transform your melody a little bit. Like when I go to the sixth, and I have learned what sort of melody that exists over there, then in some way I mirror it. So, it's like, here are the lyrics of the sixth and I sing it, to make a picture for you. So I can mirror the melody and the song in the sixth, –that's how I get access to get in. It's like being given the lyrics of this reality, and you can adapt it to your own melody. But what I said with the second is that I can't just make myself quiet, that is the difference. So I got to understand (*the melody of*) the seventh and the sixth, and even the Library. In order for me to go there, I transform into that melody and frequency and vibration that exists there, and that is how I get access, how I can get in. So if I don't have the lyrics, to make it easy for you, I can't fully engage or get in. And that is how permission is given—you get the lyrics of that specific reality. I'm still waiting for, you know, the tenth.

D. So are you allowed to interact with the new sparkles yet?

B. Pretty soon. So, as the egg has divided, I am welcomed back in some way to engage with the little ones. And they appear, if you think of popcorn, they pop around, that's sort of how it is when they first split off this big egg. From there, they are all assigned a little mentor to just sort of care for them. They're not supposed to teach them that much, but they are supposed to nurse them. And they are kinda young, so if you think of a sparkle being a baby up to one-year–old, or something, then they are given a five–year–old to simply radiate warmth and presence, because they do know and detect that they are not anymore in one big egg. So warmth is important for them to continue their wish and their need to have sunshine in the head, so to speak, to feel the presence of others.

D. So do the five–year olds stay with them all the time?

B. Yes. Yes, indeed. Before it's time to learn things, they just sit there and radiate warmth and correct them.

D. Are they in a big space together?

B. Ah, it's a big space, but it's still divided, so that's where they're at. Eventually, of course, it's all about getting different teachings and understanding. But in order for that to even occur, you have to be somewhat embraced by equals who don't demand anything from you, who simply radiate a presence and a love and warmth to the sparkle.

D. Is there distinction made to assign them to certain five–year olds, do they try to match patterns?

B. Ah, indeed. They try to bring in five–year olds that are very similar in their makeup, so it's not like a foreigner for them, even if we are all the same. As they do, the five–year olds, their teaching is to care—to care for things. So it's like having a fish in a fish bowl. So you are given a fish and you are in charge of making sure the fish doesn't die. They're taking this responsibility extremely well because the five–year olds, they really want to make sure their fish is alive and kicking.

D. So that's really their first experience in taking care of another soul?

B. It's to nurture and care, and to give somewhat of an embrace, to make sure their fish is doing well in their fish bowl. So their first teaching is just to understand that you selflessly care for another entity, –that's what you do. In some way, you are connected to that specific fish, always.

D. Do you remember when you were that little?

B. I remember being surrounded, like in a cocoon, and it was warmth and I could sleep there, and I felt very protected. It was like a big sleep.

D. Do you have any recollection of who it was guarding you?

B. Ah, it's a female, a friend to Gergen. It's like a couple thing that took place when I was a sparkle. There was me an Ia, and then there was Gergen and a female, and they were like parents to this little twin couple of us.

D. So Gergen was taking care of Ia.

B. Indeed. But then this female energy, she's like a grandmother almost, I really like her. But she works a lot with potions on other realities, so I don't see her that much anymore.

D. You mentioned her before.

B. She's like a medicine woman, that's what you would consider her to be. I really like her, she read stories and stuff, especially to me.

D. Probably about traveling.

B. Huhuh. But I liked that. I liked to just be there, and she was talking a lot to me and telling me stories, just talking about things. And I remember not understanding everything, but I just liked the presence of someone talking to me, and she did. She talked and she talked and she told about all these most fascinating things, if I only could remember them.

D. She might have told you some secrets.

B. I called her Lou–Lou.

D. Was she an equivalent of like a five–year old at the time?

B. No, she was older. So maybe this was later in sparkle life, but that's who I remember, so she was probably with me from the beginning. I still can communicate sometimes with her, but she works with the potions. She creates new plants and liquid forms. She works a lot with the realities that are liquid, –and she's busy! So Ia doesn't work with her either, that much, because we are more working with energy and solid form. But Lou–Lou is more in water worlds, like liquid. I'm not saying water worlds, but liquid. She makes samples of new plants, but plants who are in liquid. Some are not fully formed, —it's not like all are sea–grass. I might want to go there actually, because I haven't seen her for a while. But the whole process is that you have someone like a mentor who follows you, and then, you know, Gergen, he was equipped to take care of both me and Ia. So that's what happened.

D. That's really nice to know. So, the little egg that you are watching now, will you be involved with any of them?

B. Nay, it's not like all of us get a fish. I might get one later. I did have one, way back. But now I'm mainly interested to see what this new egg is gonna do. But Ia said they are not gonna know that. They (*the new souls*) are in the phase of being caressed and tended to. They're just in that phase of sleep and eat kind of thing, and to be cared for. I asked if I could have like a manual on how to decipher signals, but Ia said, "That's YEARS, –if years existed–, of training to even understand the deciphering manuals. And it's not like I can just give you one, because you're not going to understand, and it's just going to create more questions for you."

We should point out that Bob and the other spirits will present ideas in a way we can understand. Ia does not measure in "years", but Bob converted the magnitude of the effort into a time frame we could appreciate. The spirit world shares many similarities with our Universe, since it is designed by the spiritual dimensions, but certain things they say are simply to aid us in grasping the concept. Time, as we understand it, does not exist in the spirit world, but it does on Earth. In our spiritual home, "time" is a measure of learning and progress, and is cyclical in nature, not linear.

After the spirits within the energetic egg have all separated and gone through a period of waking up and becoming active, all those that came in the bundle are placed in the same big classroom where they are given the freedom to play and learn about their new environment. Just as we humans are made to forget, the new spirits, who came from the all-knowing Creator, are also without a memory of their origin. They are, however, destined to perform certain objectives, but are given the latitude to explore other areas of interest. Ia and other mentors are experts in detecting the patterns of intent given to each new soul by the Creator, but it is up to the soul to develop and fulfill its own purpose. Zachariah once said that souls who do not perform as expected can be returned in some way to be modified, but that is quite rare. The teachers and mentors work patiently to bring out the very best in each new soul, and this training begins in what our spirit team refers to as sparkle school.

Sparkle School

After the energetic bundle has separated into individual souls, which can number over one hundred, the souls are gradually introduced into learning situations under the gentle guidance of advanced spirits, such as Ia. The second dimension is considerably vaster than we can understand, because those spirits are responsible for the lifeforms on every planet in every fish tank. As we have discussed in earlier books, all the spirits who communicate with us are part of a group involved in the project we know as "Earth", even if they have never incarnated here. Souls on the second are designed for specific functions on specific planets, so when Bob and Ia were created, they came together as part of a group destined to work with Earth, at least initially. All the little spirits in the successive groups that Ia and Bob mentor or care for also have Earth as a destination. This ensures that knowledge about this planet is passed from the older spirits to the younger, and each generation contributes a little bit more to the collective understanding. There are elaborate schools set up to teach the developing spirits certain specialties, broadly broken into four main groups relating to animals, plants, aquatic life forms, or energetic patterns. All the second dimension sparkles must attend classes and learn about the types of life on Earth, but will normally only go into advanced training in one of the four groups. This decision is a matter of each sparkle's preference, but what they prefer may simply be an awareness of the pattern given to them by the Creator.

All the second dimension spirits go to physical realities to study the life forms that will be found on the planet they have been assigned. Bob, as we have learned, was drawn to study land-based animals, so he went to a place he calls the "4–H Farm". I'm sure he picked the name because we humans know it as a group dedicated to teaching children how to take care of animals, –but

I'm also sure that when Bob and Ia talk among themselves they do not call it by that name. If a soul is destined to become a healer and helper of plant life, they go to study on what Bob calls "the Greenhouse Planet", where they learn to become "gardeners". Those who prefer fish and other aquatic life will be sent to "the Water World" and will become "water engineers". The final specialty is to study and work with energy patterns, which is the path that Ia followed. (DNA is a visible manifestation of the underlying pattern.) The various planets where they go to study are physical locations in our fish tank. But as Bob explained, the planets are part of the second dimension, and would be at a slightly higher frequency than Earth. As to whether we would be able to visibly see the planet though a telescope is something he has never clarified.

The next part of their training program is when they go to Earth and blend with various life forms, which has a two-fold purpose. They practice maintaining their own light capsule, and are also expected to sense and interpret the energy patterns within the tree, animal, rock, or fish that they are temporarily blending themselves with. As they get older, they will travel around on Earth looking for imbalances in the patterns of the living beings, which they may then be able to repair. The Earth is home to innumerable entities from the second dimension who are here tending to all life forms, the waters, and the atmosphere.

In these next few sessions, Bob often is describing the activities related to some of his students. Once he became an "adult" in the spiritual world, he was given a group of ten students to mentor. Over time, as they became more independent, some chose to join other groups that were more directly involved in activities that matched their own interests. Bob still has six that he supervises, but they all have become much less reliant on him and demand less of his attention. Because Ia is like a kindergarten teacher on the second, Bob periodically drops in as a guest lecturer in Ia's classroom, where he entertains and tells stories about his adventures, –at least to the extent he is allowed to divulge information. There was one young sparkle, who Bob felt a great kinship with, named Tom (for our benefit). As Tom got older, Ia assigned Bob another group of ten students for him to mentor, including Tom. We were fortunate to have been told quite a few entertaining stories about Tom's growth from a little sparkle to a young adult, which really gives a fascinating view into what spirits are taught, as well as how they are educated.

We would like to warn you that we have knowingly left a lot of grammatical errors (as determined by modern masters of the English language) in his talks. Not because we're too lazy to fix them, but rather, he speaks the way he speaks, so who are we to judge his choice of words? Punctuation can also be a little tricky, as it is sometimes hard to detect the end of his sentences due to his liberal use of "and" and "but". But if you are a little bit forgiving and follow along, you will hear the beautiful melody he gives to his stories. I also use dashes within his sentences, either to show a brief pause, or to indicate he is about to veer off-topic, which he often does to add a clarifying remark or side observation.

Bob as Guest Speaker (April 2, 2017)

D. Does Ia ever have you come in as a guest speaker? ("*Ah*") Do you like that?

B. Ah. She says, "Make it simple, Bob. Make it simple." But I tend to be so excited about what I've learned. And she knows I like to make a little charade. Huhuh! She allows me, but sometimes she puts her hand on my arm and says, "Make it simple, Bob." And I sort of reverse and try to make it simple, and I tell them about the visits that I make. And how it's possible for them, if they want to become like little travelers, and little scientists, because these are second dimensional beings in the making. So, SOME will be like Ia, and SOME might wanna be like me. So, I wanna say there are options, and I wanna tell them about the options. So I do. And Ia says, just make it simple. And I try to, but sometimes, because no one, –they have not seen a solar system, so I can't talk about the solar system–, but I CAN tell them about you. I can tell them that there are DIFFERENT life forms that looks very different from us, on other places. So, I can say that, and that makes them really interested. I try to describe Ophelia and you, and how you communicate VERY differently. And I tell them about the stars. They have seen star falls, so they have seen stars, BUT, they don't know how they get there. So, I don't want to confuse anyone, but I want to tell them that there is some intelligence behind all the things they see up in the sky. And I do! And I say, "This star is made by light beings in the seventh dimension." And they don't know about dimensions, so I have to sort of sketch, and say, "This is we, here we are. And here is Earth." And then I draw. Ia, she sometimes does like this (*shakes his head side to side*), but she laughs and she allows me to do this, because she knows there is one or two here that will be little scientists. So, she encourages personal development.

D. Sounds like she calms you down a little bit, too.

B. Ah. She's been with me for a long time.

D. Sounds like a little couple, almost.

B. I see it like that. We went together, you know, like when we merged in trees, way, way, way back. We were in it together.

D. You're very close with her then. How did she get a job in the vault? How did that happen?

B. There is another group she operates with, it's another angelic group.

D. What dimensions?

B. It's a little bit higher up. I'm familiar with my ladder. She has a different one, because her ladder goes in a different direction. So, I don't know if it's like number 1–2–3–4–5. Because her ladder is, –if mine goes here, to where you are in your lab–, and over there is Ophelia. I see this. But her ladder goes in another direction, so she communicates with an angelic reality similar as Ophelia operates within.

D. Does she also go to train somewhere?

B. Ah.

D. So, she is a traveler too, in a way?

B. In a way, indeed. But she doesn't go to different levels. She works with healing energy, I would say. And it's also about the capsule. She learns about how maintenance in the capsule is evolved and she does a lot of evaluation on the capsules for the second dimensional beings, creatures, to go in. So, it's a different learning. And I haven't been studying that, but she tells me some. It's mostly about preserving capsules for the second dimensional beings, but it's also how to maintain capsules that exist on the third dimension, the capsules around objects like trees and certain things. Because everything has a capsule. You would probably call it an aura. But it's both from us, as an individual. But it's also something that is placed on the third dimension, and she operates with the maintenance of these capsules, which is light, –it's light only. She doesn't work with sound. She works with light only. Oxygen and light.

Because it's somewhat like an atmosphere, –we talked about the atmosphere before. The capsule on the third dimension is actually around objects, it's like its own atmosphere. So, she works with maintaining the balance within these. It's a field.

D. Does everything have its own field, all living beings? Or is it like a general field?

B. Yes, you know, there is one general field. But there is also an individual field, and she operates with that. Because there is a balance that needs to take place. If the field around each individual object, –including a person, a vehicle–, if that is not in a good health, then it will influence the general field as well. So, she works with that. In some way, I think that she operates with those in the eighth, because eight and seven, it's atmosphere and it's also light. Ophelia is light (*the seventh*), and eight is the elements and atmosphere, you know. But then again, she is not in the same ladder as I am. So, if she starts to move, if I try to make a picture for you, she will not just, whoopsi, travel through your lab. So, she's not cleared for that. And I'm not cleared to go to these places she goes, because they learn about different potions in order for the capsule to be healthy and operating. You know, once, –I will tell you how it is, –once a capsule is shut down, like a lamp, then that object doesn't exist anymore.

D. On the third dimension?

B. Yes, indeed. So, it can have an outer influence for its existence and disappearance, but it can also be that the capsule hasn't been functioning properly. So Ia and a group that she works with, they have the ability, if it cannot be healed and exchanged into a functioning field, they can actually shut it down. (*He is saying there can be outside influences that cause the light capsule to disappear, but the inner one can also have problems. Ia and her group work to correct problems with the inner balance.*)

D. And that causes the individual to...?

B. It causes the individual to fall asleep.

D. So, the soul energy leaves, the cloud energy?

B. Yep, before you shut something down, you make sure the inside has left. You know how we talked about how my creature was gone, my furry one? Before it was gone, before it was physically removed and shut down, its field, then the inside had left. So, it never experienced like, oh, I'm being shut down.

D. Well, hopefully it will have a place, somewhere in the future.

B. Well, it all goes into the vault, into the museum, because it has existed. Everything that has existed will have a place, in some way, in a vault or in a museum. Not everything is in a museum for display, but it exists in its own vault. But when a plant or something suddenly doesn't exist anymore over time, then it has actually been shut down. Because, number one, it doesn't operate correctly within its own environment. Number two, it has not been able to be repaired, its field. So, in that way, you make it fall asleep.

D. I'm glad you get to spend time with Ia. It sounds like you share what you learn with each other?

B. Ah. I like her. She likes me! So, she invites me to talk with her students. You know, she has a lot of students, and everyone likes her.

D. Well, you see her in the vault all the time. (*The vault in the Library on the fifth, where information from different realities is stored. Bob and Ia tend to different vaults, but see each other all the time.*)

B. I see her and I say, "What are you carrying there?" And she says, "You know you're not supposed to ask." And I say, –I'm just trying to say something so she notices me, because we do know each other–, and I say, "I'm not going to tell what I have in my vault either!" And she said, "I know you're not, because you're not allowed to. But you must have something that you are really proud of." And I say, "Yes, I am! I'm really proud of my boxes!" But she never asks, so she's very polite.

D. There must be something you can tell her about your work?

B. I tell her about solar systems, and she is familiar with this. And I tell her about how I am learning about more of an extensive version of the core. And she says that is very interesting because it will in some way affect her work with the capsules. She's interested in learning about the sun.

D. Well, that's all quite fascinating.

B. So, anyway, we meet here and there, because I also have things to share, –she works with the capsule and I work more with the core, and we try to keep each other updated with certain things. And we do that sometimes, we go to like a little meeting.

D. Well, you still have meetings with Gergen, don't you?

B. Team building!

D. Go on little expeditions into the third dimension.

B. In the jungles. We did before, you know. Anyway, I guess that will be it.

D. Well thank you for stopping by, I learned a lot. Hopefully we'll be talking here as frequently.

B. So, okay, bye bye. I'm gone!

Blending With Trees and Rocks (May 28, 2017)

After studying and becoming familiar with the types of lifeforms they will encounter on Earth, all the spirits on the second dimension are then instructed on what to expect when they first go and blend with trees, rocks, plants, or animals. It's an exciting time for the little sparkles, and marks the beginning of their progression towards being directly involved with identifying and healing problems they discover while out traveling to Earth. If you are tempted to think this is a little strange, just remember that you are a spirit inhabiting a host body as well, so the process is universal across the spiritual spectrum.

D. How's Ia doing? Have you seen her lately?

B. I stopped by one of her classes, and I did like a little show for her students. I talked about the vast, mysterious space that exists above that they will see once they blend with trees on Earth, and how they would be able to somewhat stargaze. So, I encouraged them to become like little stargazers, and I said, "Do you know what exists way up there?" And they don't, of course. So I tell stories about things. I do indeed!

D. So when you are inside an object, like a tree or a rock, you can still see out?

B. Well, not in the beginning, because that is only confusing. The first couple of times when you blend with an object, you merely function to adapt into being somewhat encased. Because you have to also know that you are a guest and a visitor in the tree, for instance, and you have to learn about the tree. So, if you are trying to put your focus outside the tree and looking out for the stargazing experience, then you have missed the first lesson of all, and that is to understand how to resonate and not interfere with the object that you are blending with—because you are a guest. It's a little bit different with an incarnation, because you are not necessarily a guest. It's not like when you leave someone else will pop in. So, it's a little bit different. But you still have to honor the vehicle that you are in. When the little particle, the little ones from the second dimension, when they start to blend, they learn about the respect and care for the host. And that is one of the main understandings, because they will learn to blend, first of all, with the trees. Then they will move into a plant, which has a shorter life span, and they have to in some way speed up that knowledge they learned in the tree. They have less time, even though time doesn't exist. But they have less cycles to learn about, or understand, how to fully blend and care, and also learn from that plant. So, you can see that once you start to move and upgrade yourself into different life forms, it comes with a variety of different ways to do so. The tree would be considered the easiest one, because you travel in a group and you have your tutor, of sorts, with you. It's like going to camp, like little people going to camp, it's the same thing. Then, they get a little bit more bold, and they go alone to camp and merge with a plant. But they don't have to do it so thoroughly as they did with a tree because they have to somewhat proceed faster. And then the next level would be to sort of gradually move through different objects that exist on where they are supposed to blend, and they report back what they learned. In a similar way like a soul comes back with a life review, so does the sparkles.

D. So when your little sparkles were out, did they come back and you'd talk about what they experienced?

B. Yes, indeed. And they tell me, or in this case, normally Ia—Ia will push them, really, so she says, "Once you first blended with a tree, what was the first thing you recognized?" And normally they get a sense of a pulse, which means they sense that it is alive. And they will have to report back how they operated within that tree in order to not interfere. It's also because they have to learn that it is very important not to interfere. It is a cosmic law that exists within all that you do not interfere with another life form. So it's the same thing, they have to learn the cosmic rules that exist regardless of where. So they report back and then, as they progress, Ia makes them go into a tree that carries a certain, –it's somewhat like a treasure hunt, because they have to go into a tree that carries a certain experience, let's say, and the little ones have to find that. Not all do in the first time. So, it's like a treasure hunt. The first tree you blend with is considered like a friendly, easy–going host, but then it becomes more tricky. And it's because they need to know, later on, when they blend by themselves, when they are not just sent off, where to go and what to look for in order to be helpful.

D. Wow, that's fascinating!

B. Yes, and the little ones get really excited when they go on their first treasure hunt to find the problem. And there are certain trees that are known for us to send them to, because they carry different experiences the little ones have to find. And when they report back and, let's say, there is one that has a problem with its roots, and the little ones come back and say, "This one was in full harmony. It had full oxygen and was like a teenager." And it was actually more like it was retired, and the roots were actually hurting like you want a hip replacement. Then Ia says, "You didn't really solve the assignment. You didn't find the treasure, so you missed one of the clues when you went in." So this is how they learn, because it's FUN to learn in the way of a treasure hunt. Because you get this assignment, and you get excited! I like that too; I like to be excited!

D. You're never really in danger when you are out on Earth, are you?

B. No. Just startled. Even when the little ones are in the trees, even when someone cuts down the tree, they are never in danger. They are instantly removed and retreated, so to speak. No, not in danger, simply sad when certain things happen. Simply sad. I'm sad when they spray (*poison on the crops*), even if I'm intact, from my point of view. I do see the creations and I know that everything that exists has been made by someone in my lab. So, I get sad. Sometimes I even get angry. The worms, I got sad and angry. And I don't like, I'm especially concerned about the soil.

D. The way they grow crops now, the soil is going to be dead.

B. But it is also what I talked about; those sound barriers that have been somewhat interfered with. It actually creates, when those sound vibrations or barriers that are encasing everything, like mountains and trees and so forth, and when they are interfered in their own vibrational field, then they somewhat resign. So, that's what we talked about earlier, about the cars and planes and so forth. I would prefer if it could be created a different way of moving about, because it is a fact that you do not need to make either noise or pollution. It is a fact that the knowledge exists how to make it less disturbing for nature and where you are at.

Bob described how loud noises can actually kill sensitive living organisms, such as zooplankton, because there is a protective vacuum layer around the creatures that is broken down from the high energy sound waves. I had never heard that before, so I did a little research and discovered that once again, Bob was absolutely correct. Scientists in Australia evaluated the effect seismic surveys for oil exploration had on the zooplankton, and were shocked by the results. These ships travel back and forth, sending sound waves into the rocks under the seabed, where the reflected signals can be analyzed to determine geologic structures deep below the sea floor. Their study determined that a single sound pulse from the survey ship would create a 2 km diameter kill zone, where up to 90 percent of the plankton were exterminated. When in operation, the ships send out a pulse every 10 to 12 seconds, 24 hours a day, for months on end. Each year, there are tens of thousands of square kilometers of ocean that are bombarded with high energy sound waves, which deafen whales, dolphins and fish, and also kill fish eggs and much of the zooplankton. Naval vessels also use sonic transmissions for communication, and that has been linked to the debilitation and death of many mammals and fish. Those from the second dimension are extremely concerned about the disregard we display towards their creations. Bob then makes a rather cryptic observation that humans already possess the technology to transform our society into one that does not require fossil fuels, suggesting that governmental suppression of humanity is both malicious and intentional.

D. So, what else has been going on?

B. OOOHHH, I have been visiting with Gergen and with Ia a little bit. I've been talking with them, and I have showed them my scriptures and my journals and what I have detected during my travels to this group. So, I have shared that, and they have been really interested in it, because Ia said there are some in her class that are somewhat interested in traveling, she said.

D. I wonder why?

B. HEE HEE HEE. She said, "You just put all sorts of things in their heads!" And I said I just want them to be excited. I want them to know that there are options, not just working with plants, and not just sitting still and reading up on things, you know. Not everyone has to be in the lab all the time. There is progress because one feels happier if you know that there is certain things that will come, eventually. Like my solar system; now I feel more excited to finish it and to make different adjustments, because I would know where to put it. So, if the little ones know there might be ways to travel and know what is beyond, so to speak, then they will be more excited and eager to be a part of the learning process.

D. A bunch of little Bobs!

B. They might be! They might be so, indeed! And I will tell them, if I'm allowed to, that they can travel on a rainbow, and that you can go to all sorts of different places. And I will, if I'm allowed to, I will tell about certain things that I have found. But, hehe, Ia is like, "You put little things in their heads, you messed it up a little bit." She had put in to their system to sit and work with light one time, to sort of learn how to generate light by yourself, and just be your own battery. And she said because I had been in there prior and talked about all these travels, she couldn't make them sit still and work on being a battery, because they were just, you know, popping their eyes open, so to speak, and looking around and whispering. And she said, "You made my work a little bit harder, because they didn't sit still and they didn't become like batteries." You can see it as a meditation class, if you like, and they were in training to fill up their own light capsule, because they have to be somewhat in that light ball of energy as they blend and merge and so forth. So this was in training for that, but because they were somewhat preoccupied with my discussions where I told them about my travels, they didn't sit still. But she laughed and said, "I might not invite you anymore!" So she laughs, you know. I'm sure I'm still invited, but maybe after. She said we're going to have to look around the schedule when you can come in! HUH HUH HUH. Gergen, he's laughing. He sort of shakes his head. He knows about this, because he's seen our progress, me and Ia, all along. So he knows that it's been a little bit like this.

D. She settles you down, and you fire her up!

B. I would say so, indeed. Ohh, sometimes she reminds me that I do to need to work on my own light capsule, because as I travel and as I divide, like you say, and project my energy, it becomes more important for me to return and withdraw my energy and come into my light capsule. So she reminds me of that.

D. Well, that's good, –she watches out for you.

B. She knows that it makes me happy. She said, "You were always different." When we were in class, when we were sparkles, I was always asking questions, I was always way ahead of the teacher's agenda. So, she said that I was always wondering about things, and the teachers were like, "Shush. Shush, Bob. We will come to that later." And she laughs about that, because she was more quiet and paid attention to what the teachers were saying. I heard what they were saying too, but as I did, questions popped up, and I sort of raised my hand and I wanted to know more. So, I think I'm better suited to be alone, like with you, instead of being in a group, because I can see that I might, you know, disturb and distract. So, I think it's better that I have just one teacher, I think that is much better for everyone, including me! HUHUHUH, Heehee, I can set my own pace, so to speak.

D. Well, you are doing what you are supposed to be doing, now.

B. I am, indeed!

From Theory to Practice (Oct 9, 2017)

Years ago, after Bob began to describe his reality, I asked where the Greenhouse Planet was located. He said it is within this fish tank, not that far away. He then began talking about the true problems with genetically modified organisms (GMOs), which man largely does not understand. In *Wave 1*, the spirits expressed their concerns about GMOs, microwaves and electromagnetic radiation, agricultural poisons, atmospheric contamination, sound pollution, and other ignorant actions of humans, all of which can cause severe repercussions to the carefully managed balances in nature. While we are destroying various creatures, the second dimension is struggling to repair the damage. What is not very well understood by humans is that there is Master Mind awareness in all the living beings and plants on this planet. So, the pain, suffering, sorrow, and fear we cause in other life forms is felt by the Creator. There is a tendency to ask the question, "If there is a god, why does this happen to me?" But yet, what about all the pain and suffering we humans carelessly inflict on the plants, trees, animals, fish, insects, fowl, and other creatures who carry the consciousness of the Creator? I would say we are considerably more indifferent towards the Creator, than the other way around. We lack a reverence for life, and this is nowhere more evident than our treatment of the animals, plants, soil, and air we depend on to satisfy our excessive needs. In this next talk, Bob is explaining that GMO seeds do not function the same as natural seeds, that one of the primary traits of plants, to connect with one another in a web through the soil, is broken by human manipulation.

D. When you went to the Greenhouse Planet, was it in another fish tank?

B. No, I was not. I was clearly in the same box, but it was a Greenhouse Planet somewhere "nearby", Ophelia said.

D. Was that before you started working with Ophelia?

B. Ah.

D. So you worked with the Greenhouse Planet first?

B. Uhumm.

D. Was this after you were a sparkle?

B. A lot of us actually go there first, to garden and to somewhat just learn how to grow things. Because it's also where you can see something become before it's put somewhere, so a lot of us go there to study. It's like a study area, but it exists; it's not like a made–up reality or planet, it exists. But we go there normally just like after the first graduation, so to speak, from sparkle school. So, we go and learn about that. It is an existing place, but in its atmosphere it's different, because time and evolution goes quicker, because that is what we're there to do. We're there to see how things evolve. Let's say I wanted to create a plant and I wanted it to be in a moist environment where there's gonna be a lot of rain. So I would go to an area within this Greenhouse Planet where that can be experienced. And this dust that is in each atmosphere, that is the thing that creates the different time, or what is considered to be time, but it's the cycles. So this dust is put into the atmosphere and that creates not only events, but also the sensation of movement. So in this specific Greenhouse Planet there is a lot of dust, because we have to see quicker, because I want to see if my plant is going to be operating well in that moist environment before I put it in, let's say, the Amazon, for instance. I guess this is where the Evolution Group comes in, they are the dust people, they do things like that. (*Bob has mentioned the Evolution Group uses this dust to alter the speed of evolution, even within existing solar systems.*)

D. While you were there, you didn't have an accelerated evolution, did you?

B. No! No–no.

D. The dust didn't affect you?

B. No, it did not affect me at all, which could be somewhat concerning, but I projected myself there. I went there and I did what I was supposed to do, but I was encased in my light capsule in some way, so I was not necessarily exposed to the atmosphere in the same way as my plant. The plant was more in a form shape, whereas I was in somewhat of an energetic capsule, as I projected my awareness to understand this reality.

D. So your projection could work with the soil and the plants, you could touch things there?

B. Ah, I can touch, I can touch, and I can move around things.

D. Are you going to talk more, at some point, about how life grows, how plants actually grow. You know, the way that things evolve from a seed to something?

B. If the council allows it, because I think it is important that people understand that the seed is like a little family. Within the seed, –that is what's happening when humans try to make a seed, it does not become a family. When a true seed comes off from like a flower, it has in its bubble a family unit of this specific plant to become. And a family unit, it could be like what sort of awareness it's supposed to carry, how long it's gonna live, so it carries different events within this understanding in this bubble that becomes a seed. BUT, when you man–make a seed, you only put in the awareness of growth, to become the pumpkin, to become a carrot. It doesn't have the rest. Like a human, for instance, you have several levels within you; you have a brain you're supposed to think with, you have a heart, you have all sensations, and you have a spirit. And it's the same thing with a seed. That is why when a seed comes from a flower, when it drops off and it flies away, it carries more than just to become a new flower. Do you understand?

D. I think so.

B. So within this seed to be planted, it also puts out light around it in the soil. When a man–made seed is put in, its only instruction is to become a carrot, and nothing else. But the other ones are meant to create a web in the soil to other life forms that also grows. If more and more man–made seeds go down and are not creating the light web to other life forms, then each will somewhat lose its power, its life capsule. Because there is less and less of the web underneath that connects trees, ah, even in the lakes, on the bottom of the lakes, those that create like...(*struggles to find a word*), in the lakes, those that—

D. Algae?

B. Yes indeed. It's all connected. But as more and more of the man–made seeds are put out, they become disconnected. And that is what is happening when there is not a seed that carries all the awareness to spread out, like a star. Some part of the seed will become a carrot, but the other ones are programmed to create the web to other plants in the neighborhood, so to speak. And that is what is happening now. The web underneath is somewhat vanishing.

D. Is that from the genetically modified seeds?

B. Yes indeed, because they are only programmed to become a pumpkin, and they don't know that they are supposed to send out like a little string to the nearby ones so it creates that web that exists like underneath the trees, for instance, the roots. So the roots connect to other roots, but they don't if they're only programmed to become a carrot. So that is what I'm saying about that. A real seed is programmed to connect with other roots and seeds, not necessarily some that is similar to that seed, it could be like another bush or tree or something else. That's also when life forms like the worms and others get confused, because they don't feel the nutrition in that region anymore, because that is actually what a seed is supposed to do.

D. That's fascinating and a really good explanation.

B. Ah. As I see, –I can see the web in the soil that is supposed to connect–, it gets a little bit, let's say that there is supposed to be a hundred strings, then now it's like seventy, and it goes down. So eventually there will only be like this carrot plant by itself. And that's not gonna work, because it's not connected to the whole web of growth, because that is the roots. Life forms such as this will not have roots in the same way if they are not connected to other roots. So that's what I'm saying about that. And individuals living in the soil, like the worms and even little bugs, they detect that, because they also feed from the roots. So, if there are no roots, eventually, if this continues in this massive speed of man–made seeds and food, then the little ones in the soil, they don't have roots to feed on and everything will shut down, and it will become like a drought. That's what happened on other places before.

D. Well, then the humans will disappear. Will you be able to restore the soil then?

B. It's tricky, because you can see by just here (*in Colorado*) the soil up in, –you paid attention here–, up in your mountains. You said, "Oh, it's been raining a lot, why is the soil so dry?" So it's gonna be the same. It doesn't matter if it rains, because the soil cannot take it in, because there is no nutrition left, there's no web left, so it will become a drought then. So, it doesn't matter, it would have to be almost like those torrential rains that was before, like back in the days after dinosaurs. That will sometimes have to be it. I'm just saying it's that whole chain that takes place. You don't want to have your own farming place next to an agriculture place that is not aware of using the right seeds, because you are close to that web and it will mirror off on your plants and your web.

D. That's very sad, how ignorant some of our scientists are.

B. So, you want them to somewhat stay away.

D. Those are the people I'd like to kick.

B. Ah! Ophelia says I'm not supposed to. But I'm sure she has something else up her sleeve. If I'm not supposed to, then I'm pretty sure that she has something like a backup plan, of sorts. You know, that would be the right thing to do, that you have a backup plan if something doesn't really work. I don't know how long this waiting around has been taking place, or how long we are supposed to wait around for something to be solved before, let's say, plan B kicks in. I tried to ask that, but she didn't say, she doesn't say. She smiles a little bit, so I don't feel nervous necessarily. But she is a bit concerned about the web above, and I am concerned about, and Ia is concerned about, the web below. And clearly, they interact. But I do trust that Ophelia and Jeshua have meetings about it and somewhat discuss solutions that could potentially come. Even if she doesn't say to me, I'm pretty sure there is somewhat of a plan B in operation somewhere, even if they don't talk about it. At the moment there doesn't seem to be.

D. Well, I certainly hope so.

B. Ah. Well, we'll see about that. But like Ia, she works a lot with that light in the web and tries to somewhat maintain and send down light to existing webs and roots that are operating correctly, so they become stronger than the neighbor, let's say, that is not necessarily operating as it should. She works a lot with that, with her friends, and puts in more, –it almost looks like light capsules again, but they are not sparkles, there is not people souls that you put down. But it is that you put down, it almost looks like a little crystal, if I could give you a picture, that they put down and it somewhat expands as it is put in. But there are different ways to try to help. But if you constantly need to remind and do things over and over, you somewhat get confused! I get confused why it continues, because you have been given a bigger brain, a bigger understanding, and also, like Ophelia said, you've been working with a filter to remember who you are as a soul and who you are on another level of higher understanding. So, one might THINK that it would be an easy task for change to come from this reality, if more and more uses these two, the brain and the understanding of their true home and how things should operate. So whatever disconnect someone had put into this reality to operate as a filter of choice, I can see that there is conflicting events for people to take a stand on.

D. Well it's hard for people to know what to do, because there is so much disinformation released by the big companies, the media, and many scientific communities.

B. Ah, ah. It doesn't help at all if someone puts a claim on truth, like on your spiritual rights, it's the same thing. If someone puts a claim on being, "I'm the one giving you the news, I'm the one teaching you, I'm the one telling you what to do." It is that whole fact to proclaim supremacy over others, whether it is the connection to who you are as soul, or what you are supposed to do on this level. BUT, it (*spiritual truth*) is spreading because of more and more things that cannot be controlled by these people, and that is because a lot of the technology (*internet*) that you are using at this time is unstoppable for them. It must be frustrating! I'm happy about that, though. Because things pop up that cannot be ignored.

D. It was easier when they could just burn people at the stake to shut them up.

B. Exactly, indeed. Then there was no way to find out, because you were somewhat locked in your box, there was no way to find out. Now, the only thing in the way of not finding out is if you become lazy and don't have a mind like a star, you only are still and nod and are like, "This is what I'm supposed to do," so you are in that one string. BUT, if you start to investigate, if you start to question, if you start to become that star, then everything can be found for you to start creating your own changes. AND, you don't necessarily need to talk about it with everybody, your friends, but if you start to do those changes yourself, as more and more do, suddenly those who proclaim supremacy will just fall flat, because there's no one there to listen anymore. What we want, what I want, is for people to become that star, to investigate, to ask, "Huh, what is that?" Maybe just sniff in that direction and see, "OK, is there something with that?" But there are always gonna be those who are afraid of change and who will try to shut it down, and some people will just say, "OK, maybe I was wrong," so they back off. But if more and more become a star, then those who shut others down, then they will also fall flat.

D. When you say, "be a star", could you explain what you mean by that?

B. It's like, if you are a scientist, they are somewhat in that one string. They are supposed to be a star, that is what mainstream people and society think of scientists, is that they are a star, that they go out and search and investigate. BUT they're normally stuck like a cocoon in one string. When you become a star, you start to investigate, you sniff around and pay attention. It's like not being blindfolded. So, you look in each direction and you say, "Oh, what is that?" So you follow a clue or a lead and you go in that direction. When that direction starts to light up, suddenly you will see that something else is lit up that is resonating with that first idea that you had. So, the more you start to look at that, you become a star. It's spread out, and as it's spreading out, there's no limits of what you can explore and what you can find.

D. Okay, that's a great explanation. So, what else has been going on?

B. Oh, I have actually been with the sparkles a little bit, because they crave my attention. Huhuh

D. We all do!

B. So I have been attending Ia's singing classes.

D. Singing?

B. Singing classes indeed. The sparkles love to sing. Oh, they LOVE to sing. It's singing differently than singing here. It's like toning, but high, because they're small so they haven't a whole range of it yet. So Ia has singing gatherings for them, and it's just a joyful activity, and it's also because they are about to go into the smaller cluster groups, so this is like a graduation time for them. It is similar like a holiday season for you here. It is a time to be merry and a time to be joyful and to do things with others, together. So she's trying to send them off in the most positive way she can. So I'm participating in that, and I do allow questions. Ia said that she will invite me for them to ask questions, so I do that.

D. You entertain questions?

B. I entertain questions, indeed.

D. What kind of questions do they ask, mostly?

B. Some questions are just about, you know, like they are a little bit concerned about moving in and out of trees, because they do know that that is coming up. They talk a little bit about that, and I say, "Well, you can see me. I'm perfectly fine, I'm right here, everything is fine. So there's no need to be afraid." But then I tell them the story when I went into the tree, because it doesn't help if I'm like pompous about it, so I have to tell them my story. So, I do that, I tell them how I experienced it when it was my first time to go off into my cluster group.

D. You were a little nervous, then?

B. I was a little bit nervous too then, indeed. So I tell them about that, but nervousness is a part within us that, if it's channeled correctly, if it's not avoided, then it creates a passage to a higher level of learning on our ladder. So I said, "Being nervous, it is that fact that we can feel that tickle of something greater beyond." And I said, "You will constantly feel a little bit nervous, and constantly feel like there is, 'OHH!' But if you are guided by your peers or your friends, then it is a tickle that will make you climb up on your ladder, so to speak." So, I'm telling them that it's a continuation of surprises, but if we don't follow that sensation of being nervous or being suspicious, –like I still get that, and I tell them about that–, and the curious one in the front said, "What gets you nervous now?" And I looked at Ia, and she's like, "Kindly, kindly," she said.

D. Don't scare the little ones.

B. Ah, so I said, "In this case," –because I do not want AT ALL to talk about being dissolved, I'm not going to do that to anyone, because I'm still not fully OK with that, even though Ophelia said it is the biggest treat under my tree–, but I did say, "at this point it is the fact of traveling, to move outwards of the boundaries we are familiar with. And to move beyond certain realities that are different in their structure, and even the beings that occupy this reality that sometimes can be experienced as both somewhat a little bit scary and odd. And that scary is just in our own minds, so to speak, and odd can be good." I'm thinking about the cone ears, how I was a little bit like, "Ohh, what's that?" But it expands our star within if we see more of that. We are a little bit hesitant of things that are considered new. It's still that fact of coming to terms with encounters that might be considered a little bit spooky or odd. I simply said that I'm traveling to realities that have different levels of form. And he said, "Like another tree?" And I said, "Uh, it's not just the tree, it's those who wander around." And then I said, "It's just different animal life," that's what I said to him. And then Ia, she nodded and she said that was good that I said it was just different flora and fauna. So I said, "Different animal life", and he was content with that. Because that is, in some way, what it is.

The Determination Ceremony (Oct 29, 2017)

Bob is simultaneously active in several different locations, which we will call anchor points, where he has left a little bit of his soul energy. This includes: the second dimension; the vault in the Library on the fifth; Ole's council; Ophelia's lecture hall; and he is also my constant guide and companion on Earth. All spirits, as they progress, are able to move their "traveling" energy around from one anchor point to another. But a soul is also constantly aware of all anchor points. The soul can move portions of its traveling energy to anchor points that need more attention. Then, when something else arises, move energy elsewhere. For that reason, Bob will often discuss one topic for a while, then shift to a completely different subject at a separate location. For him, there is seamless continuity. Although we have organized his talks in a chronological order, he bounces between distinctive story–lines. Here, he once again returns to Ia's classroom, where he share's a bit of his accumulated wisdom with the young sparkles. One that he notices is Tom, who Bob will later mentor.

D. So, what else is going on with you?

B. I've been with Ia.

D. Oh, what's going on with Ia?

B. Ah, I'm hosting classes.

D. A guest lecturer!

B. I'm a guest lecture! What I've been talking about is the experience of creation when it comes to other life forms that exist, other than plants and animals. What I have been talking about is that if one is interested in moving beyond the boundaries of creation that we are somewhat familiar with, when it comes to the Earth, let's say, then there are no limitations what one can create. So, I've talked about my travels to the labs, Ophelia's lab. And Ophelia has also been coming in and talking.

D. Oh, has Ophelia come to your class?

B. Ophelia comes sometimes and talks. And I am gonna invite you to come and talk when they are a little bit more ready. So, at this time I am preparing them. So, what I am doing is preparing them to understand that they (*the other entities, such those from the sixth dimension*) are very different than the ones in the seventh, so I'm talking about that.

D. The way I look will scare them?

B. Ah, ohohoho. So, I'm telling them the story of when I first traveled. And I also said that there is a difference between light and dark, and dark is not scary. So they have to be aware that there is nothing bad in either side. So we talked about different things, and I talked about how you can create certain things. I'm trying to make them excited about different ways of creation. And I also was a part of, in my own little way, to create like this light capsule ceremony.

D. A ceremony?

B. It's a ceremony, a ritual, if you like. Ia, she is more soft in the way she wants them to move into the light capsule, so I wanted to do it somewhat different. So I had, you know, like drums, and I made them go like, bom bom bom bom bom bom bom bom BOM bom bom bom bom bom bom bom BOM bom..(*repeated eight times*), AAAAAHHHHHH bom (*again, eight times*) BOM. So, I made them BOUNCE into the light capsule. Because, I said, "Sometimes, if you go soft, you glide slowly into your light capsule. BUT occasionally, there will be like an alarm, and you have to move faster, let's say, into your light capsule, so this is another technique to do so. You kind of bounce into it." (*He then repeated the entire chant.*)

D. Where did you learn that? Is it yours?

B. That's mine! Because sometimes when I move into my capsule the way Ia and Ophelia do, like with the harp, I fall asleep. So for me, sometimes it's better if I'm just tossed into it. So I thought, "What could be helpful for me, if I want to go quickly into my light capsule and just retreat?" Then I thought, "Maybe with bongs, of sorts," so I'm creating that, I'm using other frequencies. Ia's are more soft, and mine are more determined! Hahaha. I like determination in my songs! So my determination ceremony, like I call it, is to be determined and focused on your goal, –so we're teaching them different things. At first some of them were like "Ohh! Ohh! Scary!" And Ia said, "We will try this now. So, everyone, close your eyes, and we will try this. This is going to be a different technique for you all." And then, "Welcome, Bob," and she clapped her hands, and then I began. It was a great result!

D. Did they like it?

B. Oh, they liked it indeed. And I did too, because I didn't want to stop bonking. And I could see, –the way I see it, I look over them and I can see the energy in colors, and I can determine, based on what color they are at, whether they are in the right state of mind. So I look for that, and a lot of them move into a reddish color. But you might think that you move into your light capsule it has to be white, but it's not like that at all, the light capsule can be in different colors, based on what it is that you need. If you need to move into your light capsule based on a need of healing, then your capsule would become like light blue. And certain different things, based on what you need, creates a different color on your light capsule. So I look for that. And I looked to see if everyone had a color, because that is a sign that I know that they are moving into their light capsule. A lot of them actually turned into like a reddish color.

D. What does that mean?

B. It means that they feel stable. They feel like they are connected, like they're solid, because sometimes I want them to feel like that. I want them to remain and to be still in the experience, and red makes that because it's a little bit more heavier in its density than the other colors. The other colors are lighter, so they float more. I wanted them to feel solid, to be more massive and still within their light capsule. So I created my own ceremony, and Ia was kind enough to let me practice on her students, even though they were a little bit like, "Oh, what's this—what's this?" They like me, but because this was new, they were a little bit like, "Ooohhhh!" And you know, we don't always necessarily like new, until we know what new is. Huhuh.

D. What did Ia think about it?

B. Oh, Ia is very encouraging of everything that I do. So she said, "Did you create this yourself, Bob?" And I said, "Yes I did." And she said, "Well, I'm sure it's going to be lovely." And so she said, "How did you create this? And what is the intention with it?" And I said, "This is to make them more solid, to not float—to not float away, to make them remain and to feel heavier within their light capsule; to be somewhat asleep, but solid in their energetic being." And she said, "Go right ahead, Bob, it sounds lovely." And so I did.

D. And what did she say when you were done?

B. She said, –she laughed a little bit–, she whispered, kinda, "You could have had the same end result without the bonking, because there are different ways." And I said, "Well, I wanted to make a little show out of it, I wanted them to be excited." When I come, it's also like a little show. I like that.

D. I'm sure they're really happy to see you coming.

B. Ah, ah. Gergen was there too! Ha ha. And he's like, you know, he laughed. He always encourages us to proceed in the way that we are fit to do so, and to do it individually adapted to our personalities. So he said, "This is right up your alley, Bob. You did well, did well." I said, "Well, you know," (*He was looking satisfied while popping his lips.*) Ia said that I did well too, and that's important for me.

D. How many students does she have?

B. Oh, she has plenty. This was like sixty—eighty. There is one in the front that is very eager, always pays attention. I think that is one that is going to come with me, maybe later. He's like a little, –he reminds me of me, and I like him.

D. A curious little star.

B. Curious little sparkle, indeed. And I told him, "If you have any questions, simply come to my study, and we will talk about things, and we will ponder about things." But it is all in Ia's hand, of course. Because Ia decides when they can go, so they don't just randomly move around everywhere. So she is in charge of their progress. But I told her, "Once he feels that he is ready, I will be happy to assist."

D. Do they spend most of their time—do they study in small groups together, or are they still individual?

B. Oh, they're more in groups, these don't do individual. These are in groups, big groups, and eventually they are going to move into smaller groups, –and that's a big step for them. They have this big, familiar group for a long time, and eventually they are going to move into smaller cluster groups of study, based on what their expertise are, and based also on their own level of learning; so they're going to be matched with similar minds, so to speak.

D. That happens on all dimensions, doesn't it? Even the souls of humans go through the same process?

B. Ah, begin big, so you're familiar, so you feel the warmth from your friends, company.

D. And then gradually end up sitting in your study alone, waiting for someone to come. (*I was teasing him about his impressive office. He had modeled it after Zachariah's office, with bookshelves and cabinets where he stores his notes, and things he collects on his travels.*)

B. Huh huh huh huh huh, and there I sit! But I do have a lot of people coming. They do come.

D. I'm sure they do. Have I ever come to visit you in your study?

B. Well, you do project yourself a little bit, so you can come like that, but different than Ophelia. She can project more, at this time. But my feeling is that you will be able to project yourself more into my reality, but it's going to be different because you and Ophelia are different. But you can certainly have a look–see, and you can project your awareness, because I allow you to. It is all about that you have to allow someone to visit, that is the first step before, —because even if someone is ready to travel, if you're not allowed and welcome, you will not get in, so to speak.

D. Does Ia have like a group that she raises from little sparkles, and then gets another group?

B. Ah, so she is very dedicated to the little ones. When she graduated, let's say, then she started to care in the nursery kind of thing, so she raised the little ones. But then she started to follow some of them individually, and that's how she later became like a teacher of those who are, let's say, like five or six–year old's. So they're not infants, but they're still in the progress of becoming a teenager. So she likes that. She likes those who are not, –I guess she likes to mold them with her knowledge. I like more...

D. When they can think for themselves?

B. Ah, I like that more, but she likes to make them think. And I want to talk with someone who already thinks! Huhuh. But sometimes I do like to come to this kindergarten sparkle class, I do like that. It's just simply a preference. I'm not saying I don't like the little ones, at all, but she can really remain with them, and I somewhat get distracted and am like, "Oh, I gotta go." So, if I were to be in charge of that class and I would say, "OK, I gotta go," then the little ones, they might be sad. My students are not that small. They're doing really well. They're moving more and more into individual study. They're doing really well, I'm proud of them.

D. Do you think any of them will travel, like you?

B. Ah, there's one, one is really interested in this, but still a little bit hesitant to be out beyond the boundaries where we're familiar with. He asks a lot of questions about transforming his energetic being and how that feels, and what to expect and how to return, and so forth. We talk about that.

D. Do you think you're the first that ever left the second?

B. Gergen, –I don't know if Gergen has. He might have, because he knew Ophelia. So he must have gone somewhere.

D. He's never talked to you about it?

B. He said that he and Ophelia go way back, so he must have gone places, I would assume.

D. I'm sure Ophelia knows.

B. (*He looks to the left.*) Oh, she smiles, she says, "We go way back." So, Gergen has been with her.

D. Gergen must have gone to study on the seventh, as well?

B. Ah, because light is also part of the DNA. So, he went there, of course. The science of light is to increase the knowledge of DNA. And depending on how much light it is, is also based on if the DNA needs to be in hibernation or not. If there's a lot of light then it's just programmed to become, to be what it is. A lack of light doesn't mean a constant lack of light, but it means that it matures within it. So he studied that, also with Isaac. Gergen moved around in his days! Huh huh huh.

D. So you've followed in his footsteps, kinda, even though he didn't really tell you that much about it, you had to figure it out all on your own.

B. Ah, Uhh, uhh. He might have seen in me like what I saw in that little person sitting in the front of the group (*Tom*), I might have been like that.

D. Gergen said, "Oh, we've got one here!"

B. Got one here! Huhuh, that's probably what it was. Okay, I think I'm gonna go, because it seems like Ophelia says it's time to go.

D. Well, thank you for coming, and also Ophelia and Isaac. It's always good to hear your voice.

Spiritual Lemonade (Nov 11, 2017)

Bob makes a memorable comparison of how the fourth dimension is like a watered-down lemonade. It has spiritual awareness, but it is very weak, in comparison to the higher dimensions.

D. So if you compare the vibration of the second to the vibration of the fourth reality, is it faster or slower?

B. Ah, it's faster.

D. So it's closer to the fifth?

B. Ah, in some way. In some way, the fourth is more like a clegg, so it's not a spiritual vibration. If you have a lemonade, which is the spiritual energy, but a lemonade you can't drink. (*He's using lemonade to represent spiritual energy.*) So you put a lot of water in it. That's how the fourth is. So there is spiritual awareness in it, but there's too much water, so it's sort of diluted.

D. That's a wonderful explanation.

B. Whereas the other ones, like two, five, and upwards, are just concentrated, without water. Pure spiritual energy. You don't have to put water in it, you're not supposed to do that. So, with that, it (*the second*) feels like it's similar to the fifth in vibration, if you like. Again, we're talking about tones, so it's a different tone, but it's similar like a melody. That's why I get distressed when I go higher up and I hear like those brainwave noises, because it's so unfamiliar to me.

D. So when you work on the gardens in the fifth, that's pretty close vibrationally to your home?

B. Ah, ah. That's very familiar to me. That's why I kinda like to be on the fifth. And the first time we started to meet, we actually met at the Library and the gardens, so it's very similar. Everyone can feel familiar there, because the fifth carries a little bit of each dimension. If you come from the sixth, then there are parts here that resonate with you, so you feel familiar. There are separate meeting points for all spiritual realities, if you like. The garden and the Library, of course, are for everyone, but the vaults are only for a few to see. So for Zachariah and the ninth, let's say, then there are areas of big studies, like big pillars and big, huge classrooms. And there is also, for you, an observatorium for star research. For everyone who comes, there are parts here that are created so that everyone feels at home. So, everyone likes the fifth.

D. Did you go there before we met, had you traveled much to the fifth?

B. Ah, I went there first with Gergen and looked around, like a field trip. And then he showed me certain things. But I was mainly in the garden. We briefly went through the Library, and he said I was gonna be there more.

D. When do the sparkles, at what point in their development, do they go to the fifth?

B. Oh, it's like after they hit seventeen.

D. So Ia doesn't take them?

B. Oh, no, no. The first thing you do, if you're a fast learner like I was, around the age of twelve, eleven to twelve, you can actually go to the garden, because it's very similar to our garden. But normally, and I don't want to blow my own horn here, but I did go, in human terms, when I was around a twelve-year-old, eleven-twelve, I developed early, one might say.

D. A little prodigy.

B. Ah, so I went to the gardens, because I asked a lot of questions about, "What's beyond?" Because there was something in a class that talked about that, and it caught my attention. And I asked about that. I asked, "What is beyond? What is beyond? What is beyond?" And then Gergen said, after a while, "Why don't we just, you and I, take a little field trip?" It was just him and me. Ia wasn't interested at that point. So he said, "We're gonna go take a look-see at beyond." And so we did. And I said, "This is just the same garden," and he said, "No it's not. Look at the coloring, look at the textures, look at the plants. There's a difference here." And I said, "Yes, it is a difference in color. The color patterns are different." And he said, "Yes, we are in a different reality." So we did that, and that caught my attention. So we went there a couple of times, you know, him and me, and I looked around. I garden things, so I observed certain differences.

D. Did you tell Ia about it when you got home?

B. I did.

D. What did she say? Did she want to go then?

B. No. She said, "Everything will come when it's supposed to," and I said, "Well, it just did!" Huhuhuh. And she said, "I'm not in a hurry. When we're all going to go, when there is training or study, I'll go." Because I didn't go necessarily to study, I went there only to enjoy and to somewhat satisfy my curiosity. Hehehe. But she said, "Everything will come in due time."

D. Very patient.

B. She's very patient. We're different in that way. But she listened to what I said.

D. You're the bold one in the group.

B. Ah, Gergen is good with that. He looks into all the different, independent, individual characteristics that we carry, and then he tries to satisfy them. I'm sure he was tired about the questions, so he said, "Why don't we take a quick look." So we kinda did.

D. How many students does he have in total, ones that he works closely with?

B. He doesn't work closely with students like that. He comes in sometimes and holds big lectures. He doesn't really–, I mean, he's like a mentor for me and Ia, but he doesn't have students in the same way like that. But you can certainly come and ask questions at certain times, to him. But he holds big lectures, and he's also more with the council. His students are somewhat independently walking, like me and Ia. He monitors our development, but differently.

D. Ole must have monitored Gergen, then?

B. I would think so, indeed. It almost looks like he would be the mentor to Gergen. Ole, Ole.

D. He's probably very proud of you.

B. Ah, I like him. He's friendly. He would be like someone that you would consider like a grandfather who will bring you cookies and milk.

D. Maybe you can go visit him on the ninth or tenth, or wherever he's hanging out?

B. I don't know where he's hanging. He smiles and waggles his finger a little bit (*Ole was apparently standing nearby listening to our conversation, and Bob could see him.*)

D. Meaning what?

B. Meaning that I'm too curious again. Gergen says that we will leave now.

Bob's Students Study Remote Teaching (Nov 18, 2017)

Bob has a lovely study area that he designed on the second. One wall is covered with notes of topics and ideas he wants to share with us during this project. He brought a lot of his notes to my study on the sixth, where we meet before each channeling session to discuss what he should talk about. This session covers quite a few topics, but is mainly about his students and how learning and teaching becomes more difficult when they start to blend with trees and rocks on Earth.

B. So I'm in that phase where I want to learn more. I want to learn more about that travel thing. That's why I invited Ole. (*He invited Ole to his office.*)

D. What did Gergen say when you were sitting around your table?

B. Oh, Gergen, he sat and he smiled and he allowed questions, but he was also answering certain things that is part of my own windows as well. But he didn't interfere when Ole told me about the different ways of creation, and how tricky it can be to make it wired correctly, so that individual that you are creating is operating as it should.

D. Was Ole, was he Gergen's mentor? Grandpa, papa and

B. Ah, ah, and then me. So it's like a little family unit here, of sorts.

D. Did he like your library?

B. Ah, he liked my study. He said I made it really cozy, and I also made it so he could tell there was a lot of teachings in it, he said, from various different sides of the corners of the world, huhuh.

D. From your travels, collect things and bring them back.

B. Ah.

D. Does Ia feel left out when you meet like this?

B. Oh, Ia's busy. She's all sorts of busy with the sparkles. They are actually on that first little level of ascending in their knowledge. So at this time there's a lot of things to attend to when it comes to the gradual moving upwards to a new level of learning. So let's say these are three–year–olds, and now they are gonna move up to be four–year–olds, so that is to give you a picture.

D. Do they go into smaller groups now?

B. She's talking about that, that now is the time for us to start moving into smaller groups, and that is tricky. There are a lot of assistants with Ia, similar like Ia, that comes in. Because they're not gonna just have her, each cluster group will have their own Ia. But then they get confused and they think she's gonna leave, and she says, "I'm always going to be supervising, and I'm always going to be present, but you are now going to get like a teenager that is going to take care of you for a little while." So it's also that process where, you know, once you move up to be a teenager, then you're also supposed to be taking care of the younger ones. I did that too! I've done all this. I also had babies to tend when I was a teenager.

D. Did you have a little group?

B. I had a little group. There was a group of ten, and from that group that I was assigned, –and Gergen was a part of overseeing this, so when I became a teenager, I got a group of about ten–, but from that ten, it actually came down from that original group to the group that I'm now having (*about six*). I also got one from another group that was really, really intelligent, but was sort of misplaced. So he came over to my group later. They see this, because even if the intention is, "We're going to be in this group," but they all evolve differently, we all do. And even if you are, let's say, placed in a group focusing on plants, but then they say, "Oh, here we have someone who is really interested in travels." Then, you know, "Let's see if we can squeeze him into the travel group." So that's sort of how it works.

D. Is that what kind of group you have, a travel group?

B. Currently, but it didn't start out as a travel group. It started out as a regular plant group. But we did different things because I wasn't really interested in plants. So I said, "We're gonna work more on mobile life forms than those who were just still." So I said, "In this group we're gonna work on creating like little rodents and stuff," and that's what we did.

D. Like chipmunks?

B. Ah, like the chipmunks, and we also created like a guinea pig kind of thing that existed prior to the current guinea pig. It was a little bit bigger, but it didn't come in as many different colors as this one, the current one. It was more like a big brown one, but it was furry. So we worked a lot with that guinea pig. It doesn't exist anymore, but we worked a lot with that. And then Gergen came in sometimes, and others came in, and they said, "How is your plant projects going?" And I say, "Oh, we're working with the guinea pigs and the mobile ones." So he said, "Don't forget you also have to talk about the plants and the trees." So I did that, I talked about the trees and we learned more about the fact of merging. I was really good at that, because it's part of the traveling thing. I said, "Look at me when I move into a tree, this is what you're going to do," and I did like, go in...and go out, go in, and out. Like, "Peek–a–boo!" I go in and out. I wanted to make it a little bit funny, so they didn't feel just tossed into it, the tree. Because that is a big part of this first training, and the sparkles know this. That's why they're a little bit hesitant to move from the big group into the smaller ones, because now they know there are more demands on them.

D. I'm sure you're a really good teacher.

B. Ah, ah. So, when I was a teenager, I did that.

D. Then what did you do after that, after you were a teenager?

B. Then you get a pause from being a teacher for a while, if you want to, so I did that, I took the pause, and I didn't continue at that point, because I went into a new level of training and learning. I worked on my own, but with friends on a similar level.

D. Like in your lab?

B. In a lab. I didn't teach for a while, because it went in cycles, and they allowed that because they don't want no one to feel drained. So sometimes you come in and teach, and you do so for a while. But then you have the opportunity to be the student. So you have to go in cycles like that, and I kinda like to be a student. I like that, because there's no limits to what I can explore and expand and learn and ask. But if I'm only teaching, then I have to stick to a certain agenda. Like, "So today we're gonna talk about going in and out of a tree," when I want to talk about something else.

D. I'm sure you slipped in a few observations, here and there.

B. I did indeed, I did indeed. I made it into like a fairy tale, a little story, when you move in and out of trees, huhuh, so it doesn't become a big, mysterious endeavor, in that sense. But I like the fact that it is like that. And I'm sure it is on all locations, that you move through a cycle of where you are a student, and where you are teaching others. And sometimes when you are teaching others, like a human, for instance, it is that you are in training to be a spirit guide to a human. So a soul that has been going away from home into a physical vehicle, then the one left behind, –it can be like a teenager, someone that's a little bit older than you–, then it can be allowed, from the main spirit guide, that the teenager will be able, or try to communicate, with the soul encased in the human form. So that is also part of the training, you're teaching, but you're doing remote teaching, if you like. It's tricky. It's like having that little walkie talkie, and you think the walkie talkie is on, on the other side, but it's not! HAHAHA. And you're talking to yourself! You squeeze the little button and you go, "Phuu—phuu—phuu—phuu. Come in, come in, over, over." And there's no response! It's tricky! It's a higher science of teaching, I would say. It's more tricky than to teach and be a teacher when everyone is home and everyone is listening. That is a big step when it comes to the teaching aspect of growth, when you are in your soul home, so to speak. It's considered to be one of those windows. When you master them, then you can advance and you can add other teachings as you move again into the cycle of being a student. If you were doing really well in your teaching cycle, when you move into being a student, then another window will open, and you say, "Oh, what is this?" So it's like having a treat.

D. Well, that way nobody is ever stuck.

B. No one is ever stuck.

D. You help others, then you're helped yourself.

B. Ah, and then you get helped by others. So you help one, and then you get helped by someone else, that's how it works. That's why it's so confusing that it's not working like that here. Like you help someone, and then maybe they don't need to help you right back, but they can help someone else, so it's like a chain reaction. But there doesn't seem to be a system of that here. That memo didn't fly down!

D. It's every man for himself.

B. It's kind of odd, because that's not at all how you are trained in your spiritual home. Regardless of where you are patched up, or where you belong, it's one of those cosmic laws or one of those cosmic understandings; that you are supposed to share knowledge.

D. So, tell me, were you allowed to talk to Ia about what you're doing? (*His studies with me and Ophelia.*)

B. Yes, indeed, but not everywhere. When we sit in Gergen's office—it looks like a library, I would describe it to you like a library. It's a small room with really tall bookshelves in like oak or mahogany, dark wood, that is somewhat in an oval shape. This is where Gergen sits. So he sits there and this is where we meet. So, in this sacred room of the three of us, I can freely discuss certain things—and I do!

D. Are you going to have to make a presentation to the council?

B. Ah. That's a little bit nervousing (*his word for making him nervous, I guess*), because it's not only what I experienced, but I also have to investigate certain points they wanted to check off. And I do have to report, not necessarily a solution, but I have to be thorough, so I'm not just sent off like a clown. I did research, really, so it's somewhat like I have to be at my best.

D. Did you say, "sent off like a clown"? (*Laughing.*)

B. Ah, I'm not supposed to just to go off on like a road trip. I kinda want to make it known that I took it really serious, and I have collected data for our benefit. Not only about the communication here, but also what I have learned by paying attention to the discussions that have been taking place with Zachariah, and Ophelia as well. So there is a whole...it's like delivering a ball of information. And it cannot only be that I wiggled the ears, or I tried to be a frog, huhuh. So I have to somewhat report the magnitude of my discoveries, so to speak. And I will do that I'm sure, of course, so there is no problem with that.

D. I'm sure you'll do well. You're a good speaker and you organize your thoughts well.

B. I can indeed, and Gergen is going to be there. The other ones, I meet them occasionally, but I'm not really close with them.

Some of them were really a little bit suspicious about this mission. That's also why I'm a little bit concerned that they think I didn't take it too seriously.

D. Why would they think that?

B. Well, it's because they were not really sure about us delivering certain things, I would assume. And they might not have been too eager, –they were a little bit more conservative–, so maybe not too sure if they wanted to share everything with the public, so to speak.

D. So did you pass along everything they wanted you to talk about?

B. Well, what is available at this time. Yes, indeed. More to come. But there was still, because of the fact there is two or three in this group of Gergen's friends, in the council, that was a little bit more conservative. And a little bit more hesitant, I would say, about if mankind was really at that level of understanding certain kinds of teachings that we were providing from the second dimension. So, with that, I do need to take this reporting back somewhat seriously, and I am going to be addressing a lot of this to them, to make them understand that it is of value that certain teachings come forward.

D. Well, I certainly think that what you say is valuable.

B. I think so, indeed.

D. I really appreciate everything you've shared with us. It's been very informative and I'm quite happy about it.

B. Well, I think that will probably be, be, be, be, be it, today. So, this is what I'm working on. I'm gonna go there (*nodding to the right*) and report to the council.

Teaching Tom (Dec 17, 2017)

The spirits we communicate with are very careful and strategic with the stories they allow to be passed through Christine. Even when Bob or Ia are describing their interactions with the sparkles or students, we should constantly be aware that there are important messages embedded within the chronicles which they want us to interpret on a personal level. The lessons or discoveries reported by Bob, or any of the spirits, are similar on all dimensions and should not be viewed from a distance, as if they have no relevance to our own spiritual development. We each have a unique role in creation, but when Bob, Ophelia, Jeshua, Isaac, Gergen, Ia, or any of the council members express concern for a problem on Earth, we should read it as a warning to humanity, understanding that we too need to be concerned. As you read the often-amusing narratives of Bob, please be mindful that ideas with a greater purpose have been artfully interwoven into the stories.

We were first introduced to Tom when he was a sparkle in Ia's big classroom, where Bob occasionally goes to entertain and teach the little ones. Over the many months of recounting his life, Bob gave us a very detailed description of how the sparkles are taught and the very personal way they are guided and helped to reach their potential. I am reasonably sure this is the first time this type of information has been revealed to humans. Spirits have anxieties and reservations about the unknown, but also have a tremendous amount of love and happiness in their home environment. They joyfully work together for the benefit of the outcome, but have unique personalities and feel great satisfaction when they accomplish some goal or reach a new level of learning. The way Bob teaches Tom is a process that goes on in all dimensions; each spirit is encouraged and helped along the way, and is expected to help others in a similar manner.

D. So what's been going on with you? How's your studying going?

B. I've been doing a lot of reading, I've been doing a lot of studying, and it is a fact that I do create my own books as well. I'm not just reading others, I'm actually going through and reading my journals; quite enjoying my own words, I must say, that I put down in scriptures, about my adventures on several different locations. We've actually now had the grand finale, with you, so that was like a week ago from your perspective. (*He brought me in for a show–and–tell in Ia's sparkle class.*) I will tell you that it was a great success. And the little sparkle in the front, he wanted to crawl up on stage where you stood. He wanted to touch you to see if you were alive! HUHUH. So he came up and I let him, because if it would have been me, then I would have wanted to come up!

D. Satisfy the curiosity.

B. Satisfy the curiosity indeed. So, I allowed him to come up. So he was actually, during this whole ending ceremony that we had, he was actually allowed to sit next to me on the stage, and he was very happy. He likes to feel that he got favors. So he felt a little bit special, which you know, I'm all in favor of that! Because I feel like it is important that someone feels special. So I felt that I made his day, so to speak.

D. Maybe you're stamped out of the same pattern. You might be teaching him for a long time.

B. Ah. I think he wants to, because he asks a lot of questions for me to ask you. He was curious about you. The other ones were curious too, but they were more quiet and observing, waiting to be asked. So I did ask if there were any questions to be had, and there were. But they were more subtle in their approach, whereas this little one, he just, you know...

D. What do you call him, what's his name?

B. I call him Tom.

D. Bob and Tom.

B. He is so excited about traveling. Tom says he wants to travel in water. He likes the water because he likes to feel like he is limitless. So he talks a lot about that, that he is interested in the waters. So I said, "First of all, you have to master certain lessons before you can travel."

D. Are all the sparkles that Ia is teaching, are they all related to the Earth plane, or do they have other realities that they will go to?

B. They're gonna go to different realities. Like I said, Tom is really interested in waters, so he is assigned to either work on the water reality on Earth, or a water planet. So, it's not necessarily that they will all go to Earth, even though the majority will, because they have somewhat learned the basics. Because there's such a diversity here, and there's not necessarily a diversity on all different locations. Like the water planets don't have that many lands, for instance, so there's different lessons there. BUT, it's like I went to the greenhouse, for instance, and the water planet is similar—it's a place to study up and to learn the basics within that specific element that you chose to occupy and work with. They're gonna, eventually, be placed on either the Greenhouse Planet, or go to a water planet, if that is of their preference—like Tom. But then later, they are actually, –what I gathered here from Ia–, they are supposed to do work here on Earth, because this is where help is needed.

D. So the water planet would be within our fish tank?

B. Ah, mmm.

D. That's what I was wondering the other day, if everyone would be working on Earth?

B. Well, eventually, it seems like they will. All the groups are different, so one group will go to the Greenhouse Planet, for instance, whereas some will remain in the area of study and continue to study up more on facts. So they go to different places, and this is based on how they act. Like Tom, for instance, he's very hands–on. So he doesn't necessarily, at this point, want to have more study. He wants to do something where he can touch things and see results.

D. (*Laughing*) That sounds familiar. (*Bob is the same.*)

B. Ah, huhuh. Eventually we will have to teach him about self–study, because he can't go through life with just hands–on with everything. Eventually we will have to teach him about self–study.

D. What about sparkles that want to study animals, moving forms?

B. If you think of, like a 4–H Farm, that is similar what they go to, and they are in charge of a sort of a pet, and they're small pets. The biggest one would be considered like a goat. Mainly they are rodents, like different ones. Some actually take care of butterflies and dragonflies and insects. Based on what cluster group that you will belong to is also where you will go and study up. But then, there is always these shifts, because it's not like you go to one place only. Eventually those in the 4–H group, they might see that, okay, someone here is actually really good in understanding what growth can be added to animal life so they feel better. (*Studying plants that benefit animals.*) So that person might be considered an excellent student to go to the Greenhouse Planet, for instance, to study up more on that. So you circle a little bit. Just because one doesn't want to self–study, it doesn't mean that it's never gonna happen! Huhuh. That happened to me. So you can't navigate around a topic that you don't want to study, because you have to be very wide in your education. You just begin differently.

D. With the students, who kind of divides them up? Is it someone above Ia?

B. Well, Ia is the one, she has taken really close notes on each of them. So Ia, together with Gergen and other friends, they meet the sparkles individually. It's not like you just get an envelope saying "Okay, you're expected here," because they want to talk about it. So they make great efforts in talking before they deliver where they are supposed to go, and WHY they have suggested this for the sparkle. So it's not necessarily considered like a sentence, or a punishment, it's delivered as an opportunity they see in this specific sparkle. And that is the difference than to just send someone off saying, "Okay, you match there." But this is like talking about the progress they've seen, and how they are delighted to have that specific sparkle to join the program on, let's say, the Greenhouse Planet. So for me, for instance, I went to the 4–H Farm first, because I was really interested in the mobility. And I worked a lot with like hamsters and guinea pigs and I studied activity. I studied why certain ones like to be in groups and how they move, and (*the types*) from different locations, and why. (*Adaptations to different environments.*) So I studied that. I was really happy at my 4–H Farm, because there was more farm animals, if you like, that I could investigate. But then Gergen came, and he said, "You also need to learn about the plants." And I said, "Maybe that group is full, maybe there's not a spot for me there." And he said, "Well, we will create a spot for you," and he said it in a way so that I felt like it was a great honor for me to go there. But it was actually a way for him to say that I should leave the 4–H Farm and go the Greenhouse Planet, but he said it was like an opening had been made for me.

D. Ah, so you've been picked.

B. I've been specifically picked, and there was an opening— so this was a great honor for me to learn more. So I went.

D. Did you enjoy the Greenhouse Planet?

B. I did, but it was more like solitude, I would say, because I was sitting and I was observing a plant, and...

D. Wasn't as entertaining?

B. Wasn't as entertaining, but after a while, I could see that it was reacting like the animals. Just because it didn't move around like the guinea pig, it was actually the same life form in the plant. And that is what Gergen said he wanted me to see. He wanted me to observe the small signs of life in everything around that I would perceive, so I would not miss out on the awareness in plants and trees. So as I sat there, I was by myself with my notebook, and he said, "Sit here and simply observe." And after a while I actually did see, like it was communicating to me, actually. So I said something, and I could see it responded differently, based on how I was interacting with it. And I was surprised by that. So if I came in and I sat and I felt a little bit low, then I could feel like comfort from the plant. And that's when I understood that this is a life form as well. Just because it doesn't jump up in my lap, like a guinea pig, it's still the same; so I was intrigued by that. And that was the whole purpose—I understand that now, afterwards. The whole purpose was for me to see that there is an awareness of life and a quality of life within each. Even rocks carry a slight sparkle of that awareness. You can actually communicate with a rock, even if none of us (*from the second*) are in there. But EVERYTHING carries an awareness. You can get a sensation of calm and comfort, even from a rock. So, that's what I learned.

D. That's a wonderful teaching. So where did you go after the Greenhouse Planet?

B. That's when I came here.

D. So you didn't have to go to the Water World?

B. I never went to the Water World. I worked a little bit with water, but I never went to the Water World. But I worked with water when I came here, and you know, I was gonna like blend with certain things.

D. I remember you said you didn't care for it.

B. Ah, I blended with a fish, and you know, ah.

D. It wasn't your calling?

B. Nay, it wasn't my calling, really. It was the size of a salmon. Nay, I–I–I–I said, "There's an opening for someone else here!" Huhuh. And I came here actually, and I did a lot of work on this plane with plants. I sampled things, and I worked with plants and I worked with nature, and then, you know, continued to work with animal life as well.

D. Is that what you were doing when I found you?

B. Who says you found me? I found you!

D. Oh, yes, of course, you found me. I was just standing there, like a tree.

B. Uhuhuh. Didn't look like a tree. You just looked like something that was misplaced, hehehe. But I was collecting samples with my friend when you came.

D. With your little Individual?

B. My Individual. It doesn't exist anymore, but it was a friend. He was actually sort of carrying a lot of my samples.

D. Put him to work.

B. Yeah, like you have little bags on donkeys that you put things in, it was similar. He was carrying.

D. He didn't mind?

B. He didn't mind at all, because he was allowed to wander about in the jungle with me. At this time, it was a lot of vegetation going on, so it was almost like a jungle, very green, very lush.

D. The whole planet?

B. Well, this was located in South America, a little bit. That's where you came the first time.

D. I remember you said you had some projects there.

B. Ah. Well, I had projects there, and I also had projects over in India, what is now considered India. I have a soft spot for the jungle area within the northern part, center northern part, of South America, because I spent a lot of time there. I hide things there.

D. Little treats.

B. Treats. Like flowers that can become, if the group is ready for it. So I hide it there, I implant like patterns, so it exists. There's actually a plant that exists that's going to be very curing of a lot of diseases, even virus diseases.

D. That's wonderful.

B. But I don't want it to be put in the wrong hands, or to be mixed up (*combined*) with certain things, because it's not supposed to. I see that within the group consciousness at this point that you—to make it simple—you have a blueberry and you make a jam out of it. So everything that you find, instead of letting it be, you just redo it into something else that is not necessarily the intention. And if you do that with this specific plant, then the mystery is lost. So I'm waiting to have that exposed. And I will probably lead someone, help someone to find it.

D. Humans are too greedy, they want money for everything.

B. Ah. I want this to be the right cycle within your own consciousness, when everyone operates from the fact of helping, instead of just, "How can I make a profit out of this. Oh, this is mine, this is mine." So I want there to be a sensation of sharing, "This is something good, this is gonna be helpful," like it's free. It's not to make a profit from.

D. That's not the mentality now.

B. It will be.

D. Do a reboot.

B. I'm not supposed to, I'm not allowed to. Even if I had that button, I'm not sure that I would be able to push it. Hehe. Ophelia laughs about that. She laughs about our wish to reboot things. She said that changes will come. But from this level, because we are trapped within the sensation of time, then it feels like it's going really, really slow. But it's actually not. She said there is great shifts taking place, even though from our level of experience, especially yours, it looks like it is going very slowly. But even mine, because I'm not involved, so I don't see the great picture of everything. I don't see the end result. But if I did, she said I might tell! And she wants...oh. Ah, we'll see about that! But when you came, because I didn't recognize your pattern, really, I wondered if you were lost. And you were probably lost, but you seemed very friendly, and you stood still, which was something I appreciated.

D. I didn't come running at you?

B. Didn't come running at me, or danced at me like you did in the 1600's, like Charles Mustard. You didn't dance like that! Because I would have been like, "Oh, what is this, what is this?" Those who existed, they didn't really dance. I mean, they moved a little bit around a fire, but if you had been very outgoing like that, I might have been like, "OH, ohh, what is this?" But you were not, and I felt like I needed to help you, because maybe you were lost; no one likes to be lost.

D. Well, thank you for helping me.

B. Well it became a starting point for a very fruitful companionship, I must say.

D. So I'm probably not going to be coming back to Earth?

B. Well, you didn't really plan on coming this time either. But you did it because this one here wanted to come with someone from his family, and said, "If I'm gonna do this, I'm gonna do it with one in the family," so, you know, raise of hands! Jeshua didn't come, and Isaac said, "We're gonna work from this side," and it fell on you. And you were like, "Okay, what am I going to do? What do you want me to do?" And then we started to plan about it.

D. Well, the good thing is, we will continue to work on the other side.

B. Well, it's not like you're not gonna come back at all, but you might take a rest. Because you said that you wanted to take a rest from the current state of human consciousness. So, you wanted to leave off something of a treat for humanity to grab and start to ponder about. But you will come back, probably. I don't know what your plans are about that.

D. Once you build a new vehicle, maybe.

B. New vehicle. We'll see about that. So, anyway, we had the grand finale with you, and you were really calm and friendly. I thought they might want to go dance around you, like the tree, Hehehe. But it was only Tom who wanted to come and sit close, you know, next to us up on that little stage we were on. There was a lot of questions, because you did mention Siah. So they wanted to know a little bit about different life forms that you had perceived on your travels. So, I translated, and you talked about Siah.

D. It's good that you had seen Siah.

B. Ah, yes. I described Siah and I actually, in my own way, helped to draw a picture on a big cloth. I drew a picture of Siah, and then you told about the personality. You told a little bit about the planet, because in some way it is very similar to Earth. But you talked about, through me, the difference of consciousness within the leading mammal on that planet, versus the leading mammal here. So you talked about the differences, because there were several here, including Tom, that wanted to go to the planet with Siah. And then Ia came in and said, "Now we're getting completely off route. We're not going to talk about that, because they have to go to the Greenhouse Planet and the 4–H Farm. They can't go to Siah at the moment." So we talked about that, and we talked about the different societies that they will come across later on, on Earth, that might be perceived differently. But our hopes are that the civilization here will operate from a sensation of giving and sharing, like they do on the planet where Siah is.

D. Do they have any awareness of the current civilization here? Have they been shown or taught?

B. Who?

D. The little sparkles.

B. The sparkles, if they have been shown?

D. Yes.

B. They have seen a little bit. But it's somewhat kept quiet, because otherwise they might not wanna go. They see the good things. They have actually seen documentaries, which is not your current time. It's actually prior, because everything is building up, -you don't put everything in the lap, immediately. So they see the good things on this planet, because that's how we want it to come—because there is a lot of good on this planet. The majority is actually good. But among the humans, even if the bad is less (*than it appears*). Because so much of what people hear is about the bad, it triggers the sensation of fear around them, which overshadows the good, like a big cloud over the sun. But, the matter of fact is—the truth is—that it is more sunshine than it is clouds. But because of the sensation to create fear, then sometimes the sun is dimmed. Fear is put in your (*mental*) system, so you think, "Maybe the sun isn't as bright, maybe it isn't that beautiful. Maybe I don't have a soul, maybe I don't—", and so forth. People start to question the good things. That is an extension of fear; it creates doubts, and then when people start doubting within their own being, then their own sun is dimmed when it is actually not dimmed. It's actually extremely bright. But these clouds that move in over consciousness create that.

D. That's a wonderful explanation. You should be writing this book

B. I should be writing a book! Huhuh. I did!

D. How many have you written so far?

B. I have like three.

D. Are they in your library, your personal study?

B. In my library, indeed, in my personal study. Well, from this mission I have like smaller pocket books, if you like, of certain discoveries when I went working on plants and stuff like that. But, from this specific mission that we have been doing, I actually have three volumes. Oh, okay. Ophelia says it's time to go, so, I'm probably gonna go.

D. Well, I'm so happy you came today. And Ophelia, I'm also grateful to hear from her.

B. Oh, well I hear from her all the time. I'm with her in her company as much as I can, because she soothes me also, and I like that. I ask her questions about, you know, like my treats, my gifts under the tree.

D. I'm sure your happiness makes her smile.

Sunshine and Clouds for the Sparkles (Dec 21, 2017)

This story is about how young spirits are trained to face challenges. They are conditioned to see the positive aspects of life, instead of dwelling on the negative or discouraging factors. On more than one occasion, the spirits have urged us to change the way we absorb information. Corporate media is a very important part of how the Cell manipulates society. They target emotional responses by exhaustively fixating on negative and divisive topics. Truth, honesty, and subjective neutrality are rigorously avoided. They rule by way of deception, proselytizing their atheistic viewpoints to create fear and hopelessness. Once you realize that and shun their malignant propaganda, the world becomes a much nicer place. As Bob points out, sunshine stories are one way to accentuate the good that is always present. Gergen gave a magnificent talk about gratitude, which we included later in this book. Having a sense of gratitude is a powerful way to train ourselves to find the sacredness and beauty in each day of our lives.

B. (*Bob came in singing a happy melody.*) There's all sorts of activity today, you should know! Ia is here, and Gergen is here, and Ole is here, all friends are here, you know, communicating. I might see if Ia wants to say something, but she is here.

D. That's quite an honor.

B. She says she doesn't want to steal my sunshine, but I say—we can share! We share all along. I don't mind sharing, as long as it's given back to me! Ha ha huh ah.

D. So, Gergen and who else?

B. Ole. Ole.

D. Ole, really? Has he ever talked through a human?

B. (*Bob pauses to listen to Ole.*) No. But he has traveled, he has indeed. But he's mysterious a little bit here. He says, "Treats are to come, Bob. Don't get ahead of yourself." So, anyway, oh, oh, it's like a gathering, I must say, from the second dimension. And we're here to talk about, a little bit, the different aspects of our presence in nature, as well as a need to send positive notes and messages to humanity. Because there is so many sad news stories all the time. And there is constantly things that makes people feel belittled, or small, or sadder than they have to be. SO, it would be highly appreciated if there could also be somewhat of a balance in the way that communication within your species takes place, and to somewhat share the goodies of life. You know, little things, it could be like you rescued a pet, for instance, that fell into a little puddle; someone rescued it and took it in, –like sunshine stories. There's so little of the sunshine stories, and that is what we provide for the sparkles. Because if we were to bring them all the gloomy incidents, you can imagine that no one would like to go anywhere, there would be no progress anywhere! And that is the key here, it is to understand that as long as there is no sunshine stories, or at least some that balance the other ones, then people feel like they are immobile, that there is nowhere to go, because where is the sunshine, so to speak. So with the sparkles, we constantly, to give you a picture, we give like 60 to 70 percent sunshine stories, so they feel encouraged and joyful about their mission. Because if you are only fed sad stories, then there is no joy in progress or a desire to even begin to do something different, because one feels like a cloud has just moved in over one, and that's what we do not want to do to the sparkles, AT ALL! (*He takes a deep breath.*) So, in the beginning, it's probably ninety percent sunshine. And then a teeny, tiny cloud comes in that is hardly noticeable for them. And then we bring in more clouds, but it is that fact to still be able to recognize the sunshine. We bring in more clouds, meaning more challenges, and more obstacles, if you like, but the trick is that the sparkles are so used to sunshine that they are not blinded by the amount of clouds that we increase on their path. So we bring them more clouds, more obstacles, more challenges to grow from. But the thing is, they are so in tune that there is supposed to be sunshine, so they are not diverted or preoccupied by the clouds that we have popped into their system.

D. Like when their creature gets taken away, that would be considered a cloud?

B. Ah, it would be considered a cloud. Like when my Individual was removed, that was a huge cloud, and I lacked to see the sunshine for a while, I couldn't see the picture of the sunshine. BUT, after a while, when I understood that I did not want my Individual to be present and endure certain activities from the leading mammal at that particular point, then sunshine was brought back. But it is a mindset, and we put great effort into teaching this to the sparkles, to predominantly be in sunshine in their head. So, when obstacles and clouds come in, they still are not clouded or overshadowed by that obstacle, because they still see, even if it's less sunshine. The more you progress, the more clouds are put in, in order for you to navigate and to manage to overcome certain obstacles. So, in the beginning, the first time you poof in a cloud and see what happens in the group, it's like, "Ohh! Ohh! Ohh!" And then we monitor this, and some, like Tom, he did like that (*makes a brushing motion away from the body*), and that's not how you're supposed to do either. Because you're supposed to identify the cloud and what it is, and if it is of value for somewhat of a shift that should take place, or a lesson that is lurking behind the cloud. So, you're not supposed to shy away, but you're not supposed to sway away either. So we puff in the cloud for them and we see how they react. And gradually, as they progress in their kindergarten school, more clouds are put into their awareness. And it is because, when they are by themselves later and they're going to blend, then they might be subjects for clouds that are not sent from us, but comes from other sources, like the humans, for instance. And they have to be somewhat centered and understand, so they don't shy away. We don't want them to shy away, we want them to be in that mindset of sunshine.

D. That's really good. Are all dimensions like that?

B. I would hope so. Ophelia's is probably, because she has a lot of sunshine, so there's an abundance of sunshine up there! Huhuhuh. Ah, where you work there is sunshine, but differently. It's not sunshine, but more like a glow. That's why I had my lamp in the beginning. I think the modality and the principles of learning and teaching are similar from the smallest little sparkle to the giants like Jeshua. You can go back in your own memory here and try to remember when you were a sparkle how you were taught, to see if it was the same way. Even though when it came to that self-study, you probably chose that. You probably didn't want to go to a 4–H Farm, you wanted to be in that study group. And there are no judgements, because there are study groups as well in our reality who are really good with solving puzzles, for instance. I've never been really good with puzzles.

D. Well, where did Ia go?

B. Ia, Ia was actually in that group. Oh, she's an excellent puzzle solution person! She's just, –there's like nothing that can preoccupy her sunshine! So even if there's a puzzle with like a million pieces, she never gets freaked out or stressed or impatient or anything at all, in that manner. She, she— (*He looks to the left, listening.*) Oh, she said she did indeed. Because I wasn't there, she said, I didn't see everything. "Don't put me on a pedestal," she said, "because I too get impatient sometimes with the puzzle pieces." (*Ia works with the energetic basis for DNA, which Bob calls puzzle pieces.*) Huhuh. I was at the 4–H Farm, so I did not see this! Uhuhuhuh! But she said that it is important to identify where the sparkles are at, and not bring more clouds into the sparkles' awareness than it is ready for. Even though we belong in a big group, there are differences, and there are different ways to interact with these clouds, these obstacles, based on what sort of individual it is. So she said we had the same amount of clouds, she and I, but it was brought into our chimneys differently. I was more like Tom, I wanted to sort of make it go away. Whereas she took it in her little hand, so to speak, and analyzed it. I never analyzed it. I see that was a BIG mistake, that I didn't analyze the clouds. I did learn, but I see now that there is value to look at them, because they come from somewhere. It could be Gergen putting them in, but some also come from a higher source, maybe Ole.

D. What does he say about that? Was he popping clouds on you?

B. (*Bob laughs.*) Because of the fact that I was so content at my 4–H Farm, then they made my clouds move in faster. Because they were like soap bubbles coming in. They (*makes "phffoo, phffoo" sound*), poofed them in so I felt bombarded. And it was a way to make me understand that there was a shift that needed to take place within my own mind and with my own way of absorbing. So, if someone is like that, then they just puff more clouds, like soap bubbles, into them! Huhuuhuh.

D. Forcing you to analyze them.

Guinea Pigs at the 4–H Farm (Dec 23, 2017)

D. What notes have you brought today?

B. I have actually been with Tom. Ia said, because of the fact that he was a little bit, how can I say, –after our grand finale, Tom was a little bit concerned and a little bit sad because he saw that there was a long progress before he could travel, and he was a little bit sad. Whereas the other ones were celebrating and felt really uplifted, but Tom was focusing and saw that there was a long journey ahead.

D. Is that because he wants to travel?

B. He wants to travel. So Ia saw that, that he was a little bit sad and she asked him what was the problem. And he said he really wanted to go travel with me. And they had a private meeting, and Ia came to me and told me, so I felt like I wanted to invite Tom. So he came to my study and we looked at pictures that I have in my book, because my books are not only words, because that's kind of boring if it's only words. So I put great effort into creating images that would also mirror the stories within the books.

D. So you gave him a little documentary?

B. I can say that. I allowed him to ask questions, and we talked a lot about different things. He wanted to know, you know, the story of when you came, because he was fascinated that there were other creatures. And he wanted to know more about Siah. And I said, "I have not been there, I have only seen it a couple of times." So he said, "Maybe next time you go, I can join?" And I said, "We will see about that. You're gonna go to the Water World." And he said, "I also want to go to the 4–H Farm, like you did." So we talked about that, and I don't want to (*talk about the Water World*), because I don't like the water, and I don't want to put that in his system. So I told him the stories that I knew from my friends who had gone to the Water World, and also what I experienced in the 4–H Farm. There is also goodies and treats in those realities. So I wanted him to focus on that, but he said, "Now I have seen this creature with you." And I said, "That was like a treat, one of the gifts under the Christmas tree. So now you know that there is something beyond that is undefinable from the level of us." So I told him a little bit about you and me, just like random, more private stories. Not necessarily the stories like, "Oh, I did a solar system, and I'm gonna travel in a bubble, and I'm gonna go out into the universe, but you don't know what a universe is, so sorry." Haha. I did not say that, because there is no need. I talked about the more personal aspects of having a friend that looks quite different. And he said, "I also want to have new friends, and different friends," and I said, "Yes, it's great to have new friends." So we talked a lot about that. I mainly talked about our meetings on Earth. I said that you are now blending in a human vehicle, and that I help with that. And he said, "Maybe if you need assistance, I can also come," and I said, "You haven't learned remote teaching yet, but I will absolutely make a note." So I made a note to ask him later on.

D. You might be with him for a long time. He sounds like he is going to be your protégé.

B. Ah, indeed. He likes that. He said that he prefers to not to be in big groups, and I said, "Oh, I know that feeling." But I said we will talk with his main teachers, as well as Ia, and we will see where we can schedule certain classes that will be suitable for him.

D. Can you go visit him when he's in the Water World, just stop by?

B. If I want to.

D. Do you want to?

B. Not really. There's all sorts of opportunity to meet in my study. I might swing by the 4–H Farm, because it's fun and there's lots of little pets. I like them, I created somewhat of a bond to them. It's like being a child again, almost.

D. Are they in the same form as they are on Earth, or more energetic?

B. You mean the animals?

D. Yes.

B. Oh, they are similar, but, ah, not really. Nay, I must say it's not fully (*the same*), but it's not half and half. Nothing is like half and half that I've been to. So, it is a guinea pig, but it doesn't die. So in that regard they're not like your animals, because those have a life span.

D. When you said that you had made a bond with them, I thought it has been a while since you've been there.

B. Ah. It's been a long time. They're still there, because they don't die. So in that respect, it is a spiritual reality, if you like. But it is manifested, in a way. I can't really place it in that wheel for you. I can just say that they are manifested, they don't have a life span of life and death, like they die. Because, there will be sadness. Once they (*the little sparkles*) start to move to Earth and operate, then they are extremely well taught that there is a life span on the individuals that they will come across, so there is no sadness.

D. Are the ones on the 4–H Farm, do they have a little bit of the Master Mind in them?

B. More Master Mind. Ah, that's why you can communicate with them, almost like a regular friend, so it's different. You take all these patterns, but someone else has already created them. So you don't take your own pattern and put it in the 4–H Farm, you work with someone else's pattern that has already been established. But you learn what sort of pattern they possess. And later you learn, also, the way how to create these patterns, and you add the experience of life span. But in the 4–H Farm, first you play and you learn from the ones that already exist. Then you create one that is operating correctly. The last thing you do before you leave, is to learn how to add the little chip, if you like, that is considered the life span, you know, it is born and it dies. It is a little bit of a sadness, because they don't die here. The teachers have to make them understand that on certain places, most places, there is a life span, even though it differs. The life span here is quite short, if you compare it to other places.

D. For everything?

B. For everything.

Tom leaves for the Water World (Dec 31, 2017)

Bob has been working closely with his students, and now he is at that point in his story when they learn about traveling away from the second to one of the areas of specialization. Bob accompanied some of the students to the Greenhouse planet and was helping acclimate them to the new surroundings. He doesn't stay there, but he does like to visit and mingle with the little sparkles.

B. (*Bob came in after Ari, and began making faces*) That was a lot of waiting around today! But I did have a little bit of a listen, I did indeed. And I did sense that it was somewhat of a family reunion. Oh, this one falls asleep a little bit. Let's see here. (*He began making noises and smacking his lips.*) Oh, there you go. He (*meaning Christine, who projects a male energy in the spirit realm*) didn't like that. Hehehe. It is somewhat of a different energy sometimes when I come in, especially from the higher ones from other sources that I don't belong to. When they leave, they leave a little bit for me to puddle around in. And I'm like, "Take away it all! Take away it all, –clean!" It's like when you leave an apartment you clean it, huhuhuh, so the other ones just can sort of move in their furnitures. It's the same thing here, it's a little bit of an overlap, I must say, where it somewhat feels like, "Am I the cleaner?" (*Laughing.*) I may be. Anyway, okay, okay, energy's up, someone is awake. So here we go. SO, I've been gardening.

D. Oh, you have? I didn't think you liked to garden.

B. Oh, I do indeed. Especially when I'm told to.

D. Who told you to?

B. Gergen. Because of the fact that I am in charge of a group that is about to go to the Greenhouse Planet. You have to give and take when it comes to education. And I've been getting a lot, I must say, and now it's time for me to also give back. So, what I do, is that I do this gardening with a few students from the sparkle group. But it is not the whole union (*the entire class*). It is a group that is here to go to the Greenhouse Planet. So we do a lot of gardening, and I answer questions about that.

D. Are you enthusiastic?

B. I am, but mainly because I see that they are. And that is also something that teaching is all about. Sometimes when teaching, it doesn't feel like the most exciting thing you want to do. BUT, if you focus and see how the ones you are teaching, the students, how they are reciprocating and answering to your teachings, then that can be the greatest joy of all. So I feel content and happy, because I can see that they are, even though I'm not learning, necessarily. But I see that they are. And everything for them is new and I feel happy about that, – because I'm a part of that, and they will always remember me as that fun uncle who taught them something that was brand new. And that is the way that I feel it is to be a good teacher, it is to sometimes not only focus on my own progress, but to leave that behind and feel the joy of teaching others and see their growth. They are like little flowers, if you like, so I am gardening them! Ha ha ha huh. That's what I do!

D. That's probably how Ia feels about teaching?

B. Oh, Ia, she gardens all over.

D. She's planting seeds.

B. She's planting seeds all over, and they keep on blossoming. She actually said, she actually told me that this is a very fulfilling way to operate. So she encouraged me to do so. She said, –it's not like being told, necessarily, but I know that I am, from Gergen in some way–, but Ia was merely suggesting that there is a great source of joy and fulfillment by teaching others, and to see that growth. How small that might be doesn't really matter, because you are part of that development. So, I do see that, and I feel that. She said, "Before, you somewhat understood, but you didn't feel it because you didn't really engage." And that is true, because my main little student group, they are much older in their learning curve and ladder, they are much higher up. So she said, "They are already that flower. Don't you want to see somebody to become that flower?" And I said, "I can appreciate that," BUT, I never fully FELT it, that feeling, the appreciation of seeing that first flower blossom, and not just see a ready bouquet.

D. Who better to teach than you! You're a good teacher.

B. Uhuhuh. So, I'm doing that. I got myself a little group. They're like ten, and they are really eager. I can see, it's almost like they are those flowers, because I can see that they change light and color, so I see that. And when I see all these colors that starts to transform and change and become, then it's very fulfilling to me, and sometimes I actually feel like it is a little bit of a rest from my own learning. So I understand that, and that's what I do.

D. That's great. Is this on Earth, or on some other space?

B. Oh, it's at home, we're gardening at home, but they are supposed to go to the Greenhouse Planet, and we are actually on our way.

D. Kind of just giving them a little introduction?

B. Introduction, indeed, but we are on our way, and they ask me if I'm gonna come, and I think I'm gonna. Tom is also going, but Tom is going to the Water World, and I said that I'm not gonna go. He's gonna have another teacher in the Water World. But I said that I'm gonna be right here when he comes back, and we're gonna ponder about things again. And then we'll do other things that are not related to either the Greenhouse Planet or the Water World. So I'll be here and we're gonna continue our path of learning together. I'm not abandoning him at all, it's just that, you know, I'm not the expert at this. Then he said, "Maybe you want to learn? If you're not an expert in this, maybe you want to take this class again?" and I said, "Nah, I'm good. But why don't you tell me when we meet." Hahuhuh.

D. Maybe you're supposed to go swim around in the Water World?

B. Nay. I think I'll wait. I'm fully occupied here with my flowers, so I think I'm gonna wait for that. BUT we are actually about to leave. It's a similar way like you travel to your holiday destinations. You get all these things to prepare, and this is what we did. We did preparing, and now it's time to leave. So we're gonna go together and, you know, I'm very well familiar with the Greenhouse Planet. In this Greenhouse Planet there are sections that belongs to different realities, so we're gonna go to the Earth section in the Greenhouse Planet. Because otherwise it would be confusions. If they learn something and when it's time to really blend and merge and be useful, then there's nothing to be found that looks the same! Huhuh. (*Because the second dimension works with every location where there are life forms, they have prototype environments where sparkles learn about the life on their assigned planet*).

D. That's nice that Ia comes here to watch when you're doing this, and you can go to her place and watch her work, so you're both experiencing what the other is working on.

B. Ah, indeed. So I've been doing that. And then Tom, Tom is about to go the Water World now, because everyone has done their pre–meditation, if you like, before departure. Again, it's all about when you shift energy and you shift location. Then you have to move into a phase of meditation, –we can call it like that–, and it is to just prepare and because you somewhat become the new energy, the new reality. But you are helped, similar like the new sparkles, they don't know that yet, so they have to be helped by others who knows the conditions on that reality. SO every time you move into a different location, then you have to be assisted by elders. And it could be, in this case with the higher groups, they are actually assisted by those who are, because these (*his students going to the Greenhouse Planet*) are like the six to seven-year old's, and they are assisted by those who are like thirteen to fourteen, let's say. So you're always helped by those who are considered like an elder, depending on where you're going, and you are somewhat preparing for that travel. So Tom is all set to go, and he's extremely joyful now. So I'm happy to see that, that he's changed his focus and direction and he is extremely excited to go to the Water World. Because he was given a little bit extra in his medication, he was deprogrammed to not focus on things that was not in his favor. (*Laughing.*) So he was assisted with a little bit of extra dose of, you know, joyful focus to the Water World. So he forgot all about the other things (*he wanted to do*), at the moment. He forgot all about his need and his wish to be an assistant, at this point. But it's not gone. It's like it's asleep, so it's not gone, but it's a little bit on snooze. It's like when you have amnesia, when you forget something. So it's not gone, it's gonna come back alive. But they made that memory, or that sensation or drive and need, to somewhat be shut down for a moment, because it's not serving him at all when he's gonna go to the Water World. He needs to put all his efforts and his energy and his capacity in that location, so he can't be split up and divided.

D. Kind of like when a human incarnates, everything is forgotten.

B. Ah, so in this case with Tom, because he was so eager to go to other places than the Water World, then they made that memory somewhat go to sleep. But it's not like a lobotomy, like it's taken out, gone; it's still there, but it's just asleep a little bit. I was actually observing, and I saw it being shut down.

D. Who did that?

B. Oh, Gergen came in and actually assisted. Gergen is like a grandfather to them.

D. Do they know him pretty well?

B. Yes indeed. They all show up and they wander around and say, "Oh, hello." And they come and they go. It's not like a very big mystery, you can all see each other. It's not like a division where, "OK, we can't go talk with the CEO's because we're only workers, we're only babies." Everyone is somewhat familiar with one another.

D. Does Ole ever wander around?

B. Ole, nah. I didn't see Ole, because he was probably safe in his study, observing this. But some of them wander around a little bit, because Gergen does, you know, chit chat with them. But Tom is all set to go, and everyone is all set to go. But you have to prepare them differently based on both location but also, in this case with Tom because he had actually diverted his attention elsewhere, and that was not in his favor, some of his memories had to be put into hibernation.

The following week, Bob picked up on the excursion he was taking with his students to the Greenhouse Planet.

D. So, the little group that you are taking to the greenhouse, when are you going to go?

B. Oh, we're already gone.

D. Ah, so you're working with them over there now?

B. Yes, I am. I'm helping, but I'm not stuck there. I'm free to go as I like, but they are not. I come and I teach and I also listen a lot. Because the first that you do when they come into the new environment, –it's not what you do here (*humans*), where you just overwhelm them with words and teachings–, we actually allow them to take it all in and ask questions first, and to look around. It's of high interest for us who have been there already, to see what their first impression is of that location, because we also learn how we can change and adjust. If someone says, "Oh, what a scary, scary little creature!" Then we're like, "OK, this is considered scary." That's not what happened, but we want to hear their first impression. And later, then we will discuss. It's a different way of teaching. We're not just simply talking to them. We ask them to talk mostly, and we bounce back a treat of knowledge, –and that is how the dialogue goes back and forth.

D. That's a good way to teach. So, as you progress, eventually you don't have any more fun and games, do you? Do you still do things that are fun?

B. Nay. But it's more in your spare time. It's not in class, because you are put in class to learn or to teach. So that is what we do later on, because they are still not really familiar with the fact of sitting still and absorbing, so they are at first very mobile. When you are very mobile, you don't have the capacity to be just overwhelmed with teachings and words and structures and so forth. It's all about adapting your teachings to the ones that are being taught.

D. Do they then study the energetic form of plants, or do they just learn how it operates?

B. Umm hum. But first we are very interested in hearing how they observe this. So we ask them, simply, "Tell me what you see," and they say, "Oh, I see a plant." And I say, "Do you feel like it is a big or a small plant?" "Oh, it feels rather big." "What is your sensation when you look at this plant?" –so we ask like that. We want them to give their first impression, because that's also helpful later on when they are sent somewhere. If they feel very comfortable and loving in an environment, let's say in a jungle, then we know that that specific individual or group will be extremely helpful, because it can detect the energetic patterns in a jungle. There's no need to send that one to like a desert area, for instance.

D. So they respond better to things they are programmed to work with?

B. Indeed. But we don't want to put that response into them. We want that to be instant, from them. So we observe that.

D. That's brilliant.

B. Ah. Otherwise, you know, you're just sort of programming them. And that is not what we want to do. We don't want to program anyone. We want them to become their individual pattern, because we don't know. It's like a chain, one development leads to the next, while we try to figure out what the Creator has intended with that specific little sparkle. So we're really interested in hearing how they observe their surroundings.

D. So they go over when they are about six, from a human perspective. So how long do they study over there?

B. Oh, like till nine, ten. That's also when you go blending and merging, actually. So you go back and forth a little bit, the last two years or so.

D. So they introduce them to the Earth, and start showing them what it's like? And then they eventually go full time to the Earth, or to a lab, after they're done with their basic training?

B. Umm. Well, then they will go, in this case, to Earth, and they will be helpful in different things. So, it's a program and we follow it. It's fascinating as well, because we try to detect, you know, it's like deciphering a cookie. How many raisins are in it and what sort of raisins are there? It's all about deciphering what that specific cookie is made of. And if there is raisins in them, what does that mean? Because it's a raisin of knowledge and we want to detect that, and we want them to show us that raisin, we don't want to impose on them. It's all about private space as well, so we don't want to impose. We want them to blossom, and they do that individually in a different pace. So that's what I've been doing.

D. That's a really good description. (*He then looked to the left, towards Ophelia.*) What does Ophelia say?

B. She laughs. She is always smiling and laughing. She says it's joyful when we do this. She says that everyone expands, everyone is in motion, everyone learns and grows.

D. Do you as well?

B. I do indeed!

D. Even when you're not allowed to listen to others? You didn't hear anything that Jeshua said?

B. Not allowed to. Nay.

D. I'll tell you about it in our study.

B. Ophelia said we will see about that.

D. Does Ophelia have any ideas she would like to share, or do you? Does she toss you a bubble?

B. No, she tossed me the first bubble, that's what we talked about. She said that time is up. Oh, okay. She said it's time to somewhat retreat. Saving energy, she said.

D. When it's time to come here, do you travel together?

B. Ah, Ophelia and I always go together. I never go by myself. I'm always accompanied by Ophelia. Sometimes with Isaac as well. But the other ones come from another location it seems. It's not like we're all going together.

D. So when you're off working somewhere, do you kind of get a call and then you go to Ophelia?

B. It's like a buzz within. Ah, so anyway, Ophelia says, "Saving energy, saving energy," so we're gonna go. But, okay, you can tell me more when we meet in the study.

D. We're going for a walk today, so I hope you can join us.

B. Oh, I'm gonna be there. Look behind the rocks.

D. Alright my friend, thank you, and Ophelia.

B. Okay. Bye bye.

Sparkles go to Camp (Jan 13, 2018)

D. So what has been happening with your students on the second, when you're not doing something in our lab?

B. I've also been meeting with Gergen and Ia, and my friends. And we've been talking about, you know, because we just sent off that group that graduated, and we're somewhat...it's the same thing here, we are in that phase where we've sent them off and we take a step back for them to become independent. We're taking a step back in a way that we leave them with new tutors, and the tutors are actually the teenagers. The teenagers are simply there to collect their first impression of their new location. (*The teenagers observe and assist the sparkles as they adjust to new surroundings.*) And they feel a little bit lost, because they know we will not join them anymore. BUT that is a part of their learning progress. It is to rely on their own level of capacity and to build that self–esteem, —and self–esteem is not built if you are standing there side–by–side all the time. You have to take that step back and let them fly by themselves, and that's what we do. But we don't leave them, we just give them a teenager that will supervise and be close to them. It's like sending away little people to camp here (*on Earth*). The first time you go away to camp, you cry because you miss your parents. It's the same thing here, they get sad. So there is a lot comforting going on, and nurturing and listening. So there's like big gatherings with a couple of teenagers with these little cluster groups when they make, –it's like a workshop–, they make a lot of activities in order to preoccupy their sensation of distance to where they are familiar with. So they do a lot of workshops, if you like. There is a lot of listening from the teenagers, and making them work creatively, because that's also a way to bypass a sensation of being lost.

D. Get them to sing kumbaya.

B. Huh, if they want to, they can sing. But they do miss being with us, and we supervise this. It's like you going outside the room that time. You were present, and you observed what I was doing with my self–study. But you were distant, and it forced me to upgrade my level of learning. And this is the same thing. We're creating a distance, but we are present and we give them a teenager so they're not so lonely. You didn't give me a teenager; you gave me a book! (*I left Bob alone in my lab, at Gergen's request, so he would begin to study and reflect "in his loneliness", as he said.*)

D. Ophelia was talking about self–confidence. I think it's a really good idea to develop for people.

B. That's what we do with the sparkles.

D. Everyone has the ability to connect with their higher self, but without self–confidence, they have doubts.

B. Self–confidence only comes from your center point, your stillness within you. This is where your energetic being, your soul, can go in and out, and self-esteem is only found there. So we teach that. But they don't understand the idea, so they have to find that for themselves. We do different exercises for them to reach that awareness of self-esteem and confidence within their center point. And, you know, some still hold hands, and that is okay. But eventually you have to be independent. We can see that some still need that comfort, and some, like Tom, he's already set to go. He wants to be his own satellite; he wants to go. And when the workshops are done, he wants to just go and hang out with the teenagers, when it's really time to sleep! Huuhuh. So, that's what I heard from the one supervising the Water World. He said that Tom wants to hang with the bigger children, he doesn't want to go to sleep when it's time to sleep. (*Spirits, especially the younger ones, go into stillness to recharge their light capsule, which Bob calls sleeping.*)

D. Were you like that at the 4–H Farm?

B. Ah, ah. I wanted to learn more about the mobile individuals that we were with, and I wanted to hear personal stories from those who had been there for a while. But I can see that Gergen was observing me from a distance, similar like I'm observing now. They communicate with the teenagers, because the teenagers, they're our friends. So they might be feeling like, "Okay, of course you can come with me." But then, there's an intervention going on from someone like Gergen, if they see that. Like I'm doing now, I've been told about Tom, and there's an intervention going on from the one who supervises the Water World to the teenagers, to also make Tom sleep with the other ones.

D. So in the spirit world, there's a cycle of sleep that spirits go through?

B. It's a resting cycle.

D. That kind of gives a division of time, in a way?

B. Yes, because it is a change of activity, a change of awareness. The change of activity means from moving around to being still. The change of awareness is to make your inner being somewhat draw still, so that is the sensation of time, if you like. But it is that fact to move into your light capsule, and the light capsule can be created around you. But the main thing is that your inner light capsule is intact and that you focus on that. That is the first trick you learn; it is to master your expansion and rest of your inner capsule. Then the outer one will automatically follow after a while, as you master your inner ones. So you don't have to put yourself in a light capsule, because if the inner one is not already asleep a little bit, then the outer one doesn't become that full experience. So if you see it like that, how the stillness can be found within you, even if there's a lot of noise around you.

The Greenhouse Planet and 4–H Farm (Jan 28, 2018)

The primary training camps for young sparkles are the Water World, 4–H Farm, and the Greenhouse Planet, and the labs where they study spaghetti strings of DNA. The students have to attend all four, but are programmed to have a preference for one of them. That will become their main area of expertise. Bob, for example, was most fond of the 4–H Farm. His student, Tom, is predisposed towards the Water World, since some of his missions involve the waters on Earth. When Bob tells how the students are nurtured, it is impossible to miss the tenderness and care that permeates the spirit realms.

D. So what sort of thoughts did you come in with today?

B. Today I'm sampling. I've been sampling information from my group in the Greenhouse Planet, because they are really happy. It's like going to your first camp, and they are really happy up there. But they have to still send reports. At the moment they have just been playing. There's been a lot of playing with the older students who are there to make them feel comfortable. Because it is a fact that one might feel a little bit sad when you leave on your first trip, your first away time from home. But they have been playing a lot, so they've been reporting about all sorts of activities, like playing with the animals, and dancing and circling. And there's been like games of different kinds, simply to make them feel happy with their new location. And I do know that they think that this is it, that they're gonna go back now. But here comes the first level of lessons, is that they have to remain and now it's not gonna be just play and games. So now they are put in a little classroom kind of thing, and they have to work and modify soil. That is what they are doing now. So they are learning the structure and foundations and the elements that are existing in soil, –that's what they do. And this is soil from the Earth, so they learn about that. And they have little jars, if you like, that they are dissecting and analyzing, and in this little jar they are gonna plant a seed. But in order for them to be successful, because they are actually given a soil with no nutrition in it, so they have to analyze one with no nutrition in it at all, that is not alive, and one jar of soil that is ready to be able to host a seed. And they are gonna learn the difference so that they know, when they come to a place and a region where the soil is lacking, –and it could be lacking oxygen, primarily, and light–, then it becomes in a different color to them. So they're learning the difference of how the different colors are supposed to look in order for it to be healthy. So, they have two jars and they have to, in some way, learn from each of them in order to understand that they can encounter both of these. So there is no need to put a lot of effort in planting seeds in a soil that has a specific color, meaning it has no oxygen and light in it. There are ways to increase the level of oxygen, and one way is actually with the earthworms. BUT the earthworms don't necessarily LIKE to go to soils that has no nutrition for them to operate within. SO, the first level to heal a soil that has been somewhat asleep is to first create the nutrition within it so the earthworms want to come in the first place.

D. They want water and leaves.

B. They want different things to be able to feel like this is a sensation of home, if you like. Once that is established in this soil that has not been doing so well, –it's a sick soil, one can say, it has the flu–, then you give it a little bit of medicine, and you give it a little bit of nutrition, it's like giving vitamin C to someone who has a cold, it's important. And after a while, the soil is doing a little bit better and that is when we put in the earthworms, and they can, through their operations and tunnels and how they move around, they not only take away and eat the good things, but in the way they sort of poop, it comes out a new element that is actually like a nutrition for the earth, so it's a cycle, if you like. And as they move around, the further they move, and the further they eat and poop, then the soil becomes alive in a way that it changes colors. Once that is established, then you can plant a seed and it will become something.

D. Wonderful. The colors you are talking about are energy fields?

B. Ah. So the color in a soil that looks like it has a flu is kind of a greyish, grey–brownish color. Whereas the other one is really dark brown, it can even border to have a little bit of red in it, and that soil is healthy and that is a soil that can be used for growing different plants and vegetables.

D. From a human's perspective, a black, humic soil is the best, but that's looking at it through our eyes.

B. Ah. It's supposed to be really dark, and it's supposed to be kinda moist, that's also different. The other one is dry, so it almost becomes like sand. But the other one is more like, if you take it in the hand, a fresh one, a healthy one, then it is like creating those chocolate balls you like, so it becomes like that. So it's sort of sticky and you can mold it. Like that tobacco that you have underneath your lip, that's how it becomes in its consistency, –but you can't grow in tobacco. So this is what they learn. They learn about how soil can be different, and how one can identify the problem, first of all, and what the solution is. So there is several jars here where you gradually can see the change. And the healthy one is over here to the right (*nods to the right, as he visualizes the setting*) as somewhat of a role model where they are trying to head to. They work in groups, because at this point, they still like to work in groups. So there is like groups of five, and they have one to the left, which is the jar where the soil has a really bad flu, and then there is a healthy one to the right, and there are several jars along the way that they are gonna work on to progress and to make it as close as possible to the healthy one.

D. When they eventually get to the Earth, in order in make it moist, they would have to have rain, and that involves the atmosphere. So there are a lot of things they would have to work with.

B. Ah. The atmosphere, indeed. But we don't confuse them here, because they are still on the jars with the soil. Eventually they will understand, –because here we provide water in the jars. There's no need to make it rain and have them identify clouds, at this point. At this point, we provide all the elements needed, and all the earthworms; we're like a big grocery store, so they don't have to think much about it. I'm not confusing them either here with saying where the water comes from, and where the earthworm comes from, I just give them to them.

D. So are you kind of in charge of what they are doing? Do they report to you?

B. Ah, my little group of five, yes indeed. (*The original group of ten has split up, going to different locations.*) But there are several groups here, and we create the sensation of a little bit of competition here, because it's still a game. So we're gradually introducing the concept of study. First it was all play. Now it is a mixture of a little bit of play and games, versus, you know, a task at hand. Eventually, we take away the game, and I remember that being not so much fun. When I went to the 4–H Farm, it's the same way of teaching. At first, we could play with the little animals all we wanted. But eventually we had to learn about their organs and how they worked, what they eat, and so forth. But first, when we got our own pet, or our own little guinea pigs, then we could have like a race with them, and I thought that was fun. But eventually they say, "Now we're not gonna make a race. It's not gonna be like a competition all the time. Now we're gonna learn about the different organs within them." So they told the guinea pigs to not run around, and that was the change that I saw. And I was confused because I thought they were sad, because they didn't move. But they were told by the teachers to be still so we could feel them and analyze them. Analyze them with a little, –it's like an x–ray, but it doesn't harm in any way. If I give a picture for you—you make the guinea pig lay down, and it lays down on the back. And it's like a little tissue that you put on the belly, if you want to investigate the belly, and it's like an x–ray, if you like. So I put the little tissue, the little blankie, on the belly area, which is somewhat see–through. And as I look at this, –and this is an energetic tissue–, I can see inside the guinea pig. So it's like an x–ray, but it's simply a little blankie.

D. A magical blankie! Can you use that on the Earth?

B. (*Snorts*) Huh huh. Doesn't exist here! Stupid! If it did, that would be great! (*Looks to the left.*) Ophelia laughs. She says here it would be considered all sorts of magic.

D. I just wondered if you had something like that you carried in your little backpack. Maybe you could use it here.

B. I'm not gonna tell. But I have it in my possession to investigate. In some way, those who investigate wildlife, they have this in their little backpack.

D. Okay, that's what I was wondering, if you could use it on Earth.

B. But not give it to humans.

D. No, I didn't think that would be a good idea.

B. Nay. But it is a way to identify, especially, if there is an inner problem. In this case, there was no problems with the guinea pigs in the 4–H Farm, because they were all healthy. So the first ones that we had to encounter, they never died, they never had cycles. So we just learned what was where, and how it looked, and how it was connected to other things inside. Eventually we had to learn, in different ways, of course, when there was a problem.

D. That's really interesting. That's a good way to teach. I was going to ask you; how did your dancing go with Ia? This one said it wasn't very fast.

B. Ohh, it was fast, from one perspective. Gergen suggested we do this first, the turning, more than spinning and rotating heavily. So, I followed the suggestions, and thought this could be something nice, because I don't want to push. So it was a slow turning, if you like.

D. It was still pretty nice, wasn't it?

B. It was indeed. Not many laps, though.

D. Does Ia like it?

B. She humored me, it feels, because she said, "Okay." So we did. And then she said, "Is there a purpose to this, Bob?" And I said, "This is like happy. This is like an expression of emotional happiness from a human standpoint." And so she smiled, and she did turn with me and she seemed to have liked it. But I'm not sure she will adapt it into one of her classes, necessarily. But, you know (*as he pondered, popping his lips*).

D. Does anybody on the second dimension ever pair up, like humans do?

B. Like penguins. (*Some penguins do mate for life, so he made a true observation about their behavior.*)

D. Is Ia—

B. *(Interrupts)* She's not a penguin! Huhuhhuh! I'm not a penguin!

D. Cute like a penguin.

B. In many ways we might look like penguins. But, no.

D. With a little blue robe on. Are you and Ia like a couple, in a way?

B. It's like, similar like twins. You're born with someone. You (*on other dimensions*) are born more differently, like one at a time, and you have more close soul companions. And we're sort of born as a couple, in some way. We always keep in contact, even though we might drift and have different areas of expertise as we progress. But we are always a part of our couple unit.

D. So you gave Ia a slow turn, to show her dancing?

B. Ohh, the dancing was, you know, I did actually show the spinning, so I did actually do that, because Gergen encouraged me after the rotating incident. SO, I did actually spin. I did!

D. How was that received?

B. It was received with a giggle. So I think that she approved of me spinning. But I don't think that is what you do in a group. So, I don't think that she might spin, but she understood the process and she understood that it was an end result that could be creating a sense of happiness in the vehicle. So, she could understand that because she does see all the little students, and they sort of bounce around. Even if they might not spin, but they still are very active. So, she is very well familiar with activity being an expression of happiness.

D. Maybe you can go to her class and demonstrate?

B. I might do so, indeed.

D. Get them all to spin.

B. (*Ia, who was listening, must have corrected his assumption.*) Oh, no. She said not. No–no–no, no–no–no, because they're not ready to spin, and they might get confused. She doesn't want them to spin. They can move, she said. But spinning, is considered physical activity, and has a tendency to create disturbances to mental activities and learning. So, she doesn't want me to show that. They're not there fully. They have to, in some way, master their physical activity. Because their focus lies, at this point, not to be moving around, but actually to create and to be still and focus their attention on the learning and the mental capacity. So, if I come in and spin, that somewhat disturbs the whole lesson of where she is at with them.

D. That makes sense.

B. So, you have to sort of respect that. Not everyone is on the level of combining mental activity and emotional activity, as well as the physical. Because it takes a lot of focus to spin.

D. When the little sparks are in the classroom, is a 100 percent of their energy there?

B. The little ones are not split up, if you would like to call it like that. They are where they are, because there is no way, like I said, if they divide, then it would be the same as creating the division between the mental activity and the physical. So, in this case, they are encouraged to remain somewhat still within. So, if I come in and show what spinning is all about, that might, or that will, actually, only disturb where the little ones are at.

Bob has occasionally mentioned the difficulty he has with understanding the languages that exist within the spiritual realms. I would have thought that telepathic communication is uniform and common throughout all the spiritual levels, but it seems there is a difference between the second and the other dimensions. They have never said if the sixth and eighth, for example, can easily interpret one another, but it seems that each dimension has a faster or slower pulse. In order to hear and understand a spirit from a specific dimension or reality, the foreign soul needs to be granted the keys to the melody present in that reality. Therefore, Bob will sometimes say that he needs a translator when he meets with certain groups. The translator will be an intermediary that sends thought bubbles to Bob on the frequency of the second dimension.

D. So, what sort of language do you have? Have I learned your language pretty well?

B. Well, I'm more clear because it's easier for the upper levels to read us. We're somewhat more transparent, I would say. Okay, I will put it to you like this. Let's say we communicate with dots, EVERY one of us. But my dots come in like, dut......dut......dut......dut. And then you go up and you come to, let's say, the fifth; then it's like, dut...dut...dut...dut, so it's a little bit faster. So, as you move up, the dots come more in a faster pace. So, it's easier for those who are in that shower of dots to understand the little rains that comes from us. But you still need to slow down because you are programmed to communicate in a faster dot frequency, but it is easier for you to come down and somewhat understand what I'm saying.

From a Sparkle to a Star

Bob has given us very detailed accounts of his progress and growth from the time he was a sparkle. A major turning point in his growth came when Ophelia interviewed him to see if he was interested in learning more about the creation of form. He was patterned by the Creator to do this, but other spirits such as Gergen and Ophelia were there to help him realize his potential. Young spirits in every dimension are first taught in a large group setting of about one hundred students. Gradually, they are moved into smaller groups that share a common interest or pattern. Gergen saw that Bob was destined to follow a different path than most of the spirits on the second. He was very eager to go traveling to places that most of his fellow classmates had no desire to explore. Ophelia seems to be the one who is coordinating his training with Gergen, but I seem to be his primary companion outside of his home dimension. We work together in our lab on the sixth, in the Library on the fifth, and he is my spirit guide when I incarnate. Bob did continue his studies on the second, but began to travel to the Library on the fifth to work with me in one of the vaults (see *Wave 1*). There, he studied the contents of certain boxes and where the designs of various solar systems and energetic forms were kept. He said I spent a lot of time explaining different concepts to him, which was preparing him for additional training on the sixth, seventh, and eighth. Later, he started attending classes at Ophelia's lab on the seventh, followed by trips to my lab on the sixth dimension. Part of his learning, which we will discuss later, involves making his very own solar system. Those minds indoctrinated by current scientific interpretations of reality may have a logical objection to solar systems or galaxies being designed by a higher consciousness. But our spirits are very much in agreement that the Creator and all the spiritual helpers are responsible for everything that exists. Deep–field images from the Hubble telescope suggest there may be 2 trillion galaxies with 100 billion stars each, so if our Little Friend makes and launches one little solar system, I don't think that is an unreasonable stretch of the imagination.

When we organized this book, we tried to categorize the talks by topic. Then we put them in chronological order, so you will see that we begin with an earlier session than where we left off in the last chapter. These talks are mostly about Bob's transformation from a sparkle on the second dimension to a luminous star and a great traveler to other dimensions.

Bob Reads from my Journal (Dec 11, 2016)

This session was only two months after Bob first began communicating with us. Jeshua had just finished speaking when Bob came in. He tells an interesting story that he read from my book of records. This current project of delivering information from the Elahims and other groups is not the first time this has been done. Based on his description of a pillared temple, scrolls, a ship, and the destination of Constantinople, a similar effort occurred sometime after 300 AD. Otherwise, Bob would have identified Byzantium as the destination. Zachariah came to Earth as a "walk–in". He kept an open link to home and communicated a treasure trove of spiritual knowledge to a group of nine priests. All of us worked to compile and organize this information. Once done, I sailed to Constantinople, where it was intended to be kept for posterity. Upon arrival, this lifetime of work was recklessly destroyed by fire.

The main religion in the Middle East (Iran), prior to 600 AD, was Zoroastrianism. It was the first true monotheistic religion and was practiced in the Persian Empires for a thousand years before Judaism began to be created in the 7th century BC. Zoroastrianism taught people to think good thoughts, speak good words, and do good deeds. Their ideas of a single god, heaven, hell, and a day of judgment, were repackaged within Judaism, Christianity, and Islam. The new religions parroted some of the Zoroastrian beliefs, but excluded the most important parts—freedom of thought and a tolerance of the religious beliefs and cultural traditions of all people. When the Islamic Arab armies invaded Iran (the Persians) in the 7th century AD, their first targets for destruction were the accumulated knowledge of science, philosophy, music, art, culture, history, and religion. The great Zoroastrian library in Ctesiphon was burnt down, and the Persian religion decimated. The moon cult of Al–Ilāt has, over the centuries, deliberately destroyed every library it encountered. The spirit realm foresaw the cultural and intellectual degeneration associated with the Abrahamic religions, and wanted to redirect peoples' beliefs in a more positive direction. This was the purpose of the mission that Zachariah undertook the last time we did this. Unfortunately, the forces of ignorance prevailed, as the last two millennia attest. So, once again, the spirit world is attempting to enlighten mankind.

D. Hello, Bob.

B. Oh, the big one just stepped back. I didn't want to walk on anyone's toes, or anything. You want to have respect for the bigger ones. You don't walk in on some else's subject. Especially if there is an information meeting going on, you want to wait your own turn. Sooooo, let's see. Oh, yes, he left.

D. Well, we were glad you could join us today. Did you hear what Jeshua said?

B. Oh, there was a lot of pictures coming from him. He shows himself but it's like more from a distance. I don't really engage; I don't think everything is for my ears. Ophelia has a little head thing covering my ears. I don't want to interfere in any way, yet I am aware of their presence. They sometimes fly around a little bit, so I know they are there. They're part of a future wave, he said. (*This was when Wave 1 was being delivered, before the spirits from nine and ten came forward.*) At this point they do not communicate, but they are in future waves. Those waves are a little bigger than the first one. Let's see...OH, OH, they're way back. That wave is bigger, and it looks wider. I think it will stretch over a longer period of time for you, my friend. It's more of an intense wave coming in over a longer period of time. Not to disregard the other waves, of course, because everyone has something to say.

D. Well, until that time, we'll enjoy your company.

B. Yes, and today we go and see something in the vault. So, if you'll excuse me, I need to just see what I am supposed to do. Ophelia says that we will open...there will be one box, and there's a book. There's a book ready for me to read in. And this book is on a little stand. She placed it for me to take a look in the book, and there is a little candle for me to see, I assume. Oh, it's a little bit high up, so I WILL use my little stool at this time. So, let's see. It's a big book and there is also a little box, and it's almost like preparing for Christmas! It's a little box and there might be one more, but one I see. So, we will begin by looking in the book. So, let's see...this is your book, this is where you have reported about different visits in the past. Is there something you wish to ask, my friend, from this journal that is yours?

D. Is this my book?

B. This is your personal book. Yes, indeed, personal indeed. Oh, it's like taking a look in someone's diary! I'm not sure if I'm supposed to. Well, I'm sure they only show me what I can see, of course. As I see, I cannot really move the pages. It's almost like it's open where I'm supposed to read.

D. Well, let's hear what Ophelia pointed at, what does she want you to read?

B. Oh, it's about something in an ancient time when you were here, and you were all going on a ship, and you carried a lot of stuff in boxes. It's like scripts, scrolls in boxes, on a big wooden ship. You are transporting it from the northern side of Africa and you're going north. You're going, oh, this is it, indeed, you are supposed to bring stuff to this place, Constantinople. Okay, this is a huge ship, a wooden, big ship, it's in ancient times. You have guards around the box of these scripts that you are in charge of delivering. So, the boat arrives, safely. You do not wish to release the box to anyone, you wish to follow it to its safe destination. There is some sort of disagreement with individuals in the harbor about the need, they want to check the boxes, they want to check what's coming in. There is other things on the ship that is not your responsibility, like little spices and some sort of golden cups and knick-knacks. But you don't care about those, so you toss that box to them. But they are really interested in one box, which is your box with the scrolls. You don't wish them to meddle really, and look into this box. So there is some sort of disagreement and there are some soldiers that comes and try to take your box. And there is a little bit of a riot and there is a fire and you are really concerned about this box. Oohhh, oohhh, there is fire and they put this fire, oohhh, the box, the box, your box—your box of knowledge is lost. Oh, this is a sad moment. You have to begin new. Oh, so much work.

D. Was it my work?

B. Yes, you and others from a temple in the northern side on the African continent (*Christine saw an area around Alexandria.*

This was the same life when Zachariah came down to physically assist with the transmission of knowledge from the Elahim.) Okay, I understand this. Because this is similar to what you are doing now. Also, Ophelia says because of this occurrence in the past, there is a blend of energy with emotions of redoing something you already have done. The massive work that was placed in the past, lost, and then to do it all over again. There is a combined joy and sadness in this work (*our current project*), because it also creates a heavy cape over you, because you have to get it right and you have to protect it as well. So, I see. This is a little bit of dilemma in this because you also feel very protective of the work that is coming. You don't want to do this over, it's so unnecessary. I get it. It is also a sign for you to also be very careful when you deliver it to someone else. It is a memory, and it is to understand that it is a massive work, and it has been done in the past. If you feel the pressure of combining all these different things you want to put into the script. Then, there were more script rolls in the box, because you were a group of individuals working on those scripts. You don't have to feel that it has to be the same amount in this life. You are only TWO working this time. Last time it was a little bit of a council group. So there were several doing similar work as you are doing now, and there was more information in the box. So, know that you do not have to provide the same volume, that is the lesson from this. You're only two! You're not like a council of ten individuals anymore. So you do what you are supposed to do, and you do it good. Because you don't have to bring the whole box, as you did last time. But, it is sadness that you have to redo things again.

D. That's fascinating!

B. But he (*Zachariah*) worked with you when you did that in the temple, you know, with your scripture that was in the fire. They (*Elahim*) were involved, very much so, because of the education they wanted to transmit.

D. And this was in Alexandria?

B. In the northern part of Africa, in the temple, where you were a group. He's involved with cycles of learning.

D. Was he incarnated at the time?

B. He was part of it, he was here. He was a part of this group. He chose to come in. He was pure in his being. He carried all the knowledge with him, inside, like a container.

D. He didn't have to forget?

B. Didn't have to forget. He just went through like an x-ray. His soul just went in and picked a body. And he was only the messenger.

D. Did he come in as an adult?

B. Yes.

D. That's the way to travel.

B. Now he's doing it differently, through you.

D. In some ways that may be harder, for him.

B. No, because you will remember, because you were there as well, and you worked with him in this pillar place. So, you will remember. That is why you are so connected with him. He communicates to you, instead of directly in front of you. So, that is it. That will be one thing in the book. Let's see if there is something else.

D. Okay.

B. Oh, here you describe the physical body—the body is something that you do not really like. (*He is reading from another part of my journal, which Ophelia must have shown him.*) You feel it's heavy, you feel it's in some way dirty. You don't really like to blend your energy fully because the physical is not completely clean. And because it's not clean you have a concern that your energy will be affected. Not being clean on this plane means inhaling food; you don't know what it has within it. Other places where you reside you do not necessarily eat. So, if you manifest a physical form somewhere else, it is what it is, and it is created from a pure sense of manufacturing, really, and it doesn't get affected from pollution caused by the inhaling part (*ingesting food*). The food thing is something you don't really approve, that you have to do that here. Because it effects the physical and you feel it is something that is beyond your control...Okay. (*He was having a silent side conversation with Ophelia.*) This is not what you prefer, you do not like to be affected, because you understand in some way it affects the mission that you have on this plane because of the pollution that can manifest and stay in the physical vehicle. It creates a little bit of a burden on this plane. Oh, okay, you agreed. But then again, you don't feel like you want to be here.

D. Well, that's interesting. Thank you.

B. So, let's see what we can learn from that, because there is something with that that is not being said, so I will ask if there is another page that I can maybe take a look–see on, when it comes to this. Because it is important, because your physical body is not working correctly, and it is almost like you on the inside, you know, reject it! SO, you might actually try to embrace it a little bit better. But if you fight it, you fight everything. It manifests in the engine and it doesn't really work in your favor once you're here. Because you ARE here. So know, when the soul fights the physical—and you chose to have a really strong physical layer working on this plane—it creates a little bit of warfare within you! So, what can we learn about this? We can say, okay, you will do good with having those periods when you clean out the body with the liquid fasts, you know, those times when you detox. Detox periods. You should have it with two to three months in between, and it should be two to three days, a week tops, but not longer, because you will get tired in the head. And you will get sad in the head as well, so here is another conflict. So, if you like, 3 to 4 times a year, with cycles, do detox, then it will help. Because it also sends a signal to the soul that its vehicle is taken care of best it can. As for now, we wish for you to do detox two to three days, THREE DAYS, she says, THREE DAYS, with about three months in between. You will be sad in the head, but it will be good for you. Okay, we will leave it at that, but just know that it is a good thing for you to do detox. It will help the engine to run better for you.

D. Okay. Thank you. I appreciate the information.

Our Original Solar System (Dec 11, 2016)

After Bob had read from the journal, Ophelia then gave him a box to look into and describe for me. The box contained an energetic model of our solar system, which is different than the one we presently have. There had originally been three planets in a row, traveling in the orbit we call the asteroid belt. At least one of the planets had been inhabited by other beings. Also, the current moon was put in place after the three planets were partially vaporized and destroyed. Bob said there had been another moon at an earlier time, perhaps further away in orbit than the one we know. Bob seems to be talking out loud while he investigates the box, and as he ponders questions, he is either being told or he figures it out himself.

B. So, let's see, there was this package as well. Ohh. There's like this miniature stuff in here. It's like a baby version of a—I will not touch it. I just take a look, okay, so I won't touch it. (*Ophelia must have cautioned him about poking it with his fingers.*) So, let's see. There is something moving in here. There is a baby version of how a little solar system could be placed, could be done. So, I'm going to see what it looks like. It has one–two–three–four–five–six...oh, it is the (*our*) solar system. However, it is also something with the asteroid belt. It wasn't really fully optimal, –how it was done. The asteroid belt is a stabilizer, of sorts, between different vibrations. There is one vibration from the center point to the asteroid belt, and there is another one from that spot going outwards. So, what does it mean? On the inside of the asteroid belt, oh, it (*the vibration*) is faster in there. I'll have to see what this could mean. I need maybe a little map to understand. Sometimes, with the box there is like a little envelope stuck to it so you can read! Huh, so you understand what it is inside! Hehehe. There's no note, so I will have to guess. Inside the asteroid belt there is a faster frequency the closer to the sun, the core. So, it is vibrating faster and everything is more in its intended form, shape, and place. Outside, it is more silent. And it's colder, of course, and it is moving more...Okay, so the outside of the asteroid belt is actually communicating and resonating with another solar system, close by. So, they actually are in between this sun in the middle as well as resonating to another one (*solar system*). SO, this is a model of the solar system. But there is something with the outer planets that is—

D. Is this asteroid belt a place where there is a missing planet in the solar system, or is this something else?

B. Oh, it was, it was. There was not only one. OH! This is it! This is what it was. Because it is a known fact for the scientists that they think one planet exploded and created the asteroid belt. In some way, that is true. However, there were actually three planets in a row in that specific core. So, that is why the asteroid belt is so massive, because science can't understand how so much junk can come from only one. (*Based on what the spirits have said, some of the planets were vaporized, and as the planets exploded, sending dust and debris in all directions away from the orbital path.*) And there were actually three in a row. They were placed in order for some sort of interaction with the planet Earth, as well as the planet Mars. But this is not very common. This is not common. at all, that you have three planets in a row, in the same path—like a tail.

D. What happened to them?

B. Something with it that went boom. It was from outside, coming in, disturbing. It's like a comet coming in, and that's how it looks, like an incoming ray of comet, making the three of them go poof!

D. How long ago was that?

B. Oh, who can tell?

D. Long time?

B. Oh, indeed. But it's way after the planet Earth came along. So, it's not that long ago. It's not like billions of years, actually, but it's still a long time ago. But know, it was not one (*planet*), it was actually three planets in a row. That's what this model is about. Because, for some reason, someone outside the solar system wanted the asteroid belt because there was some sort of protection for the inside. So, they make these...because, first of all, the three were placed in some sort of observation spots, almost. But then it didn't function that well. So it was decided, I assume, to make them...oh, let's see, this is longer I think, because it created a change in the climate on the Earth. It was a time when more clouds were...

D. Is this before you came in?

B. Oh, no, no, no. I did see the three, you know.

D. You've been here a long time then. (*Based on his statements, the Moon has been placed here within the past 60 million years. But he also said there was a previous moon that was moved out.*)

B. Indeed. But it actually created, when this occurred, it created heavy clouds and heavy, –it was like coughing. A lot of living beings coughed after this, because it poured into different directions from this source. Cough, cough. So, that wasn't really good. From my perspective, maybe they could have done it differently, you know, who wants to be surrounded by dust and cough. Oh, I'm not really sure about the time frame here with this. It's probably more in the past. I get confused with human years; I normally refer to cycles of the planet. You know, like I have different markers. I know the dinosaurs come in, I know they don't come in, I know there is a cloud and heavy rains, so I follow different time frames than you do.

D. You came in with the clouds, didn't you?

B. I came in with the clouds, indeed. So, it's been a process here. I sometimes struggle putting it into the numbers, because there are no numbers, so I normally guess. I know it sounds strange, but that is how I see it. SO, this is a model about the solar system, but it was actually three planets in a row.

D. I guess they were following each other with the same speed?

B. Indeed. It's like they were really close, so one could almost see them, similar like the moon. But the moon came later, you know.

D. How did the moon get here?

B. Oh, it's placed. It is put there. It is not from the original model, because in this model there is no moon. So, there is the Sun, there are planets, there is the three in a row that later became poof. And there is a couple...one, two, three, there is actually four from the asteroid belt and out. This is the original model of the solar system. Let's see, so we have the sun, then there is one–two–three–four, then there is the three in a row, then there is the one–two–three–four.

D. Were the three in a row the next bunch of planets after Mars?

B. Fifth. Yes, indeed. That would be it.

D. Who put the moon there?

B. Oh, it's part of your group, because you're the ones who place stuff everywhere. And then, you know, the rest of us just have to sort of adapt to it. And we said, "Whoooa! There is something new!" So we ask, are we supposed to go, is this supposed to be where others go? And then we get yes or no. The moon is more placed. It came after the big poof of the three. So, instead of those three, they put something else closer to the planet. It carried the same purpose. But the three planets in a row, they carried three different beings. Beings, –more like three different awareness's, being close to the project, which was the Earth plane. For some reason it wasn't optimal, and it went poof, and instead they put like a little thing on the inside closer to the planet. They observed.

D. That's fascinating, thank you for the information.

B. This is your box, you know more about this than I do. But I am just seeing the model of how it was, the basic model of how it was meant to be. But it was very different, it was unique, with the fact of having three planets in a row.

D. Was I involved in building the model?

B. Uh–huh.

D. How about this one, was she involved?

B. Uh–huh. (*Suddenly laughs very loudly*) HUHUH! This one WANTED MORE!! UH–Huh. Wanted like a whole series of planets in that course (*orbit*). Because it was the purpose of observing the Earth planet, and this one was like, "Why not just put in a whole group? It's just engineering school." This one wanted more planets. You're very different in the way you do your science projects. You are more careful. Oh, there are models in here where this one had done something. There are less planets, but there is more speed. Do you know what is causing that?

D. No, I don't.

B. It's the center of the models, the center sun, the core. That creates the foundation of how fast things can move around it. Every star is different. Every core is different. This one likes to work with bigger ones. All exists. It exists the slower, which is this level, this solar system is considered as a slower sun. There are other solar systems and galaxies where the suns are more massive and it carries a different construction, so the planets orbiting that star actually, it's more suitable for other things than plants. I don't go there. It goes too fast and there's no plants. The sun is bigger, there's one place that is created where the sun is almost 50 times bigger than this one!

D. That's huge!

B. It is. But sometimes size isn't everything! You both work on this. You both create the foundation for other groups to work and create evolution in different ways. Also, not all models carry solid planets, like this one. And that's not for me to know at this point. But there's actually some that aren't solid. I know there are, because I've seen those boxes. The core is kind of similar, but it's smaller, it's not as massive. But it is orbiting with something that is not fully like a solid form. Those realities are different and do not necessarily need the same core for them to function. So, there is more density the bigger the core, the bigger the star. Everything is bigger and more solid. The little ones are more with energetic realities.

D. Is the energy from the sun just a conversion of spiritual energy?

B. Ah, that can be said. But it's also the engine of the whole thing. So the bigger the center, the more possibilities lies for manifestation that is physically shown. The smaller ones almost looks like a little rock, those realities are more of an energetic form. They're different, not really as easily detected as they float around.

D. Could humans see them? Are they in a physical reality or something else?

B. Something else. But they move between the physical, so in some way they interact. But it's like a little solar system. It looks the same, it's just not as fully solid. But it has the same structure; a center and little realities orbiting it.

D. Is it less visible than gas?

B. It's like a gas form, but it comes with different colors—I can see one here. One is more—it carries different colors and some actually come with tones. They are more...you know, this solar system doesn't move as much as others. The other ones aren't as stuck in their placement like this one. Everything is moving, of course, but not as freely as those realities that are not solid form, fully. It's a whole different mobility with them. I don't know what they do, but they sort of snooze around between, and they're not affected if they crash into those who are solid. You don't want have two solid solar systems meeting, necessarily. But these are more snoozing around. There are different realities, but it's the same structure, the same model, just different.

D. That's extraordinarily interesting, I really appreciate all this information.

B. Well, this is what you do, because I have seen it in the boxes you have shown me. I don't really fully understand how they–they–they...what's the purpose? You know, you want to know that. Someone like me, –you want to know, you want to see, what's the purpose? But I don't know, I can only see. You said it's important and it creates different possibilities. And you're all about expanding the universes. So you are expanding different realities within each section, if you like, just to see how it interacts and if it is detectable and if it creates occurrences on the solid ones. That's what you said.

D. Amazing, if I could only remember.

B. Yes, indeed. But it is created to sort of hover around within already solid realities. And it creates a presence of sorts, so I'm sure it carries a spiritual awareness that is moving in to more solid realities. It's almost like it is a living entity by itself. You know those creatures in the water, those who look like jellyfish? That's how it looks. And they carry colors. I don't know who they are, but they come with colors and tones. Some have both, some are silent, but they move around like those jellyfish, around solid objects. I don't know why, but it is what it is. And this is what you showed me before. We did have discussions here in the vault, and you showed me different things. You put boxes way up high that I could not reach, and you gave me a stool. But the little stool only has two steps, Hehehehe. You said you'd give me a bigger stool as time goes by. Now I have one with two—two steps, but the shelves are really high. But as we go, so will my stool. But now it is two, two levels. So I can reach up one, two. I tried to reach the third, but I can only see the boxes. I don't want to push, because if I push them and they fall, I would never be able to get them back up, you know. It's a responsibility when you get clearance to do something. So, you know, I wait patiently for you to give me a stool with three steps. You reach all those floors, there's like 6 levels on this bookshelf with boxes, and I reach two. Those on the bottom are more related to the Earth plane. It's not very much...we've gone through those already.

D. Well, thank you for all the good information. I know we have been here awhile. Is there anything else you or Ophelia would like to add before we close?

B. Ophelia just smiles and nods. She just smiles.

D. Do you like Ophelia?

B. I do. She's very caring, and she always cares for animals. And when there is something I wish to ask about the animal kingdom, how I can improve, she's always very helpful. She's very close to nature. So she travels between all realities. She seems to be a little bit equipped everywhere, really. But ah, her heart is really with caring for the planet and animals, and soil is important to her. So, she is like, broadly educated! Well, she is the one I always ask questions to, and she is the one that tells me what I can look at. She's very helpful.

D. Well, that's nice. I'm glad she is working with us. Bob. Thank you for joining us today. I guess we'll talk later in the week?

B. Uuhh. Where do you want me to put the box? Do you want it to be open? Oh, I'll put the box back. Maybe I'll put it back, because it belonged on the second shelf. The book is yours, so I leave it to you. I don't know where you want to have it. Oh, Ophelia says that she will take care of it! Okay. So, yes, we can leave, because the box I can put back, but she said she will tend to the book.

D. Well, thank you both. Alright, my friend, we will talk soon. Goodbye.

B. Bye bye, bye bye.

Bob Begins his Travels (Dec 25, 2016)

In the next discussion, Bob is describing the different types of knowledge we work with and how we share that information with one another. Christine and I work on the sixth and ninth dimensions, engaged in the design, launching, and maintenance of form and structures within the twelve fish tanks. Solar systems and galaxies are created as a joint effort by all dimensions between the sixth and tenth. The sixth and ninth work with the cores of stars and planets as well as moons and other bodies, including what scientist call black holes, which are actually a different type of non-light emitting stellar body. The seventh is the dimension that creates stars, using the cores supplied by the sixth and ninth. The eighth helps everyone, as they supply the patterns for the elements, atmospheres, and electromagnetic energy. The second dimension is responsible for the implementing life forms containing DNA on all the living planets within each of the twelve fish tanks.

The vault is a storage area, below the main Library on the fifth dimension, where documentation from all fish tanks and spiritual realities are archived. Ophelia and I (*my higher self, Lasaray*) gave Bob the task of maintaining records in the vault. It is here that he first learned about the energetic models of solar systems and galaxies. He has reported that he and I spent a lot of time looking at and discussing things before he eventually began taking classes with Ophelia.

B. I want to say something that we help each other with; we help each other to understand the combined work we do on ALL planes. On the other plane (*the fifth*), in the vault, I learn about how you create the form, how you make things move around. Which, you know, it still moves, but it is very different from the way I think that something should move. (*The motion of planets, solar systems and galaxies, as compared to his knowledge of animals.*) You want to learn about things on the surface (*of the planet*), because that's not what you do. So I tell you how things appears on the surface, what different things you can put on surface. So, you tell me, "I created this", which can be somewhat of a planet. And then I say, "On that one, there's no way a tree can grow because there's no atmosphere." So, we learn from each other in that sense. You're kind of interested in trees, you're fascinated by trees. Because you have seen different entities, of course, in other places you have created, but this sort of vegetation is something of an interest for you.

D. You're an expert in that.

B. I am. Because, you know, there is something also that I teach my little beings, my little friends who are still sparkles, ah, there is also this; souls are a little bit skittish, a little bit tense to come into body, because it is a trap. Those who live in my reality are a little bit afraid of blending with solid objects, like a stone or a tree. So, there is a little bit of an encouragement that takes place. My little students, some say, "What if I can't get out? What if I'm locked there and can't get back home?" There's a lot of encouragement that takes place to make them understand that we come in a certain way, but we can also leave a certain way. It's the same way with souls. You come into a physical body, but when the body dissolves and falls down on the ground because it can't operate anymore, you still have the possibility to leave. So, it is the same thing. I have a class with little, oh, they're smaller, let's see if I can tell you. There is a group, -they look like balls from your perspective, so I teach them about how to enter a solid object. They don't seem very fearful about the entrance, it's more the exit they are concerned about. Some think they will be locked there.

D. So if they enter objects, there's millions of trees and rocks, how many of those have little light beings from your dimension in them.

B. Oh, more than you think!

D. And what is the purpose of them being in these trees and rocks?

B. Same purpose as you grow into a soul and incarnate in a body—it is for the experience.

D. They learn about the form they are going to create at some point?

B. Ah, and to observe its surroundings. I represent a little bit of that thing, you know, what you see when you're out in nature, when you think that no one is there. If you look into a tree and you see something that sort of feels like it is staring at you, it could actually be some of my friends. I am concerned about that a lot of people only pass by and don't necessarily pay attention to nature; and we do all sorts of tricks so people will pay attention. Even, you know, —BOO! sometimes. But it is a struggle, –it is a struggle when they don't hear you. This way of communicating is, of course, clearly in favor—when you have someone to talk through! It's a bit different with a tree! You try to, but it doesn't say anything, because you're in a tree! It's the same with a rock, really. However, if you start to look around you a little bit, if you pay attention, you will see there is actually little individuals, sparkles, normally, in the trees. When I say sparkles, that means the little ones that are in the making of, similar like a soul. The soul is born and the soul progresses, and then it chooses to go into an incarnation. It is the same in the second dimension where I belong. There we have little sparkles. First, they take studies, they learn, because they don't incarnate in the same way, –we blend. We go in and out of objects. So it is not an incarnation, similar like into a person, where you sort of (*makes sucking sound*) jump in, in that way. So, it's kind of different, we go in and out. The little ones, the sparkles, my students, –because I don't blend any more–, but they are a little bit afraid to get stuck. So, you have to encourage them, similar like your guides did when you came the first time to this plane. So we tell them, "You can go into this object, but you are free to come back out. You have to learn to blend and leave, in and out." Some objects in nature actually possess more than one sparkle. Trees actually is a favorite spot for unions from my sparkle family to go to. They like to merge in trees, if you have seen that. A lot of people don't see that—it makes me sad, you know, when they don't see it. It's the same thing like rocks. Some people they just see like, ohh, like a boundary for them almost, instead of seeing it like something that is of a living life form, really. (*Popping his lips.*) It makes me sad that you are not paying attention. We also create a lot of different treats for you, like what you can eat and so forth. We don't like all this manufactured food that is on the market, like plastic food. We don't like that at all, at all, at all.

D. So, who are the teachers you report to, what do they do?

B. Oh, it is somewhat of a little council, you know. All have a little bit of guidance from their elders. I have one that I really like. He's old now, he has a white beard. He's been here a lot of times. He almost, from your perspective, would look like Santa Clause, but he's very wise. He's been like a grandparent to me, and he's been with me as a teacher on my journeys. He looks at my reports and he puts them in the vault. (*The second dimension has their own vault of knowledge related to Earth.*) He's always very encouraging. It's like a chain, you know. So, I give him my final reports. At the moment, I'm looking into those things I can communicate through energetic waves like this. (*Information he can share as he blends and communicates through Christine.*) So, that is my main focus and what I would like to explore more. Because there is so much with the solid form from where I am (*He has worked mostly on solid forms, such as animals, trees, etc., and wants to learn more about energetic form.*) So, I'm moving into the vibration of frequencies and energies. Ophelia knows my teacher; they go WAY back, I'm sure. You're more new. Before we met, Ophelia said, "I have a friend and I will introduce you," but I didn't know what to expect.

D. Ophelia's friend, or your friend?

B. No, it was you! I was selected to learn. Because of my advancement in the group studying form, I was selected by Ophelia. She asked if I wanted to visit those masters of form, - and I didn't know what that was. But I said yes, because I'm curious. And because of my teacher, he agreed. He nodded and said it would be okay. So I said, "Okay." And then I waited. And I didn't know really what would happen, because I thought I was gonna' go somewhere, -but I didn't. So, I waited and you found me in the forest. And from that time on, we became somewhat of a little couple, a friend couple. First, there was this part where we didn't communicate that well. Because I couldn't understand you really well, so there was a lot of pointing and such. In the beginning, I never went anywhere, it was more you coming to me. Maybe it was because I wanted to feel safe. Maybe they thought I would be more comfortable in my own setting. As I progressed over time and our friendship grew, and I became comfortable with your appearance, then I was allowed to travel to your lab. I'm somewhat of a scientist, so I do prefer labs. I prefer to do things hands–on more than read. Because you just read the same thing over and over and I want to see that it becomes something. That's why I also write in symbols, because it carries more than a word form.

D. When we communicate, is it a form of telepathy? Do we pass pictures back and forth?

B. Oh, I showed you pictures, and then you garbled. But I learned to understand you, because I hear your answer in my head. But you can't verbally talk like I do, so it's more like, khhkhuh, kkhhk, like gurgling. But I understand because I get the pictures in my head. In the beginning, you sent me pictures and I drew it and I returned it; and you said if it was right or wrong. So, that's how our communication started to take place. And then I wanted to know about how form is created, because you are more of the first level of form (*the planets in various solar systems*), and I'm more of; fur or no fur (*the plants and animals*). So, I don't create the original form, but I create what comes later. It's like getting an Easter egg, and at first, it's completely white and plain, and then you can color it. (*The second puts life forms on empty planets, if they are designed for that.*) Plants, – you don't do plants, so that's why you're sort of interested in that. Because something you work on has to do with the atmosphere, it's your project, you said. That's why you're interested in the trees. I tried to show you rocks, but you said, "I already know about those," so you didn't really want to listen. But sometimes, I show you a rock and say, "There's someone in here." And then you look at it and flip it, but I don't know if you understand what I'm saying. You're more interested in the trees, because you're studying atmosphere, shifts in atmosphere around celestial bodies. You're interested to understand the resonance of the trees with the atmosphere. Where there's no trees, there's all sorts of exposure. This is what you are learning. Because you, on your progress, on your journey, are interested in understanding what is surrounding the planets. That is more of the eighth and ninth dimension of work; the elements. So, it's not just to create a ball.

D. So, Ophelia is the one who originally picked you?

B. I was with my teacher, discussing my progress. A lot of times we only sit around and talk, because we go way back. And then she came in and she looked friendly. I didn't know who she was, but she was big and kind and, you know, like glowing almost. And I felt like, "Ohhh, this is someone pleasant!" So, she came in and my guide, who is more of a, his name is Gur–gurgur, Gergen! It's hard to say. (*This was delivered not long after he began speaking through Christine, so his skills were still developing.*) But Ophelia came in and then she smiled like she always does and she said hello. And she said, "I've been following your progress, together with your guide. Are you interested in moving up a level and learning more about form?" And I said yes, but I didn't know what that meant. But then I thought I was going to go with her, but I didn't. She said a teacher would come to me. So I waited and didn't know what that would be about. But she said, "He will come to you and he will teach you another level of form." And I was very interested in that. (*How Bob and I met was presented in Wave 2, so we will not repeat it here.*)

D. You told us about Ophelia's lab. Do we have a lab that you practice in? What's it like? Do you like this lab or is Ophelia's better?

B. Ohm, very different, very different. Oh, there's not that many students in your lab, so I haven't really met anyone. I'm merely observing here, but I'm FASCINATED to be a part of it. I don't know why we always shut down the light though, but I stand and (*laughs loudly*), ohohohohoh, because you thought that I was a little bit scared of no light, so you gave me a little torch and said, "You can hold this, but just don't wave it around too much, but you can have it so you won't be scared of the dark the first time." Now I'm not scared any more. (*He said with some degree of confidence.*) But the first time, I didn't know why we were standing in darkness in there. But there was darkness and there was like colors in the ceiling, spheres that moved, rotating, if you like, and then your friends came in. It's very silent in here. That's the difference, you know, because in Ophelia's lab, and in mine, there's all sorts of noise. Here you have to be quiet. It's hard because I don't ask questions as much, of course, because I feel I am supposed to be quiet. And I am! I am. But afterwards, you say, "Now you can ask your questions and we will go outside." But I don't really ask questions when you're working with your friends.

When Christine is in trance, she can often see images related to what is being discussed, so she described what Bob was showing her. On the sixth dimension, there is a working lab area where a handful of spirits will gather to manipulate or evaluate energy fields within the different fish tanks. Apparently, we work in darkness to better see the color patterns. In the center of the room is what appears to be a large, round table, except the table is like a glass–bottomed boat that can bring parts of the fish tanks into clear focus, projecting a holographic image into the room. So certain groups of spirits on the sixth are able to remotely view and modify sheets of galaxies, on a large scale, down to individual planets or stars on a smaller scale. In addition to this room, I also have a lab that is well lit, where Bob and I spend most of our time working together or with other spirits on various projects. Since Christine and I are brothers (*at home*) and good friends, he also spends a lot of time with Bob.

D. That doesn't sound like as much fun as Ophelia's class.

B. It's different, it's more structured. No, it's more, I do prefer...it's just the polarity here. You don't invite anyone in here, but I do see those that are similar like you each have their own little beings with them. It's like one for each, it's not like a whole colony coming in. So, I'm there to see.

D. What about the area where we work in groups?

B. It's like energy waves, but it's like lightning. It's like blue and white lightning primarily, –and purple. Purple also. Blue, white, purple and green. In Ophelia's lab, it is primarily yellow and white. You also have a little room with a big sphere with energy, electric stuff in it. Oh, I'm not supposed to touch it, but you can have a look.

D. Is this close to our lab?

B. It's in a room. Where Ophelia's is one big space, here it's like several rooms. There's one big room in the middle, but then there are like two to the sides. And there is one where you keep a big sphere, and inside of it, it's like electricity of colors inside of it. Oh, you just said, "You can have a look here," because you know I'm curious, and you're kind enough to drag me around here. (*We have come to know this as the "sphere room", because he mentions it occasionally.*) I don't practice as much here, in the big room, but I participate and I pay attention. I don't ask questions as much because it's very quiet. You might think because of all the electricity and flashes and stuff that it would be noisy, but it's not.

D. Is it quiet?

B. It's completely quiet. And because I can't understand, this is also something that, you know, probably because of where my level of understanding is, but I can sense that you are communicating. But I can't read it, because the other ones don't give me a picture like you do. It's like I'm standing there like I'm blind. I take notes and then I ask afterwards, but I get a sense you're not telling me everything. You're all taller, and I can't understand when you communicate. So I'm sort of limited in understanding here. So, it's mainly visual at this time.

D. Well, it's a long–term project.

B. It is. And I'm grateful to be here, because this has to do with the form, but it's also the core of stars and planets, the core of what causes planets to become and to move, and I can see there is an idea here! Clearly, there is something.

D. Have you actually seen Ophelia create a star? (*The description of Bob making a little star in a glass–like fish bowl can be found in Wave 1.*)

B. Because they (*the teachers on the seventh*) know we are really curious, sometimes they humor us by showing off a little bit. So, one time they made a huge one, a really BIG one. This fish bowl in the middle of the room had several pipes and there were all sorts of light beings, and we were put way to the side against the walls, –so we wouldn't be in the way, I assume. There were like twenty light beings, including her, and they created a MASSIVE sun. If I created an orange in my fish bowl then this would be considered...mmm, no, because there's nothing...OK, if I created a pea in my fish bowl, my sun was the size of a pea, then this one is like those balls you have in the swimming pool.

D. A big beach ball.

B. Big beach ball. So you can see mine, that I thought was kind of big, but in comparison, my fish bowl was like a pea and theirs was a beach ball. Oh, they showed off. Made my little, my pea almost...

D. Oh, it's all the same.

B. (*Laughed loudly.*) That's what she said! HA HA HUH. She put her arm around me and she said, "It's all the same, it's all relative to where you put it. So, it's the same," and that made me happy. The teachers are extremely skilled, but I'm still more interested in your lab. Because I can't understand the communication there, I'm somewhat limited to what I can see, and because you shut down the light a lot, that's why you gave me that little lamp, that little torch.

D. It will all come in due time.

B. Well, that is the whole thing, I guess, with everything, whatever that means. So that is what we do. My lab is more like Ophelia's lab, there's all sorts of activity there. You would consider it completely unorganized, but it's not. There's a lot of movement, you can see all sorts of individuals moving around, and there is all kinds of questions being asked out loud.

D. With your training on the sixth and seventh, are you eventually changing the type of work you do?

B. That is the thing–that is the thing. What I've been TOLD is that I'm being trained for something that will come in the future. But, in order for that to BECOME the new car from my factory, I have to understand the engineering behind it. I still don't know what that is.

D. Well, you should be very proud that you were picked.

B. Ah. Ophelia knows, you know probably as well. But you're not telling. It's because I'm still learning, but you smile a lot. I know you like me.

D. Who wouldn't? You're easy to like.

B. That's what you said. Ophelia laughs, but she teaches me a lot, because there's something new coming in. Oh, I do think I know what this is! It is the upgrade of the human body. So that is why I'm learning more about form and light, and the engine! (*Explained in Wave1.*)

D. See, you were told. Is that coming up pretty soon?

B. Nah. What do you mean, soon? Everything is in due time. I would assume this is in another cycle. It's not from one day to the next. It's not like a new thing is going to be born within a few years, you know. Oh, this is complex. This is just in the beginning of the process. It's what we do. It's what is supposed to happen, I assume. And when it is happening, when it's done, I will have that manual in the cloud and I will use it for my final step. Because it has to be operating well in the environment, so you can't do all sorts of changes. And that's also a little bit where I come in, because I have a little bit more knowledge about what works on the surface, than say, you do.

D. I'm sure you do, you're very wise.

B. Thank you. I've been studying elements, and seasons, and conditions for a while, so I kind of know what goes and what doesn't go.

D. When you look around your lab at the other second dimension spirits, would you say there are many as curious as you are, or is that kind of rare?

B. I do, I do like my students, because they are like me. I've always been inquisitive; I've always added to my knowledge. You should never grow out of being curious, because that is how you progress. But there are some that are like me, the personality can change of course, but most are very friendly and concerned about the environment and they don't necessarily like to blend with other dimensions as much, but they do like to communicate with Ophelia's people, –they come here sometimes. You don't really come here, so when I tell them about you, I don't know if they all believe me. But I do tell them about you, and I tell that I have been to these magical places, and some, –I don't think all of them–, believe me. That's too bad. But, SOME, especially my students, they're very intrigued. They are like sponges, they just absorb everything you tell them, so you have to be careful what you tell them.

D. That's probably why they were given to you, because they match you.

B. That is actually correct, because you get the sort of student that is compatible to you on personality. But, you know, in general it's a very merry surrounding, and it's very happy, –you can hear singing, for instance. There is a group that likes to sing a lot, and there are all sorts of happy expressions, I would say. But the difference might be that I like to leave a lot, go to other places and come back and tell stories, because I feel like it might help sometimes. But I don't know if everyone believes in you.

D. Well, I'm sure they will, eventually.

B. They will. I tell them stories about you and what I've been seeing.

D. So your students were hand–picked by Gergen and others, to learn as you do?

B. Hand–picked, indeed. So, I'm primarily by myself when I'm traveling. I spend a lot of time in the labs, studying, because you give me assignments and I try to look into it. You send me an image in the head, and then I try to draw with my symbols and I try to explain what I think happens, then we discuss it. And then you say you want to know more about the functions of the trees, so we talk a lot about that, because you are concerned about the atmosphere. It is the whole thing that needs to operate well.

D. So, when you take your notes, which vault do you keep your notes in?

B. Because the notes I do with you, they are not supposed to leave. So they remain in the box, my box, where I have my notes. And when we go to the Earth vault, for instance, you have your ideas in a box. So, you don't move them from one place to the next. You don't want to confuse anyone else.

D. Does Ophelia keep her notes in our vault?

B. I don't think so! And if she does, they are on the top shelf, I'm pretty sure, because I haven't seen them. And sometimes she just smiles; that's the difference, because she always smiles, which almost appears that she is gonna tell you. But she doesn't, always. So, I wait and she smiles and she put her arm around me and then you kinda think you will be answered. Sometimes you are, but sometimes you're not.

D. Do I answer your questions?

B. (*Laughing.*) Because I poke you! Because we're working more in a way that I teach you and you teach me, then when you say you're not going to tell me or something and laugh a little bit, then I say I'm not going to tell you about the trees! Then you laugh in your own little gurgle way, then I say—you're kind of fascinated by the pine trees, because you think they are operating more in favor of the atmosphere—so I say, "If you're not going to tell me, I'm only going to talk about palm trees!" So, it's funny like that. Then you say, "OK, I'll give you a little bit," and I say, "I'll give YOU a little bit!" That's sort of how we trigger and learn. But I can't read your thoughts, necessarily, because you communicate differently. I try sometimes, but it's like a fog. So, it's harder to see what you're thinking than it is with her, because she always smiles. You always sort of look a little bit neutral, so it's kinda' hard to know if you're hiding something from me. Oh, I know what you also do sometimes, because I'm shorter, sometimes when you stand up and I can't see your face or your top, then you know it's even harder for me to know if there's something you're hiding from me. And sometimes I ask, "Why? Why? Why hide?" And then you say, because you also want to encourage my curiosity, you say, "You WILL know, just not now."

D. In due time.

B. In due time—in due time. A lot of times I feel like both of you, when I ask questions I'm not supposed to, you sort of divert my attention with bringing me another box. "Oh, look at this, Bob, look!" And then I look. But I remember, I know—I know what you're doing.

D. Well, you catch on pretty quick to our tricks.

B. I do! I have tricks too, you know! Just because I'm smaller, don't expect for there not to be tricks! Because even though you can see the top of my head, you don't know what's inside the head all the time, even though you have some sort of laser beam you can use to read things. Seems unfair. You both read my mind better than I read yours, for some reason. That's how it's operating.

D. So when you compare your size to Gergen, is he a lot bigger than you?

B. Oh, no. About the same size.

D. What about the sparkles?

B. Oh, they're small. They're like blueberries.

D. How high do they come up on you?

B. To my knees.

D. They are little.

B. They are, but so were you when you were an infant. I don't know how you looked when you were an infant. Maybe you were born that way. I doubt it, though; I think you were smaller once. But my little students are interested in learning about, some are already asking about gravity. I say "No, in due time!" Hahahaha. So I do the same thing, it seems!

D. That's a good lesson.

B. It's a good lesson, really.

D. I guess if you spend most of your time alone, you must enjoy our little talks?

B. I do, I do.

D. So do we.

B. And also, because I do have questions that sometimes aren't answered, I try this way to see if something comes. Like I say,

I'm also a little bit tricky! (*Lasaray is my spiritual name, which Bob uses all the time in our conversations. He mistakenly thought my incarnation would have some of Lasaray's knowledge accessible.*) But it's that fact that there is some sort of bigger, or a new engineering that is in the making, so because I would be considered a master designer from my level, I'm sure that's why I was picked, combined with my curiosity.

D. We certainly appreciate your knowledge.

B. I feel chosen.

D. Yes, you are. You're one of the chosen people.

B. I'm the chosen child. Not to blow my own horn, but that is what I feel, actually, –very privileged, very privileged indeed.

D. I think everybody is happy to work with you. You're a pleasure to be around.

B. I don't know about your friends, though, because you are all quiet. I don't know what they think or what they believe. So I try to just be still next to you and not move around too much. I don't go off route! You're not supposed to, so I kind of remain still.

D. Are there other people there with you, or are you there by yourself with us?

B. I'm by myself, but sometimes I see that the other ones in your group have some sort of little student with them. I don't know who they are. (*Most of the Elahims are mentoring a younger Elahim student.*)

D. I'm sure everyone is friendly; they're just quiet.

B. Quiet, indeed. Quiet and sparkly. A lot of blue light here, and purple and green. So, that would be it.

D. Thank you very much for coming, and we look forward to talking to you soon. Zachariah as well—we appreciate his information.

B. Zach likes the words. He's very smart. He's actually writing a lot of big books.

D. Like manuals?

B. Manuals, indeed! He's putting it down like on manuals, and in books. He's also working with scriptures in the library, so he's involved with the general education on several levels. Highly intelligent. Education is good.

D. Do you know if he is the one this one saw as the professor? (*Christine saw a spirit guide who looked like a scholar, about a year before she and I met.*)

B. Indeed. You share his education. He operates all over, there's no limits really, he can operate with several at the same time. It's like an umbrella of education, –kind of huge. He's very intelligent. He's somewhat involved with what sort of advancement should take place (*on Earth and other planets*), when it comes to technology and things like that. He implements thought bubbles into the right individuals who can understand it and make sense of it. He not only puts thought bubbles into you, on what you're going to write, but his group also puts thought bubbles in to those who work in science. Oh, he has his own group.

D. What dimension does he work from?

B. He operates from, –I would say he's like you, in some way–, six and nine. He travels between. Because he is somewhat involved with education as a whole, he travels between dimensions, and even to Ophelia's lab, but it's not like he has a class there.

D. Just passing by.

B. Passing by. He's like, oh, what would you call that, —an ambassador of knowledge! That's what he likes to be called. Oh, indeed, The Ambassador of Knowledge.

D. That's a good name, probably appropriate, too.

B. He did not like the fact with the bible thing. I'm just saying that and then I'm done, since he's involved with education.

D. It's anti–education.

B. Anti–education. It's misleading. It did not come as a thought bubble. They proclaimed it to be a thought bubble of intervention from a higher source, when it was actually not.

D. I suspect most religions have a similar foundation.

The spirits on the second dimension come in many different sizes and functions, because they work directly with their many creations. Some are large, like the gardeners, who tend to the plants, trees and soil. But others are exceedingly small and move in a large group through the soil or in the atmosphere. Because all spirits are created with a color pattern, the activity that each one does is reflected in their primary color, as Bob explains later. Souls have the capacity to divide, and Ia explained how sometimes a soul will come in on the second with the ability to sub–divide into a million smaller pieces, yet act in a coordinated way to achieve certain goals. She said that this type of spirit could bring light to a large area of land, as it moves along repairing damage to the soil and its inhabitants. Bob, Ophelia, and Ia describe the little light bearers from the second as being just at the very edge of our ability to perceive. These little helpers interact directly with plants and other life forms, or they can work in a coordinated way with many of the small physical creatures, such as insects and earthworms, as they move about repairing and adding light energy where needed.

As we have said many times, each spirit is created for a specific role, so the types of spirits and their activities are extraordinarily diverse. It also happens that most of the spirits who work on Earth for long periods of time are very sensitive to the environment where they reside. The loud noises we humans generate are very disturbing, so these nature spirits will tend to leave areas that are too stressful or inhospitable. As a result, nature will become weak and sick in places where humans congregate. Bob and I were talking about one of my medieval lifetimes, when he shared how he and his friends feel about our modern way of living.

B. You were in Italy, southern part, and you moved a lot between different cities in, –oh, let's see–, Italy, and you moved over to Turkey, and they were not necessarily familiar with nature spirits. If you had been somewhere else, like the northern climates, then your visions of me and other beings would have been welcomed more easily. So, in many ways, the northern climates, like Iceland and Greenland, if you were there and told that you saw someone like me, or a sparkle or something, they would just nod and understand. Because they are not necessarily so much misled by outer influences like in this era of technology and all sorts of noise. All this noise makes us want to not come, because we don't like the noise, even though we're kind of noisy by ourselves. We talk a lot and we laugh, but that's different. It's not as high and it's not rumbling, which disturbs our energy frequencies. Like cars and trains, for instance, are a little bit scary! I do like those that are a little bit quieter, but they're still scary, you never know what that is all about. A lot of my friends that lived near where the trains took place, they left. Because when the train comes, it creates the vibration down into their tunnels and in the trees next to it, and it became unbearable to be in! And you know, it's not like there's a warning so you have time to think, "Oh, here it comes," –it just comes!

D. So, do some of your friends that don't work in labs, do they just live on Earth?

B. Indeed, they can if they want to. You can be a scientist, and that's when you are in the lab. Or you can be on the mission of merging and learning, like I did when I tried to be a fish, which I didn't like because I couldn't navigate in water that well. That's when I knew that water would not be my primary element to work in.

D. I had a question about the second dimension. This one and I were wondering if you have to do anything to get any external energy?

B. Only, similar like a human, like we are saying to you that you should meditate, –and that is to fill up your energies. We do the same thing. In the spiritual realities, as well as different energetic existences, you only recharge with adding energy, if you like. So, it's not like putting something in your mouth.

D. That makes sense. How frequently do you have to recharge your light capsule?

B. Oh, not that often, anymore. Because you don't lose energy as much as you progress. So, the little ones, it's like if you have a puppy, you feed it all time. It's the same thing. The little ones, because they lose so much energy when they're learning, when they're moving around and are more active; so they need to recharge more often. Gergen, he doesn't need that much at all, he's more still. I move more, so indeed, I do need to recharge, because I'm traveling more. As I travel, I tend to lose slightly. It's almost like docking to an energy pole, if you like! It doesn't really happen like that at all, but that was amusing, I think! Huhuhu! But I can tell you it's like being still and just sort of allowing yourself to be filled up.

D. Do you feel better when you're done?

B. I do, but it's not like here, of course. It's not like eating, but it is the same result, to feel full. You can also share energy, if you want to. We can, we can provide if we see someone that is lacking a little bit, you see it in the color they radiate, so you can actually, from your own little warehouse, your own source, you can help someone out that you meet and just give them a little energy. That's what you can do, if you see someone that maybe forgot to go and refill, and you see that, you can be friendly and just give a little bit of your own. Because sometimes as we work with things, we lose energy; it's like when you forget to eat, similar I would say. We actually have those also, that work only as givers of energy, that sort of move around silently and can detect these kinds of imbalances.

D. Within your dimension?

B. Within my dimension. I'm sure it exists everywhere; they are givers.

D. Do they work on the third dimension as well?

B. Yes, the procedure is the same. They can come in and provide energy, but they're normally, –like we talked about before, about the flies and insects that land on things–, they can work that way. They send it through a physical entity that already exists. But it is the same process and the same result we are aiming for.

D. Fascinating!

B. Well, it's just how it is. It's not so unusual, it's just how it is. If you see someone that is lacking energy, you should give them a little energy, that's what we do. But there are those who exist somewhat in the layer between the second and the third, and they operate with providing certain areas with more energy. In the waters, for instance, –and here we're not using bugs, of course–, so here we use different things. And this is the water group, so I'm not really working with them, but they are actually working on providing more oxygen to waters.

D. Does the water group have the same physical appearance as you?

B. Different colors, we see things in colors. The water people are more like blue-green. I'm more like brown-red in color. Not necessarily like a skin color, don't get confused here, but it's a way to see where someone's profession and skill lies, really. You can see, oh, there is someone working with water, or there is a little battery, a giver. Gergen is yellow.

D. What does that indicate?

B. It indicates that he works a lot with light particles.

D. So, will you always be the same general color?

B. If I don't completely transform into a completely different expertise, then I will probably remain. I'm working with organs and insides, and that is why you and I have come together, of course, because you work on the inside as well (*cores of planets and stars*). I am at this point, in this field of expertise where I work, in my case, with the engine (*his word for the digestive system*). I also like to work with the liver. Engine and liver.

D. What about the feet? (*I asked because he is always talking about paying attention to the signals received through the feet.*)

B. Well, that is external, that is not inside. I'm talking about the inside. We have groups that work with circulation, with blood, for instance. They're not brown, they're more like orange–red. They work with circulation. That's also something that is up for debate. Because we work really tightly, me with my engine and the liver, and those that work with circulation, because if they change something, it IMMEADIATELY affects my organs. If I change something, then they have to adjust after that. So, we work really close.

D. That's good. Do you enjoy that work?

B. Yes, because I do want to improve. It's like, I don't believe in a ready product. I believe that there is always room for adjustments and improvements, and that is what I am working on. So, in that regard, I'm working closely with the circulation group, because we adjust after each other. If I'm going to upgrade my engine, they need to sort of adjust the movement and rhythm and circulation, in order for it to function properly. So, that's what we do.

D. Well, you'll be much better informed after you have studied on the sixth, seventh, and maybe eighth.

B. I will indeed! Because I will understand how important the core is for a new surface.

D. When we work together, I'm never mean to you, am I? Or too demanding?

B. No, no. You tease me and I tease you right back. I know when you tease me. Sometimes I hide. You left me to self–study and when you came back, I hid! So, I'm tricky too! And you said, "You didn't self–study, Bob!"

D. Can you blend with objects in the lab?

B. It's harder, but I can blend a little bit, but it's not the same, it's not a manifested reality like the Earth here, so I have to hide more, so I do. And you say, "You didn't self–study, Bob!" I say, "You lost me! You lost me!" And you said, "You're still in the room!" I don't want to go out, I don't want to leave the room. If

I get lost, there's no one to ask, and I don't want to get lost. So, I stay put. But I do trick you, and I can tease you! So, anyway, that will be it.

D. Thank you for coming, always a pleasure.

Traveling through the Fish Tanks (Jan 8, 2017)

One of the teachings in Bob's next talk is about how spirits are given access to locations, levels, or realities. He uses types of music as a metaphor for the vibration within fish tanks, although the concept also applies to the spiritual realities. The vibration of a fish tank can be disturbing to some souls, but appealing to others. Each soul has, within its blueprint, the keys to travel to different universes of form. If a soul is intended to travel to fish tank five, then those tones will feel welcoming. Otherwise, the soul will be repelled. It is similar to how spirits advance in the spiritual dimensions. Early in its development, a spirit may not be able to tolerate the vibration from the level of the councils, for example. But later, after enough learning has been accumulated, it will feel at home on the higher levels.

When Bob was deep in his comparison, he took a little detour and recounted an amusing experience he had in Scotland, when he was knocked over by the noise from a troupe of bagpipers.

D. People are always talking about aliens coming here.

B. Yes, because they carry a different tone from their home, from where they depart.

D. So, are there indeed other life forms that come to visit Earth, that we can see?

B. Yes, indeed, yes indeed. Because they come from a different vibrating system, solar family system, which allows them to move. First of all, that is the whole thing—IF you are allowed to move.

D. So, humans, even if they figured out how to travel, would not be allowed to go anywhere?

B. So, they try in a somewhat clumsy way to go in a rocket to different places, but it doesn't bode well. It doesn't go that well either! There's a reason why they don't get so far! (*Laughing*) It's like, "Ohh, why's that? Why can't we go that far? But if we could potentially figure out the fuel system, maybe then?" But they haven't figured that one out. We actually divert science a bit. Because, you know, it's better for them to think there's something wrong with the fuel, –than them! Hehehe. Oh, Ophelia, she gives me the green light, but she's still a little bit—she laughs, but she doesn't want me to say it in a critical way. But sometimes you have to be a little bit humoristic about things. But there is a reason why they don't get that far. It's somewhat clumsy, but they can send out little satellites with a little camera and have a look–see, but they are still limited to what they can see. Because this is the fish tank where certain conditions exist that makes it impossible to move as freely as other fish tanks.

D. When you say fish tanks, do you mean specifically the Earth and the solar system, or the visible universe? (*This was early in our talks, and I was still unsure about some of their terminology.*)

B. Oh, it's the visible universe that exists in the fish tank, –certain conditions. I will say something for you to put in your little computer that you carry here. If you see this fish tank (*our Universe*) at five o'clock, those who come most frequently (*visitors to our planet, whom we call aliens*) come from the fish tank from four o'clock. They're kind of similar, but as you move into six, seven, eight, nine, and so forth, it's more of a vibrating, non–physical form experiences in those. So, there it is.

D. Do those other fish tanks occupy what we perceive as space, are they within the same space as we're in, just a different vibration?

B. Yes. Yes, different vibration, indeed. But they carry the same dimensional structures. Everything is the same. To make it different, see it as songs, if it's easier for you. You know, this fish tank can be like rock–and–roll. It's really fast, like drums, all sorts of noise. Another one can be like those songs from the '50's, a little more solid and settled in its way. But as you move into the other fish tanks, it's more like harp sounds, or classic tones, like Zen music, like, ding—ding. That's like in the eighth and ninth. It's really still there. You can float around there, so that is how you should see it. They carry different songs, really. And within those songs, some carry more motion, and then others are more in stillness. And when there is more stillness, you might think that everything is still, but that's also the foundation for motion within a floating scenario. This is what you showed me! You said, "Bob, look at the boxes and see the tones, because that is the basics of understanding what exists within that reality." So, I listened to them, together with

Ophelia, actually, because she's really musical. She operates well with harp music and making music. I like drums, like native drums, I like those. But it has to be in some sort of order, of course; I don't like rock and roll drums because there's no order in it. But, if it's a drum, then this will actually activate my group (*those on the second*), because if it's a drum that resonates similar like a heartbeat, then we are actually activated.

D. So, do you ever work within those other fish tanks?

B. I'm studying them, I'm learning about the different sounds. At this point, I haven't looked at the light in them. I'm at the point where I'm trying to establish what sort of reality exists within them, based on what I can perceive as sound. The ninth dimension is involved a lot with this. Jeshua is involved; Ophelia's higher council is involved. It's almost like an orchestra, a symphony. Either you like it, or you do not! I don't like some of them because they sort of have a lot of high-pitched sounds. And from the perception of me, from having somewhat of a hearing device, it actually creates disharmony within my physical being. I don't know why anyone wants to be in that fish tank. Ophelia says that it's more of a liquid experience. It's not supposed to be solid...she doesn't tell me more. Maybe that's where those jelly people came from. They might like that kind of music, who knows. I don't. I like more like singing, and drums. I like the drums. I don't like guitars, because it's like pitching in my ears. Electric guitars I don't like at all. Sometimes I like trumpets...OH? (*Looking to the left.*) Ophelia says, "But you didn't like those pipes, the Scottish pipes." She said I was confused when those came in one time when I was in that region. She laughs, and she reminds me of that experience. I was actually TOSSED to the ground by that! I didn't know why, because it looked like a trumpet, but it didn't sound like one! I was hiding behind a rock, actually, because I didn't know what it was. There was a group of those trumpet (*bagpipe*) people that came. It was some sort of joyful experience, it appeared to be, but I can't combine it with that expression of noise, really. But Ophelia reminded me, when I said I do like trumpets, she said, "No you don't!" (*laughing*). I must have forgotten about that scary experience, really. Especially when they come in a group. It might be better if there was only one. I was really close by, you know, minding my own business, and when they came, I was not prepared at all. It's somewhat disturbing when you're caught off guard and you've never heard it before.

Lonely Work (Jan 25, 2017)

Bob tells how his traveling serves a greater purpose. He is an explorer who is also an emissary from the second. As he learns things on his travels, he is always thinking about how that knowledge could be utilized at home. In fact, that is one of his main goals when he is out traveling, which may explain why he takes so many notes.

D. Well, what have you been working on lately?

B. I do journal myself, –everything isn't about you! Hahaha! I've been working with my own projects a lot, which is to connect the understanding from what I learn when I travel through the sixth and seventh dimension and how it can implement in the second, where I mostly reside. So, what I do, I collect data from all different realities, but it has to come into fruition in the second dimension. So, I'm actually doing a project where I'm trying to connect both sixth and seventh in how it could take form, or become something, in the second. So, that's what I do, it's a lonely work. I do work with my guide, Gergen, a lot, because he's done something similar before. So he's a great source of inspiration and learning about how you can combine higher levels of vibration, which is sound and tones, into a manifestation in the second. So, that's what I do. And sometimes I ask Ophelia, because she is familiar with a very large spectrum of the levels. So, a lot of times, I ask her. And then I ask you a lot, mainly from the sixth dimension, how I can combine it and mold it into a second dimension reality. So, that's what I do. I also work with my students a little bit. They are at this point working with energies around insects and especially those with wings, because they move and travel and resonate with a field of gravitation and vibration and they radiate light. So, in many ways, insects actually radiate light. That's why you should not just kill bugs, because they move on gravitation and vibration, but they radiate light, which is in some way absorbed in atmospheric shifts. So, a place where there is very few bugs, the atmosphere is less healthy, you should know that. Mostly people think, oh, there is vegetation like a jungle, here is probably a lot of oxygen. But they forget about the beings that move it around and spread that light and oxygen that radiates from plants.

D. There are not very many bugs here where we live.

B. No, it's not.

D. Is this unhealthy?

B. It becomes a little bit more silent in the atmosphere. That's how I would put it to you. When there are less bugs, even though you can physically hear them, it actually creates a sort of a vacuum, a stillness in the atmosphere around it. And not necessarily in a bad way, but if there isn't vegetation that balances it, then it becomes a little bit of a problem. But it's a whole, it has to work in harmony. Those places like South America, with jungles and so forth, are considered healthy atmospheric surroundings in that region. So don't go and knock down the trees, because you don't have a lot of that jungle anymore. In the northern part of India is also a healthy spot of vegetation balancing with creatures that flies. It's like a big greenhouse, so don't disturb, don't touch. It's best if you don't do anything really. If you don't know what you're doing, don't do it! That's what I would say in general. Just do what you can to be in harmony with your surroundings. Where there is something still and solid like a rock or tree, or if it is a living being that moves around, if you don't know how to interact, – don't. That's what I would say.

D. So, when you're travel around on the Earth, I guess you can see humans in their form, physical form? (*"Indeed," he replied*) You must be invisible to humans?

B. Not always. You can see us if we want to. Especially, we are mostly visible in the morning, just before sunrise. That's when we're actually mostly visible for those who are up at that point. Just before sunrise, because we're out, then we hide, or you know, merge. I don't blend anymore with solid objects here, because I've already had that experience. Now I'm learning about motion and form, and how to potentially move some object from one vibrating code of tones and light into another one. Understanding that the conditions from the departure area is of significance, whether it is movable or not. "Something within can be transformed," you said, "but it has to be almost like a chameleon. It changes vibration, but it's still visible on some reality." When you came and went from Earth, you said, "I didn't dissolve." I said, "Yes, you did." But you said, "No, I didn't. From my perspective, I was the same." And I was like, "Why couldn't I see you? Why couldn't I see you come and go? You just were there, and then you were not." And you said something about the conditions of transforming your vibration into another reality. And it's also something with those cracks (*portals or openings in energetic fields*), –that is a puzzle! I want you to tell me more about that, because it seems to be some sort of condition or foundation for any sort of travel to occur. Maybe there were more cracks before than there are now. It seems like that is the case. But you can find them, you said, you can find the cracks, but I don't know how, or maybe you will tell me. So, I'll probably just tag along when you try to find one. And then I'm gonna' stand there and see what happens, see if I dissolve. I hope not, because I don't know what would happen to me on the other side. It seems like a lonely journey, it's not like a group activity. So, I don't know.

D. Yes, you can sneak right through.

B. It's almost like going through those doors in security, those beep–beep–beep doors, similar in some way. If you're not allowed to go through, it will beep. And if you can, then it's a green light. In some way, it's similar. And then you pack your body in through, on that belt, and you pick it up on the other side. That's how I see it, I have no idea how this works, and you don't tell me! So, that's how I see it, when you explained that you brought your physical in some way, but you moved your soul vibration so you didn't feel a change. But I see it like the airport, like you put your body in the bucket and you snooze it through, and your soul energy goes through the beep door. And if you are allowed to travel, then it's a green light. And then on the other side, you pick up your physical and you just continue. That's how I see it. This class I'm gonna take. I'm gonna take this class for sure! You laugh at my way of looking at things, but you said, "Well, it's similar." You actually gave me this picture in my head, so I could sort of relate to what you're doing. But I STILL have questions about how this occurs, because, you know, who moved the physical? How is that even possible? But you say it's something with that crack. So it's not like the airport, but you gave me that as a way of understanding. And I kind of like that—but I just don't understand.

D. Well, I like it too, thanks for reminding me (*I was joking*) and sharing it.

B. Ah, so if I walked through the door, it would probably be a red light and all sorts of people will come and stop me. But what happens to my physical body, then?

D. It's gone.

B. It's gone into that tube and into that tent, where someone's sitting inside and you have no idea what they're doing with your stuff.

D. Stealing your belt!

B. Stealing my belt and my stuff and my notebook, my notebook! It's somewhat disturbing, in some way, when you don't see your things going into the tent (*the x–ray machine for baggage*).

Bob's Individual is Removed (Mar 19, 2017)

Leading up to the introduction of the humanoid, the spirit realm had to make adjustments to minimize the anticipated damage. One of those was to remove Bob's Individual from Earth. Its pattern was put to sleep, which we would see as becoming extinct. The patterns of all creatures continue to exist in databanks on certain planets.

D. What about in the future, can you see what is to come?

B. I cannot. But others, I'm sure, can. I can't see if something isn't energetically there, or put there at that point when I'm standing in a specific location. I can't see if Gergen, let's say, has planned on putting in a new palm tree. If it's not in–place, I can't read that and it's not for me to see. So, for instance, it would be MAGNIFICANT, if I could see like the shifts of the continents. Let's say, if I could see that this specific plane would be closer to...you know, the other side, like the Russian and the Japanese. But I can't see that, because it's not in the Earth's memory bank, as of yet. So, even if those who works on the grander shifts, let's say, like moving continents, they might have it already figured out. But I can't see it, because it isn't in the near vicinity of my ability to reach my energy. So, if that is the case, if this is where the continent is heading, then I can't see it.

D. But you can see where it's been?

B. I can see where it's been.

D. When you came in during the big rains, were the continents pretty much where they are now?

B. Nay. No, because, you know, it was more connected, this continent with the one to the east. More connected. More like solid.

D. Huh, that's been awhile in Earth years?

B. I don't know, I don't count. I see changes of cycles and especially like the environment, like elements and rains and so forth. I can see that. But there were different animals at that time as well. Some of my friends (*he calls the animals he created, "friends"*) that I created together with my other friends, and Gergen. I was really sad when some of them were taken away. There was this little creature that looked like, similar to, —like if you think of the armadillo, but with fur. So, they were really friendly. They didn't harm anyone, and I really liked them and they didn't interfere or eat anyone. So I didn't understand why they had to go. Gergen said it was part of a bigger plan. And I said, "They didn't harm anyone, why couldn't they stay?" This was way back, and Gergen, he sort of comforted me because I was part of them being established. And I felt like, maybe they just put them somewhere else. And Gergen said no, they cannot be there anymore. It was something with their brain. It would not be good for them, because the brain was a little bit too intelligent, and they were kind. They were removed. They were removed and I don't know why. Gergen said they will be victimized. There's no need for them to be there anymore.

D. Well, their patterns still exist?

B. It does, indeed, in my vault. Everything exists.

D. Maybe they can be put on that other Earth you found.

B. I'm not putting them anywhere if they're going to be extinct again, because how will I explain that to them? If I create them and then I say, "You're going to be here a little while. Enjoy while you can because, you know (*makes clicking noise*), gone!" I'm not going to do that again. But they were kind, they didn't deserve to be removed. But then again, I didn't want them to be victims to something. I didn't understand what was coming. Gergen said they would not be...(*He trailed off and was quiet.*)

D. Treated well?

B. They will not be understood and left alone. There was something with the fur, someone would take their fur, which I didn't understand. Why would they take their fur from them? Why? They were kind. Why would you want to take someone's skin?

I didn't understand that. But he said there was a new cycle coming in where something with fur will be highly attractive to someone. Because these were very spiritual, in a way, they carried a lot of awareness from the Master Mind. So they would have understood what happened to them. Gergen said, "We don't want to do that to them, do we, Bob? And I said, "No, I don't." So, when I understood what was coming, that someone would take someone's skin, then I didn't want that anymore.

D. When I first met you in the forest, was that one of the creatures that was with you?

B. Ah. You tried to touch it.

D. So, this was back before humans.

B. Yes, indeed. Gergen said, there's gonna come creatures that are more physically inclined, but not with a big brain. So, they will not understand that my Individual, that I've already put there, that it had a higher mental vibration and spiritual awareness than the (*physically*) bigger one that came, and they will only see the fur. It was soft, very soft. But you don't take someone's skin. That's not what you do.

D. It is not right that humans treat animals so poorly.

B. With choices comes responsibilities. That's what I want to say about that. And Gergen said that it was because of this new individual coming in. That's why we removed my creatures, who were almost like friends. They didn't harm anyone, and they would understand what was happening, because they were actually more on the inside like a humanoid is now. So they understood more than the new creature that came in with more of a physical attribute. So, that will be it about that. So, this is clearly something I think of when I'm creating my solar system, that I'm NOT going to put something on it if later there is going to come someone that acts like that. I'm going to create something maybe like a creature that is not so much inside, like a Master Mind inside. (*He is saying that if a creature has too much awareness from the Master Mind, it suffers more from abuse by other creatures, such as humans.*)

Self-Study is a Virtue (Mar 26, 2017)

When Bob first started going to the Library and vaults on the fifth dimension, he was unaware that Gergen had instructed Zachariah and Lasaray to act as a tutors. Bob would be left alone and given free rein to dig around in certain pre-selected boxes in the vault, knowing it would spark his curiosity. He would then have questions, but since Lasaray was gone, there was no one to ask. So he would go up to Zachariah's office on the main level to quiz him. Zachariah, however, made Bob memorize a lot of information before he would answer. So this process became the first step in Gergen's lesson to teach Bob about self-study. Self-study is the term they use for the planning, data collection, and what-if analysis.

D. (*Bob came in as Zachariah stepped out.*) Hello, Bob.

B. I just wait and wait and wait and wait. You know, I don't get like a schedule, like, "OK I'm gonna talk for fifteen and then you can come in and talk." Sometimes I'm just hanging around, waiting for that opening when it's my turn. I don't want to be so far away that I don't see the window when it's my time to come in. But sometimes I feel like I'm just hanging around and I don't see the window. But, I DO like to listen to Zachariah, because he tells a lot of things that I put in my book and in my notes. You know, I learn as well.

D. Yes, he's very wise. Do you ever meet him away from our group?

B. He is indeed. Yes, indeed. I meet him when I need help journaling. When I work on certain scriptures, he gives me books, and he makes me interpret them. He helps me with the interpretations of certain scriptures. So, it's like, you know, you have that google translate? (*He laughs loudly.*) He's like that! He helps me with certain things that need translation, so to speak. I thought I would bring your book with the pictures, but he did not approve. He said "This is a book where you need to talk with him." But those books that exist in the Library, if I don't understand certain things, and I'm allowed to study them, then I actually call for him if there is translation that needs to take place. He spends a lot of time in the Library. He has all these scrolls, like scriptures, in his own office, a little place in the Library. Since I'm down there, a lot of times I can go up and, – I'm not allowed to bring things UP from the vault, BUT I can memorize it–, and I can go up and I can meet him and I can ask him, "Could you please help me with the translation? What does this mean?" And for some reason, he always seems to know EXACTLY what it is that I have memorized. It's almost like he is energetically connected to me. He must read something, because I memorize something in the vault, since I'm not allowed to bring the boxes up, SO, I memorize it really, really well, and then I go up and then I ask him. And for some reason it's like he always knows EXACTLY what box I've been in. So, I say, "Why don't you just come down, instead of having me making all these journeys? Why don't you just come down then?"

D. What does he say?

B. He said it is the fact that I learn more when I program things in the boxes, so I remember more if I program it in my inner computer and bring it up to him. He also says, "Don't be lazy, Bob, –don't be lazy. Nothing comes easy, nothing comes by being lazy." It does not, it does not indeed! So, HE told ME.

D. I'm sure he said it in a nice way.

B. Oh, indeed he did. He's very generous with teachings. Even if I come when he has all these scrolls out, and I come with my one note, he takes the time. So, I like that. I don't disturb when he has meetings, it's only when he's by himself. Otherwise, I just walk back down and then I come back at a later time.

D. So he spends a lot of time at the Library?

B. Ah, not in the vault. Up, in the Library.

D. Is he one of the main keepers of knowledge?

B. Ah. He is. He's like an ambassador and keeper. Like a real professor, a tutor of grand scale. Having all this knowledge within your reach must be EXTREMELY satisfying. He can read all sorts of languages. He's not limited at all! He doesn't need translations. He can read all sorts of reports coming in. He channels reports, you know. Almost like a post office, I would assume. (*He laughs.*) If something comes in, he immediately understands!

D. So does he help file things and direct where they go?

B. Indeed.

D. When information gets in our vault, how does it get there?

B. Oh, I don't know. It's there. I never see you come down with boxes, if that was your question. You don't carry things a lot, at all. I never see you carry things, not the jars, not the boxes. Somewhat a mysterious way you move around. But, they are there. Some of the boxes that I see in the vault, they have little tags on them. I can see yellow tags and I can see red tags. And I ask about that one time, and you said, the red tags mean that it is not completely satisfied, it is some sort of progress yet to be made within that box. The yellow ones are in somewhat of the late process of being stored. So, there are little tags I can see. So, it's not like ready boxes only come down here. Some boxes are still in need of more information before they can have NO tags on them. So, that's what I see.

D. So, what exactly do you do in the vault?

B. I'm allowed to look at the boxes with no tags. You say I'm going to be confused by looking in the other ones, because they're not done yet, they're not ready yet. SO, I can look in those boxes with no tags, because they are already organized in a certain timeline, and also, what took place and occurred. It's also about the experiences. The experience and evolution, I would say, in certain different areas, and some are still in progress. I guess some evaluation needs to take place before they are completely filed (*with no tags*). So, I'm not allowed to touch those with tags. You made that clear. I can't reach them anyway, so there's no need to say that, because I can't reach them. The red ones are high up, and then comes the yellow and then, you know, there are some levels under that that are more like with no tags. I cannot reach all, even though they are with no tags. I said, "If there are no tags, why can't I reach them all?" And you said, "It's still confusing, so there is no need. You don't want to be confused." I think it's more that you don't want me to ask questions, rather than it will confuse me. Why would I be confused?

D. Well, it's like your little students. You don't tell them everything, do you?

B. No.

D. And why is that?

B. Well, because, you know, if they don't understand what they see, the discussion will not be very productive and also, it might disturb where they are at. I don't want to disturb their own thought process of learning. So, if I put in too much, –it is what Ophelia said one time about providing things in cups, and not the whole barrel. So, I can see that, I do see that. BUT I am curious and I want to know what you are doing. And maybe I can join, like when you file the boxes. I never see how they are organized within. When I work with my drawer, I get a lot of time to self–study. So you say, "Bob, now you go and self–study." And I do. And I sit with my notes and my books with pictures. So, when that takes place, when I self–study, I know you go somewhere. You're not far away, you don't leave me, really, but you are working on something, privately. And sometimes I feel like it is some sort of haste in it. So, I'm doing a lot of self–studying, and I don't know why. You know, I kinda prefer to self–study with you next to me, so as I'm self–studying, I can ask if something comes up. But you said I need to reflect and not simply just burst then and there. I need to reflect on what I see, read, and also the way it comes about. You said, "Self–studying is a virtue, Bob." (*Christine and I still laugh about Bob wanting to self–study with me next to him, because it would then no longer be self–study.*)

D. Almost sounds like you somewhat disagree?

B. It's different. We don't learn that way, necessarily. I mean, I do, in some way. I can sit and be by myself, like Gergen, but we are more group activity. So this is different, –to reflect in my loneliness. And then I wonder, "Where did you go?" And then I kinda drift from that self–reflection and self–study, because I wonder where you are. I like to do things all the time, and move things around and discuss. Being still and reflecting, it's different.

D. Maybe that's an aspect that's being worked on. Is Gergen reflective?

B. Oh, he reflects.

D. Maybe it's a trait you have to practice?

B. Oh–oh–oh–oh. Oh, that might be, when you say it like that. "It's a different way of learning," you say. "Let the words speak to you, instead of you speaking them out loud. How does this knowledge feel within you? Does it resonate, Bob?" And I say, "How is that supposed to feel, if it resonates?" And then you say, "Because it is a sensation," you say, "once you have understood a certain message." And I can relate to that, but I do prefer to discuss things. So this is what I do. I self–study occasionally, because you are off to some sort of haste. It's almost like you rush off for something. And I say, "Can I go?" And you say, "No, Bob, you have self–studying to do." So, it's like, "How long is that going to take?" And you say, "As long as it will, because there is not an ending in learning." I'd kind of like a timeline, a deadline, when self–studying is over. It seems like it is a constant thing here.

D. If you have a question, can you send a message to me? And I come back and answer?

B. Well I tried that, you know, I send out an SOS almost, a little bubble of thought. And you did come back, you did come back. But you wanted to only talk about the self–studying. And I wanted to talk about where you had been and what you've done. And then you laughed, and you stood there and said, "Let's talk about the self–studying, Bob. What have you reflected on?" And I tried to trick you and I said, "What have you been reflecting on?" (*Laughs loudly*) And you said, "You're tricky!" And I said, "You're tricky, too!" So, I'm trying to know more, because you don't bring me everywhere.

D. I've taken you to see a lot of stuff, haven't I?

B. Indeed. There is some kind of museum here, too. You take me there! It's similar, like in the vault. It's like different energetic structures, the progress of those cores, like different cores. I don't see planets, strangely. I see different cores.

D. Like the one hanging in the room? (*He had described a huge multicolored ball floating in one of the rooms, which silently flashes light around inside its structure.*)

B. Oh, that's a big one! You're not supposed to touch that one! That must be for show. You did not create that one by yourself, I'm sure of it. That took a group activity for sure. But the other ones are on display. You talk about different cores, and where they were put. These are models of planets that no longer exist. So, they are brought back for being analyzed, (*to see*) how they operated within their hosts. There are little tags, a little note on each, with dots in your language that describe how it operated within the host. The host is gone, but the core is here, and you analyze them and you can teach and learn how to make more optimal cores to resonate better with the host. Everything looks the same, from my perspective, but you say, "Look at the differences, you can see the colors, can't you?" I said, "Yes, I can. But I don't know what they mean." But you say, "Not now necessarily, but—"

D. After a period of self–study?

B. (*Laughs.*) Self–study! But this is just a museum of how different cores have been used and how they were operating. It is a memory for you to learn by, to create better cores, more functional cores. And some, you said, actually existed in celestial bodies that are not created anymore. So, you know, it's like a museum. It's not very big.

D. How many different cores are there?

B. From where I'm at, I can see like a hundred different tanks, like little glass boxes, I can see that. I don't know if they all relate to here, or if they relate to other places, because you don't tell me. You only say, "This is for display for students to learn to visually get an insight on how a core resonates, operate and how it—", there are like students in here! They look kinda odd!

D. Do they look like this one and I?

B. They're smaller.

D. What do they look like?

B. They're thin, and like long faces, kinda, somewhat human features, like the mouth doesn't move, it's still, like yours, it's still, and the nose is like two dots, two holes.

D. That's not very attractive.

B. Well, who am I to say what is attractive! But they are here with their mentors, and based on what their project is in their drawer, they come in here and look at earlier cores and how the evolution of cores have progressed. So it's like an understanding of what did not necessarily function, but how it looked before in a specific celestial body.

D. Well, you're a student. You'll be learning about that.

B. I will, indeed!

D. Are you the odd one out?

B. It's like, I can't read the notes on it. Everyone seems to understand, because I can definitely see communication going on between them, and they seem happy. I can see the movements on them, even though I can't understand what they say. So, it seems like they understand something here. For me it's just like sparkles, with flames and balls, a lot of dark green, dark purple and black. But I'm not trained, like them.

D. Are you going to learn the dot language?

B. I don't know if I will learn the dot language. Like Zachariah, he understands, for sure. He doesn't need anyone to translate, he seems to understand all sorts of languages. I'm sure he's self-studied! Hahahaha! Oh, you know. But, that's what exists. So, you can go and have a look-see here. But if you don't understand what they really are...it's only like older models. If you think of something like, okay, this is an old car, and this is a new car, and here are the improvements. This is why we improved the car. This is the same thing. It's like a little museum. It's a STUDY room, you say. Study room. But, if I don't understand the note on it, then, you know, it's more of a showroom! You know? But I do have questions about where you go.

D. Maybe we'll take you along someday.

B. We'll see about that, you say. We'll see about that. First you reflect, then we'll see about that. So, back to the drawer, you know.

D. All the other students have drawers as well, don't they?

B. Yes, they have, but they're not in my room. This is like your private room, I think. You have stuff in here too.

D. It's our own area, then.

B. It's like an office. Yes, they are on the other side of this place. I don't ever meet them. This has just happened because we were in the same show–room, or room for "study".

D. You're undergoing special training for something.

B. It's about understanding the inside, and how to make it optimal for the host. So, you know, the outside, the celestial body itself, that is not as tricky as the inside. Because, say, "Okay, I wanna have trees." And those who create trees come and have a study. And then the atmosphere people come in and say, "We wanna have clouds." —BUT, if it's not functioning from the inside, the clouds will just drift all sorts of places, and the trees will not become, or grow, or blossom. So, the inside is important. It's more about the inside. Oh, Ophelia says time is up, so that will be it.

D. Alright, my friend. I hope you help me write.

B. I will be here, and I will help you and I will stand next to you, EAGER to help. Zachariah also says he will help you with the scripture when it comes to the structure and how to organize it. So, if that is what you want, then you send out your color spectra and ask for guidance, for him to come in. And also try to see what colors you see within you, because that is a key for you to use in further communications. He will help you with the division of words, he says. The divisions of words, cleaning it up. That's what he says. Dividing it into different boxes, properly. That's what he says, —PROPERLY. Indeed. So, that will be it. And I say, that we will always be here, and I will soon talk with you again in some way.

D. Alright my friend, thank you.

B. And then you give me the answer to why it stopped! (*He returned to his questions about evolution on solar systems and galaxies, and why things happen.*) What happens if it stops? What happens to all my stuff that I put around it if I create something, put all this trouble into action in doing something, and then it stops? And WHO made it stop!? WHO? You want to know these things before you create something. You don't want there to be like, "Ohh, all my dinosaur friends are gone because something swept in or did something," you know. You kinda want to be prepared if you are doing something of that scale. So, WHO decides, and WHY? So, that is something that I would like to know.

D. Those are good questions.

B. WHO, and WHY? What happens if it stops, and what sort of cycles are we talking about? You said it has a destined lifespan of experiencing. But, experiencing what?

D. I think everything has the same destiny, doesn't it?

B. Ah, it all has a sort of destined lifespan and cycle for some sort of purpose. But WHY, WHAT is the purpose of it? What is the experiencing thing when it's a solar system, a celestial body family, -what is the purpose of it? Or why? You know, those things. I ask those things. It's not in my book. Well, maybe you can answer—that will be appreciated! Then I will tell you about the blueberry! Huhuhuhuhuh! Tit for tat! You give—I give. I tell you more about the blueberry and you can tell me more about that! Heehee!

D. It's only fair!

B. Well, that will be it, and I'm grateful for your friendship and for helping me, and for being with me. So, I would say goodbye, and I will soon return.

D. I'm grateful for your friendship too, and for Zachariah and Ophelia and Jeshua. Alright, my friend, goodbye.

B. Bye–bye, bye–bye, bye–bye.

The Individual and Evolution (May 7, 2017)

I have to admit that before we began conversing with the spirit world, my ideas about creation were a bit more conventional, being a mixture of evolutionary adaptations mixed with my own interpretation of intelligent design, the controlling force behind everything. After hundreds of hours of talks with those who are intimately involved with creation, and having never found a single error in their logic or statements, I find the spirits version of creation to have a beauty, harmony, and sanctity that is pleasing to the heart, mind and soul. In comparison, the modern theories devised by atheists, secular scholars, or religious devotees seem hollow and vacuous, soulless or mindless, depending on whether the theory originated at the universities, or from the pulpit.

Most of the spirits on the second dimension, after completing training in their chosen specialty, are given the opportunity to design and create their very own plant, animal, or organism. They follow the general patterns established by their predecessors and the Creator, but are given the latitude to make what we would consider a new species. Bob worked on many different life forms, but had developed one that looked like a little red panda bear with very soft fur, but it had fingers and could hold things. It actually had more spiritual awareness (from the Master Mind) than the modern humans. He called this gentle and playful creature his "Individual". It was created in the lab and then placed here as a new species, but later removed before early humans first made an appearance. Bob was very saddened about having his Individual removed, but he didn't want it slaughtered by man. Based on the geologic records, it would have been introduced within the last 30 million years, and removed several million years ago.

Another observation Bob makes, which negates evolutionary theories of human origins, is that Caucasians were introduced on Earth 35,000 years ago by the Evolutionary Group. There may have been several varieties, because the race of giants that lived in Europe and North America had fair complexions and red hair. Bob describes the smaller white–skinned people as having red or blond hair, and likely had blue or green eyes. They mixed with other hominins, and their genetic imprints are still among us. As Bob points out, they did not follow the general evolutionary path of the other humanoids. Most of the older versions of the humanoid were also unique creations of either the spirit realm or alien visitors. The Out-of-Africa hypothesis is a fable the evolutionary biologists have clung to, despite overwhelming evidence to the contrary, especially in the field of archaeogenetics. All lifeforms on Earth were designed or placed here to fulfill a specific purpose in the web of life, and are not a result of random mutations. While the different species of humans had unique origins, souls can come in to any type of vehicle. So, on a spiritual level, bodies are tools to be used for soul growth, but do not define the soul. As Zachariah pointed out so brilliantly, bodies are like glass bottles of different colors. If you pour water into a blue bottle, the water appears blue, yet it is only an illusion. When pure soul energy merges with a bottle (vehicle), it only appears to take on the attributes of the bottle. The bottle only influences the soul during life. When the soul returns home, it carries no trace of the vehicle, other than the record of its actions and decisions.

D. When you were first working with creations, like on Earth with your animals, you probably had to learn by making mistakes, didn't you?

B. I did indeed. Yes, indeed. Some didn't blend in that well. I learned about that.

D. If you only give them three legs, they don't get around as well.

B. Indeed, they have to be moving around properly. The tail, also. I had one that had a really long tail, and it somewhat stumbled and it got stuck. So, upcoming models did not have that long of a tail. We created it to have a really long tail, almost like a snake—it was furry. But it wasn't good for it, because as it moved around, it got stuck. So, I learned that you have to slim it, in order for it to be able to move comfortably. Especially if you put up a lot of vegetation, you have to make sure that the individuals in those regions aren't too clumsy and too big. So, you don't put the dinosaurs where there is a jungle. It's harder for it to move, because then they bump down trees, and you want the trees. It's a chain reaction and a side effect of creation when you see that. So that's why I want to make sure I launch my Individual in a place where it has the best option to operate properly.

D. I'm sure he'll be happy, finally.

B. I think so. I think so indeed.

D. Were you responsible for developing him, pretty much?

B. Ah, I was assigned to create something all by myself. So I did—similar to your solar system, it was done pretty much by myself. I did have a friend who worked with circulation that came in. He came in with a final touch about the circulation around the organs, a little bit. But I created the Individual myself. Because I wanted there to be a mark of something I did, just by myself. Similar to what people do with graffiti, you know—I was here! (*Laughs at his analogy.*)

D. You put a lot of master mind in it?

B. I did indeed.

D. So it was really smart and had soft fur?

B. Ah. Soft fur. And it was highly intelligent because I thought it would gather information about where I put it. I put it in the South American region, and I also put it in what is now India. So, I wanted it to collect data about the environment that was on that specific place. So, it collected data, and because the Master Mind, for some reason, had an interest in especially India, at that time, so we looked at that through this Individual. It collected data. There was a change after that, based on vegetation that took place, and insects as well, because there were insects that didn't function that well within the environment. So my Individual collected data about that. We changed the flora or insects based on its mission and understanding of the regions. That's what it did. It was more work in the India country, north India. It sort of wandered around and collected data. It was more content in the South American region, so those who were placed there, they were more on a holiday. Where the other one was more working. But there is actually a key element between these two places that can be found now, because there are certain things that only exists on these two continents, in the northern part of India and the Amazon part of South America, that is still there, only on these two places.

D. What is it?

B. It's a flower, which is actually to cure cell disease.

D. Do we know what flower it is?

B. It looks like, –because it is somewhat hidden, it's mainly in the South American region, but it actually exists in the jungle part of India as well. It has to be left alone. It cures cell disease. It makes cells become white again. Dirty cells that have become red and poisonous, this specific plant has the ability to make cells white.

D. Is that something that humans are supposed to know about?

B. Not this group. Upcoming groups. I'm not giving this if you don't know anything about it. Upcoming groups will take care of this.

D. I had a question about the different races of humans. Were they all sort of initiated from different types of mammals that were here?

B. Well, like we talked about before, some followed what you know as the human timeline, but then again, there are those that were placed here that didn't have an evolution that you are familiar with.

D. So, they were just put here, they just started out?

B. Yes, indeed. That's why they are somewhat different, because if you study its past, it doesn't have one. Scientists are like, ohh, it must be some sort of offspring of–, you know, they come up with all sorts of different ideas, really. But it's useless to try to make sense of everything, because they don't understand that evolution can be somewhat placed. Like the Evolution Group comes in and just puts their start–ups down. And it just kick starts that specific group. There was actually a group that were put in the Russian region, and they were like extremely white in skin. They were launched, and you can see their offspring, they are somewhat pale. They came after, they don't follow the general evolution timeline of man.

D. What color hair did they have?

B. These ones have, they can come with a little bit of reddish hair, but they can also look almost like albinos. SO, they are really pale, but the hair can differ somewhat, but they don't have dark hair. Like reddish or white. Normally very slim, they don't gain weight as easily as the other ones.

D. Was that around the Caucus mountains?

B. Somewhere in the middle of Russia. So they were placed. Scientists think that they are some sort of alien, I'm sure, because that's what they say, that everything is alien when there's no evolution to follow.

D. How long ago was that?

B. They came in, let's see, about 30,000 years ago, that's what I would say. They came in 30 to 50,000 years ago, so they are somewhat new, but they operated not very publicly. They got the chance to simply develop in hibernation, like the greenhouse. (*He is making a comparison to plants on the Greenhouse Planet.*) They were not disturbed, and that's why they were put where they were. If you put them somewhere else, like the African region, they would have been detected. But they first came down around 35,000, around that time. There are still offspring from this group, and they are different than the other ones, they don't follow the same—oh, there you go.

Ophelia says that will be it about the lecture of time and man. Okay. (*He said to her.*) So, you know.

D. Well, thank you.

Bob Practices to Blend with Christine (June 4, 2017)

Since Bob has never operated a physical vehicle, he was a bit concerned how well he would do when it came time to do the channeling. He knew that he would be observed by his mentors and hundreds of council members from many dimensions, so he felt the pressure to not disappoint. He did a lot of planning before we incarnated to start the project, and he does a lot of preparation before each session. His commitment is evident in each wonderful story he delivers.

D. Hello Bob! What have you been doing?

B. I'm writing a journal, actually. I'm writing a journal how to do this, because I think others will come, and once they do, I wanna be helpful. (*He's talking about those from the second, blending and communicating through a human in the future.*) So I have written down in a journal, step–by–step, how this really works. Because it is the same as a blend, like with a tree, however, it operates differently. The blending would be considered the easy aspect of this, because it is somewhat the same. BUT, if I were to blend fully, like I did with a tree, then I will be unable to communicate the same way. So it's a different kind of blend, even though it would be considered similar. If I were to fully blend, like I did with trees, her physical would not really like that, because it's not what you do, really, there's only supposed to be a soul in there. So you blend differently with the energetic field. In many cases I actually blend with, –I don't become the physical–, I blend with the mental, number one, and a little bit with the emotional. But mainly with the mental capacity and the voice box. So, it's a different kind of blending. Uhh, huh huh.

D. Well, you're doing really well. You're really good.

B. Oh, one might say it has been a work in progress, because I didn't have that much to train on. It's one thing to train when everyone is in the lab or in the vault, because we practiced before coming. But it's very different once you two are in a physical vehicle. I didn't know that—I didn't know how that was gonna play out. Because I said, "Oh, this is gonna be like blending with a tree." And Ophelia said, "It's not going to be like that, because you can't do it fully, like with a tree, because her physical will reject you. And then it's not going to happen and you're not going to be able to talk at all, because she will reject you. So it's not going to be that same physical blend, as with a tree." There was not that much to practice on, really, until it was time for shooting sharp! Huhuhuh! I said, "Maybe we can train doing this, practice in the vault, or in the lab?" And you were standing like on each side, and I was like, "OK, how do I do this?" But we all were in our own energetic form, so it didn't really become the same thing. So, it's not possible in that reality. It has to be manifested in a physical form for it to be, – I could not blend with your energy in the lab. So there were not many places for me to practice. I did try to practice with a frog, and that's what you saw me doing, with the blowing up of the toad (*He said he practiced blending with a toad, to see if he could make it "speak", which didn't work very well. Then, after he started speaking through Christine, he tried to puff out her neck like he did with the toad, which did not work, either.*)

D. Trying to make the frog talk?

B. Because I didn't have anything to practice on! Huhuh, I said, "Maybe we can practice?" and you said, "But we're not physical, so you can't come in and talk through me." And I tried to study up, but there was no way to practice.

D. Well, you're a true pioneer. You're the first to do this.

B. I am, indeed! I am considered like a voyager of knowledge from the second dimension. I am considered like a voyager by Ia and Gergen. And they say I am like that, indeed, because I sail on the vibration of knowledge that is supposed to be spread out. And they are happy, too! Sometimes they come and they ask me to deliver certain things, –and I do. Like when we talk about the soil and stuff like that.

Ophelia's Big, Big Harp (July 4, 2017)

Bob's early travels away from the second dimension were to the Library, and later to Ophelia's lecture hall and lab. He next talks about being in a large class on the seventh, learning about light and sound. Ophelia and the other instructors had previously shown the students how to make stars, and now they were showing the source of the energy that creates stars, planets and other forms. Cosmic light and cosmic sound combine to make melodies and colors. The patterns, in some mysterious way, create gravity, vacuum, and structures we see as elements and electromagnetic fields. The students in the class are from different dimensions, but Bob is the only one from the second.

Bob came in and began singing what we call the harbor song. It is a boisterous Irish pub tune he remembered from one of my lives in the 1700s. He likes the song and sometimes uses it to raise Christine's energy.

B. I'M HAPPY!

D. (*Laughing with him.*) I've never seen you otherwise!

B. (*Continues singing for a bit.*) I would like to, –maybe we can have an orchestra! Oh, let's see, Zachariah did not feel like that, at all!

D. Zachariah didn't sing along?

B. He doesn't sing that much. Ophelia sings, Ophelia sings. She has like instruments in her place. She has one that is one big harp. You might think that it is to create an orchestra, but it's not, really, because it is actually to mirror the light waves. They use like a big harp, –big, big, big, big harp that she, not necessarily just she, but like her equals, are using to mirror the waves of light, how they travel in some way. Interesting.

D. Light or sound?

D. Light, it seems, with the harp, at least. She is secretive about that harp. I'm curious about it, because it's really, really big.

D. Does she keep it in her lab?

B. No. Ohh, well, sometimes. And this is tricky for you, but it's so big, so there are several playing it, on each side of the harp. There are like one–two–three on each side, and they are all plinking on it. They actually did that one time in that big hearing facility. (*Ophelia's lecture hall on the seventh.*) They took this out and it was completely silent because no one knew what was gonna happen, if something were to come in, or if it was just like a show they did. So, this big harp came in on that stage in the center, and there were like three on each side. Ophelia simply supervised, and if you know Ophelia's size, this harp is probably like three times the size. (*Ophelia is seen by Christine as about three meters tall.*) So, it's a big harp and it has a lot of strings, and her helpers are walking on each side as they create the noise. And as they did, it was almost like we all became entranced. I almost felt like this was some sort of magic.

D. Did it emit anything like light, or did it make sound?

B. Well, from it came like waves out into this big hearing, and everyone became like in a trance, –it was almost like we all fell asleep. It was like the air became really dense from those waves that came. And normally you can use this to create the patterns of light waves, how they resonate with sound. Because even if I say "light" waves, it actually, as it moves from its source outwards, it creates a melody. And this is what they tried to mirror with this big harp. But I think they wanted to make some sort of effect, because this one is clearly really big, and it became like we were all entranced. Some actually fell asleep! I don't know about the cone people, because they have such big ears. But it was actually a feeling in my physical being like somewhat, at first, of a vibrating. And then, like I said, the whole surrounding became like dense in the air, so to speak. Maybe they were tired of the questions and just wanted us to go to sleep?

D. After it was over, what did they say about it?

B. They said it mirrored the way that sound and light travels and how it creates a melody. And when you combine it, you can understand what different realities exist within, because it is a knowledge that light actually comes with a tone. And once you understand that, it is not necessarily a difference between light and sound, really. They actually merge into one being. And as you understand that, –and that is what they tried to mirror with this harp, I would assume–, then it is the foundation that makes gravity come in and to become its surrounding. So, in some way, it is the foundation of—it lays the foundation of...Ophelia showed me this, and it looks odd. It's like those waves of sound and light, they merge into one beam. And as it travels, based on its different components and structures and speed—one here believes that light only has one specific speed, BUT, as it is combined with sound, it actually becomes in a different speed as well. (*Light is constant, but as it interacts with sound waves emanating from the Source, the speed of light and the density of gravity are altered within different regions of the Universe. The manipulation of light and sound energy is integral to the process of creation, and is therefore controlled and under the direction of the spiritual realms.*)

D. I've always suspected that.

B. It is, it's not constant. Nothing is constant, really. (*He turns towards Ophelia.*) Am I supposed to? Yes, I can. (*As he turns back.*) Nothing is constant. On this level things becomes constant because of the polarity thinking. So, you see, light is one thing, sound is another. And then you have like male—female, black—white, and so forth. But nothing is constant as you progress outside this reality. But light, in order for it to change, the sound is added. And that's what they tried to do with this thing with the harp, I would assume. I'm gonna take more of this class, I haven't fully understood this whole process, but I'm interested. You can simply take with you the fact that nothing is constant, not even the speed of light.

Bob, the Professor in his Study (Oct 15, 2017)

D. Well, what are you working on? How are your travels going?

B. Oh, I did bubble training and preparing myself. I had to prepare my own vehicle. Similar like the sparkles, they learn about maintaining their energy. So it was suggested that I also went into somewhat of a training with my energetic being.

D. Do you have to work on your light capsule, then?

B. I work, not necessarily in the same way, but I do work with my energetic levels, and I'm increasing them. So instead of shutting them down in my light capsule, I'm trying to expand. I don't know why, but for some reason Jeshua said it would be good if I expand my energetic being, so I'm supposed to be...I'm not growing, of course, but it is a way to ride the waves, in some way.

D. Float like a cork!

B. Ha, float like a cork, I do! HUH HUH HUH. I thought the bubble would just take care of everything, and I'm sure it in some way does. BUT, you know, it's not like I'm asleep in there. So I still will have the sensation of change and experience, and it's also the fact that I'm a little bit lonely in the bubble. I ask if it was possible for ALL of us to be in the bubble, because I would prefer that. But Jeshua said that you don't travel in a bubble, but you will all be around. So, I've been doing various things to prepare.

D. Well, we're not going to leave you all alone to float around.

B. Nay, that I expect! I don't think Ophelia—

D. She wouldn't approve of that.

B. She wouldn't approve of that at all! Nay.

D. Is Ophelia the one who oversees your education with all of this stuff?

B. Ah, she encouraged me with the change of vibration, because she knows that I don't like that. I get stressed when the vibration changes within my physical, –or my energetic physical vehicle, if you like. So she encourages me to do these adjustments, because she knows that I want to travel. And she said, "It's similar like when you started to travel to my lab, and the vault, and to Lasaray's lab." I went into training for that as well, to change, because it was unfamiliar for me. I don't do well with new experiences, necessarily, unless I feel secure. That is the whole thing about this. So, Ophelia, she knows my progress and she knows where I struggle. And she also knows where I'm a little bit like, "Ohh—feels a little bit scary!" She encourages me to do certain things, because we all have knots. Some of my knots is the experience of change, you know, like when the surroundings change. So she encourages me to work on that. And if I embrace it, then I will also get a treat! Ha ha ha.

D. Well, you now travel back and forth to the labs and places like that with no trouble at all.

B. Ah, ah. It's just because I project myself, it's not that big of a deal, really. But before I knew, it WAS a big deal. It's the same thing - everything that is new is a big deal kind of thing. So, I too need to be reminded of the treats.

D. When you work on withdrawing your energy to the second, where do you spend your time when you go back? What do you do?

B. I do talk a lot with Gergen, because of the fact of our work, we're sort of wrapping the whole thing up. He asks a lot about how the information that we provided from the second dimension is received. And I do like to sit. And sometimes, –this is new–, but sometimes I actually like to sit just in quiet, in a room of study. So I do sit in a sort of library, similar like Gergen's room with books, I do like to sit and reflect on my notes.

D. Wow, that's a change!

B. That's a change. Sometimes I feel like they (*the others on the second*) are kind of noisy.

D. So that self–study really paid off, huh?

B. Ah. I do like to sit and reflect, and not be disturbed. So sometimes I sit there.

D. Do you ever sit with Ia and contemplate things?

B. Yes, indeed, because she soothes me. I always seek her out because I like to be with her, and she tells me what she's doing. And I do like the little sparkles, because they're kind of innocent and they're just in the beginning of their journey, and I like that. OH, I feel old! It's almost like being a grandfather here. HUH HUH. To just look back and be like, "Oh, I do remember—" like that. Huh huh. I do like the youth.

D. Do you spend more time with them? Do you try to teach them?

B. I do, indeed. And I also listen to them, I like to answer questions. I liked that when I was a sparkle. (*When older entities shared knowledge.*) I had so many questions, so I try to accommodate questions, because I do know how important that is.

D. Were there other souls, like Gergen, who talked with you then? Were there other mentors you worked with?

B. Yes, other teachers, indeed. I had one when it came to like geometry and so forth. There were different teachers. But I had questions which were sometimes not answered, so I try to be the type of teacher that I always wanted.

D. I'm sure you're good with them.

B. Ah, so I do that. And then I sit in my study and reflect, huhuhuh, on what I thought.

D. Did you make your own study? Did you create your own space?

B. Ah, huh huh, ya.

D. What does it look like?

B. Well, it's like book shelves with plenty of material to study up on, you know, additional information for my own studies. It's similar like Zachariah's, being in that center of knowledge (*Library on the fifth*), so I created that.

D. You kind of imitated Zachariah's study?

B. (*He laughed loudly.*) OH, I DID INDEED! HA HA HA, oh.

D. That's a nice feeling, though.

B. Hehehe. It's all part of growing up.

D. Do you still seek Zachariah out in the Library?

B. I do indeed, because I like to discuss ideas. Like if there are certain things we have put forward in this group (*our channeled sessions*), for instance, then I like to elaborate on that so I get it correctly down in my journal and other documentations as well. So I do that. I do seek him up. So, in some way, I have imitated him, huhuhuh.

D. He's a good person to imitate. Quite the scholar.

B. He is indeed. He's like the greatest professor of all, like an ambassador of everything. So he's not a bad role model, really. I try to imitate, so when the sparkles come, they think I'm like Zachariah! HAHAHA.

D. Do they come visit you in your study?

B. I allow them to, it's like having an audience. Oh, I'm playing a little bit. But I DO like to sit and reflect. I have risen to the fact of enjoying the company of my own mind, so to speak. Huhuh.

D. What sort of things do you contemplate?

B. I contemplate on, you know, where we started and what we have accomplished in these sessions. And also, if there is maybe something that was missed that I would like to move forward in a later time, and in what way. So, I study up on all sessions that we have had that I participated in, and to somewhat try to see that everything is covered, from my perspective. Other ideas I will move it forward to Ophelia and Isaac, to talk about in our meetings between sessions. So, in some way, I have risen to a little bit more of a professor, a little professor like Zachariah. Hehehe.

D. You can go and visit with Ole, ask him questions.

B. Ole, he can move around to all sort of places, so I might ask. But I'm concerned that Gergen comes as soon as I pop the question. Because he knows that whatever I ask, if it is not fully answered, then he is put in that position of answering.

D. Well, he's your mentor. It's just like Tom, I suppose. You have a sense of responsibility to what he hears, don't you?

B. Ah, his ears cannot hear everything, you know, because it might end up in all sorts of new ideas that doesn't belong. And I'm waiting to talk more about the travels. He asked, similar like I asked about beyond, he asks about travels.

D. You know what that means; he's going to be a little traveler, like you.

B. He wants to know more about what I do, but I'm cautious about sharing. So I can see that there is a resemblance with Ole, probably. He's cautious to tell me too much, like I'm cautious to tell Tom too much.

D. So, if Tom were to ask Gergen something, you might want to know what he asked?

B. Indeed! Because he might bypass the whole line–up I have of teachings, so I might put a foot in over there and say, "Oh, hello, Tom! What is going on over here? Do you want a cookie? Do you want to go somewhere? What's going on over here?" Oh, I can see what you're saying now. I might ask Ophelia though. But Ophelia can play the harp and make me somewhat fall asleep. And when I wake up, it's long forgotten.

D. That's a nice trick.

B. She has always tricks up her sleeve. Ophelia says upcoming discussions here, ahead, mainly next year, she said, would be to access information on different centers. Siah's place is one center we will visit, she says, so we will look into that. And when we say we, I'm pretty sure that I'm gonna join. Because now I've heard it, so I might be able to, if I can't travel, I might be able to watch it as a documentary and participate in that way.

D. That's wonderful.

B. So we are gonna go, Ophelia says. So, okay, Bye bye.

Bob Ponders his Education (Oct 22, 2017)

B. I'm working now with Isaac and the plants, trying to create new versions of patterns. He's an excellent teacher, I must say. He smiles and he encourages me, but he doesn't really say the answer, he just nods and smiles, so you feel like you're making progress, even if you might not! Huh huh. So, I feel constantly encouraged by him to do things. And he's taking his time, he does indeed. He understands my nature.

D. Was I a good teacher, or have I been a good teacher?

B. Yes you have. But you were more firm in the way you taught me. But you and I are different. Because we have so many different levels of meeting points, like here and there, and so forth. So we are like friends, and you want me to be the best that I can be. I'm sure the other ones want that too, but they are not as closely tied to me, in that way. It's like having a parent, and then you go to your grandparents, –it's much more fun, because they can send you off later in the day! Ha huh huh! Zachariah is also really firm. He's firm, you and Zachariah are more equal. This one is more like, you know, joyful. And

Ophelia is like a mother, caring. She always takes time for me. And Isaac is like that too.

D. Ophelia must be really close to your development?

B. Yes, she is. Yes, she is. And so are you. You have two very different approaches on how to learn. And Zachariah is like you, a little bit. Both ways make me move forward. Because if I'm too pampered then I might just want to remain in that setting and just have fun. But because you pushed me in a different way and challenged me, then I combined those two ways of learning into a modality that made me move forward.

D. Ophelia hugs you, and I rap you on the knuckles.

B. Uhhuhuh. You don't do that. But you are more like you bounce questions back, in a way. She smiles and she nods. But with you, it's like sometimes talking to a mirror. So, I ask a question, and it bounces back. It changes a little bit, but it's still the same question, -and that makes me think. And Zachariah is doing the same, bouncing it back, so the knowledge comes from me. And Ophelia encourages me differently, like Isaac. They are more like grandparents, if you like to see it like that.

D. It's probably fun to get out of our lab and go visit them?

B. Well, I like to be everywhere, to be in different places to learn. I like that. I don't have a preference, but I can see in rewind that all ways of teaching helped me to move into the best designer, the best creator of form and creator of new ideas, as I could be.

D. I'm sure you're really well-respected at home. We were talking this morning about you having a really nice office next to Gergen's.

B. Ah, ah, a little bit away. But I do like when they come and talk with me. I ask questions, answer questions, and they can sit, because that's what I like, I like to sit and talk.

D. Which way do you teach? Are you like Ophelia and Isaac, or like me and Zachariah?

B. Ahhhh, I try to be both, and I try to mirror that based on the individual I'm talking to. But I'm actually using both techniques, because that clearly worked. So sometimes I'm a little bit stiff and firm, and sometimes I'm more like, you know, I am who I am. I like to make jokes about things because I think that is a good way to learn. Hmmhmm.

D. I bet you're a really good teacher.

B. I try to be different, based on who I'm talking to.

D. I'm curious, does Ia ever come and ask for your advice about things?

B. Ah, we both do.

D. So you ask her things, and she asks you?

B. Yes, indeed, because we're operating with different things. She is working closer with DNA and light and so forth. And she's also operating now up with the eighth, so we have a common point. Even though she's working with the teeny, tiny details, and I'm trying to make a big, huge planet, but it's still from the same source, the eighth, with the DNA and so forth.

D. Well, Isaac is a master of that.

B. He is, indeed.

D. Does she meet with Isaac, or someone else?

B. I don't know, really. I've only met with Isaac, like him and I. But I am gonna ask if Ia can come, because she will like Isaac, and Isaac is friendly. But I also want to be a part of it, I don't want to be excluded again.

D. Like how Ia and Gergen kind of work together?

B. Ah, so I don't want that. I'm happy to share, but I want to be a part of it, too.

D. Understood. Does Gergen ever ask for your advice?

B. Uh, in some way he asks for advice. Well, not advice, but he asks, "What would you like, Bob, to put forward more information about? What would you personally like to lift forward to this reality, if you could?" And then we talk about that. And he also wonders sometimes about how humans react to us. That's also what he asks. So I say, when we were there and there, the response was this and this. So, he can see, clearly, but he asks about that a little bit. We do talk about that. (*They constantly monitor our interactions in public forums or trance sessions, gauging how their messages are received.*)

D. How do you feel the response has been?

B. A lot of people who are already familiar with nature spirits, they are more ready, if you like, to communicate with us. And some are just in that first beginning phase, where they don't really know what to believe. It's still a part where some might wonder if ALL of this is true, if it's real. But the only thing one can do is to move into your soul particle and sense if it's a vibration, if it's a tickle, if it resonates with you. But it's also a fact of where each soul is on its own level of learning. And if someone comes with several knots, and we try to provide a treat, then they might not be ready for that treat, as of yet. But I don't worry about that, because I'm only here to somewhat talk and try to deliver a message. And most people will see this as something good and that something is providing them more insight about who they are and their true nature. But there are those who will question the authentic message from it, and they are still in some way locked within their own cocoon, –they're not a star, or they have too many knots.

D. Yes, it's a problem. I struggle with the same concerns, that people have preconceived ideas they don't want to release.

B. So, it's like, "Loosen up that knot!" It's because they are not there yet, on their level of learning. And some will, from this—either the scripture that you provide, or the work that you do—it will make them move up a step on their ladder, and that's all that we wish for. But I am happy about the response, really, because I feel like people are happy, and happiness is the key to progress. If you're angry or if you're narrow minded, then you are in that cocoon, and this is just one way to make them become a star.

D. Well, you do make people happy. You make us happy.

Bob Stands before the Council (Nov 11, 2017)

Bob recounted how he was brought before the council (*which he has since joined*) to describe what he learned and how the information from the second dimension was received during the trance sessions leading up to the end of *Wave 1*.

D. So, what's been going on, my friend?

B. I've been in my study a little bit, and I've been talking to my students, explaining...oh, it feels like its falling asleep again. I'll sing again, (*The spirits that come in from the ninth and tenth dimensions carry a slower vibration than does Bob, so he struggles to adjust Christine's inner energy up to his level when he comes in after them. As he continued singing, he was able to get her tuned up*). So, there you go. Wakey–wakey! I've been in my study, and I've also done my reporting to my council.

D. Oh, you did?

B. I did indeed.

D. How did that go?

B. It went well. Gergen was there for moral support, if you like. So, I came in all dressed to the occasion. Like here, you would say you come to an interview in a suit and tie, so I was well prepared.

D. What color did you wear?

B. For the day, I actually wore blue, light blue, because I wanted to mirror calm, huhuh. But first I wanted to go with red, –I like red–, but Gergen said it gives too much of my personality. So he said, "Why don't you just go light blue, because that will reflect calm and make them pay attention to your words, more than just your personality." So that was the trick with that. They all wore white. They have white, always white.

D. How many were they, in number?

B. Oh, they were a lot. They were like sitting in a row on a podium kind of thing. They were (*paused and mumbled as he counted them in his memory*) —twelve.

D. Wow, that's a big council.

B. Ah. And the one to the right, the far right, I thought at first, he was like a beginner, because he didn't say anything. The other ones asked me questions, all of them, but he didn't, the one to the right. So I thought he was an apprentice of sorts, but he was actually above them. But he was friendly, –I wanted to talk with him more. I was disappointed that he didn't ask any questions. Gergen stood next to me, and the other ones sat up there, and each and every one was asking different questions, you know, along the way, and he was just sitting there smiling and taking notes. I wanted to talk with him, but he was like an elder, he turned out to be.

D. What sort of questions did they ask you?

B. Oh, they ask about the progress of the information. A lot of it had to do with, aside from the soil and the seeds and that sort of thing, they also were interested in knowing how it was perceived about their existence in nature. And that is something that some of them were a little hesitant about sharing, because they were not sure they wanted to be detected. And I said, before the mission, "I want to be detected, I want to be found, and maybe more wants to be found!" Then Gergen said, "Sshh, don't say it like that, Bob. Just simply say that you encourage us to be known, because otherwise, how would they (*humans*) know what changes can be done in nature? Put it like that, Bob." So I did. And that is also why, combined probably with higher councils, like Ophelia's and so forth, that this mission came about that we participate in. Everyone was supposed to participate; so if we didn't participate, then it wouldn't be a complete picture, would it? Huhuhuh

D. Well, that is true.

B. So, we talked about that, how that came forward, and the part of how we operate in nature and how we can be seen, and also how we see and sense humans and their mental activity. There were a lot of questions about that.

D. That was good, I really appreciated that knowledge.

B. Ah, ah. They wanted to know if that came forward, that we see everything in energy. That we can see what is manifested that man can see, and also what is only like an energetic memory. So I said that I did say that. That was one of the things. I had points that they wanted me to deliver, and these points were important to them, so I told them. I gave like a report and checked off the list, so to speak, of what I told you, and also what is available to be released in the first book, but also in upcoming scriptures. They were happy about that. After the meeting they really started to smile, the whole panel of people, not only the one to the right. He was in favor of all of this. I'm sure he was the one initiating it from our level. Maybe he's the one that talks with Ophelia, for instance, participating in the higher councils on the ninth? Because on the ninth, everyone from all levels are welcome to come. I'm sure, if I were to guess here, I'm pretty sure that he went. Ole, Ole. His name is Ole. Huh, he is like a father to Gergen, almost.

D. How does he look? Is he bigger?

B. No, he's a little bit smaller than the other ones, like he shrinks.

D. Like a raisin.

B. Like a little raisin, but a very intelligent one! Huhuh. I like him, I like him. (*Bob recounts things in chronological sequence and has, since he first began speaking, presented his memories as if they are real–time occurrences.*) Oh, he said that he was like me one time. I'm like a grandchild, almost. He said he likes to watch me when I'm travelling. He said it makes him happy, because he doesn't travel anymore. He does more like...office work! Ha ha ha. He said, "I don't travel in the same way, it's more like paper work!" HUH HUH huh, but he likes to watch it, he says, "I follow you, Bob." (*Ole was telling him that during the session.*)

D. Well, he probably picked you, I bet. He and Gergen.

B. Ah, I didn't meet him, I only talk with Gergen.

D. He's kind of like you and Jeshua, he knew all about you.

B. Ah, knew all about me, and I didn't know. But he said he followed all my endeavors, he said. All my adventures on different locations, he followed. Huhuh. It's like a TV show. I'm like a TV star! Huhuh. He followed all excursions, he said. He was particularly fond of when I went to Ophelia's big classroom. He said that he laughed about that. Because those times I didn't get to sit in the front seat, he said he laughed, because he could see I was a bit frustrated. He followed and observed how I interacted with other participants on this little stage. (*When Bob hears a call to come join a lecture at Ophelia's, he always rushes to the auditorium, so he can sit up front, close to the stage. Ole wasn't laughing because Bob was frustrated at being late and sitting in the back. He was amused by how Bob reacted when he saw all the strange entities in the auditorium, whom he normally didn't notice. However, in the spirit realm, because thoughts travel differently than sound waves, it really wouldn't matter where he sat in the forum.*)

D. How did that come across to him?

B. Ah, I can see that! (*He was looking towards Ole, who must have shown him a response to my question*). He says that I put forward that I was just glancing on them, but I actually stood up and stared, he said. And he laughed about that. He said, "In your mind, you glanced to the right towards them. But you actually stood up and stared." (*This was described in Wave 1, when he showed up late and had to sit in the back and was able to see the other students. It was then that Bob noticed the little group of students who looked quite odd, having what he described as cone-shaped ears, about whom he was very curious.*)

D. Get a better look.

B. Get a better look. Some of them are actually bigger in size, so he said that. So he watched that, and he also looked at the development of my drawer (*his project in the lab on the sixth*), he was interested in seeing that. And he said that I was protective, you know, that I guarded my drawer like it was a treasure; and he doesn't take that away from me, because it was a treasure for me. But he said I was suspicious of the other ones in your lab. He said that I carry that characteristic a little bit, –that I'm suspicious. Huh huh.

D. You didn't know them.

B. Nay, I did not know them. And they did not really say anything, they only, like, —stared.

D. It's good to be cautious when you're out traveling.

B. Ah, one should not rush. But sometimes I do rush. But if I rush, it is only because I feel familiar with those that I'm with and the surroundings where I am at. Otherwise, I tend to be more cautious, –and he pointed that out here. But that's also one of the criteria they wanted. Because if I had only been in the state of mind of rushing, then they would not have allowed me to travel. So they wanted me to be a bit cautious as well, because they wanted me to not just eat everything that came my way, so to speak, and to somewhat look at it from an angle, from our level, as well, to see if it resonated with the way we operate.

D. So what characteristics did you experience in the lab that helped you, from his perspective?

B. The self–study, you know, the details. He said that was part of the characteristics that was improved over time, with me being mainly with you.

D. Was that intentional on their part?

B. Well, it was intentional because he told you to! Apparently...this I didn't know. (*He was given images so he would know that I was instructed to leave him alone to self–study.*) You've also been around, you've been sneaking around here, it seems. So Gergen must have given you indications on, you know, pointers, checklists to follow. Maybe that's why you left me. You left me to self–study, and I didn't really understand why. I thought we were just going to be friends hanging out and do things together. So I was confused and a little bit like, "Oh, where are you going?" And then you said, "I'm just around the corner." And SOMETIMES, IT SEEMS, you did not go to a matter of haste. You just left!

D. I just stood outside and watched?

B. You just left, you didn't want questions, –oh, here comes all sorts of secrets! Because you didn't want questions, sometimes you said there was haste to attend to, but there was not, –you just went and stood outside the door. Because this was a time when I didn't leave the room! (*Laughing.*) You just went outside and stood next to the door. If I had looked out, I would have seen you. Oh, I see the picture now, they show me the picture, Ole shows me the picture. Oh, you stood just outside the door sometimes. Ohohohoho.

D. That's not very nice.

B. Ah.

D. But you know you're one of my best friends. I wouldn't do anything—

B. Ah, and you did feel bad about it, because you said you didn't really like that. So after that experience, we did a lot of things, –you took me to the sphere room, you showed me places to collect certain materials, and you took me to the museum. So you took me places, because you did feel a little bit bad about it. But you were instructed to leave me and it did pay off. But you were not really sure about it, so you said, "I'm gonna go, there is haste." And sometimes there were haste, but not all the time.

D. You probably never had an opportunity to be all by yourself before, like in your lab on the second?

B. Nah. First, we are big, big groups, then we go down to clusters, smaller cluster of like ten. Then we go down to four or five, and the next level is to be by yourself more and to do individual missions; and my mission was to go with you and do this. In order to do this, I had to be operating from my own capacity, because this is not a group activity. I had to be by myself, but I was uncomfortable with that, so you have to learn different ways to master it. So I was in a setting of friends, but I was also gradually taught how to be and reflect and study by myself.

D. You're really good at it now.

B. Ah, and I was also meeting you in the vault. So as I was down there, sometimes you left me by myself with boxes that I was allowed to look into, –and it was the same thing, I can see this now. That there was like a strategy on your part to warm me up to do this independently, because it's not like a group activity from my part, —except for Gergen, of course, who observes, and clearly Ole. The other ones (*council members on the second*) probably look too, but they're not so, –they're not smiling, so you don't know what they're thinking. They are friendly, but they just don't want humor and other traits of joy to overshadow the purpose and the task at hand (*he's back to describing his meeting with the council*). They said, "It would be easier for you if we were sitting here laughing, but the whole agenda that you were on would somewhat be overshadowed with laughter. So we are giving you this personality trait as a group, so that you only focus on the task at hand, and then afterwards, when we're done, we can have a festival." Like a graduation festival!

D. To be a little star, like you are, you were taught to rely more on yourself.

B. By myself, by myself; because I was gonna communicate by myself, so that was the whole thing. We all, in some ways, learn to be by ourselves, eventually, but this was different.

D. Are you still studying much on six and seven?

B. Ah. I take classes.

D. Is Ophelia still watching over your development, pretty much?

B. Ah, she's never far away.

D. What about Isaac?

B. Isaac comes by too. He sort of pats me on the back, you know. I like him. He can just swing by wherever I am, he just seems to show up and be like, "How is everything going? How is your drawer proceeding? How is bubble training?" He always remembers everything, so he asks about that, –and he seems to show up everywhere, so I'm thinking that there's no check points for him! He just travels everywhere he wants to go. Huh

D. He says, "Where's my little buddy now?"

B. It's like having those key cards, and you sort of move around. I kinda have a key card.

D. He has a master key card.

B. A master key card, and you can maybe go and see if it click–click, maybe works. You can go up to the Master Mind, or maybe go and sit and have a listen when Jeshua and those on the ninth have a little meeting, and you can just sort of scoot over and have a listen. So I feel like a star within is lit up. Sometimes my star is more, –you can see the star as a lamp, so sometimes it's more dimmed, and that is when I focus on tasks at hand that I already know and I'm just trying to make it function. BUT, when I'm in the phase of that I want to learn more, then my star is not as dimmed, so it's more lit up.

D. Does it get bigger over time, your star?

B. Ah. It gets more strings, if you like. It began like with a little teeny, tiny star, and then it became like four lines to each side, so to speak. And then it became more, and eventually it looks like a sun, huhuh.

D. Blinding to the eye. Well, congratulations on getting a good review from the council!

B. Congratulations to me!

D. A job well done.

B. Well done. I got a little thing on me, it's like a medal, a golden star with a little stone in it.

D. Is that like around your neck?

B. No, you attach it to your robe, so it's over my heart, so to speak. It's like in gold, and there's a big red stone in middle, and there's smaller ones on the edge of the star.

D. Do you keep that with you always?

B. I'm gonna have it on. I'm gonna have it on when I sit in my study, so that people can see that, huh ah, because when they say, "What is that?" And I'm gonna say, "Well, this is like a reward for well-done, executed work." So I'm gonna say that. Everyone likes a treat, so I'm very happy about that, I'm proud about that.

D. Are you going to get something after every wave? Will you have to give a report every time?

B. They are curious about knowing what I have seen.

D. Can they not see that as well?

B. They might have, but they don't share. These are not big talkers or very sharing. I'm more sharing, and these are more listening to what I say. But they're happy, so when it was done, the one that was kinda strict, he came down and gave me this star, and then everyone applauded to me and smiled. So I felt like they were being strict just to make me a little on edge, so I would focus on my report, but after that it was all friendly, so maybe it will be a festival!

D. Well, that's wonderful. Congratulations, my friend.

B. Ah, ah. Anyway.

Before we leave this chapter, it might be good to retell the story of how Bob described his perception of objects on Earth, since it was important to his council. We talk about frequencies and vibrations all the time, but as humans, we are consciously unaware of the actual energy field. The physical eye only picks up certain bands of light waves, which are converted into electrical signals, that are then interpreted by the brain. If we take a tree, for example, to us it is solid and dense. To those on the second, it is a bundle of energy, organized and held together by a pattern that emits certain sounds and colors. When Bob, or any other spirit (including your soul, when outside the body) observes a location on Earth, the currently active trees and plants can be seen, along with the residual energy from previously living flora. The further back in time (and yes, time does exist on the Earth), the more faded the energy appears. A spirit does not see through eyes, but directly reads the energy field with its being, in all directions at once. Those spirits on the second dimension are responsible for maintaining these patterns. As they move around on Earth, they evaluate the colors and sounds coming from the living plants and animals, and try to assist, should they find imbalances. Everything carries the awareness of the Master Mind, so they can communicate with the trees, plants, fish, animals, insects, worms, and birds, because they work directly with that inner intelligence. If we learn nothing else from the immense volume of knowledge they have provided, we should at least accept that we are surrounded by a web of awareness that can detect our presence and intentions. A tree, for example, is more aware of you, than you are of it. The second dimensional spirits are calling on us to view the world in a more sacred way, because it is their work and efforts we are destroying.

Building A Solar System

The lab on the sixth is the setting for most of the discussions about the solar systems and the fish tanks, as that is where Bob comes to study. Our previous books, *Wave 1* and *Wave 2*, went into quite a bit of detail on the function and purpose of the different dimensions, so we will not repeat those observations here. However, we will remind the reader that Bob is a master designer of different life forms found on Earth, and he began traveling to different dimensions to expand his knowledge about how form is created. He is also going to be on the team that works on the next model of human, which is planned on being introduced in the next few hundred years.

The sixth and ninth dimensions are the realities that design and plant physical objects like suns, planets, moons, and other solid forms in our Universe. I say "plant" because the solar systems and larger objects are designed as energetic patterns of sound and color within the spiritual dimensions, much like DNA. After the energetic model has been fully prepared, it is placed at a pre–determined location within a fish tank, just like a seed. Then other elements (also energetic patterns) are added and the system begins to grow into the intended form. Once the system has expanded and the material has coalesced from light and sound into solid form, it is put into hibernation. What we understand to be matter is only solidified patterns of light and sound energy, so as new solar systems are added to the Universe, new material comes into existence. The aetheric field of the first dimension holds the patterns of solidified, visible matter on the third dimension. I know this is completely the opposite of modern scientific theories, which claim that all the existing energy and subsequent material in the Universe instantaneously came into existence from a mathematical singularity smaller than a gnat's toothbrush, i.e., the "Big Bang" hypothesis. But you have to ask yourself, which theories are more illogical? Scientists have a great fondness for certain physical principles, such as the first law of thermodynamics dealing with the conservation of energy, which they believe to be immutable. Fortunately for us, the Universe is not a closed system, meaning that most of these "laws" have only limited validity beyond Earth. In addition, the spirits also tell us there are galaxies and solar systems that are not fully materialized, which float around within our fish tank but do not interact with the vibrational fields we can detect with our senses or equipment. It is important to set aside any theories you may have learned in school, and consider that the spirits are describing how the process actually occurs, stripped of all hypothetical pontificating. All dimensions are involved in creation, and many souls on Earth who have a home in the sixth and seventh dimensions are very familiar with what Bob is studying.

This chapter is predominantly about how he studied and executed the steps of creating a solar system in our lab. Later, he gives a lot of information on how he learned about sound and melodies related to stars and planets.

A Drawer in the Lab (Jan 15, 2017)

We introduced a few of Bob's experiences in Ophelia's lab on the seventh and in our lab on the sixth, in *Wave 1* and *Wave 2*. Over the years we have listened to many amusing stories as he recounts things he has learned and discussions he has had on his travels. In our lab, he and I spent a lot of time talking before his training began on how to build a solar system of his own. We had a drawer where we kept his model, and as we went over different levels of teachings, he would include that knowledge in his project. We began with a little sun, since he had made one already with Ophelia, and then moved on to the planets, one orbit at a time, spending considerable effort on the living planet. You should think of the sun and planets as energetic objects containing certain elements and color patterns. He was often frustrated and confused, but as he came to master the basic concepts, he was rewarded with many gifts of knowledge. And now, somewhere in our Universe, floats his solar system with his Individual on it—but we will let him tell the story.

Even though he is now known as a great traveler, it took a lot of courage on his part to begin going to unfamiliar places, like our lab on the sixth. To feel less anxious, he carried a little apple with him when he first came to visit, because it gave him a sense of comfort. This talk was very early in our discussions, so his language skills were still improving. When he first began speaking, his mind often ran much faster than the words he spoke, so a lot of ideas never quite got vocalized in the fullness he intended, or that they deserved. In the spirit realm, entire ideas and conversations can be transmitted in a single thought bubble, so he had to learn how to parse out words one-by-one, in order to flesh out a topic using our primitive style of communication.

B. I carry my apple just for show, because it symbolizes home and it's something that is familiar to me, and it's solid and it's round—I do like round.

D. Do you have it in a little backpack, or how do you carry it?

B. It's like in a little bag on a stick.

D. Do you have a notebook?

B. On my back, in my backpack. Different. Some notebooks you say, "You have to leave them here, Bob, but they will be here when you return." So, some of my notes, which relates to the projects in the drawer, I don't carry them around. But the apple I have in a bag on a stick, a little brown cloth that I wrapped around a stick, sort of. It's small, it's not that big. But it's just to feel familiar, really. I don't really need it, you say, "You don't need it here."

D. Well, it's comforting.

B. It's comforting to me.

D. I've always planted a lot of apple trees, I like them.

B. I do too. They're friendly, it's happy to see apples grow, because it's a symbol of health and fruition and cycles, you know—spring and cycles of warmth and fall. Cycles, I do like that.

D. So what do you and I talk about in the lab?

B. You create more the solid objects in space, where it's floating in gravity. And how much of a certain element needs to take place around a celestial body for it to function at best. It needs to resonate with the star inside, as well as being encased, in order for it to progress. Because even solar systems and galaxies, they have their own evolution; it's a life form—it is! I'm interested in that, you know, because it's a different part of evolution. It goes slower, though. You can't really see it as much. You pay attention and you think you're going to see something change, but it doesn't, really. And after we wait a while, I ask, "Why are we looking at this, because it doesn't seem to be an obvious change?" And you say, "There are molecule changes that take place between celestial bodies for them to function at best." I ask a lot of questions about why we are creating these things, because I don't understand, really, the purpose of creating it.

D. That's a good question, why are there so many stars and planets and galaxies out there?

B. I do know, but this is just from my level of understanding, of course, and I'm sure this will be answered by those who understand the bigger design of things. But I do know, and this is because Ophelia told me that when we created our little suns and stars in our fish bowl, they're not just shut down when we leave. They're actually placed somewhere so we can follow them. Some of them that I see actually are our little training projects that just float around, but they don't cause any harm. It feels very good to know that you created something and you can see it, and it's out there. But it's put where it can't necessarily be disrupting other systems.

D. So, your little creations in the lab, they are taken and put somewhere out in the Universe?

B. Put somewhere, put somewhere you can see it. I made a couple. They don't really operate. You know like when children make something in day care, you don't toss that away. You put it on the wall so they feel good about it. It's similar. So, we do get to put them somewhere. (*Laughing*). I do get to have my projects on display. But they don't have anything going around them at this point. Maybe that is in the future. (*He practiced making tiny suns in Ophelia's lab, before coming to study on the sixth, where he made a whole solar system.*)

D. Maybe your next project will be to make little planets for your little star?

B. I guess that is why you come in, because I follow you both. But, ohhh, it's like I ask you, "When will I get to do a planet? I did a star, when can I get to do a planet?" And then I started coming up and doing something with you. Oh, let's see. We began with small, it's like little rocks, really. You say, "Before you can make a big one, you have to know the model." So, you and me—we have a table—and then you teach me and I show you how I would make a solar system, but it's not for real. It's on a table with little rocks, or round balls. There is this ball that looks like the hematite, the black sparkle one—that is an important thing here, because it carries a lot of gravity keys in it. The elements within it is actually similar to what can be found in plenty of solar systems. It's divided though, so this is the solid form you see here, but I can get it in a liquid form. The hematite in a liquid form is somewhat of a key thing to create solar systems. You should study up on that, I guess, –that's what you show me.

D. Well, iron is very common.

B. This is more than iron, this is like attracting. Attracting and releasing in some way. Hmm, interesting. So, I'm learning here. I make a model first. I think I've come a little bit longer (*further*) in Ophelia's class, because I did make something that was put out there. And here in your lab, I'm still on the drawing table, so to speak.

D. Making progress.

B. Yes, I do indeed. But it's saved here. You put it in a big drawer, and then you take it out so we can continue. So, it's a long-term project of mine, I'm learning.

D. So, how do you travel to our lab? Do you think yourself there?

B. Well, when we meet in the vault, we meet as we are manifested in our own reality. When I go to your lab, it's more like I'm beamed there in some way. I don't really see; I'm beamed.

D. How do you know when to go to Ophelia's classes?

B. I'm called, and I also have a schedule.

D. You hear her call and you rush right over?

B. She assists me there. It's similar with you, you sort of assist me, so I am traveling with you in some way. It's more like beaming yourself to different places. That's the best way I can describe it to you.

D. And you normally keep the form you're in?

B. I don't know any other way! I don't dissolve like you do. When you travel, you can dissolve and manifest. I don't really do that. I merge with another thing, but there's nothing for me to merge with at your place. It's just different.

D. So what do we do with the little model solar system in the lab?

B. I do like the models in my drawers that you make me do. There is a class about the liquid form of the hematite that I will attend, I'm going to learn more about the minerals in space. Quite different than minerals here that I'm used to. There's all sorts of different minerals, depending on where you put it. I'm going to learn about minerals, components.

D. How are they in a different form than they are here on Earth? Is it an energetic form?

B. It seems like a lot of your things are, in the beginning, a liquid form. Then they are molded, almost, into a solid one. This is FASCINTING! I'm taking this class for sure! This I will go to.

D. Do you have a lot of options for classes you can take?

B. I sign up for plenty. But I also need time to reflect in between. A lot of times I see classes, upcoming classes on the board, and "Ohhh, I want to go to that one!" But you say, "You haven't done the first one!" So, you sort of divert my attention, because I can see it, and know what's coming. It is that fact of learning things at a certain pace. But at this time, we're moving into understanding how a liquid component is the foundation, how you mold it into a solid one. Why is it liquid? It's like tanks and bottles, glass bottles, and it floats in there. Everything is in liquid form. It can float almost. I don't understand it. This is the next class, I guess. You laugh, you see how eager I am. And you show off too, because you reach for something on the higher shelf and said, "Look here what you can do, eventually." I don't know when that is, but you take something in a liquid form and sort of roll it in your fingers and toss it up. And it floats, it floats in some sort of vacuum. It's up in the ceiling, so I can't touch it, but it floats there. It's something with the vacuum.

D. Do we use electricity for any of these processes?

B. Sound. You like sound. Ophelia likes light. You work a lot with sound. Sound is some sort of foundation for the vacuum. Sound energies. There's like a cloud in the room you put up in the ceiling, and you just shoot this little thing up, the liquid ball, and I look up and it's just floating up there, completely out of reach. And you say, "It is the sound vibration combined, where sound and gravity creates this vacuum, making things float and stay in its place." (*He then got really excited.*) OHHHHOHHHH!! That is what it is!! That's how it stays in its place!!

D. What's that?

B. The sound and gravity combined, creating the vacuum, that is how it stays in its place!! You shoot them up and say, "Look, it doesn't go anywhere else." And I look up and it doesn't, it does not. I see this energetic cloud that we're looking up to, that you shoot up these little silver balls. I don't understand how it holds them, but they hang there and they don't move. You say, "Sound and gravity and vacuum are the foundations of holding a form." And then you say, (*gets excited again*) OH HOHOHOHO, you say, "There can be a rip, and when the rip is in the cloud, this is when you can move between."

D. Move between?

B. From one side to the other, within, you create a rip. (*He is talking about portals between locations in a fish tank.*)

D. It's very interesting. I can see why you like coming to that lab.

B. Oh, it's all sorts of effects, like, hmhmhmmm. (*Laughing*) You know how people get happy with fireworks and stuff like that? This is that times a hundred! It's fascinating.

D. So do we just work one–on–one?

B. I prefer that, and you know that. I want to have my own teacher; I also don't understand the other ones. I see that they communicate with their person. (*Each older Elahim has a student*) It seems like you are more individual, so you talk with one. But I DO want to go and observe, sometimes, when you operate with your friends. I haven't been allowed yet. I would like to see you create something BIG like Ophelia's friends did. I would be quiet; I would be quiet.

D. I'm sure you would.

B. But you say, it's something with my protection. It's like I have to have some sort of energetic shield, because I don't belong. So I need to have some sort of energetic protection bubble around me. But I would like to sit in and observe. I would be quiet, and I would like to sit in.

Cores of Stars and Planets (Jan 15, 2017)

NASA defines the gravitational force as a field of influence. Some scientists think that it is made up of particles called gravitons, which travel at the speed of light. But NASA honestly admits we do not know what gravity is in any fundamental way. The conventional Newtonian principles relate gravity to what is referred to as mass. But as noted by Henri Poincaré in *Science and Methods* (published posthumously in 1914), "What we call mass would seem to be nothing but an appearance, and all inertia to be of electromagnetic origin." Bob tells us that on the sixth dimension, gravity is an element that is added to cores, but is also a separate field that exists external to planets. In the future, scientists will revise their gravitational and standard model theories to incorporate an electromagnetic plasma cosmology. Gravity will be revealed as a force that transmits nearly instantaneous signals. Scientists will discover tachyonic fields, proving the speed of light is not a limiting factor. Albert Einstein's postulates of curved spacetime and the mass of an object increasing as its velocity increases will be revealed for what they are—fantasy. Albert's vacuity has misguided mathematical meta-physicians to dream up theories about dark energy, dark matter, black holes, event horizons, a big bang, singularity, and much other nonsense. These conjectures will also be reclassified as illogical medieval science. The Universe is filled with an energetic field of cosmic light and sound known as the first dimension. Patterns introduced into this field cause vacuum, matter, and electromagnetism to become manifested within the vibration of the third dimension. The patterns are part of the spiritual design and are ultimately controlled by the Creator. As Bob next explains, the cores of stars and planets are important to maintaining the order of the cosmos.

B. There is an order here, because the closer to the star, the core within that celestial body is more like a pea. The further away it gets, the core is more bigger, it's more solid. But I don't know what that's about, but I'm just telling you what you showed me. So, you showed me the closer to the star, the smaller the core. And it's something with the resonation with that heat. So, the heat from the star triggers and communicates with the core of each celestial body that operates around it. And based on that little receiver within the planet that moves around, it communicates with the star in the middle, so it determines the way it moves and how fast, and distance–wise (*how far from the sun*).

D. That is fascinating.

B. The closer to the sun, the smaller the core, that's what you said. Okay, but how am I supposed to put them there? And how do they move? I can somewhat understand that the sun, the center, is responsible because it's like an engine, it creates heat. So it's maybe like putting a flame behind it so it sort of moves, you know. Who wouldn't move if you had someone putting fire up your ass!? (*laughing*) You would move, for sure!

D. Doesn't the inside of the sun turn? It rotates, doesn't it?

B. It rotates, the whole thing rotates, actually.

D. Doesn't that create a field that pulls? (*I was thinking in terms of gravity.*)

B. It creates, yes, INDEED! But sometimes they move faster and slower. So, I don't know. Because once the star is put there, WHAT MAKES IT ROTATE? WHAT MAKES IT STILL MOVE? What is the engineering within that makes it still MOVE? And how long does it move? What happens if it stops? And if it stops, what happens with, you know, the other ones? Will they just float, will they fall? What happens if it stops? And if it never stops, what sort of fuel inside exists that never stops? Uh, you know. SO, that's what I ask. What happens if it stops?

D. (*Laughing, since he seemed to expect answers.*) Those are very legitimate questions.

B. Indeed it is! Indeed, it is, because you know, we see motion, but we also know that objects have the possibility to choose to stop. And if it does, what happens then? No one tells me! And I can't understand. It's not it my books, –you gave me books to read, which is mainly pictures, of course. But sometimes I feel like you are not telling me everything, because I DO have questions about THAT. But you said, "Its conditions determine, from the day it is born, how long it will live. Similar like a body here, it has a life–span." And then I ask, "What are those?" And then you say, "There is no way to understand the terminology of cycles, because there is no time." So, you point out the fact of progress of the cycles within the solar system. So once each (*exhales loudly*), –mmmm. So, you say, "It is similar to: once there were dinosaurs and then there were not. And when they are not, that cycle is over. So, it's similar, everything carries a determined cycle of progress for it to travel within. And it has a destined path, really." And I said, "Who decides that? And where is it going? Where is it going?"

D. And what was the answer I gave?

B. YOU POOFED ME, YOU POOFED ME with that cloud. YOU POOFED ME. And I said, "I can't see! I can't see!" And you said, "Maybe there's nothing TO see." And I said, "I don't feel like that is the case!" And so we had a big laugh. You gave me my apple, and that was it. And then you said, "Oh, Bob, time for a break!" And you know, I felt like it was a diversion of question time, really.

D. As we are talking about astronomy, I have a question about the first dimension, since you're closer. What we call gravity, is that directly related to mass, or is that an energy field that's controlled by the eighth?

B. It's more energy than it is a solid form. You can see it because it's actually in one of your containers in your lab. So it is an energetic form; everything that becomes a mass or a form actually origins from a liquid form. It is the components within the liquid form that decides what sort of mass it will become. Gravity is not a solid form, it's not like a stone. It's a living entity, so it is motion, it moves because it is a liquid form, so it is not necessarily eh, –locked in its place.

D. It's not a fixed structure?

B. No, it's not a fixed, it has the ability to move, and it has the ability to transform and change regarding what it touches. So, within the Earth, the first dimension, there is a source of gravity and it is attached, if you like, to the solid form of the Earth planet, creating the foundations on the surface so that things don't float away. If it's inside a celestial body, encased, it is somewhat locked, clearly. But gravity exists in space and around celestial bodies as well, and it has the ability to move. It operates differently if it's free, you say, than if it's locked within a physical, celestial body.

D. So, is the gravity around the Earth free to move?

B. Indeed.

D. But there is also gravity within the Earth that's locked?

B. Indeed. Everything inside, locked in the sense it doesn't leave the core. However, it is movable in its case. So, it's actually something, oh can I say this? (*He was speaking to Ophelia.*) Oh...the strings from the core, the gravity within, is actually different on different places on the planet, because it moves a little bit. Oh, I don't know if I'm supposed to talk about that.

D. That's very interesting. Gravity is stronger at some places on the surface, I guess?

B. It's not like you float away in some countries and you're stuck in other countries! Some areas that have less gravity are covered with mountain areas or seas. Seas more, I would say, oceans. There is a less density of the gravity on those zones; landmass carries a certain degree of gravity, so there will be no disruption on the surface. You can imagine if some groups were flying a little, bouncing, and some were sort of still and parked and couldn't even move. That would cause mass hysteria almost, I would assume. It's not that obvious, but it is shifting within. In space and around celestial bodies, it's actually in some motion within the vacuum. It's in motion, but in an organized fashion because of the vacuum. So, gravity is a wave that can move. It's something that also connects with frequencies, noises, pitched noises. High tones make things move; low tones, lower tones makes things more still. In space, which you don't hear, of course, there are different tones. Where there is faster frequencies, (*he makes a high pitched sound*), ding, ding, ding, ding, ding, ding, there's actually more motion. And then when there are galaxies and celestial environments where it goes like, (*he makes a much deeper sound*), hhuummmm, hhuuummm, then it's more still.

D. Is that a frequency that humans can hear, or is it a spiritual frequency?

B. You can hear the hhhuuummm, hhhuuuummmm. This is why natives used the drum rituals, because they connected with that. It is for the grounding, stillness, placement. The other one carries the high-pitched ding, ding, ding, ding, ding, ding, it's somewhat like those experiments with brainwaves that some institutes are working with. So, that will be it.

D. So, I guess that must be how heavy stones are moved?

B. It is actually both. It's in combination of the high pitch and the lower. The high pitch makes it...ooh–ooh–huhuh! (*Ophelia must have come close, because he looked to the left, a bit nervously.*)

D. There comes the finger, eh?

B. I don't know yet, but she's very close! Let's see what she says. She says I can say just this—the high pitched (*make high pitched sound*) ding, ding, ding, ding, ding, ding, makes things move. To put it into place, you use the other vibration, which is like the lower one. So, it's the combination of both. One moves and one places. Ohohoho.

D. Thank you.

B. She nods. She says it's a little treat for the new year. (*Laughs really hard*) Hehehehe. High pitched (*make high pitched sound*) ding, ding, ding, ding, ding, ding, makes it go up. Lower, sets it into place. Oh, they used them both. There were these...oh. (*Ophelia must have said that was enough information*). Just know the technique was to operate simultaneously, high pitched and lower. And this can be found as well around celestial realities as it becomes something, I would assume. I'm not a master designer when it comes to the galaxies and the solar systems yet, but I take my classes and I teach and I learn,

–you give me books to look at. Your books don't have a lot of words, so it's mainly pictures. The way you write is more like points, it's almost like how you see the scripts for the blind. So there are pictures and there are these dots. I don't know what I'm supposed to do with this book, but I'm sure it will come to me. But you like to read out loud to me, and I like that too. So when I say, "I don't understand this," you say, "Then I will read." When I say read, it's like you transmit dots into pictures into my mental realm.

D. I was wondering if I gurgled the book to you?

B. No, you gurgle when you laugh. But otherwise, you are highly skilled to lower your vibration and to move into your way of transmitting pictures. Because the way I receive pictures is different than the way your friends, how they receive pictures. So, in many ways, I think you send pictures of dots, which carries a picture, –if you understand the dots. But I can't understand the dots, because it's just like snowflakes coming my way, or little raindrops. So, when you talk with me, you create, –you sort of sample the dots and put it into a new bubble and that's how you send it to me. You are very skilled because you understand that I don't understand the dot language. I call it dot language, because it looks like those blind scripts that you see.

D. Well, that's a nice way to spend time together.

B. Yes, and I send my pictures to you of the animals and so on, and what did exist. You're very interested in what did exist, –we talk about that.

D. I have a question about this one. Do you see him in the lab? Do you see him around? (*Christine is a male energy at home.*)

B. Indeed, indeed. Likes to work with heat, energies that are heating, something with heat and lightning. Operating, adding, molding things with heat.

D. Are we working in the same lab?

B. Sometimes.

D. Do you ever talk to him?

B. Mmmmm. I do.

D. Does he communicate with you?

B. Yes. She–he's more teasing, you know, likes to poke me. The difference is that you can appear very serious. but you also have this side. A lot of times he chooses to radiate a very human side to me, because he's been here in very optimistic characters. So he sort of transforms his personality a little bit, like more of a joyful person, so he sort of transforms.

D. Oh, that's nice.

B. I know that both of you spend time in the vault. I haven't seen this one's book (*personal journal*), but I don't follow him that closely. But he comes by and sees my progress, and we are actually together many times and discuss. You know, sometimes I turn to this one because he's more eager to do things explosively, which I like. But he's not as close as you and me.

D. Do I work with anyone other than you?

B. Not from my place, no. But maybe I share you with, –you have students, I'm sure, in your place. But I'm by myself here with you. There's not that many from my realm here, you should know.

D. That's because you're a master designer.

B. Ah, (*laughing*) Huh huh huh.

Cause and Effect (Apr 23, 2017)

Bob gives a masterful explanation of how to visualize the density or vibrational levels between the dimensions. It always amazes me the instantaneous way that he and the other spirits can summarize and condense very difficult concepts into elaborate imagery that is comprehensible to us.

Since Bob talks about choices that souls make, it may be helpful to remind the reader about the relationship between the Coat of Karma and reincarnation. The spirits say that the Coat of Karma is like a third body. For any incarnation there are three parts; the soul, the Coat of Karma, and the physical form. The incoming soul must put on its Coat as it merges with the body of the infant. Each soul has its very own Coat. Their Coat holds the intention that the Creator had for that spirit, plus the history of that spirit's activity on this plane. The Coat holds the lessons learned and yet to be learned, along with the patterns of thought and behaviors of ALL previous lives. Before each new life, a group from the ninth dimension, whom Bob called the "tailors", sew into the Coat belonging to that specific soul, the goals and objectives planned for the upcoming incarnation. This is a simplistic way of describing how energetic patterns are activated within the Coat, which will manifest as certain experiences on this plane. (We will discuss this further in *'The Spiritual Design: Wave 3'*.) Upon death of the physical body, the soul must detach from the Coat, before it is free to travel home, since the Coat of Karma remains within the mental realm of Earth. The process of detaching from the Coat can be seen, from the human perspective, as releasing attachments to physical cravings (food, sex, alcohol, drugs, etc.), emotional bonds to material things (wealth, objects, activities, homes, etc.), or people who are still alive on Earth. The fourth dimension, also called the mental realm, is a vibrational field that encircles Earth. It has a vibration somewhere between the physical and the spiritual frequencies. It is within this field that all soul–to–soul communication occurs. It is essentially the source field for psychic abilities. It holds the thought forms and history of all memories generated on the physical plane, including those from plants, animals, and the Earth itself.

D. I was going to ask you something about your energetic form. When a human dies and their soul goes into the fourth dimension, that field of vibration is less dense than your body, isn't it?

B. It is a transformation. Because of the difference between the second dimension not being incarnating in the same way as a soul coming from the other ones upper, above. The transformation that takes place in the fourth is not necessarily comparable to the way we appear. But if it makes it easier for you, you can somewhat say that the fourth dimension, the transformation from the third up to the fifth and above, is similar to the density that exists in the second, even though they are not the same.

D. That's what I was wondering about—your density.

B. It's similar, like that. So, if it makes it easier for you, you can say that it is, but please do not put me in the fourth. But it's similar, density–wise, like the fourth.

D. But you have a different structure than say, on the fifth?

B. Indeed. To make it easier for you, if you see it like the soul leaving the third and it's somewhat spread out. And if you see all these dots in the soul, let's say, to make a picture for you, and hundreds of dots in a celestial form of a soul leaves. But there is a distance between the dots in a soul, so it creates somewhat of a loose web, if you like. The same web exists in me, but there is less distance between the dots. I will put an image of what I'm trying to say to this one, and she can explain it. But if you see the physical, and it sort of drops, and then out of this emerges the soul, and it is still somewhat attached to the physical as it departs into the fourth dimension (*it is still attached to the Coat of Karma*). So, let's say a hundred dots encased in this capsule are leaving, and there is somewhat of a distance between the dots. As it continues on it might be simply fifty dots that continues on, so it gets spread out more and more as it progresses upwards, to make it easy for you. However, I have the same amount between my dots, so I look more dense. But I'm not manifested like a vehicle on Earth. Ohh...(*Gives a big sigh, as if it were a real struggle to describe.*)

D. Can you change your size, can you become larger and smaller?

B. Indeed, if I want to.

D. So you can compact your dots together, or spread them out?

B. I can, indeed. I can somewhat, you know, it is like expanding your awareness, really. In some way, we are what we are, here. We don't transform in the same way as a soul, but the awareness within. Ohh...

D. It's the same, though?

B. I can expand it. So, before I sort of projected myself to different realities, I practiced the way to expand my awareness. As that was learned and adapted within my system, I had the possibility to project part of this expanded awareness from the second. It's somewhat different, but I'm not sure if other realities operate similar. But as I come back to the second, everything, regardless of how much has left, somewhat draws (*makes a sucking sound*) back down into my capsule. That's why I never look like I'm different. However, in some way...

D. You don't look quite as solid?

B. In some way, like that, yes.

D. So if you have like 100 dots, do you send like 50, is it like taking part of those dots and projecting them to another place?

B. It's like, let's say, I have my 100 dots, and they are more congested than the ones in a soul, which has more space between the dots, because a soul in a human is somewhat different. So, let's say, we all have 100 dots in our system, so I begin by expanding, looking similar like the one in the fourth. So I expand, making the distance between my dots to become wider. So that is the first you learn. In and out, expand and contract. So you do that, out and in and out.

D. Like a frog.

B. Like a frog. So that's what I do, you know, in and out. And that takes a while because you have to master it. And then you project part of this. In the beginning I only projected, let's say, two dots, from this expanded awareness of me, into the Library, or let's say another reality. I was at the time in the garden, the greenhouse that we talked about. I did not need to take that much, really. So the first level is to merely take, let's say, two dots, and sort of shoot it off to that greenhouse. But I still sort of looked and remained the same in the second. As I learned this trick and progressed and somewhat refined it, I learned how to take more dots and project them to the Library.

D. Who helped you with that, was it Gergen or someone else?

B. There is a group that works with this, because it is a part of learning for everyone on this level. So, Gergen was not necessarily in charge, like a mentor, when it came to understanding this, because you take classes on this, later on.

D. Was this after you merged with the trees and things?

B. Yes, indeed. So to make it easy for you, this would probably happen around the age of 30.

D. How old are you now?

B. Well, if you want to put it in human years, you know, you don't live that long, so I would say that I'm maybe like 47. And Gergen is like maybe 66, 67—67, he said. So, to make it easy for you, since it seems important to you. (*I laughed at that.*) Maybe it creates another picture for you.

D. You don't have gray hair, like I do.

B. I do not. Mine is somewhat brown. It's a preference, though. Gergen's is white. So, you know, you expand and blow out, and you go in.

D. That's really interesting. Thanks for the description. What else have you been working on lately?

B. I've been working on understanding time. Because it is a fact of when it (*a life form*) comes into a manifested reality, like on this plane, it falls under the spell of time. So, I'm learning the different levels and what sort of awareness should come in at certain levels of growth. So, time combined with manifestation is what I'm looking into a little bit, because this is what I teach my students. I'm sort of reminding myself. In some way, it is a little bit like you, —it's not like once you have read it, everything is fresh like a fruit salad. Sometimes you need to look back. That's why we go to libraries and vaults. It would be considered highly desirable if everything that you read once was just kept. But sometimes you have to go back, especially if you're going to teach it out to someone else, you want to be somewhat prepared and not confuse. So, my students are working on certain plants. One is a little bit further ahead and actually working on an individual. So we are, at this point, talking about the fact of adding the timeline. So they know when they create this, this group that works with the flowers, they have to understand when they create the flower, that it has a certain evolution in its own growth. And it's important that it happens in a certain manner. A tree, for example, carries a lot of the functions that resonate with oxygen on this level and protects the atmosphere. That's why we don't want them just taken away. There's a whole science when it comes to the trees. That's why we don't want you to interfere, because it has its own timeline, if you like. And that's important to understand, because the end result of that specific tree has an intention why it was put there in the first place. So, on this plane, which is under the spell of time, that has to be considered, once you are operating and creating objects. That even applies to organs within the system of humans. Everything has a "best before" date. Hehehe.

D. So every individual tree has that, or are you talking more about species or groups?

B. It depends. Every tree in a specific area has, normally, the same program to follow. But it's not the same program all over. So, let's say that there is an area on this plane where the atmospheric groups feels like there needs to be more oxygen. Then, it has to be changed within the ecosystem below, it has to resonate in order for the atmospheric layers to be in harmony. A lack of vegetation creates somewhat of a thinner atmosphere over that region.

D. Okay. That makes sense.

B. That's the short version for you. So, yes, I've been working with that. I've been working with my students.

D. Where do you study about that? Do you go to the Library and talk to someone there?

B. I don't talk, necessarily, because I've already mastered this, so I just go back to my notes.

D. Ah, your notes! Where do you keep those?

B. We have vaults too, ya' know. Both personal and collective. As I took this class, ahmm, (*he giggled a little bit*) because this was when you have to understand the elements as well, because in some way the elements resonate with certain timelines. Don't be confused about this, there's no need to know, no need to know, but, —it resonates. That's why the concept of oneness, that everything is connected. It is, in some way, just maybe not as a human considers to be connected. But dots here and there are like reference points from all levels, so to speak, and there are unique ones, of course. Sooooo, I've done that! I have also been studying up, because I do want to master some of the teachings that exists on the seventh and sixth dimensions as well. So, at the moment, I'm learning a little bit more about how light is the foundation within certain objects, and how that can be implemented within cores, like yourself with planets, or as well in new organs or new objects. So, you know.

D. Are you studying in Ophelia's lab?

B. I've been going a little bit back and forth. Because for some reason, my solar system in the drawer, it has some of the learnings from the seventh that need to be implemented in order for it to resonate. And I think that is because of the sun. The sun, in some way, can actually change over time. Whereas the cores (*of planets*) are supposed to be where they are located, their patterns are fixed. But the sun has the possibility to change. So I'm learning a little bit about that, because I don't want to create disturbances on my living planet. So I want to understand if changes occur over time in the sun, how that will affect my Individual on my living planet.

D. That would be good to know.

B. So, it's a little bit of study that I do. It's just to implement this thing in my own solar system, because it is supposed to go through a manufactured, if you like, evolution, this solar system. So, I want to make sure that I understand the principles of the star, and how that affects the ones that are moving around it.

D. Do you think that will be part of the information that's explained to us, those types of processes?

B. I'm sure I will be able to disclose some of it. Because as I can see it, I can talk about it. And if I can talk about it, you hear it. So, I'm pretty sure that it is a green light on this one.

D. Ophelia hasn't thrown a bag over your head?

B. Noooo, no. (*Laughing.*) But, you know, it is somewhat of an understanding for you. And it is the fact of the change of the sun in the middle, how it can affect the other ones. And it's not like you on this plane, as an individual, can do much about it. But you can get an understanding of what is happening, and you can adapt to the best of your ability. And also, because of the little ones, my students and so forth, they also need to know this. Because when I come back to the second dimension, then we're going to talk about what sort of engines and individuals as well as vegetation can exist. So we need to understand how the changes from within this system will affect this living planet. I am studying it in some way to understand and to create my system in the drawer, but in the long run it's also to understand what effects occur that can be seen and experienced on this plane. Because we don't want to work in vain and have something done that is later on taken away. That's why the elements are involved when it comes to the evolution of time that exists on this plane. Because of the gravitational field between planets and the sun, it is a whole science, you see, that I am looking into.

D. You know a tremendous amount about so many things.

B. Ohh, I'm learning about more than just an apple. So, I–I–I'm always sniffing around on all sorts of levels. So, that is what I do.

D. I was kind of curious, if they brought humans into this plane, they must have been able to foresee what activities would occur? A lot of what humans do is destructive and in opposition to what everyone else is trying to do.

B. (*Sighs.*) Well, there is a reason behind it all. Because, how can you understand how to make something better, if something bad hasn't happened first? How will you know to make improvements if everything is perfect from the beginning? On this plane, the physical might have been perfect all along, but events need to be put in so certain lessons take place. Otherwise, they don't know how to improve, let's say, the computer (*the brain*), if no events have taken place, then it doesn't interfere with the evolution in the specific individual.

But the individual on this plane needs to have experiences to stumble on, like events and certain things, so they understand the matter of choice. And some things, like if a group keeps on repeating the good choices all the time, then they know that this needs to be part of the upgrade in the computer, let's say, in the humanoid. Then there might be certain things that everyone, let's say, like 100 individuals, and 99 of them are doing the same wrongs on certain things. It seems to be related to a lot of the emotional and mental activities, –where they choose wrong. That's also part of the understanding in how to make the upgrade in the computer more suitable for upcoming vehicles. If it's perfect from the beginning, if they create what is already perfect, but, based on the changes where you put this individual, that's how you know if it actually was perfect.

D. Huh, that's interesting. That means nothing, in an environment that changes, nothing can ever be perfect, because the changes create imbalances.

B. Indeed. But, in order for you to know what is suitable on certain levels and planes, in this case, Earth, it has to experience something. And it's not just a human. Let's say they have to understand and experience drought. And you will see, these clearly do not work in a place where we will have the elements that will create drought in certain places. You can mix and match with trying to work with certain vegetation in order for it to not appear as a drought. But it has to occur, certain events. And it's the same for the Earth as a whole as it is for you, as a human. The human vehicle will somewhat collect the experience as a group, as well as in their own Coat of Karma.

D. That's very wise. That's a good explanation, Bob.

B. Well, you know, one does the best as one can. I'm not part of creating, necessarily, the whole new vehicle. I'm simply trying to explain why certain things occur. It is because they want to see what this individual, meaning you, what choices you make. Let's say, with the food intake, –we talked about that–, if you see an apple looking shiny for a long time, and then you see one that is wrinkly. It's not necessarily that you will buy the wrinkled one, that's not what I'm saying. But you have to stop and ask yourself, "Why is it looking wrinkly? And why is the other on looking shiny for three weeks?" They (*the spirit realm*) want to see what choices you make if you are forced to do so. (*He was comparing genetically modified apples that don't shrink or brown, to a real one that the second created, which will wrinkle as it ages.*)

D. That makes a lot of sense.

B. And it's also about the bigger events, of course, when it comes to what we see occur around the globe in different warfare. It is the fact of choice when it comes to interactions, or not, and how to somewhat leave certain individuals in order for their own evolution to be where they are at. Sometimes the choice is also to take a step back, and sometimes it is to take a step forward. What we see now is that there is no thought behind taking a step back or moving forward, it's simply an action. Again, we are talking about the fact of choice. So a lot of the things that you see that occurs around you is to make people aware and take a stand. And depending on what stand they take, and what they stand for. That will also be part of the collective report that will be part of the upcoming computers, because the events might change.

D. It seems like there a lot of really young souls that are down here, now. How would you see that?

B. I don't see that. I can't see, necessarily, what is tapping into the vehicle. The only thing I can see, and what I can say, is that there is a group of souls that have come in that don't know how to operate in the vehicle, simply acting on instinct. And that instinct is also part of the choice. Will the instinct come from the source, your soul particle? Then it is the correct instinct, of course. But if the instinct comes, especially from the physical, which is also part of this reality and it has an awareness, and if you simply act from the physical and mental realities, then it is not necessarily for the highest good. So a lot that are coming in are not blending that well with the levels they are merging with. A lot that are coming in are also only in the emotional levels, and that is to simply be and radiate some sort of comfort, because of the other ones that roam around uncontrolled. So, that is what I will say about that.

D. I had another question about the radiation, or the energy waves that come from the sun, –do they effect humans?

B. Yes, they do.

D. Is that energy controlled by the spiritual realm?

B. Indeed, they can dim and increase. As they increase...oh, well, let's see, no. Ophelia says, "Regardless if you dim it, or if you increase the activity in the star, both choices will actually, from this level here, appear as those solar storms and activities that will radiate from the sun."

D. Does it affect people's emotional or mental layers?

B. The mental. It's overheating in the head, the chimney. Because the computer is supposed to be somewhat in a cooler environment—oh, this is a higher level of understanding. But there is actually a cooling device or layer, like we talked about different fields, the vacuum fields around all organs. Around the brain it is encased in somewhat of a cooler layer, because it (*the brain*) is more sensitive to heat. We talked about this before. If the solar activity increases, then it effects the mental, the computer. So, in your design, you actually already have around that organ somewhat of a cooling device that encases it.

D. I didn't know if there were other energies, besides heat, that could affect humans?

B. Yes, radiation, like magnetic fields, overusing the magnetic fields—that influences the computer, causing all sorts of different, strange actions, sometimes. You don't want to overheat it. That's one of the organs that should not be overheated. The other ones are more adaptable to heat, but the computer, the brain, is not meant to be overheated. Doesn't help if you put on a hat, it's not always from the sun. It is a clue for you, like if you get dizzy, or a faint feeling if you are in the sun, that is a signal for you. It's not supposed to be overheated up there. Makes all sorts of different disturbances. So, that is what I will say about that.

D. We really enjoy your company, Bob, you're a real pleasure. I'm sure you're happy that you can finally communicate like this, aren't you?

B. I enjoy yours, too! It's been a long time of preparation. Then again, time doesn't really exist, like Ophelia says. She's reminding me of that. BUT I can sense that there has been a lot of preparation. So that's why I say a long time has been before coming to term and to do this full–out. But she says, "There is no time, Bob, don't be confused." But I sense that it has been a cycle of preparation that has gone on for a long time.

D. You must be the first one from the second dimension that has done this, aren't you? Ask Ophelia.

B. Oh, she says it's not that common, because of the tendency to look upwards, you know. Some people hug the trees and they communicate directly with us. However, to communicate through a vehicle, like this, is somewhat of a new brand...brand? What are you saying? (*He's was looking at and asking Ophelia.*) BRANCH. New branch.

D. Well, there's probably not that many spirits on the second with your personality and interests?

B. Some are shy, but you can communicate directly with them. But I don't know how many would like to do this. They might like to, but some are shy and they don't know what to say really. You have to sort of encourage them.

D. Who knows, maybe you will train your six students to do this?

B. They're curious, because I tell them, sparsely, about what I do.

D. I think the hard part is finding a human that is capable of doing what this one does.

B. Well, you have to be able to blend fully and to sort of trigger certain personality aspects within the vehicle that exists on this plane. So, it's a good match. It's a good match indeed, because this one takes on a completely different shape (*than at home*). I'm thankful for that, because it can somewhat mirror mine. He did say, in the meeting before coming to Earth, that I would have somewhat of a free room to move around and play different aspects in the personality. Give me a lot of free room, it was said, so I would feel like I was seen!

D. Be yourself.

B. Be myself! Huhuhuh! So, that was approved. I remember this one said something like, "I'm gonna have all sorts of different aspects that you can play with, personality wise." So I said, "What would that be?" And this one said, "A little bit you're going to have to figure out by yourself. Let's just say there are like little markers and dots that you can press, like buttons, and you will somewhat appear like who you are, similar like you really are." So I was happy about that, because I don't know if I want to, like an incarnation, that you become someone completely different. So I didn't know if I really wanted that. I wanted to be somewhat myself, and that is what this one was saying, "There will be buttons that you can press within my physical vehicle that will be related to expressions that you will feel familiar with. You just have to find the buttons! You don't get a map of that, you will find it more amusing if you find the buttons yourself,"

D. It didn't take you very long to figure out how to express yourself well. It's been a lot of fun for us.

B. Ohh, well, anyway. I, I will go back and continue my studies and continue the training with my little students. I have been away a lot, and they have been somewhat self–studied. Hehehe. They don't, really. At this point they study in a group, which is what we prefer. But they have been left alone. I left a task for them, or several tasks, and then I said, "I will return and I will see how you solved it." Because they are at that level of group activity solving things.

D. Are they pretty sharp?

B. They're sharp! They're inquisitive. I like that.

D. That's a very good trait. I appreciate it.

B. (*Popping lips*) Anyway. Uuhhhhh! I go.

D. Thank you for joining us.

B. Okay. Bye–bye.

Moons are Different (Mar 5, 2017)

The observations about the moons being structurally different than planets is very interesting, because it is something that may be verified in the future. NASA estimates that if the Moon has a core, it is only about 20 percent of its diameter. Whereas Earth has a core that is around 50 percent of the diameter. Astrogeologists tend to view all planetary bodies through the lens of how the Earth is interpreted. The assumptions of mass, density, internal gravity, and composition are all based on properties and theoretical equations that have a terrestrial origin. Gravity has been described, by our spirit friends, as something that is added to cosmic light and cosmic sound. It seems (to me) that gravity and its counterpart vacuum are what actually create quarks and the subsequent hadrons. Gravity precedes mass, meaning that mass is related to gravity, and not the other way around. The mass and density calculations for Saturn, for example, may be completely in error. Based on its orbit, its mass is assumed to be 95 times that of Earth. Its spherical volume is 765 times the volume of Earth, so its overall density is one-eighth that of Earth, presumably. But what if gravitational force is a combination of forces, include some that are unknown? Such a reinterpretation would completely alter cosmology and the related fields of study.

Bob previously had discussed the importance of hematite to the design of solar systems. All planetary bodies are assumed to have iron cores. When iron bonds with oxygen, it forms hematite (Fe_2O_3). Another oxide of iron is called magnetite (Fe_3O_4). Mars, the red planet, the moon and many other nearby planets have significant concentrations of hematite and magnetite. Bob also clarified that gravity is adjusted by the amount of oxygen that is mixed with certain elements.

D. So, what would you like to talk about today?

B. I do want to address the fact that I am learning more from your lab. When I started with my drawer, with the model with the rocks, you said, "We begin with three planets," even though I know there will be more. The third tends to be where I come in (*the second dimension*), because of the distance to the star. So you said, we don't need to go further than the third. However, I'm kinda fascinated by moons, because I understand the planets and their different uniqueness in its own evolution, where some carry conditions where water can be exposed, and some actually have volcanoes and stuff like that. However, the moons, they're different, they're not the same. It's not the same material like the other ones.

D. Do they have the same core?

B. No, that is the thing! They don't have the same core. Different! Everything is different about them. And it's actually more–, it's like they can float more than the other ones. The other ones (*planets*) are PUT, and they move accordingly. However, those moons that you put out around certain celestial bodies, they appear more hollow. And I don't know why they are there. Because, what is the purpose of it? And you don't TELL me because we haven't GOT there yet. But I can see them and that's why I ask, because they're different. They're not created similar like a planet.

D. They create wave movement on the planet they circle, I guess?

B. Yes, but inside it's more liquid. It is the same material, yet it's not concentrated into a ball. So, within the moon it's a liquid that sort of fills the whole thing (*based on other conversations, the liquid he refers to is the energetic pattern of the material in the core, as found in our lab. Once the moon is in the fish tank, the liquid patterns create elements out of light and sound energy, that stratify and solidify. Moons are not designed the same as planets.*) That's why it appears hollow! SO, it has the gravity, it has some sort of magnetic resonation with the host it circles. BUT there is not a core. So that is why it appears different. But it creates conditions on its host; it works with the water and also acts as a calendar. SO, that's what it does. But I can SEE they are sort of hollow. When we x–ray the model, I can see there is not a dot inside it, so it looks hollow. But you say it's not, it's in a liquid form filling the whole thing. So, a moon is different than a planet because it's placed to operate like a, oh, what did you say? It's like a timer to the host. The host being the planet, of course. It's like having an assistant, I would assume!

D. Does Ophelia's seventh, do they make them?

B. They're not involved with the moons.

D. Oh, really? So it doesn't have like a living entity within it?

B. No. It's like filled with that liquid that I saw in your lab, in those glass tanks. It's filled, it's not congested like a dot.

D. So the Earth is a living being, and the moon doesn't really have an entity in it?

B. No! But it still operates like some sort of companion to its host, whatever that is. Oh, this is probably way beyond my level of learning.

D. How's your drawer coming? I know we started with three, but how many planets do you have now?

B. I'm up to five.

D. What specifically do we talk about?

B. You talk about the distance between, and the relationship between. There's an order here. The first one (*Mercury, in our system*) is merely to create like some sort of channel of heat from the star in the middle. It's like a second heater, it's transforming from the sun to the rest of the other ones that comes after. So, it's not the sun, of course, but it sort of directs the whole thing. So, it's NOT not important, at all. Even though it's like, "Ohhh, there it is, floating inside. Maybe it burns, maybe it doesn't." But it actually creates the conditions for the other cores. And based on where it is, if it's lining up with the planets to come, it creates certain cycles when certain planets need like a rest, to go into hibernation almost. So, it blocks, sometimes, certain waves from the inside out.

I will interrupt to make a comment about Mercury, the regulator. The most simplistic interpretation of what Bob is saying involves the gravitational influences of Mercury on the Sun. As it turns out, there is a cyclic and measurable relationship of Mercury's 88–day orbit to sunspot and solar flux on the surface of the Sun. Mercury has a tidal influence on the unstable subsurface magnetic flux near the surface of the Sun, causing pockets of flux to periodically float up through the convection zone and emerge as sunspots in the photosphere. Solar flares, which shoot large amounts of energy out into the solar system, are often located near sunspots. So, in that regard, it is easy to see Mercury as a conductor of energy. However, it is likely there are other, unmeasurable processes that Bob is talking about; processes that are spiritual and beyond the scope of conventional science.

D. Huh, that's very interesting.

B. You can see that when you study the movement, you said. When they are aligned in a row, it is to create some sort of hibernation, like pausing. Everything, it's like the whole system recharges when they're all aligned in a row, out. It doesn't happen that often, you know. But when it does, it's like the whole cycle ends, it's like rebooting your computer.

D. That's incredibly interesting to me!

B. I think so! And I say, "Why does it reboot? What is it leaving behind, and what is it going to do next?" And that is something we haven't talked about, but I can see them in a row. You show me the planets, in the other model that's yours. You say, "Look here, Bob, if they are aligned in a row directly, then it's like the system gets to be rebooted." I wanted to know how often that happens, and you said it is designed to do so within certain time frames, which is probably big cycles.

D. A lot of revolutions.

B. In my drawer, I have the core, which is representing the sun, and then I have a little one that is orange, which is the one that sort of directs the whole thing. A lot of astronomers don't think it is that important, but it is. It creates the foundation of heat which effects the rest of the system. They only think of the sun, but it's not. You say it's a very big part that the little one has. Just because it doesn't carry any sort of water or stuff like that, it's kind of forgotten, that inner one. (*Apparently, most solar systems are designed to have a planet with a small core in an orbit very close to the star, which assists in the transfer of energy out through the system.*) But then it goes outward, and my system is up to five planets. Now we're moving into the one that I have that carries the liquid form of mercury, and how that makes it really heavy, it sort of balances the whole group. When you come a bit further out, it has more magnesium, you said, but also mercury, which is heavy so it balances the whole thing. I can see that it bounces like this (*Bob was moving Christine's hands up and down*) There is somewhat of an order here.

D. Is this within our solar system?

B. Uranus is one of those that balances. (*A stabilizer.*)

D. So, you're working with our solar system?

B. I'm using ours to compare, and you said Uranus is one of those. It's very heavy. Heavy. That's also someone quite interesting that people don't pay that much attention to. You told me, actually, that all planets in this solar system carries somewhat of an entity of a life form. However, not all are manifested like an individual on legs. But it carries different components for the whole group to be in harmony and okay. Even though number three (*Earth*) might be the big star within this group, the other ones are actually assisting number three to be as prosperous as possible. It's sort of embedded between different energies. The Sun on the inside with heat, but a more structured, solid energy comes in from the outside that sort of balances it. So, it's sort of embedded, I would say. They carry different qualities in order for the whole solar family to operate, even though only one might appear to be the shining star within it, like the Earth. The other ones assist to make it prosperous.

D. That's really fascinating.

B. Well, I'm just repeating what you're saying to me, so I guess you are fascinating! (*Laughs loudly*) Huhuhuh! So, this is what I learn in my lab with you. It's not my lab, of course, but it is my drawer. It is only mine, it's personal, –it has my name on it.

D. Do any of the other planets have any types of lifeforms on them?

B. Pluto did. DID.

D. That's a long way out!

B. Behind. Oh, they were not necessarily sensitive to the dark and the cold. They were behind, behind the planet, back. If it rotates you might see leftovers. We don't talk about that much, you say. It was not like your best project, so we don't talk about that much. But they did exist at one time, way back, observing. They're not there anymore, you said. Looked kinda like a big ant. They didn't have a purpose, really, I guess that was like a Monday project at the factory. Oh, that was not very nice of me. I didn't mean that. Because you said it wasn't one of your finest projects, but they're not there anymore. (*I make a habit of researching anything that can be verified, and it seems about twenty-five percent of Pluto is in continuous darkness. Also, Monday is the day when most manufacturing errors occur, due to human error.*)

D. Do we, on the sixth dimension, work with different life forms, helping to develop their civilizations, or monitor their activities?

B. Uh, you're aware of them. It's like those were some sort of helpers. There was a time when Pluto was very important. This was way before.

D. Before the dinosaurs?

B. Uh, it was the time when the Earth was a greenhouse and it just needed to start blossoming. So, it was way back in the beginning, of sorts. There did seem to be life forms on Earth at the same time, but it was more left alone. So, once you create a greenhouse, you sow all your little things that you want to flourish there, and it takes a little time before you can start to grow. And this was the face (*surface*) of the Earth at that time.

D. After it came out of hibernation? You weren't here then, were you?

B. No. I don't know what they were doing back there. At that time, there was also another one directly after, so they moved in between. Between what is now Pluto and another after that. (*He's saying there was or is another planet beyond Pluto.*) Moved back and forth. They couldn't really adjust energetically to move further in. That's why I see them kind of glued on the back. At that time, the energies within the solar system, out to Pluto, I would assume, was more congested. If you think of it as a vacuum, the vacuum can carry different vibrations. At that time, in order for the Earth to become what it is at this point, the vacuum had a higher density. So, there was no way for outsiders to move inwards. It was sort of in its own creation, you said. So they couldn't move further in. It's FASCINATING when you say it like that, that you can somewhat adjust the energy within the solar system. It's almost like you can dim it, –similar to the sun, it can also be dimmed in some way. Because

Ophelia says you dim it, adjust it like a lamp. But it's also the energy or the vacuum, which you said is conditioned by gravity, so it was actually more dense at that time. At that time, there was NO WAY for my Individuals to be able to operate on the Earth, because it wasn't ready. Because it was too much gravity, it was heavier around it, and the atmosphere wasn't in place at all, so they couldn't operate, really. So, as you create a solar system, the energy within it is more congested and it is heavier, because it is about to become a solar system. After certain things happen, then you change, you can remodel the whole frequency within it. That's how I see the waves. So, when this took place (*the creatures on the backside of Pluto*), the planet didn't move that fast around the sun, they were more still. But as you started to decrease (*the density of the vacuum*), they just started to move! When you create a solar system, it is intact, and at that point planets are somewhat still. As it progresses, you said, you change and decrease and you can dim, so you have it on high, let's say.

D. Kind of like baking energetic bread.

B. And you shift it and things start to move, like a merry-go-round. You put in a little penny and suddenly it goes (*he started singing a carnival song*) toot da toot da doo da doo, and everything starts to move. So, I guess it's something like that. But at this time, nothing on the outside could get in. It's not supposed to, because it was in the process of becoming a solar system, you said. And it was to create the best way possible for the project of the Earth to start blossoming before it started to rotate. The sun, at this point, sort of slowly spun on the inside. That's how it looked, you said. It doesn't rotate when it's in its cradle for becoming, it's more still. Then something starts to move. But, it's not like they start moving at the same time, it's from the inside out, they start. When someone, and who knows who they are, decided, "OK, everything is cooked, everything is ready to go." So, you changed and then the inner one was the first one to start and it just gradually started to move. There were only three operating for a while, up to Earth, and the other ones were still in that congested part. So after a while, all of them started to move. Oh, it's a big project, you can see. So, I pay attention and I look down in the big drawer and I can see what you are saying. I just don't know why.

D. Are the stars and the planets sort of created in place. Do they just materialize?

B. This is what you don't tell me. You don't say how they get there. I can only see when you say, "Oh, here they are, Bob. This is the congested era, when things are about to become." Because it's like planting a seed. It takes a while before it becomes a flower, –in this case a planet. You have to let it be. And then it starts to become and then it's like someone changes the conditions, so the first one starts to move. It's almost like a merry–go–round, and something starts to move. But the other ones are like, "Oh, we're not moving cause we're not ready." And for a LONG time, there were only three moving around, you said. And then the fourth came, and it just continued outwards.

D. Wow, that's really interesting. Thanks for sharing that.

B. Well, this is you. This is what you say, this is in your journal, I guess. You talk to your friends. I'm sure this makes a lot of sense to you. I can see what you are saying, and I can understand. I'm fascinated by the moons, because they came after, you said, the planets started to move. And the moons are almost like little adjustments, like little helpers to its host, I'm thinking. From my perspective, it might be an assistant of sorts. But it has something to do with the conditions on the host. Something with the shadow, it creates a shadow. It's a completely different group, you said, that works with moons. It's like a special group within your group, I guess. (*Several months later, he began calling them the "moon people"*.)

D. On the sixth dimension?

B. Ah. They put them (*moons*) on all sorts of places, I see. You say we can go talk with them sometime. I don't know who they are. They work in disguise in another lab.

D. You said our moon, the Earth's moon, was put in after the three planets disintegrated? (*Forming the Asteroid belt and throwing asteroids and material in all directions through the Solar System.*)

B. After. It came way after. It was to help the host, in some way. Something with cycle and calendar, but also with shade. Put a shade on it. I haven't talked with that special group. You don't seem very eager to introduce me there, so it must be way in the future. I don't know who they are. You also say that they don't communicate as much, not even with you.

D. That seems secretive.

B. They seem to be very mysterious. But they work only with creating moons for hosts.

D. That would be a specialty, I guess.

B. Yes, it is, it is very different. They put it on certain specific places, and we haven't talked about why. I see they are different and they are put in afterwards. Like perfecting a painting, I would assume.

D. Like putting a nice frame on it.

B. Huh huh. I'm putting frames on stuff. That's what we talk about. I guess that would be it, and I will be back to talk about more things.

D. Other things in the vault?

B. In the vault, yes, we haven't been in the vault for a while. Maybe Ophelia thinks it's time for us to return to the vault. Maybe we should just dust off some of your old journals, because they're there, you know. Oh, Ophelia says, "You would like that, would you?" I say, "It's not for me, of course, it's for Lasaray." Then Ophelia smiles and says, "You just hang along for the ride when we report, but you remember, you see things." That's what Ophelia says.

D. Well, thank you all for coming. It's really nice to have you back. Alright, my friend, until we meet again.

B. Oh, we're not very far away. Hmm, okay, bye bye.

Isaac, the Gravity King (Mar 12, 2017)

There are always unexpected bits of information that come through during our sessions. In this one, Bob once again mentions an Earth-sized planet beyond Pluto. Astronomers have yet to discover the planet, but if the spirits say it is there, I assume they are correct. Planets only reflect light, and at distances more than 40 times further from the Sun than Earth, they are difficult to detect.

Bob first talks about how gravity, or the patterns for gravity, will be added to the model of his solar system. If it is designed correctly, it will float. Otherwise, it will collapse or sink.

B. (*Bob came in after Isaac, making popping sounds.*) Is it my turn?

D. Did you step on any toes?

B. No. He's friendly though. Hehehe. He's not as scary as some of the other ones who just glances at me. He sees me and he laughs and he poke me in the belly. He's like a friend, like

Ophelia, he smiles. He's tall, as big as you, but he communicates similar like Ophelia. Oh, I KNOW WHERE HE BELONGS! HE MIGHT BE THE ONE THAT COMES AND SEE IF MY SOLAR SYSTEM FLOATS! Did not see that! But if he does, I'm good! Huhuhuhuh! He likes me too! I'm good. Hehe

D. Are you afraid someone would come and not approve?

B. I don't know, I don't want there to be anyone who I can't read. I don't want that at all. Isaac is like on the border of eighth and ninth. He's a gravity king, of sorts!

D. So, he's the one that's going to see if your solar system floats?

B. I hope so, I don't know. I hope he's not sending an assistant. I hope he's the one putting gravity in my fish tank, pour it in. If it's Isaac, I'm definitely taking classes up there! He hasn't invited me, but I'm going to ask. Because now I've been operating on six and seven, and also in the library and the vault, but you know, –I'm open! I can go on a little tour, maybe. I'm gonna ask, I'm going to send in a request for that! Maybe I need to go and take gravity classes before we put my system in the tank, because how will I understand what's happening otherwise? I can claim that. I'm tricky too, ya' know! Hahhaha. I think I would like to go with him one day.

D. Is he friendly?

B. He's friendly! He's like Ophelia, friendly, he smiles! The other one didn't smile that much; he just glances at me. (*Referring to Jeshua, who he did not know at this point in his story.*) But I'm sure he's friendly on the inside, but I can't see it when I can't read personality waves. I know that Ophelia has the ability to just transform her wisdom and her being into an emotional frequency. It's like you are collecting those dots, creating pictures for me. Ophelia does the same thing, but she sends out an emotion, and I understand and I resonate with that very easy. And Isaac has the ability to do the same. He's really close with Ophelia. Like a couple, almost. I wish they were, –they could adopt me! Huhuhuh! (*Popping his lips while he's thinking.*) I would like to go with him one day, but I don't know if he's going to take me. He's happy, friendly.

D. I'm sure that will happen. Since he's going to be coming to our meetings all the time, you can ask him.

B. I hope he's going to be the one who decides if my solar system is approved. I DO think he will approve. I hope it's him, because

I think I would be a little bit ahead. But he's friendly. HIGHLY skilled! He has a lab that is different, I'm sure! Something that is very flowing.

D. I'm sure you'll be able to go visit.

B. So! You have a question?

D. Well, let's see...

B. Tick—tock—tick—tock—tick—tock.

D. (*Laughing*) Well, how is your project in our lab?

B. Well, I'm pretty content with the inner ones (*planets*), because they are the easier ones. They don't come in so many varieties. As you move outwards, it comes more in choices that interacts (*with the planet*), and that is the trick with learning. So you create something first that only has like two components, then you might have like four, five, and so on. The further out you get, it's more tricky, because you have to coordinate the materials used, but also you have to add the color map that's gonna resonate from within. It's been mentioned about the core and how that is the foundation of everything. So, even if I create a planet, a ball, that is highly functioning in what is supposed to do as a host, BUT, if the inside, the core, isn't matching what I'm planning to do, if I'm planning to create something with life forms on it and my core is too big and it's not concentrated with knowledge and resonating with the Individuals I'm gonna put on it, THEN, it's completely useless! And that is why there are more choices when it comes to the core. Sometime I wish I could just make a moon, because it's floating inside. But you said, "That's not what we're doing. That's not what you wanted to learn, anyway." But that seems easier, because it's just floating, it's constant. You have a form and it is in a certain big or small size and you just fill it up like a balloon. Pphhhhhffttt! And off it goes. But if I'm gonna create a planet, then I have to take from the jars that exist for cores, which are different than the ones that's going to be for celestial individuals (*planets*). So, I have different jars based on what I am trying to do. AND, I should tell you, the first thing you do is create the body itself, the planet itself. Once that is established, you put in a core, –in this model, at least. I'm not sure if that is done when you actually release it, if you're going to make something for real. But I create first the form, and the INTENTION it has. You said, "What intention do you have, Bob, with that one?" And I say, "I don't know. Maybe it's just gonna regulate heat?" And you said, "No, because you already have one of those." Then I said, "Oh, okay." And you say, "What's the intention, Bob, behind this one?" And I said, "Well, I would like this one to have some sort of water and life forms, –maybe fish." And then you say, "OK, let's try to make something that will have fish and sea." And that is what we do. And then you say, "Based on what you've been taught, what jars will you use?" You know, just for the form, of course, here. And I say, "Okay, I will use these jars," –and I do. And then you say, "Okay. If you have this established, what sort of core resonates with the surface, if you are going to have oceans and fish?" And I said, "With no trees?" And you said, "You did not create trees." So, you know, this specific example did not have trees, so the core has to be adjusted for oceans and fish, ONLY. So, SEE how many different options there are? (*Christine and I laughed about this because of the innocent way he inquired why there were no trees, even though he had not included any in his design. Part of the underlying reason Gergen sent him to our lab to study was so he would reflect and analyze various scenarios before settling on an intention.*)

D. Indeed, it must be confusing.

B. It is! But the good part is, only one is going to be a living creation of sorts, like Earth. Only one in my solar system, but that one takes time!

D. You have to add patterns for everything you want?

B. Indeed! There's plenty of jars, and you said, "What is the intention? What intention do you have with that one?" And I said, "Oh, you know." And then I try to see what you are thinking, but I cannot. And then I say, "Maybe this one is just gonna be just for show." And then you say, "Nothing is for show, Bob, everything has a purpose." —It's a lot to take in.

D. Within our solar system, what other purposes are there on different planets?

B. Oh, we don't talk about all of them, yet. Oh, let's see what you said...Mercury is some sort of little conductor, almost, to the rest of them. It resonates with heat. Pluto, on the other end, similar importance, but resonates with the outer frequencies that makes it (*the solar system*) intact. So, the outer frequencies, all the way into the star, the Sun, holds the whole thing in position. As well as Mercury is the conductor for the sun, in some way, Pluto, way out, operates similar for ah, what is that? It's like the whole grid, the whole field. So, it's like the

Sun in the middle, versus something else outside. I don't know what that is. Pluto operates similar as a conductor, but with the outer frequencies. There's actually another planet outside of Pluto, sort of in motion.

D. How big is it?

B. Little bit like Earth. Something outside sort of moving around, not still. But this is complex. I don't see outside, but it holds the whole thing in position within the family.

D. Are you glad you started studying this?

B. I am, even though I'm not sure how I will use it in my second dimension lab. But I'm sure it's going to solve itself. Because it is about creating form, and I'm learning about different ways of creating form. And it can be adapted in other realities as well, –like the new humanoid. That's what I think. If I'm creating a new form, or if that's gonna come in the cloud, the manual of a new humanoid, then the inside has to resonate similar like the core of the planet. What INTENTION is it with this new humanoid? And then when that is established, then we change the insides, the organs and the engine and everything within. (*The second dimension get instruction manuals on how to create or modify life forms from "the cloud". The manuals are put there by the higher dimensions who work with the Earth reality. See Wave 1 for more information.*)

D. You are an expert on the engine.

B. I'm becoming one! (*He thought I meant the sun, but realized I meant the engine in a human*) Oh, that! That I am! Yes, I am, the engine I am, indeed. So, I guess that would be it, but you can see that it is somewhat of a challenge. Because when you looked at me and asked, "What is the intention, Bob, with it?" And I said, "You haven't told me about the cycles and what it is supposed to experience, so how will I know what intention I have with it?" And we laugh a little bit. But you push me, really, and I like that. I know you push me in a gentle, happy way, and I can push you right back, I can tickle you. But you're kind of firm in the way you teach as well, so it's not just play. I guess the tricky part is to understand what intention I apparently must have with things. I get that, I do. So, I will think about that, –what intentions. You said, "If you don't have an intention, and you put it and create it, and if the inside is sort of hollow or it doesn't resonate with the intention on the surface, or its location among the other ones, then it's not going to float, Bob."

I don't know if I need intentions with all of them, but you said that I do. But it's more tricky with that one, when there is supposed to be creatures on it. I do wanna have that, of course, I don't wanna have just like dead objects. So I do wanna have that, it's just more tricky than the other ones. Sometimes I wish I could just make a moon.

D. That would be relaxing, almost.

B. Sometimes I feel like that would almost be a little holiday.

D. Maybe we can do that, just work on a moon.

B. Work on a moon with the moon people. Well, that would be it, and I will return to my projects and the jars, and I will have some sort of intention, clearly. That is what I will focus on.

D. Well, thank you, my friend, for joining us today. I look forward to talking with you soon.

B. Well, bye bye, bye bye.

Side Effects in the Drawer (Mar 30, 2017)

As Bob retells his memories of us working together in the lab, he is able to give a moment–by–moment narration of how we resolved problems he encountered. There is a lot to be learned about the process of creation, simply by listening to his steady stream of questions and comments. Learning in the spirit world never ceases, so as certain knowledge is acquired, other doors are opened that direct the soul towards another distant goal. In this case, during the testing phase, he noticed the surface temperature on his living planet was too high. So, he began tossing out options to fix it, before realizing what caused the problems.

B. Ahmmm. Opp. (*He began making a popping sound with his lips, which he did for a long time.*) Oohhhh! I do make my presence known, so here I am! And sometimes I like to begin with a grand entrance. Maybe not all the time, but today I feel like I wanna talk more about my drawer. Because there are like side effects that I have encountered with my project, and I wish to come to a solution. And it is because, you know, the–the–the one that regulates heat, it doesn't really regulate as it should, because my other ones (*the planets in his model of a solar system*) don't seem to get access to all their supposed energy flow from the heater on the inside. So, it is some sort of side effect of what I created as number one after the sun. (*The sun is the heater, and the first planet is the regulator, which acts as the conductor of heat into the rest of the solar system.*) I wanted to begin new, or maybe add another one, because I did see that you had three in a row, one time. So, I wanted to create another one to regulate heat, because it seems like my Individuals on the one that I have life forms on, it's a little bit too hot. So I wanted to maybe push my living planet further out. But you say, "It is where it should be; the measurements are correct, based on where they are located from the central star in the middle, Bob." BUT I wanted to change the regulator, because I'm pretty sure I can't change the star. But you say, "Everything is correct." But something is clearly wrong, because it is TOO HOT, too hot on my planet. And I created creatures with fur, –and then I thought maybe they shouldn't have fur. But you say, everything is correct, there is something else...ohhh, I haven't done atmosphere yet! Ohhh, I see.

D. That will cool it down!

B. That will it cool it down, definitely! Oh, I haven't done the atmosphere yet. Oh, okay. So, that is gonna be next. You say that I'm taking classes about the atmosphere. You laugh about this. You knew about this all along, –that my creatures would sweat! But you didn't say anything. That's kinda shady! I put them there and they almost melt! You didn't say anything, but now I know I'm gonna need to make atmosphere.

D. They needed shade.

B. They needed shade from the clouds! Oh, that's a completely different jar, the atmosphere jar. It's more liquid in that one, it never gets solid. Oh.

D. Where do you take classes for that?

B. Everything is with you, so I don't go to a big lecture room here. However, there are certain mentors that have been introduced to me. But they don't speak directly to me, so sometimes I'm sitting and I'm waiting and I hear like, tick click tick tick, and I wait for you to sample it into something I understand. As we have progressed in the drawer, there have been different tutors that have made themselves known. Atmosphere is up.

D. Do you like them, are they friendly?

B. Uhhh, I don't feel either way, because they don't talk directly to me, but they are highly skilled. One gave me a book. That book was also tricky, because as I opened it, it wasn't papers at all, it was energetic, like it was three dimensional. He said, to–you–to–me, "This is atmosphere, because it carries different layers, like vibrational states. It's not just one vibration, it blends. Atmosphere has a depth in its original structure. So, this book is about understanding the depth that exists in certain things that are created." Atmosphere is one, because it's moving, — unlike a planet, it is what it is, it doesn't change and move around, becoming like a square! (*Laughing loudly*) That would look stupid! So, it is what it is; if it's round, it is round; if it's rocky, it's rocky. However, atmosphere, for instance, it's shifting, —and that is tricky! This is highly advanced! Because you know, it's almost as advanced as the core.

D. How are you doing with that, how many planets do you have?

B. It's still only five. Because my creatures, they melted! And I wanted to change the regulators. And you said, "No, everything is as it should be, Bob, we have measured the distances between them all, and it is as it should be. What is missing?" And I was like, "Maybe if I add another regulator on the inside?" And you said, "No, that's not it," so I said, "Maybe I move my planet further out?" And then you said, "No, it's exactly where it should be, based on the distance from the sun. —What can be wrong, here?" And I say, "Ohh..." and then you send me a picture and suddenly I understood that I did not have atmosphere. I need rain and I need clouds. Because clouds create shade, and as shade comes it actually creates, -that location can go into a natural hibernation, like a snooze. And that is what I didn't have. So, that is why there are not so many living life forms in the desert, for instance. Because in the desert there's not that much clouds, and it doesn't create shade, so there is no way for life forms to not overheat. So, clouds create that certain time to rest, if you like. It's important to have clouds, if you want to have living creatures on that specific area. And then you say, "Where do you want to put them?" (*His Individual and plants.*) And I say, "Well, you know, I wanna put them, -not on the poles, because that is tricky-, I wanna put them located somewhere in the middle." So, you say, "Okay. Then we have to adjust, because there is motion that goes on, based on winds and certain things, to create passages where clouds are moving through." So NOTHING is just made by chance here, at all. So, this was what was lacking. I can clearly see this, because all my creatures were overheating. And I said, "Maybe I shouldn't have fur on them." And then you say, "It doesn't matter if you have fur or not, there's something else missing." And this was it. So, this was the back of the coin, so to speak, on my solar system. I clearly had everything calculated right, everything was where it was supposed to be, but my Individuals were melting, and that was not good at all. So, atmosphere is the class that is up. Uhhhh.

D. Did you have to include patterns for atmosphere when you make the core?

B. No, because...Oh, well, well, yes, indeed, that is true. They have to communicate and resonate. The core is not in place in my planet, anyway, yet. So, in this project, the core is put in in the end, when everything on the surface, and this is clearly also connected to the surface, is established. So, the core and the atmosphere in this case, do communicate. So, that is correct. But, at this specific point, my planet with lifeforms have...neither! That is where we are at.

D. Well, you're making progress, though.

B. Yes, indeed. It was just the fact that they were melting that I didn't get. I do understand about the clouds, I do know that creatures need the shade in order for them to move into a rebooting phase, if you like; hibernation can be called the same thing, but it is the fact of being able to reboot yourself, gaining your energy. As you are in a warmer climate with no clouds providing shade, you simply release energy from your vehicle, and that is why there's not that many creatures in that region. I didn't want to have that at all, because I know it's tricky. Nothing can survive, so I didn't create that, I went around that problem quite easily. You asked me what I wanted to have on my planet, and I said I'm NOT having deserts on mine.

D. Is your solar system going to be put somewhere, like the little star you made?

B. It's highly unlikely. You don't make solar systems by yourself and just launch them, either. You work in a group where you release. So, you know, I'm learning. A lot of this has to do with how objects resonate, not only to the sun, here, but also to the neighbors on each side, primarily. But it is the fact of correlations between energy sources that I'm learning here. If my solar system would be launched, I would be pleasantly surprised, but it's still a ways off. I do have ideas about maybe how you can improve your work, with different things. Maybe you can make planets where emotional stress is not to be found, and maybe where there is not a lack of empathy. (*Sometimes*

Bob speaks in double negatives. What he would like are planets with no emotional stress, and for a lot of empathy between life forms.) So, I'm actually making you aware of creating foundations for individuals who are, or could be, less aggressive. Why not create hosts where the conditions are different? So, I'm asking about that; if the host in some way triggers certain reactions on its surface, or if it's something else, –so I'm curious about that. We haven't talked about it really, but I feel like there's so much more to this, and it's not just a dead, round object with a core in it—so I'm wondering if it can be improved. If, let's say Earth, carries certain elements that create events on its surface, that whoever we put upon it stumbles upon certain events and lessons, then maybe we could change the core or the planet itself? So, if it's dirty, maybe those who walk on it becomes dirty, regardless of how pure they are. So I ask about that, if maybe that can be improved. Because we improve organs, of course, based on certain shifts and changes that are upcoming, so to speak. I'm pretty sure—because you talked about a planet in another reality with a lot of metal in its structures, not iron, it was magnesium or something. Anyway, it created angry individuals, it created frustration in their mental realm. THAT wasn't good, clearly, so that reality has been on pause. "It was something with the elements that actually created dysfunctional minds," you said. So, I–I–I–I...we don't talk about that in my drawer, but since I know this, then I wonder about Earth and I wonder if there might be ways to improve. And I ask, "If you have the power and the ability to create peaceful realities, then I'm putting that request forward." So, that is what I do, I put that forward. Because in that case, my furry beings will never have their fur taken, and no one will make the worms look sad. So I'm simply saying, since we are creating creatures on the surface, if you do your job, maybe differently, then it might be easier for the others of us to follow in a more harmonious manner. So, that is what I ask. But you don't really answer. But you did tell me that I need not to worry about that in my creation.

D. I still like the way you think, though. If we created a planet like that, would you want to leave Earth and go work on it?

B. I know of planets that are more like a big greenhouse. You can visit and put your project (*plant or animal*), just release them there and they will just flourish. And you can go have a look–

see to see how they progress over time, because they are not going to be interfered with by other activities. So, whatever you put there, and whatever destiny or life purpose you had for that specific creature or plant, will come to term. Because there is not any outside factors that will interfere with each individual, each entity there, because it is like a greenhouse. So, anyway, just a quick hello, to sort of ask about the side effects in my drawer. I will continue to look at the atmosphere, because I do need the clouds, and I do want my Individual to have fur.

D. Thank you for coming to join us today. It's always a pleasure.

B. Oh OH, OOOHHHHHOOOOOHHH, so I go. Okay, Bye bye.

Atmosphere is Operating Correctly (May 7, 2017)

D. So how are you progressing on your drawer? How is it looking?

B. Oh, I have the atmosphere in place. And the cycles, –I wanted to have cycles, to create night and day, because that is a part of the atmosphere, actually. So, that is in place. So, you have the atmosphere, and you make the planet rotate, and that is how you create the cycles of day and night, as well as months, you know, the cycles in general. So, I put it in motion. I put the core in, and it is moving and the atmosphere is operating correctly, –so I have cycles now. I am in that position where I'm going to put back my Individual, because I actually removed it. I said, "I'm not gonna put it there as I experiment. I'm not doing that." (*He temporarily removed the energetic pattern of his Individual.*)

D. Well done, my friend!

B. I can clearly see that the atmosphere is operating correctly. And also, the rotation is in harmony with the atmosphere, so it creates day and night cycles. So it's time to put the Individual back in. It's not like putting the Individual itself, clearly, but you implement the pattern that the Individual carries. This is how I create the solar system; I add different patterns, like a little map, carrying colors and tones in order for things to become. It's like planting a seed, but instead of planting a seed, I'm planting, into the awareness of my project, the pattern that my Individual carries for it to become.

D. So you don't have to give it grass and things to eat?

B. It's already there. Everything is in place, except for my Individual, now.

D. Will he be mobile and move around?

B. Yes, indeed. He doesn't swim that well, so I'm having him far away from water, and I give him a lot of room. My continent that I have, I only actually have one big continent at the moment, because I haven't made the continents to move or shift yet. And that is also part of, in order for the continents to start moving, you implement an additional pattern in the atmosphere. So, it's the eighth that makes the continents move. But, before I do that, I want to make sure that my Individual is adapting well on the one continent that I have. It's a big one though, so it has a lot of room to move around. And now it has vegetation for it to eat. So I can watch, because I can somewhat speed up time, and that's what we do. If we were to sit in a regular timeline and wait for something to occur, then that would take forever. SO, we somewhat manufacture time here, and this is tricky for you, but there is a group within this group that comes in and there is an additional, mmm, I wouldn't say element, because it's not something you can touch, but they add something that looks like a light sparkle. And it creates a manufactured time, so I can see what will develop on this specific project of mine. You add that so I can see, you know, how one becomes two, and two becomes four, and so forth. So I can see all my Individual s. And then when I see that that is functioning well, I can add additional things. If you want to see projects before you launch the solar system, then you create the manufactured time evolution. The Evolution Group, they're a silent group. They move around silently. I call them the Evolution Group, because they, in some way, they can trick time, because time doesn't exist. Even though time doesn't exist, cycles still take place. AND WHY IS THAT, you think? Because the Evolution Group has been there and done something with that sparkle. That's what I see, I see sparkles. It's like creating, it moves things forward. Magical, almost.

D. Magic time dust!

B. Magic time dust! Huhuhuh (*He is laughing loudly.*) Evolution Group, they belong somewhere up in, where are they? They do operate with atmosphere and the eighth, because I see it as an element, but yet not. But they come in some way from the tenth, Evolution Group. I don't know them at all. I don't feel like I want to go, necessarily, because they are really silent. I–I don't think they will speed up MY evolution, but I will not blend in at all—

so I'm not going there. Maybe if you invite them, maybe that could work, if you invite them here. But I don't feel like I should go there.

D. They might look like the one you saw last week, the big orb.

B. Might be. Quiet. I don't feel comfortable, because they...It's like putting you in Japan, you know, you don't understand at all what the signs are saying, or anything. It's the same thing. I don't want to go there at all. I am curious, but I am content with you telling me, or Isaac telling me, instead. So, I'm not sure I want to go. Maybe they belong with the Master Mind? If they do, I might want to go.

D. You could follow them, at a safe distance.

B. My feeling is that they could detect me, and I, I don't want to, because if they detect me, then what if they put some sort of evolution dust on me and I go somewhere else? Because they just emerge from out of nowhere, and then leave. They come and leave, come and leave, and I DON'T KNOW THEM. I don't want to be detected like somewhat of a spy. (*He then gave a very weak, nervous laugh.*) Hu hu hu hu hu.

D. If they sprinkle the dust on you, you'll end up somewhere else.

B. I don't know what happens then, if they sprinkle the dust on me. What happens with my evolution?

D. You'll suddenly get really old!

B. Oh ohohoho, like Gergen! And in a second!

D. You'll bypass and miss out on all kinds of things.

B. Nay. Nay, nay, I don't want that. Anyway, they come in and they can do this, but I'm not sure they are gonna do that with my solar system. But in general, they do that when they work with you, when you work with big systems, like galaxy systems. I DO know you are doing that. And I DO know that there are council members from eight, nine, and ten, that are observing the galaxy work that you are doing. So, I am willing to go with YOU to observe this, because if you're there, I'm sure it's going to be fine. Maybe they have some sort of stage, or a little seating, where I can watch you work?

D. Like Ophelia's classroom?

B. Like Ophelia's classroom. I kinda would like that. If that is on your agenda, on my learning ladder, then I think I'm ready to climb!

D. That sounds like fun.

B. It could be. But I'm not sure if I'm allowed to bring my notebook. It might be that I have to see and remember in my computer area. There might be secrecy here.

D. Maybe that self–study is good practice.

B. Ahh. But yet, this is like a really fascinating show indeed, because there are just so many involved. The Evolution Group, the Element Group, atmosphere...why isn't Ophelia there? She didn't go. I don't know, maybe you tell me. But I am fascinated by what I can see here, because it's not a solar system, it's like a major galaxy. It's supposed to balance, you say, where it's going to be launched. It's like a hole somewhere that has occurred. And when a hole occurs, you say, it's like the system next to it, what scientists think sucks in (*makes a sucking sound*), but some actually moves away from it. So it creates this space of emptiness in the middle, and those need to be patched up. SO, when there are certain, which scientists call black holes, in some way it is a hole, but it is an empty space. And you have to patch it up, you say. Something occurred in some web, not close to here, it's further away, but it still needs to be patched up.

I am going to interrupt here to make a comment about "black holes", which are not at all what scientists think they are. The spirits said that these are not suns or planets, but another type of stellar object with a very high amount of gravity. These objects are used to stabilize galaxies and hold them in certain patterns. An interesting note to Bob's observation is that recent research by NASA confirms that what they call black holes actually repels over eighty percent of the nearby matter, instead of gobbling everything up, as the mathematical oracles predict.

D. Those spots release a lot of energy, don't they?

B. Yes, indeed. They can suck things in, I'm sure. But a lot of it is actually moving away from it. When things are moving away from it, that emptiness that looks like a black hole becomes larger. You said you patch it up with a major one (*galaxy*), so you somewhat create another one and put it in, so they balance as a whole in the web, and so that specific fish tank is intact. If it's not taken care of, things will wobble, you say. If there are too many unattended zones that appear to be empty, like a vacuum, then it wobbles. In order for things to not wobble, because there is motion here, similar like summer and spring, like cycles. But if there are holes, then those cycles do not take place. It either goes too fast, or it stops. You want the motion to be in sync, and in harmony. Everything works anti–clockwise, you say, and that's what we see here. This is clearly high–tech. I can see that; I can see that. But you are patching up a big hole here. And that's why the Evolution Group is there, because they have seen that the intention of the fish tank, or this area, has not been operating according to its predestined timeline. So the Evolution Group is here to give their expertise, I would assume, in order for you to understand how to create this galaxy when you patch it up, so we're back on track again. That's how I see it, that's what you say.

D. Pretty impressive work, from a human perspective.

B. Yes indeed, it is! So I AM willing to go. But the problem being, because if you don't speak the way I understand, it might just be me sitting there, and it is somewhat dark in this lab. And it's not like I can just trot down and stand next to you. Nay, oh, maybe it's better you just tell me afterwards. But I AM fascinated, I am indeed. But this is what the haste was all about.

D. Okay, that's good to know.

B. Because too many dots like this creates dysfunction in the evolution that is intended for that region. Then it creates an effect in the entire web, you said. But it's not like you are a patch–up police, like you get an alarm, an SOS, and you have to go. This one has been going on for a while, and it's too big. That's why the Evolution Group is there. But this one is a big one, and it creates disharmony in the web. That's what you said. And that is the haste, and I don't want to be in the way of haste, of course. So, I self–study, I do. I study up on my Individual, where to put it. And I made the atmosphere. And I'm going over and adjusting details on my project, in order for it to be as optimal as possible when I launch my Individual.

D. Well, at least you are not forced to wonder where I went.

B. Nay, you told me. You said, "I'm just around the corner, Bob." But I don't know what corner that is, because I don't leave the room, necessarily, so what corner is that? You are going to a big lab place, a different one than I've been attending to. (*Popping lips as he contemplates.*)

D. I guess, if everything works, are we going to launch your system?

B. Well, if it floats, because it's not supposed to collapse—like yours wasn't launched because that would create a hole, I would assume, a black, empty space. But you said my little solar project would be somewhere. At the moment my planet has a core, and it has an atmosphere, and the cycles are in place, so it has the night and seasons and so forth, so the Individual is about to be established in its memory, like a color pattern that I put in.

Bob is shown my First Project (May 7, 2017)

When Bob became discouraged about how his solar system was progressing, he was shown Lasaray's first solar project. Bob saw the model had collapsed, and he quickly identified the problem. He realized that everyone goes through the same stages of learning, and he was actually doing better than Lasaray did. So, with that simple demonstration, Bob's confidence was restored.

D. You've become a very good communicator. (*He pops his lips, listening.*)

B. I have, indeed. I have absolutely, indeed. Because at first, I didn't know how this would operate, really. I focus a lot of my energy into the voice area in this one. I learned that if I focus all my attention in that region, instead of spreading myself out, it will operate at its best.

D. That was in the manual, wasn't it?

B. It was in the manual, it was in the manual. (*He was nodding in agreement.*) That was what I was supposed to do, according to Ophelia. She said, "Only focus on the throat area, you don't have to spread out." But I didn't know, so I wanted to spread out and see how certain different things operated. She let me, but then again, I understood it wasn't functioning that well at all. With the Master Mind, when we merge with like trees and stuff like that, we move around and spread out, if you like. But Ophelia said there's no need for me to focus on the feet here. So I don't ever project my awareness into this one's feet. She said, "The only thing you are here to do is project your energy into the throat area, and somewhat into the computer as well. Because it's about sending up signals into the computer, in order for images to take place." So that's what I do, I send pictures up into the computer in this one, that's why she can see things.

D. And you also share your delightful personality.

B. Ughhh, heeee, you know, because in many ways, I also feel like people are taking a lot of things too seriously. So I want to blend in a little different angle to this reality, to just make a little more sunshine in the head. Because no one gets happy if they're told with a whip how to do things. No one gets happy about that. So if you say something, and you do it in a way that is a little bit funny and happy, which I try to do, so maybe with my perspective they will listen more. That's how I learn the best! I don't learn at all if someone is not happy and joyful. That's why I somewhat struggled the first time in your lab, because I didn't know, they didn't express any joyful activities, so it was hard to learn. That's also why I don't like the self-study, because it doesn't come in a joyful frequency, the messages. So I learn best when there is motion and also the vibration of sound, tones, and joy. I learn best like that, and you learned that quite quickly. Because first you gave me all these books with pictures and dots, and I didn't like that at all, and I started to drift quite quickly. You recognized that I wanted to engage in my learning more, and you somewhat adapted to that.

D. So, do we go out and look at things now?

B. Yes, indeed. That's why you took me to the sphere room and the show room, because I do want to move around. So you show me things and we go places. What we have been doing, actually, is that we have gone and seen your prior projects, like your drawers. Then I see what you have done. When you were a little sparkle, you had drawers as well. You encouraged me to understand that this is my first project in my first drawer. And then you showed me your first drawer, –and that made me happy, because that didn't float AT ALL! HUHUHUHUH! And that encourages me to continue, because I see where you are at now. But when I see your baby project, your first one that didn't float because the cores were too close in between, that makes me feel better about my progress. They didn't bump into each other, necessarily, but they were operating in disharmony, so they never progressed into their full potential, that's what you said. That's why I need to understand the distance between the cores, where my planets are traveling. The trick is to have the exact measurements between the two on each side, because each celestial body in the system carries a different elemental structure. If they are too close, they somewhat rub off on each other so no one is operating correctly. If they're too close, they somewhat rub off—that's what you said. And if they're too wide apart, they don't communicate with their neighbor. The elements put into the solar system are different further out. It is not by chance. You can't put, let's say, the one (*planet*) that has a lot of magnesium in it closer in, because the whole system will somewhat wobble. But, if it is too wide apart, it's like they don't hear each other—you can see it like that. They do not take in the signals from each other as they are supposed to, in order for the whole system to operate, and this is when the solar system doesn't float.

D. Huh, I understand that. That makes sense.

B. So, you want to make sure everything is exactly correct. Everyone thinks, you know, that it is only to the sun (*planet and sun, only*), but it's not. The ones on each side are equally important. But if it wobbles, like up and down, then the planets are too far apart. But if it they don't move forward in their course, then they are too close.

D. Ah, that makes sense.

B. That's how it looks when you put it in. (*He begins laughing.*) Huh, your solar system didn't float! So you encouraged me, when I get a little bit like, "Uhhhhh" (*sounding frustrated*), you remind me that we are all beginners, at one point. And you show me this little model that I can look at that didn't float. In your specific case, number three, four, and five were too close. So they became somewhat like a lump. I can see that in the drawer you showed me here. This was your first baby project—when you were a sparkle, I would assume.

D. Could you tell what was wrong with it, just by looking at it?

B. Yes, indeed. Because the sun is correctly done, and number one, outside the sun is correct. Two is also okay, but then there is something with three, four, and five. And as I can see in this drawer, they merged so the cores are not in line. They clogged up together and they didn't move forward. They were stuck. And that is why the rest of the solar system somewhat collapsed. So, you remind me of that, and you say you can only learn by making mistakes. If you don't make mistakes, you never learn. You only learned by textbook, but you don't get to be a super-designer if you have not encountered certain mistakes and falters in your system. This is why, in this case, in order for mistakes to appear, you are left alone. And this is what you say about the self-study. Because you got books, and you created this, clearly, all by your lonesome with only your books. And then you showed me there is a progress with things. And I know now you do big galaxy work with your friends, and you would never have become a master designer of galaxies, if that didn't take place in the beginning. That's what you say.

D. Huh. That's a good lesson.

B. So, you are forced, in your training, to reflect and operate only by manuals. So, you don't get someone telling you what is wrong and not wrong. But you humor me, because I'm learning differently. I'm not supposed to make a galaxy, I'm sure, anyway. So, the conditions are somewhat different. But I can see by only MY training that that didn't work (*my first project*).

D. See, you're better than I was when I was a starting.

B. (*Laughs loudly.*) OH, huhuh. Well, you know, the difference being, is that you help me and we talk as we progress, and you did that all by yourself with a manual. I guess that is why you sort of tried to introduce the manner of reflection into my system, but then you realized that it didn't really work as well, anyway.

Solar System as Chakras (May 11, 2017)

The idea that the solar system is designed as chakras makes it easier to see the whole unit as a single living entity, which it is. Just like the different layers in a human, each planet has a role within the group. The planets communicate with and assist each other on their journey. The outer planets protect and stabilize the inner ones, making life possible on Earth. Venus and Mars have a significant role in the rotation of our planet, as well as the atmosphere.

B. (*Bob began making noises, sucking his lips and snorting.*) That was a funny noise! (*Laughing.*)

D. Hello, Bob.

B. Hello. Hello, hello. I drew new maps. I've made new maps and gave to Ophelia. Isaac saw them too, and Zachariah saw them too, because they're going to be filed. I did new maps, color patterns. Color pattern maps.

D. What were these maps of?

B. One is just for regular berries, you know, but then I also learned more about the color pattern when it comes to my solar system.

I'm moving outwards now, and I am going to make the one that comes after my Individual planet. I'm making that yellow, because...you wanna know why I'm making it yellow?

D. I do!

B. Indeed, because it's gonna resonate, what you taught me as a trick, when I made my solar system, is that they can somewhat resonate with the chakra system. You told me that when I make my first model, I'm gonna work with it in a way of like the chakra system. Meaning that the sun would represent the head, the crown chakra, let's say. I'm moving actually from that direction, which was somewhat of a surprise, but that is what it's supposed to do. I'm familiar with the way, not necessarily chakras, but centers, power centers, and what tones they follow. You told me when I created my system that if I studied up on the centers that I am familiar with, that exist in ALL different parts of nature, then I could mirror that in my solar system. So in this specific case I'm mirroring that. So in the next planet I'm using a lot of the vibration of yellow. And yellow resonates, you would think, probably with the sun, but it does not. So the sun in this case would resonate with the vibration of white. So, it's a little bit different. But the next planet is gonna be vibrating in the tone yellow, but I also implemented a tone in it, because you said you can do two things. You can either have it with only color patterns, or you can add color patterns AND sound patterns. And I chose to do both.

D. I sort of follow what you are saying.

B. Ohh, I studied up on all these centers. And you said they have to come in somewhat of an order, because they carry higher vibrations. And in this case the higher vibrations are inside, where the sun is, and they go slower further out. Let's say the regulator of heat, next to the sun, that is that one's main agenda. So everyone has somewhat of a first priority agenda within the system. And the motion of the planets—just because you put atmosphere around your object, it doesn't mean it's simply gonna operate. So you have to have multiple additional effects to create the exact motions you want it to have. There is no "just by chance" that the winds here (*on Earth*) go in a certain motion, for instance. The inner one (*Venus, in our system*) influences the rotation within, so the planet moves around its axis as it should, whereas the one after (*Mars*) is more involved with the movement of the atmosphere surrounding it *(gives a big sigh)*.

D. So what about Mars?

B. Ah. There are mysteries to solve, indeed, with Mars. (*Popping lips.*) That is tricky. It happened, something, on that planet. And it wasn't that long ago.

D. Did it used to have life on it?

B. Yes, indeed. Yes, indeed.

D. Anything you worked on?

B. I didn't work on it, but I knew them. I saw who they were. It wasn't that long ago.

D. Did it have plants and things like that?

B. Oh, some were like those half-and-half, because the atmosphere was different there. But, once the atmosphere was dissolved, based on actions and things that happened, the Evolution Group came in and did something. It actually had atmosphere at one point, and that is when they had the half-and-half things. But when an atmosphere disappeared, -and I can't say that I saw that-, but I know it HAD atmosphere at one point. That was cycles back. But atmosphere was taken away and everything somewhat dissolved. It's still there in a memory. So if atmosphere were to come back, then it would all be emerging again, because the patterns are still there, in the memory. Even what you talked before, here, about karma being a karma Coat, placed in the memory here. Everything is placed and remembered and is somewhat in hibernation. So if someone chooses to, it can be woken up again. That is why it is important that you do it correctly from the beginning before you launch it, because the patterns are always gonna be there.

Although Bob did not say, based on the order of the chakras, the Earth would be located on the green, or the heart chakra, and Uranus would be where Bob's favorite chakra, the feet, are located, which corresponds to the stabilizing chakra. He later in this chapter refers to Uranus as a stabilizer in our solar system.

D. So you have made progress with the patterns for the plants on your living planet?

B. Here, with my Individual, I put in all my best berries, because I know it likes berries. So I put in the things I know it likes, and it doesn't matter if it eats them all, because it's gonna come in new, because I said that I wanted atmosphere that's gonna be providing a lot of rain.

D. Have you been back down to the second lately?

B. Oh, it's been a while. But I talk with Gergen, because as I proceed with my color maps, there were a couple of samples that needed to be adjusted with a refined DNA match. Because he is somewhat of an expert, I took his advice on how to create the match, as the DNA needed to be compatible for the tones to emerge in the way they are supposed to, on my planet, the yellow one. So that was it. I do tend to my students, because you can't neglect the little ones. So, I've been down there and they are learning a lot about motion and how to maneuver when they merge with living life forms, like animals, and so forth. A couple of them are interested in circulation, so they're taking classes with the circulation group. There is a couple who are interested into moving more into the scientific area, meaning learning more about shape and form. So, there are a variety of skills in my group.

D. Does the ten percent that you leave down there spend time with them?

B. Mainly. But they are somewhat left to operate in a group and learn together, which is like a self-study group form. By that, I'm not present in that I'm sitting there with my ten percent, like you said. But I am always connected to them, and I can hear questions coming. So, I'm always able, in the same way that I can project myself when we meet here, when I hear a calling from them, I can respond as well. So you can move in-between, if you feel so. But you lose a little of your power when you move more of a percentage, like you say, into other realities. They have evolved into the place where they are solving a lot of tasks in a group now. I come in and we discuss their projects, but they are already starting to display different skill sets in this group. They're not going to be all gardeners, or all in one specialty. But they are all going to work with a specific mission later on, but from unique angles. They are designed, this group, to work with specific matters that from this second dimensional reality will occur in future cycles, not necessarily on Earth. They are specially designed for a project that is coming, but they are going to work with it from unique angles, but the joined project is one.

D. That makes a lot of sense.

B. So, yes, indeed, I tend to that.

D. How's Ia doing? Do you swing by to see her?

B. (*Makes a shy sort of laugh.*) Mmmm, ah. She reads a lot. She, she's not very–, she doesn't even go around a lot down here, either. She reads a lot. She's studying up on something, too. She's taking an exam on light, something with...it is somewhat healing, but it's transmitting light. As Ophelia sends light from the seventh dimension into the atmosphere and into plants, Ia will do the same, but from the inside—up. So she's learning about similar transmission of light into objects in order for healing processes to take place, and also to create new capsules.

D. That sounds like really good work.

B. She's similar to Ophelia, so she is taking an exam in that.

D. You both have to take exams, don't you?

B. Ah. Ia works a lot by herself. She doesn't mind the self–study. She's always been a little bit different with that. She likes to sit and read.

D. Well, she's a little more quiet than you.

B. She is a little bit more quiet. She samples her thoughts more than I do, and goes in an organized manner when she collects information. I'm more spread out.

D. I appreciate that. I'm a little like that too.

B. But I AM organized in your lab, I don't mess around, and you don't either. We just work on different things. I'm doing MY exam in your lab, and she's doing her exam with transmission of light to, not rejuvenate, but to revitalize when the capsule is gone and everything has somewhat died. Ophelia can do something from above. And Ia is learning the same, from within. It's like waking things to life. There's a lot of white, light energy they are working on sending into this plane, because soil has become dirty. I don't like that. So, Ophelia and Ia are working on that, where Ophelia is providing the light in the atmosphere so it provides rain, and it will fall down. And Ia works from the inside of plants and trees. So, it's a joined mission.

D. I guess that's why Ophelia gets so upset about the atmosphere?

B. Ah, because the effort that she and her friends are doing is being disturbed. And it's the same with what Ia is doing, when she's trying to help soil come alive again. When someone has put in seeds that are not supposed to be there, you know, like man–

made seeds (*genetically modified seeds*), the soil gets dirty. Then Ia tries to put light in it to make it come alive again, and then another one just puts back the same BAD SEED. So then Ia has to do it all over again, like Ophelia. I DON'T LIKE when someone tries to do something that TAKES AWAY LIGHT. I get REALLY, REALLY UPSET!

D. Yes, I do too!

B. I DON'T LIKE THAT! Because I KNOW how much WORK they put into it. I see how much Ia and Ophelia are doing, and I GET UPSET. I don't like that AT ALL, because it just STOPS the work they are doing, and they have to do it all over again. I just, I want to create A STORM, almost, so they can't TOUCH the soil.

D. Just need to get rid of some humans, thin 'em out. They're troublemakers.

B. I want to change the computer. I want to change. That's why I also want to make SURE it's not gonna happen on my planet. I didn't put this on my planet. It's not in its memory, so it can't happen. That's what you say. Because I asked, "What happens with the evolution? Will evolution just be out of control, or is it in my hand to create evolution as well?" The Evolution Group, I haven't talked to them yet, because I don't know them, but I would like them to come and explain to me how this really works. So it doesn't change after I launch my system.

D. And someone comes in after you.

B. Comes in after. Who can? Is it only me, and maybe you, that can create conditions on my living planet? Or once I launch it, have I lost control of it, so that anyone else is free to put in patterns on my planet? So, I wanna know that. Because I can see what happened here, and I don't know who allowed it, because there are several doing this, with this planet. So I don't know, once it was launched, if there were others coming in and having an effect. (*He's talking about the visitors who came and interfered with the Earth.*) I think I need to know more about this evolution thing, before I launch my system. Isaac is kinda close with them, because it is with that element thing. I just don't want there to be someone who just takes away my atmosphere, saying, "Oh, we need it somewhere else." And then my Individual doesn't have atmosphere anymore. Then I hear, "Oh, this is just part of the general evolution." So I need to know about this evolution thing, I need to know more about that. We haven't discussed that, and there are questions, clearly, before I launch.

D. You don't want someone coming in to take the fur!

B. Nay! I feel comfortable that the cores are going to be where they are, unless another system crashes into it, but I also want to make sure that my system is encased so there is not going to be interventions. I feel like we need to discuss this—I want to know more about this evolution thing.

D. The people with cone ears will show up and start eating your berries.

B. If they do, that ruins the whole agenda of putting those favorite berries for my Individual, because I know it likes them really, really much, then that's no good. I do wanna have a real solar system. BUT it comes with conditions, and I don't know if that is part of evolution, that you can have conditions for them. I don't know. At the moment we haven't discussed that, so I'm just creating tones and colors that will resonate. So that's what I do.

Why were there Three in a Row? (June 19, 2017)

Bob has discussed the three planets that used to exist in the Asteroid belt between Mars and Jupiter. What I find remarkable is that one of the main arguments astrogeologists use to dismiss the idea of a planet having existed in the orbit is because the debris contains three separate chemical signatures. Another argument is there is not enough residual debris to reconstruct even one planet. However, the spirits say that something came in and vaporized parts of the planets, and they exploded. The explosion would have sent debris in all directions, even perpendicular to the plane of the solar system. Jupiter and Saturn would act as gravitational vacuum cleaners, capturing or propelling a lot of the material out of the solar system. One only needs to look at the surface of the moon, which has very little gravity, to get an idea of how much cosmic material has been flying through space. Bob is fascinated by the idea of building a similar model himself.

B. Wait, ohh, ohh, secrets are flying here! Oh, this is why I'm not left alone. Hahaha. I kinda know what I can tell, but sometimes I drift and I get excited because you ask me things. And then I say, "Oh, yes, I know," and then I want to tell you, because we do talk about this in the vault and in the lab. And I'm also a little bit tricky, because, if I answer *your* questions, then you will answer *mine*!

D. So you have some questions that you want answered? What's one you have not gotten answered?

B. It is that purpose, again. It is the purpose of the solar system. I kinda understand the purpose when there are living creatures on my planet. BUT, what's the purpose of all the galaxies, the big ones, and why do you do that (*make galaxies*), and where is it going? I kinda want to know that. And I'm curious about the—the—the cycles of things. I would kinda like to know, let's say, you make your galaxy, and I ask, "How long is that gonna be around?" And you say, "Well, we don't know that, because evolution will change, and there will be different things that come in and interfere. You see here that changes took place from the original plan of this galaxy, and we patched it up. So, you never really know." And then I ask, "What was the original intent? How long was it supposed to be around? And when it came from being a baby sparkle to like, old, what knowledge did it collect, and what happens then? Does it report back, like everyone else does, somewhere?"

D. So, what did you learn from all those questions?

B. I did not! Huhuh. So, that's why I feel like if I answer your questions, you might remember this and feel grateful for it. And then later on when I'm in your lab, then I can say, "What is the intention, how long is it supposed to live? Do they have like a predestined life cycle, or is it different based on the center point? Are all galaxies and solar systems designed to have the same life span?" Then maybe you'll answer me. (*He then gives a big sigh of frustration.*)

D. So, like with the Earth and its solar system, there were those three planets in a row originally. That must have had a purpose?

B. Indeed, also something we need to discuss more about, because we have not. And I said, "If I'm gonna have eight planets, can I have three in a row?" And you said, "No, it's too tricky." And I said, "Why is it tricky, there just going to follow each other, how tricky can that be? It's like a little worm, like a little train." So I wondered about that. And then I thought, in some way that will reflect on my stabilizer. If I have three in a row it's gonna be more heavy in that region, and then the stabilizer, further out, has to be more dense, and it has to be filled up differently than my original stabilizer that I planned on doing. I don't want anything to mess that up, so I'm not gonna have three in a row. BUT I am interested in understanding WHY, because it's not very common, and why was that placed here? (*The three planets were where the asteroid belt is currently found.*) So, there are questions.

D. How far apart were those planets, originally?

B. Well, they were kinda close. You would think, because I ask, "Why didn't you put them with distance between them, like noon, four o'clock and so forth?" But they were actually, if we talk clockwise, then one was at 12 o'clock, the biggest one, and then one was at like 1 o'clock, and the last was at 2:30.

D. Was the third one the smallest?

B. That was kind of small, indeed. And then I wanted to know, if each, because everything has a purpose, so what was the intention with all three of them, and why were they in a row? The little one seemed to merely tag along, in some way. BUT, I do know that everything has an intention and a purpose, so the little one that only looks like it's tagging along, it did not necessarily do so. Number one and number two, they were kind of similar. The little one almost looked like a moon.

D. What came in and caused them to explode?

B. It looked like rain. Not from above, it looked a shower came in and just poofed them.

D. From outside the solar system?

B. From outside. It looked like rain, sparkle rain that came in when they were like, from where I see it, at 3 o'clock (*Bob is shown the orbital position from above*), every one of them. Then something came in.

D. Then all the debris from them flew out through the whole solar system?

B. Indeed.

D. Is that about when you came in?

B. Uh, because I was actually in place, when the clouds, I was in place when all this took place. At this specific time, Mercury was on the other side of the Sun, so it managed quite well, the first influence of the rain that came in. Earth was not as lucky. But then again, they circle, so everyone had to come into this, so it spread.

D. Is that something we're going to talk about?

B. Maybe not me, since I'm asking you! Hopefully, we will discuss this further, but there will be others that come in, bigger ones, bigger ones with the big robes. I don't know them at all (*referring to Ari and Eli, whom he had not met at this time in his story*).

A Division of Labor (June 19, 2017)

Bob covers a lot of topics in this session. As we have learned, creation of solar systems and life forms is a joined effort from every dimension. And all spirits work in coordination with the original intent. Or, as Bob says, "It's not like you can go in like a single-handed person and just create something. The whole intention comes from one Source that knows much more than the rest of us."

D. When you come to the lab, do you pretty much stay there all the time? Are we together somewhat continuously?

B. Ah.

D. And then you occasionally go back to visit people?

B. Indeed. Because I also journal in my own place, and in the vault. So sometimes I can be in the lab, and then I can go to the vault, because there are certain things that are stored that I need, in order to proceed with my drawer.

D. When you go to the vault, do you combine the 60 and the 30 together, so you have like 90 percent of yourself there?

B. Oh, I know you like to think of that in those terms. But I can somewhat, let's say we have 90 at our disposal here, and I want to go to the vault. I still have like 10 at home. I'll still want to leave some in the lab, so I can still leave like 10 percent in the lab and go with the rest. I can split and I can divide. But I normally only do that if I need to go gather information that exists in the vault, for instance. When I'm here, I still have a little bit left in my lab and in the vault, because that is how we can access information from those two places.

D. So what are we working on in my lab?

B. Ohhhh. (*He makes gulping sound.*) Let's see what I can tell you. Oh, we did discuss my rocks a bit, because I wanted to know if I move them, shifted positions, if you like, how it would affect things. And you said, "Don't." So I said, because we talked about the drawer, and I said, "I kind of understand that the inner one, the orange one next to the sun, has to be left alone because it is the regulator, sort of conducting the whole system in some way, even though it is very small." I also wonder about the sizes, if that has some sort of correlation to where it's located. We haven't got to that yet, but you say, "It is clearly based on where it's at. It has a destined core, and you can't just move them around because you feel like, 'Ohh, I wanna have a bigger ball closer to the sun.' You can't do that because it's not suited for any other environment." So, it actually seems like there are different environments from the inside out (*from the sun outwards through the system*), which you can understand because of the difference in the heat. However, it's also based on the relationships between the cores. AND this is something we talked about because we're coming into the subject of magnetism. Some of them are like magnets in the beginning. It's almost like hematite, like a magnet. Uranus was one of those. There's something with Uranus. We talk about it ALL the time, even though we don't unfold its mysteries yet. But it's that thing again, it's heavy, and it's like a magnet. It stabilizes, you say, and it also keeps the whole thing in its position within the bigger solar family. You know, this is a baby family, but it also resonates within a bigger one. It's like a whole family tree. It's like having one solar system that is located in Europe, and there's another part of the family tree located in the US, so you know, it is similar like this within the galaxies.

D. Are there other ones nearby with life, like on Earth?

B. Not really nearby, I would say. There's like a band, like a band of clouds in the middle. Ohh! (*Ophelia shows him a picture*) On the other side there's a similar one, like this one, only it is behind that band. And it's designed way after our one, the Earth. But it's exactly the same model. That's kind of surprising. Why is it like this, you might wonder? Is it to exchange this one if it breaks down?

D. It's like a spare tire.

B. It's like a spare tire, indeed! (*He laughed loudly.*)

D. Have you worked on that one?

B. No. I just found out! That there is something behind that band, that fog band. It's like a fog that is sort of reddish and gray, but it changes color though, like an entity of sorts. But it's like a wall. (*There must be some visual obstruction within our galaxy that appears fog-like, behind which hides a similar Earth-like planet.*) But it is something similar like this one, behind this band. I don't know where it is in relationship to your galaxy. But it started later, so I don't know if it's still in hibernation.

D. Maybe they got the dinosaurs.

B. Huhhuh, maybe they moved them there! That would be interesting. It's like a spare tire, like you said, maybe. Who knows what you've been up to here? You don't tell me; you just show me these things. You say, "Look here," and I look, but then it doesn't really continue, because...oh...I do look, but then nothing more comes. So I don't know. But what we did talk about was that I had a question if you can move the planets around. Let's say, if Earth doesn't do well, can it be removed and moved outwards and take another one from the outside and move in and just begin new? But you said, "No, because it doesn't work like that. You have to create the whole thing from scratch again. It's not like you can just change positions. Once its core is established, it is where it's supposed to be." So they don't switch based on, "Okay, I'm getting tired of this experience, I need to hibernate." And then another goes, "Oh, I'd like the experience of having dinosaurs, so I will go in." It's not like that at all. You said, "It is what it is. Once the intention is set, it follows that certain life span, and it is what it is." And if it doesn't work out, I guess you begin new. BUT, you said, before you just begin new and toss it away, it's like you do that rebooting thing. So, there are little tricks to kick-start the system if something is broken, I would assume. But I don't know how that is done. I can't see that, but I guess it is probably one of the councils that decides. I'm just guessing here because you don't tell me. And when you don't tell me, I begin to think all sorts of different things. Then I wonder and I ask. And sometimes you just stand there and don't answer at all, which makes me talk even more. Maybe YOU go into hibernation when I talk! Huh huh huh. So, we discuss things in the drawer, and you say, "It is important that you understand how they are all resonating within their own core, but also with each other. And also, WHY they are placed where they are placed. Because nothing is done by chance here. It's carefully designed," you said, "to operate at its the best for its destined journey." That's what you said. It's a joint effort. But the eighth dimension, they create the foundation for it to travel. These are the atmospheric group, they are highly involved, you know, six, seven, eight. I'm sure you have meetings about this. I don't attend. We don't talk about that. But this I DO know that there are different individuals, different groups that operates to create something majestic in order for it to become something of a creation. So I'm SURE there are meetings taking place. We have that, Gergen and I and the other ones, we have meetings when we discuss things. So, that is what happens here.

D. So after your solar system is done, will you and I continue to work together?

B. Yes indeed, yes indeed. Because you said that we will add another level of understanding. I don't know what that means, maybe I'll go and do galaxy work! Huhuhuh! Even though you laughed about that, you didn't say no, you did not. But you somewhat laughed. And I have met your friends, but I don't think they understand me. They kinda look at me like you did the first time. But you say they are friendly and they laugh on the inside. "Even though you can't see it, Bob, they are laughing on the inside." And I say, "Oh, is that how you look, is that happy?" And I try to see if maybe there is another way of happiness to be expressed that is not laugher. I think you laugh, like gurgle laugh, just to make me happy. I don't think that is what you do, but you do it because you know that I understand that. So I don't think you necessarily need that, but it is a way for me to understand that you indeed are happy. But the other ones, they haven't got that memo yet! Huh huh huh!. They are like standing there like a pole, just staring, and I was like, oohhhh. (*He gave a nervous laugh.*) But you say they're laughing on the inside, it's gurgle on the inside. And I said, "Oh, okay." I tried to talk with some of them. I feel like I'm not excluded, but I'm not included, either. So I can sense...it's like when you are at pre–school, and you go to visit the big school, because you're going to join, eventually. And the older students are somewhat, "Oh, who's this?" But I do want to join, and I'm happy to meet your friends, but I can't communicate that well with them. One is more, eh...

D. What about this one?

B. Yes, indeed. But this one transforms and communicates in like a human way to me. Like I said, he transforms into personalities and characteristics that he had on Earth. So, in that way, communicates in a way like human waves. Understand that your mouth is not really moving, so it's coming out like waves, if I say it like that. This one, because he knows that I follow, takes on waves that is more familiar to me. You both do, but different. This one plays with frequencies and waves that belong with other lifetimes, so to speak. But I have seen the maps. I went there and he rolled out all the maps for me, and he showed me where his systems were. Because I wanted to know if maybe there were some of his systems that are gonna be neighbors. But he said that he works on other dimensions, mostly. His systems are located outside, in another fish tank.

D. I had a question. You have intentions to make things, –how do you know that's the same as the Creator's?

B. Because we got the manual from the Master Mind, and that is connecting to the Creator. It's not like I'm creating new manuals, because that would not be allowed. I get a manual and I'm creating from it. But you also have to somewhat have it approved. It's not like you can go in like a single–handed person and just create something. The whole intention comes from one Source that knows much more than the rest of us. I am not able to create manuals, but I would like to do the reboot. So clearly, I'm not the Creator, because my manuals would look very different. I don't have the whole picture. I don't have the picture of incarnations versus atmosphere versus, you know, the web around the planet. So I don't have the whole picture like those, whoever they are, up in the Master Mind. So they are the only ones that can create manuals.

D. Well, how about your solar system, did that conform to certain manuals?

B. Indeed, because you provided certain things that was allowed for me to operate from. So you got manuals, –probably the basic ones that you get when you're a sparkle–, and you gave them to me. And then, because I had seen stuff in the vault, then I asked about that, like having three in a row. And you said, "No. No, we don't do that now. Maybe later." And I said, "How am I gonna put them there later if I'm already set? How can I create a new core later?" And you said something, but didn't really answer. Maybe it's another system.

D. Another system indeed. You know how to do it now. So, I've kind of been wondering about the difference between what Ophelia's group does and what our group does, when it comes to a planet, for example?

B. You are responsible for the core inside, because (*he always mimics me by talking slowly and deliberately*), "Everything has a core, even the star." So, I'm pretty sure that you are responsible for the core within celestial bodies, regardless of if it's a planet or a star or a comet, or if it's some sort of entity in space.

D. Except for the moon?

B. Well, those in the sixth and ninth are in charge for that one too! But because it's not a dot (*core*) floating inside. It's filled, so it looks like it has the same density as a dot, it's just more spread out. But you do carry the knowledge of the core inside, because it resonates with sound. Whereas Ophelia's expertise, really, resonates with light. So, the sun is a very easy object to identify, of course, "Oh, there is seventh dimension people." But there are sun frequencies to be found in the atmosphere around celestial bodies, so in that way they are responsible for being a part of even planets. Because they create light waves, frequencies, –like impulses.

D. I remember you said she put something that glowed around planets.

B. It glows, indeed. But not around all planets, of course, but some. Some they put this glowing atmosphere around (*a planet*). I would say atmosphere because that is what it looks like. So that's when they are involved, indeed. It is for some sort of protection, for places similar to Earth where there is supposed to be some sort of growth. There's no need to waste all this magic on rocks who aren't supposed to have evolution. It's like saffron, it's probably very precious, you don't want to just waste it. Mmmmm–huuhuh! Made a joke there, did I? (*He was laughing about his comparison of Ophelia's atmosphere to saffron, the most expensive spice on Earth.*) So, indeed. Because the eighth dimension works with atmospheric settings, not only around celestial bodies, but also within everything that appears as a vacuum. And the density within, that is from those gravity people, –they're mysterious too, you know.

D. Which dimension do they work in?

B. Eight. Gravity belongs in the element world, you said. You work so closely that it is sometimes hard to know who is responsible for what. I can see, I can see what you're doing. It's just that the eighth dimension is more about the elements. "Gravity is considered an element," you said, "because it creates a foundation for life forms, as well as–", oh, what did you say? Oh, "it creates the conditions on everything that is created. But it's not constant, it changes."

D. Even within a planet?

B. No, that is what it is, inside. However, we talked about the solar system being in its cradle (*in hibernation*), and that's when the outside of the planets have different, or a variety, of change when it comes to the gravity and the magnetic fields that's around them. But inside, it's constant. It's not like you can just (*make sucking sound*) suck it out and put in something new. It is what it is, you said.

D. Yes, I think you've mentioned that before.

B. The core, the core. You're responsible for the core, which is kind of heavy, and it resonates with sound. Even gravity resonates with sound. You can hear it, you say. I'm listening, but I can't hear it because it's not in my drawer (*gravity is added towards the end of the project, before it is launched into a fish tank*). So I don't know where I'm supposed to listen. If I'm gonna stand still and listen out in space, or if I'm supposed to listen down in my drawer. Because I said, "Are we gonna add it (*gravity*) in the drawer?" And you said "No, because this is a model." Once we leave the drawer and we put it in some sort of tank, I guess, then we will add more of the elements. I'm going to meet some sort of specialist, you said, from the eighth. BUT FIRST IT HAS TO BE CORRECTLY DONE in the drawer, before I move it out in the tank to add the elements and the conditions, to see it floating.

D. So, we're going to make a model of a solar system, and then put it in a fish tank?

B. I'm gonna make one. I'm not sure if it is gonna be set off, I'm not saying that. This is a long–term project, I would say. First you create everything, –everything has to go in a special order here. I did the class with the sun, and now I'm learning about the planets and how to put them in a certain order. You don't move me forward just because I want to. I have to fix things; I have to manage things. But you said once my solar system is intact and you have approved, then it's gonna go into some sort of little tank, and a specialist of gravity and magnetic fields will assist. It looks like he will come in and do something. And then I would see what happens, –if it actually floats. What if it doesn't float? Then, you know, we go back to the drawer. It's almost like creating a boat. If you create a boat, then you have to put it in the water, –and hopefully it floats. It's the same thing here, it's like a test. You put in your own project, everyone has their own, you know. I'm not letting anyone touch mine. This is mine. (*Bob is very protective of his project.*)

D. See if it sinks or floats.

B. First it has to float, you say. It's similar like a boat, it has to float. And that is based on how I put them, and the distance between, and also how heavy I make my planets. Because it has to be the same. (*The core density is related to distance from the sun*). The density combined with the core has to be properly divided and measured in its course, so it operates correctly. So, that's where we are at.

D. Have you done anything else in Ophelia's lab?

B. It's been a while. I'm more focused on my drawer now, so it's been a while since I was in Ophelia's lab. But we have talked, she and I. We have talks, I like that. I like to sit alone and talk with you and with Ophelia. We talk about things. She's very encouraging about the work we do here, and the work we do there. And she tells me to tickle you to start investigating your past and your memory; there's something in your past, and she wants me to tickle. So, we talk about that.

D. This life, or a previous life?

B. No, a previous life. (*He then gave a detailed account of one of my past lives as a painter in Italy during the late 1400's, before resuming his discussion of the solar system project.*)

D. Thank you for showing up today. Is there anything else you would like to add before we close, any thoughts?

B. Noooo. I just feel very humbled, actually, that I will meet this gravity engineer later on and see if my solar system floats. So, that will be interesting.

D. I wouldn't let you test it if it didn't work, would I?

B. Nay, because you have to sort of certify it, so it's your name on the line if it doesn't float! Huhuhuh! No one can blame me, because I'm not licensed! (*Laughing*) However, I want to do well, because I have a little bit of a pride about what I learn.

D. Well, it will be fun.

B. I do think so too, to see if it floats.

D. Oh, it will float. I have a lot of confidence in your abilities.

B. Hmmmm. Oh, well that would be it then. And we will see if it floats at a later time, because we're still only up to five planets and I still need to rearrange a little bit, because they're not really, —the density, you said, isn't properly measured for the distance to the inner ones. So, that's what I do, I'm gonna study up on that. Some things I study by myself. I'm sure you have other things to do than just hang along with me.

Uranus in Resonance with Sun (Dec 3, 2017)

Uranus was designed as the stabilizer for our Solar System. The energetic field that holds the system is what Bob calls gravity. Scientists assume that mass creates "gravity". But that is not the way it is described. So clearly, there is a disconnect between what we think it is, and what it truly is.

D. We never really talked about Uranus, the stabilizer. You never really told me what you learned about that.

B. It holds everything in somewhat of a stable movement. So the stabilizer makes it, –I thought it was so it wouldn't wobble–, BUT it is to regulate the motion within it. So, combined with the sun, it creates a resonance with the other ones, in between mainly, for them to operate in a desirable pattern and manner, meaning how they move. This is also why they can appear to somewhat stop at certain times, so it has to do with motion within the solar system. (*I assume he means they appear to stop from the perspective of someone on Earth.*)

D. Okay. The stabilizer in our solar system isn't the densest planet, is it? Is it a physical mass, or an energetic?

B. It's the inside. Even if it could potentially be the smallest one, but it is based on how it is filled, within, based on how much of, and this is actually a little bit of gravity involved, here. So the inside of the stabilizer has more, it's not only one condition of gravity, it's several. So the other ones can have one or two components from gravity to create the core, to create the foundations within the celestial body you are creating. However, the stabilizers carry multiple parts from it, because gravity isn't just one, it is an element that can change and shift, and it comes in different shapes and forms. It doesn't matter if it is the densest or the biggest, but the stabilizer has, per percentage, the biggest amount of gravity within this whole system. It also has to do with the vacuum, it resonates with that. But a stabilizer is important for the motion, in general.

How it's filled up is a little bit tricky, because it's not like a living entity, in the same way, it's almost like a ghost planet.

D. There is gravity that we measure as humans, I guess there are other types of gravity that we can't detect?

B. Ah, ah, it's more, it's more, oh, it's so primitive here! It's more, it doesn't have to do...I would say that the stabilizer is like a ghost, or a dead object almost, because it's simply there to make sure that speed and motion are maintained at a desirable fashion. Without it, it would be somewhat exposed more to the sun. I'm not like an expert on it, so you might want to ask yourself about this! I don't know why you ask me! Huhuhuh.

D. If only I could remember.

B. Well, stand in front of a mirror and ask a question and see what happens! (*Laughing.*)

D. An empty gaze, most likely.

B. I'm constantly wondering about Uranus, because it's heavy, too heavy. And I have one in my system as well, because it's a stabilizer, you say. And all systems, regardless how small they are, needs that stabilizer. It operates somewhat in a resonance with the sun. If it did not exist, a stabilizer, way out a bit, then the system will fold; and I don't want my system to fold. But you don't talk about it, because we haven't got there yet. You want me to focus on the details of the living planet, and the ones on either side of it. But this is the part of being detail oriented, because I can see, and I know, that it's gonna come. I see it in the corner of my eye, so to speak, and I wonder about that. But you make me go back to focus on the project at hand, before we get there. It carries a really high density of iron, and it is like a hematite, in some way. The core is bigger, not like a moon, like it's filled up, but the core is bigger, I can see it in models that you showed me, that the stabilizers have a bigger core than the ones with living beings on it.

D. Is the gravity and iron, or hematite, related?

B. Indeed, with the hematite. Hematite is the magical element, that's what Isaac said one time. He knows about that. But he's not telling, because I haven't got there yet.

D. Is gravity independent? Is it like a separate element that is added to things?

B. Uuhhh, it's somewhat like a chameleon. It becomes whatever the surroundings have, in some way. That's why it's not constant. But it carries its own individual map, like all elements, so in that regard, yes indeed, it is somewhat unique. However, it has, Isaac said one time, that it has the possibility to become its surrounding, and that is why it is somewhat changeable.

D. Mixes with other things?

B. In some way it does, and that is how much of its original structure or components will be manifested in that region. So, gravity has a variety of expressions. Ugh. (*He made a sound like he was exhausted from trying to deliver that idea. It must be very difficult finding words that will convey the proper meaning. The spirits have said there are multiple modalities of gravity. The stabilizer must be filled with a type that we cannot measure or detect, yet is important to maintaining the form of the solar system. Certain expressions of gravity seem to somehow interact or create properties within the vacuum field.*)

D. So, you've been talking to Isaac lately?

B. I've been paying attention! Like in the hallway (*in our lab*), when I hear the big ones talking, I pay attention! Because the only thing he has been telling me, based on my solar system, based on what I created, is that the gravity that he will put in my fish tank will resonate with the elements and components and color maps and light that I have wanted to create in my solar system. So, it changes in some way, it becomes its surroundings. Which is different than a regular element—that just is what it is. It almost appears to me like those lizards that changes color based on where they are at. I don't know, because I haven't gone to class with Isaac, but he says I do not need to worry about this too much. It's the same thing with Uranus, you know. It gets me distracted if I try to figure out the vacuum between. So I need to be able to put my attention to the project at hand. He said there is no need to worry too much about understanding the gravitational field. The only thing he said is that it is not constant, and it changes, and it can be perceived differently in different fish tanks, as well as in different realities. And he makes somewhat of a period after that. So I felt like it was not continuing, the discussion, so I would assume I have to be content with that. He also said that it is not helpful for this plane to fully understand, because it was misused prior to the civilizations that are walking at this point. So it is somewhat of a knowledge that it has the potential to transform and to create new possibilities, based on what you use it for. So it is adaptable, and like that lizard, it changes, depending on the conditions. And if you know the secrets of it, then limits of what you can do with it becomes somewhat overwhelming on this plane. There is actually one part, he said, within science that would be allowed at this point to work with gravity, and that would be in some sort of spacecraft work. But like I said, if gravity has the potential of, let's say, one thousand different modalities, then he is saying that only one, potentially, possibly, he said, would be launched again on this plane. So, you can see, this is not like just having the element mercury, gravity is changeable.

D. Huh, that's incredibly fascinating.

B. It is, indeed. But he kind of put a period after that sentence, so I didn't feel like it continued. I tried to ask you, because I'm pretty sure you know. But you somewhat look over my head on this one (*topic*). I know you hear me! I do know you hear me. But sometimes you sort of glance into the distance, and that is when I know...

D. I'm not going to answer?

B. No. Or you just sort of change the subject. That's also one of the things that happens when avoiding questions. Anyway, it's not constant, and it changes, so it's not like he will just put whatever gravity in my fish tank. It is based on what I first created. The gravity, number one, will be put in my solar system to see if it floats. Two, IF it floats, it will be put into hibernation. Three, it will be launched. So, there are steps, clearly. I don't know where we're gonna put it though. You said we're gonna find a place for it, but that sounds somewhat vague, so I don't know.

D. Maybe we'll put it where everyone on the second can see it!

B. Ohh! Huhuhuh. Ia would say, "You're showing off." That's what she would say and, you know, I'm not supposed to do that. She says that to me sometimes, that I have a tendency to show off. But it's just because I'm excited and I want to share. There's not that many people to share with.

D. Oh, that's too bad. What about your friends?

B. Gergen listens, but he's busy. He doesn't have time to just sit and listen to me ramble on about solar systems.

D. Well, I listen to you, don't I?

B. Yes. Yes, you do.

D. And Ophelia?

B. Ophelia listens to me. Isaac listens as well. But because I haven't got to his level of knowledge in my drawer, then he's doing the polite thing, he says, to not confuse me. It seems that is the general theme within the group, to not confuse me.

D. Well, you're familiar with that, because you do the same with your students. Look how well they progress.

B. Uhh. That's because I allow them to be within their level of learning, and I did not confuse...(*voice trails off*), confuse them. Oh, I see that, I see that. I did not add more than they were prepared for. That is what Isaac probably means. He's not adding more than I am prepared for, because that would divert my attention from the project at hand.

D. I was wondering, like with Gergen, does he get new students once the ones he has have graduated?

B. No, you can come to him, and you can have specific questions, like I do with Zachariah, but he is on somewhat of a board with others of similar, equal levels of learning. He comes sometimes and talks about certain topics in classes, like bigger speeches. But he doesn't have students, except for Ia, because Ia and Gergen are really close, they are working on similar things. I'm close, too! But I, I, I have drifted off somewhat, off the grid.

D. You're not working on the spaghetti? (*He calls the DNA strings, "spaghetti", and, unlike Ia, does not have any interest in becoming an expert of these tiny details.*)

B. No, I'm not working on details. And sometimes I feel like I might want to take on that, just to be part of the group, to belong. But I AM welcome, I am welcome. I know I am. But then again, it's not really what makes me tick. But he doesn't necessarily take on new students, but he conducts lectures, indeed.

D. Do you think you'll get new students?

B. If I want to. Ia, she really likes the students. She has a lot, and she really likes that and she's a really good teacher. She's diplomatic, and she sees everyone, and they really like her. But because I too, I want to sort of take-off, it's not necessarily that nice to engage with students when you are not fully putting your attention on their projects. So, I have my little groups, and that is it for the moment. But the older ones are very much working by themselves as a group. Not individually, but in the group, so I don't feel that bad about leaving. But Ia takes great pride in seeing the progress of each sparkle, and she can focus on many, and I tend to drift.

D. But she's not travelling around.

B. No, she's not travelling around. She reads a lot. She studies up on the light capsule and the DNA modalities of light, and how to improve that inner map we talked about. How, in a human form, for instance, how and in what way, if part of the inner map has been shut down, if maybe up to fifty percent of it has been shut down, if it is possible to gain its capacity back. So she's working on maintaining and upgrading the light within certain DNA that exists within cells, if it is possible to make them come alive again. So, she's a scientist as well, but different. However, if the humans operate in a certain manner from this plane, then yes, indeed the plants and animals have a tendency for their capsules to be shut down. There are several different components that exist on this plane, that is why it is known as a project.

D. When you say the capsule is shut down, is that an individual or a species?

B. It can be a whole species, indeed. So, like when the dinosaurs went away, for instance, that general capsule, that pattern that existed on this plane was not forgotten, so, in theory they could return because it still exists on this plane, in its memory. Just because a capsule has disappeared doesn't mean it is lost in its memory. However, it's not very likely that they will return, there's no room for them. Maybe in the seas.

D. So is Ophelia going to discuss this more, later?

B. I think there will be other ones discussing this. But there is going to be other discussions when it comes to why it is more tricky to be here (*on Earth*) and what those contradicting, challenging realities and elements are, –and the cause of them, so that you can be more prepared. When you are prepared, you can make your choices better. So it will be discussed more. And it has to do a lot with the atmosphere, so I'm pretty sure that Isaac will continue talking about this. Ophelia says that this is not in this book at all, and that you have not let go of things in your computer, so this is not gonna be implemented in your computer at this time. That is what she said. So, that was it about that. So, I think she wants me to somewhat wrap this up, but she says, for you, because we drifted into something you were not supposed to hear. So you need to let go of certain things in order for you to give your full attention to new information coming in. Oh, she laughs now.

D. Curious minds, we both have!

B. (*He was laughing.*) Oh, she laughs at that! Hehehehe. She laughs at that! So, anyway I'm probably gonna take off and go somewhere and do my things. Well, she says, "Just know that there are two major components that have to operate as a receiver and a transmitter, so to speak. And in the solar system, that is considered to be between the stabilizer and center point, which is the sun. So, you can see how these two are extremely important. And," she says, "it's also the same as how the spiritual dimensions and realities operates. You have the first dimension that resonates with the tenth. So it's the same structure in everything." Oh, she laughs at this, she said, "This should make it easy for you to solve!" Hehehehe! She knows it's not. (*Laughing loudly.*) She's tricky too!

D. Well, that won't help me at all, but it's good to know.

Bob Gets to Choose a Location (June 25, 2017)

Bob was nearing completion of his solar system, and was told that he would be allowed to travel to different locations to help select where it would be launched. He became very excited and happy, and it fired up his enthusiasm to finish the project and begin bubble training. Three locations were selected by Jeshua and Lasaray for him to experience, and he was very motivated to go have a look.

B. (*Bob came in, looking nervously to his right, where Jeshua was standing. Jeshua had been speaking and stepped away from Christine.*) Let's see if he comes back in.

D. He's watching you, huh? Does that make you nervous?

B. Ohh, I don't know if he's gonna pop back. And what happens with me if he pops back? But he laughs now, so, hehe.

D. See, he's friendly.

B. He's friendly, indeed! Oh, let's see what he wants to say. He says that I tickle you, I tickle you. And he encourages me to do that, because you do need to be tickled. Because sometimes you're asleep. And he says, "Tickle him, tickle him!" HA HA HA, –I will tickle, I will indeed! He says, "Sometimes you need to be tickled, because you do prefer to go to sleep and snooze, sometimes when you're not supposed to." He sees that, he sees everything! So he likes that I tickle you. He says that I have his full support to tickle whenever I want to! Oh, I think I'm gonna ask him questions about when I can come up and maybe join and see what he's doing. Because I haven't been to his office. I don't know what he's doing, to see what is on his table, so to speak.

D. Well, since he's my father in spirit, you're part of the extended family.

B. Like a grandfather, indeed!

D. So, he's in your family tree.

B. AH. I might go, and just maybe see what is on his table, and what is in his journal. (*Jeshua sent him a few thought bubbles.*) "No," he said, "No, I cannot look in the journal." But he's gonna come later, he said, and he's gonna tell me what he's doing. Oh, I'm gonna go with him and Isaac! You're gonna go too! Because, uhh–oh, they know that I'm not really eager to go somewhere if I'm not familiar with where I put my feet, that's what he said. So, it's better that I go with those that I am familiar with. So that's what I'm gonna do. The three of us are gonna go somewhere, and I'm invited on some sort of treasure hunt with the three of you. It's gonna be like going on a holiday for me—I'm gonna go somewhere!

D. See, they're really happy with your work.

B. Ah. They said I'm gonna travel somewhere. He said I can travel on a rainbow. I don't know how that is gonna happen. –Oh, I don't need to worry about that, he said. But, I'm gonna go on like a holiday, of sorts.

D. That will be fun!

B. Somewhere different. He said that I've been too much in the lab and inside, and he's gonna make me go somewhere. You all are gonna make me go somewhere. OHHH, I KNOW! We're gonna go and see where to put my system! OHHH, HEHEHEHE! (*This was probably the most excited I have ever heard him.*) Oh, I'm gonna go with all of you and see where we will put my system! Oh, there are three choices, he said, three choices that have been selected for me to put my system. It's in MY hands! I'm going to be able to decide. Oh, that's a treat! That's better than the step in the vault. Much better than the step in the vault! OH, OH, I think I wanna go right now! Right now, I wanna go. I'm gonna go and I'm gonna decide. Three locations have been selected, three have been selected. We're gonna go, all three of us. It's gonna be an excursion, of sorts.

D. In a nice friendly galaxy.

B. I would assume that they are all friendly, because I did put that in my request. So, I would assume that they are all friendly ones. But maybe something else, like conditions within these three spots—but it's been CAREFULLY selected, he said. You and him have been carefully selecting some places here. You said that it would better if there were different ones, and then I can choose. I'm really grateful for that. It's much better than getting another step on the ladder in the vault, clearly much better. It's like a medal, it's like getting first prize! If I know where it's going to be, then it's much easier for me to navigate and to create on my living planet as well, because I will see the neighbors. I wanna see the neighbors! That's what I want to see, and that's what we talked about because I was clearly confused and concerned about the neighbors. Because I do see that there are different solar systems, all circling with all sorts of different intentions. If I knew that it was all your solar systems—and I kinda know your intentions, at least what you told me about the intentions you normally have. So if I knew the neighbors were your solar systems, the ones you created, I would be happy. But I don't know that, and if they are just random solar systems, then I kinda want to know about the neighbors. Who knows, there might be something that happens along the way, and neighbors are good. You know, you run out of milk and you can go to the neighbors. It's similar, so neighbors are good. I kinda talked about that. So, there are three spots that I'm gonna go visit. And we're gonna travel on a rainbow, that's how it will be perceived from my perspective, I would assume, because I don't think there are rainbows, really. But I will see it as a rainbow. And he said, Jeshua said, "It's going to be similar and I'm not going to be afraid, because nothing bad can travel on colors." So, I will go on a colored road, so to speak. (*He then began to contemplate about all the different concerns he might have, once he is allowed to travel. So this is an example of what we chat about in the lab, I would assume.*) I will be able to ask about the neighbors. And once I have decided where to put it, –and it might be that it is in the center of a galaxy, or it might outside, or on a corner somewhere–, so there are all different things that are details to consider, here. I kinda would like it to be not too dark. I would like it to be somewhere okay, but it also has to mirror my atmosphere. If I choose something that is closer to another sun, a center (*point*), then my atmosphere might need some adjustments. But I don't want to have it somewhere dark, because what if my sun doesn't shine as well, and then my creature might be upset. It doesn't do that well in the dark. It sleeps during the night and if it's too much dark, then it will be confused. So it has to have a lot of natural light. So I want to make sure that it is a correct place. And it is a fact about the neighbors, because who knows what the neighbors are capable of. They might be far, far, far ahead in their evolution, and they might be able to travel, let's say, and they might travel to my planet. And I'm all in favor of visitors and guests, but they have to be friendly. SO, this is up, this is where I'm gonna go! (*He always seems very concerned about the neighbors. He observed visitors coming to Earth. Some of them must have interfered with the animals or plants, and he doesn't want that on his planet. Most visitors to Earth are friendly.*)

D. That's wonderful. Well, congratulations!

B. Congratulations to me!

D. It's a real honor.

B. Indeed. We're all gonna go. You, me, Isaac, and Jeshua, all are gonna go.

D. A little family outing.

B. Ah, might be. That was a surprise, indeed. So, anyway, that was the highlight of my day! One might say. I like him. He's full of surprises, and he can fix things and make things happen. I like that.

D. You were afraid of him when he first showed up.

B. Well, that's because he didn't show that much of an interest in me, and he was just coming and going, just passed me by. But now, I can see that he HAS paid attention to me, and he has listened, probably more to you than to me, but he has taken my wish into consideration. And I'm happy and I'm extremely grateful for that, and to all of you who listened to my complaints and my concerns, really.

D. Well, it's just because you care so much about your animal, your Individual. So, that too is appreciated.

B. Yes, indeed. It's not going to be that far away, because I said I do want to tend to it, so I don't want it to be in a fish tank I don't have access to. That is the only thing that I say. If it's going to be launched, then I want to have access, otherwise I am content with having it in my drawer and in my tank, here, in your lab, if I can't follow up. If it's put somewhere I can't see it, then I don't want it to be launched.

D. That would be nice, then the whole thing would be yours. You would have made the creature, and the planets—

B. (*Interrupts.*) And the sun! I did that too.

D. Your own personal solar system.

B. My own, my own. But it has to be in a fish tank that I have access to, otherwise I don't want it to be launched. Otherwise, I can't see it, and what if it needs me? So, I want to be able to monitor the evolution and the cycles, that it operates correctly. You say you will always tend to it and make sure that everything is functioning correctly. But then again, I do want to see that as well, too. That will probably be it about that. (*Popping lips.*) But it's something to look forward to, don't you agree?

D. Oh, yes, that will be a lot of fun. That will give you some incentive to finish off your system.

B. That will give me all sorts of fuel to get it done! Because then I know exactly where to put it, and I know about the neighbors after I have a little visit. That's helpful.

Bubble Training Begins (July 16, 2017)

When spirits travel out into the universes of form, they often shield themselves inside an energetic layer, which they create around themselves. Because Bob had never traveled in that manner, Jeshua introduced the method by creating a separate bubble for him. It served the same purpose, and also gave Bob a sense of comfort and security. With a bit of practice, the traveling spirit learns how to master the art, and the bubble is no longer necessary. Bob is not capable of traveling out into the fish tank without a protective layer, so he has no other options to visit the location where his system has been placed.

D. Have you gotten any other information on your solar system?

B. I'm in training. I'm in training for departure.

D. What's involved with that?

B. Well, at the moment I've been in somewhat of a space room, that's how I can picture it for you. It is the fact of being floating. I think that it's going to be like traveling through vibrational states, and the physical being of me tends to be stressed about vibrational changes. (*Even though Bob is a spirit, he has an energetic physical body, as all spirits do.*) Either it's with the harp, like I fall asleep, or I can feel it like a disturbance in my being. So I'm sure that is why this training is ongoing, so I will be familiar with waves of vibration. It feels like boom—boom—boom—boom—boom, that's how it feels in my system. And I'm also gathering my notes, so that when I am in a certain location, I don't have to think about all these questions. I have already things that I would like to know, things that are important for the system as a whole to be in harmony, –what I consider to be in harmony. But there are also certain things you said, "Just because from your level of opinion something is in harmony, doesn't mean that it will be in harmony where it is located." So I have to learn about that. And since I don't know that, those questions are not on my paper.

D. I'm sure we'll talk about it.

B. Yes, because you kinda know my intentions here. So I would assume, and what I would hope for, is that you will add questions and add information—like saying, "This place has a lot of natural light," if I don't have that on my paper, then you will help me so I know. And I might go, "Why is that needed?" And you will say, for instance, hypothetically, and you will say, "You wanted your Individuals to have natural light, so this place has that." If I don't know to ask that, then I want that to be provided to me, so I don't get lost. There are certain things that I don't know how to phrase as a question. But I have, over and over, in many ways, told you about my intentions. Since you have more knowledge about the locations and what they provide, then you will be able to describe it for me. Let's say that you say, "This place will not be able, in any near future or cycle, to change the atmospheric surroundings. So what you have on this living planet will be constant." Then I will take that into consideration. Do I want it to be constant, or do I want to have changes? Do I want changes in my seasons, for instance? And then you say, "Well, if you pick this location, hypothetically—," then you can describe that to me, so I don't get confused. I would assume that once you have put it somewhere, it will somewhat remain. I don't know how I would be able to remove it, so I kinda want to know that.

D. There's a lot of things to plan for ahead of time!

B. Ah, and you know about my conditions, because I made it perfectly clear about it being friendly and the neighbors and so forth, so you know that. But you also know the little details that I might have just said in passing. Just said it, and you paid attention, hopefully, and you would say like, "Here it will come in contact with evolution." And then I can say, "What is that?" And you say, "Well, what we planned for this specific destination, let's say, is more of travels." Then I will take that into consideration. Okay, the general evolution in this galaxy is about making creatures travel. Am I okay with that? And if I am, then I will say, "Okay." So, little things once we have departed. But at this point, I am preparing. That's what I do. Jeshua is not part of this. Maybe he's just gonna come when it's time to leave. Isaac comes sometimes, he comes.

D. So how are you preparing to travel?

B. Because there's gonna be, clearly, a lot of impressions going on around my bubble, then Jeshua said I need to still my mind, otherwise I'm not gonna be able to decipher and make choices correctly, because I'm gonna just fully engaged with all these new impressions that come. So the bubble training is also to protect me from that, in some way. When I was training in the bubble, the first time, it was somewhat empty. BUT, when I'm gonna travel, it's gonna fill up with an element that is like heavy air that will make me float inside, he said. That is why the bubble itself is gonna spin, but not me inside.

D. Is that to protect your energetic body?

B. That's what you say. But it also has a side effect that it makes me go to sleep in my brain, a little bit. So it's a fact that I'm not gonna be bouncing around inside of the bubble, I'm gonna be locked in my position, but I'm gonna be protected, and I'm gonna be somewhat asleep. So, it's like, he said, my whole system will move into hibernation, except my receiving centers, my so–called "center point", the heart and the computer. They're gonna be activated, but they're gonna move slower. Similar like if your heart beat goes from a hundred beats a minute down to thirty. So when I'm in this bubble and I'm off, my centers are gonna be on a minimum capacity, so I can perceive the signals correctly. I don't know about the brain. So this is what I've been training for. I've been floating around in a big tank, not my bubble, but a big tank, and Isaac was there. It was like a big tank of this materia, and I was floating in it.

Because it was somewhat dark, you said, "We can put in colors for you, so it feels better. What colors would you like?" And I said I would like red and blue. So you put in a little bit of red and blue, so it would not feel so scary in this big tank. But you were standing above it, and I was below, in the tank, training for the bubble. I could look up and see you.

D. Did I smile and wave?

B. You said, "Everything's going to be okay, Bob. We are just going to add colors, so it feels a little bit more fun for you. Focus on the colors. Which one do you like the most?" And when I was floating around there I said, "I like red most." And you said, "Look at the red, look at the red," so you were guiding me to focus on the red color, so that I forgot I was in the tank.

D. So when you go floating around in the universe, what kind of information are you going to collect?

B. I am interested in not only in the neighbors, because Isaac said we cannot always decide about the neighbors that we are going to have, –and we don't know their evolution, he said. So even though you might think, "Oh, this is a nice neighbor," you don't know the master plan behind their evolution, so that might shift. So he told me to not only focus on the neighbors, but to focus on the general intention of the area. Let's say, if it's going to be developed; that is more interesting. He said, "Let's say that you want to have a silent experience for your solar system. Then you want to have it in an area where there's a lack of development, so you want to focus more on that," he said. And I said, "I don't want it to be lost, like in silence. So I want there to be activity, because I get confused myself, if there is a lack of activity, and I want my system to be somewhere where there is progress and commotion in some way." But I was so focused on it being nice commotions that I forgot about the main agenda of my solar system. And my main agenda is that it's not gonna be secluded or by itself, because evolution and progress sometimes go hand in hand with your neighbors, and if you see a neighbor not doing so well, then you yourself, who might have more knowledge, can affect that neighbor. My system is gonna be a prototype for goodness, and I want that to be placed where it has the potential, if needed, to be a role model.

D. That applies to a lot of things. That's really good.

B. Ah. So, Isaac said I should focus on that a little bit, –so I have.

D. How long do you plan, once you set your creature up on this planet, how long do you think it will be there?

B. I–I–I have planned for it to be there for a while, a long period of time. You said that normally a good thing is to have cycles about, from a human point of view, of one hundred thousand years. You said that is a good cycle to put creatures into certain evolutionary spans. Then you said, "After that, it is a good idea if you then upgrade or change it, or remove it, based on preference." So I kinda know that is the general idea. A cycle of a hundred thousand years is somewhat of a theme that you go by when there is physical reality. And it doesn't mean it has to be removed, but everyone wants to improve. So then it is suggested that you do some sort of an upgrade. It could be like either mentally, emotionally, or physically. This specific prototype (*of his Individual that was removed from Earth*), the first one, is planned on being there one hundred thousand years, then we will do upgrades. And that will make me constantly be in the space of creation.

D. Well, that's good. You probably already have plans for things you'd like to do?

B. I do indeed, I do indeed. Because it is actually only operating single, or as a couple unit. So my next upgrade might be that it should be like in a flock. It doesn't do that, right now, and it never became that on the Earth plane, because it was removed. So it never became, but that was my intention, for it to be in a flock and to operate with the intelligence that can exist within a flock. I wanted that to be part of its next phase. Here, with no disturbances of guests or other things we will have to consider, it might be that I can make that next step for it.

D. Does it have hands, or hooves?

B. If you think of like a bear, but with fingers.

D. So it can grip things?

B. Yes, it has a thumb. If you're that intelligent and you can't grip things, it's frustrating. It's like being in a straitjacket. You can't move, you know, so it's the same thing. You have to match, mix and match. Since it has a lot of intelligence and understanding within, if it wasn't able to grip things and to elaborate and play and to create things, it would be very frustrated. They actually build nest differently than regular animals because of their ability with the thumbs. They have like four fingers, including the thumb.

D. Can they stand up on two legs?

B. Yes, they can, if they want to. They do when they look, when they are scouting.

D. Like a prairie dog.

B. Similar like a prairie dog. The back feet are bigger than the hands, so they are not the same size, all four, not the same size. So, that will be what I'm gonna do.

D. That's a nice project.

B. It's a nice project. So I'm gonna do that. Anyway, okay, I will continue with my training and my questions and my notes. And sometimes you force me to think. Because I say, "Have I missed any questions?" And you said, "I don't know. What could that be? What's the intention, Bob?" And I said, "Well, I have like fifty questions. Is that enough?" Then you say, "Well, what have you covered, Bob?" Then I try to make you say, "Oh, but you missed that. You asked about that one time." But you don't. So I'm back into the self-study phase, where I need to reflect back on all the questions that I have, or had, up to this point.

D. You've had a number.

B. I've had a number of questions, indeed. Sometimes you're helpful, and sometimes you force me to look in rewind and reflect, from the beginning of my solar system, on what I was concerned about. That's what you say, "Focus on what you were concerned about. And then, from there, you will remember the questions that you had at that time. And if it has not been answered at this point, you can put it down on the paper." So, in some way, you force me to not be too lazy, because it is my project, and you don't want to take that away. You say, "This is going to be yours. You will be completely satisfied, because you made all the conditions and you made everything by yourself." (*Whenever Bob says "paper", you should understand he is implying how he is making notes. He explained that he records information as symbols in an energetic, yet somewhat of a physical book. It's for our benefit that he calls it paper.*)

D. The end result is that you'll be able to design everything by yourself. And you'll know why.

B. Ah. Indeed. And I do appreciate that. Because once this is settled, I'll be completely satisfied because it's all mine. I will not say, "I did that planet, but then you and Jeshua and everyone else, you did everything else." And then everyone would be like (*gives a big yawn*), you know, maybe yawn. So, – I want it to be mine!

D. I'm sure when it gets right down to it, we'll help you to remember things if you have overlooked something.

B. Ah. Yes, indeed. Jeshua doesn't force me, like you do. But we're a friend couple, so you sort of tease me in a way to trigger me to think. And Jeshua is more like, he just tries to look after me, I would assume. And then you say, "Let's make him think." So, you're more involved with teaching.

D. Good cop, bad cop.

B. Huhuhuh. I think that will be it, and I'm gonna continue with my reflection and try to remember what concerns I had in the beginning. I did have concerns about the evolution thing, and we have covered that, somewhat. But still, I want to know about the general idea for the specific region I'm putting it. But you said, "You can't study up on everything about this place, you have to experience it," and I'm all about experiencing.

D. I'm sure it will be a nice vacation away from the lab.

B. Ah. I have to be REALLY alert so I don't miss anything. I don't want to miss anything on my travels, you know, I'm sure it's going to be fascinating! But, it is that fact of the changing vibrations, that as we move through these different realities and also into certain areas, then it will affect my being. You somewhat transform like that lizard, that chameleon, and you just become the new energy wave. I don't have that training, so it's gonna be different for me, I would assume. Jeshua said I'm gonna be in a bubble! "We'll put you in a bubble," he said.

D. Once you learn how to do this, you'll be able to travel anytime you want.

B. I don't think so. Jeshua said I will be put in a bubble, like a soap bubble. That's interesting. You don't travel in a soap bubble, I would assume. I don't know, but he just told me, "It will be similar like a sphere."

Spin Like a Dryer? (Sept 24, 2017)

Bob was given different exercises to prepare him for the sensations associated with the vibrational fields that he will pass through. Then he was immersed in a tank to simulate the floating sensation from the dense air–like material that will fill the inside of the bubble when we actually travel. Then it was time for him to try moving into and out of the empty bubble, which is basically an energetic shell. It was a sphere about twice his size and was placed in a space he calls the sphere room. He was quite reluctant to go into the bubble because he was not sure if we could hear him, or if he would be able to get out again. Christine described what she saw while he was telling his story, and said Bob was walking all around the bubble, trying to build up the courage to get in, and looking very nervous.

B. (*He began making faces as he adjusted his energy into Christine's. But he didn't say anything.*)

D. Hello, my friend.

B. Peek–a–boo!

D. Long time, no talk.

B. Well, on this plane at least. But I talk all the time. I talk indeed all the time, because I have questions that continues as I progress with my training program for everything to unfold as it's supposed to. So we talk all the time! Maybe you're somewhat tired of the questions, because I do sense that it comes to an end with my solar system project, and we are about to launch, Jeshua said. SO, Jeshua said that my bubble training has gone well. I must say that I was a little bit intimidated about going into the bubble, because it was somewhat floating. Jeshua said it was supposed to do that, but I needed to be somewhat encouraged because there was like no doors in this bubble. I could see there was like no emergency exits in the bubble, so I wanted to know about that. And Jeshua encouraged me and calmed me, and Ophelia as well. They actually called her in, because I wouldn't go into the bubble. So everyone was there the first time I actually entered the bubble. All of you stood around it and said, "It's not going to go anywhere, Bob. It's just going to be here in this sphere room." It's similar like the sphere room. And you said, because I was wondering if there was like a gate thing in the ceiling, and if it was gonna just shoot off, but you said it was not gonna do that. So the first time I got in, because I can see out, but there is like no exits, so as I get in, it seems like I cannot get out. And Jeshua said that I will get out, and you said so as well, but I didn't want to go in. So Ophelia came and Isaac came, so we were all standing around the bubble—and then I did get in, into the bubble.

D. You were like the little sparkles going into a tree for the first time.

B. Ahahaha. HUH HUH, AH, I see that, and I remember it being somewhat the same as when I first went into the tree. I see that. So I can see that going into something, not being sure of how to get out. So it was like that, yes indeed. When you say it like that, it was actually like going in rewind, and experiencing something that was somewhat unfamiliar.

D. So how did you get out of the bubble?

B. It's not a door either in or out, I simply (*he is struggling to find the words to describe*), I simply, it's like it's absorbing me. Jeshua said that you don't have to look for exits, or windows, or anything, because it's just going to be like going through the surface of the water, like we talked about before. (*Related to souls moving through the fourth dimension after death.*) So he said I'm not supposed to just go out anywhere, so I have to be in the bubble. And that is where I became a little bit confused, and a little bit distressed. He then said I only go in and out when we are in the sphere room, so to speak. (*Jeshua advised that he would remain in the protective bubble while he is out traveling, but Bob interpreted it as being stuck inside all the time.*) And I also wanted to know if you can hear me inside. (*He sounded a little nervous.*) He said you do. The first time I–I–I entered the bubble, it was simply like going through the surface of the water. And as I was inside the bubble, you were all standing around it. And it was floating like maybe one meter from the ground, so I could see you. And then I could hear you, and Jeshua said, "We're going to make it spin a little bit." (*He started laughing.*) And I said, "Like a dryer?" Oh, you laughed about that, and you said, "It's never going to be like a dryer. It's not like that." Huh. So Jeshua said, "We're going to make it spin a little bit. The bubble's going to spin, but you inside would not spin." So I would not be feeling like I'm getting sea-sick or anything. But he said that he's gonna make it spin a little bit—so you did. It was like moving in one direction, clockwise, it never went the other direction. It was to make me familiar with this way of travel, he said. So that was the first time. But I have improved, indeed. Now I go in and out, and you don't have to observe me all the time as I go into the bubble. Because I know now that as long as I am in this room of training, then I have the ability to go in and out. But it is somewhat like you said, it is the same way like the sparkles need to know, to be aware that even though there is no green sign saying “Exit”, or “Emergency Exit”, or like a little button that you can press, you’re never locked, really. But he said I’m not gonna exit as we are traveling. I would still see you and communicate with you, even though you will look different. As we all go, you will be more like stars, he said, but I would still recognize you. So he said that you’re gonna portray yourself like stars, from my perspective, BUT in different colors so I know which one is which. Because clearly that is of importance to me, that I feel who is who, and so forth. But, because you don’t travel in a bubble, he gave me this whole outline of how the departure would be, so I know I’m not floating by myself.

D. Well, that’s good. We would never leave you alone.

B. No, he said that you’re going to be in front of the bubble, and he would be to the left, and Isaac would be to the right. I don’t know if there is gonna come someone from the back, but that’s what I’m gonna see. I’m going to constantly look straight ahead and I will see you, so to speak. So that’s how we’re going to travel, he said.

D. This will be a lot of fun when we go out exploring.

B. (*Popping his lips, listening.*) Jeshua is mysterious. He has stuff up his sleeve, so to speak. I know that he knows things about the center pole (*the Creator*). I do know he does, I know he does. I tried to ask questions about the wheel in general. Mysterious.

D. He didn’t really answer?

B. He smiled.

D. Like Ophelia.

B. Like Ophelia, similar like Ophelia. Isaac is doing the same, always with his arms crossed and smiling. And you are more like diverting my attention, saying, “Look over here, see here,” and I’m like, “Uhh?” And I look. You’re different because you know I get confused when you get silent, and you also know I continue to poke you. I don’t poke Jeshua, I don’t. I don’t do that. But with you, you know that to be silent is not working that well, because I’m more myself with you—I continue to ask, so you’re more doing the diversion maneuver.

D. Well, that’s because we’re such good friends.

B. Ah, ah. I have added, on my little planet, certain vegetation and flowers and trees and so forth, because of the adjustment of the atmosphere. I had like a jungle, but I changed it a little bit so it's more like forests, only a smaller part that is a jungle.

D. Well, it might like that better. More room to roam around.

B. Ah, I created lakes as well. I wanted that because I thought maybe I want fish. I thought about that, different things, so that is in its memory now. If I later want to have a fish, I have a fish tank, I have a lake. Huhuhuh. So if I'm like, "Oh, I want fish." Then you would say, "You didn't create a lake, where are you going to put it?" So I thought about that; so the self–study has been rewarding, I must say. So that's what I've been doing. I'm happy to be back, and we are moving closer to where we're gonna take off. And now I know where, somewhat, where we're gonna go in the universe. Big thing, this. I would like to see this pole in the middle, because I can sense that there is some sort of awareness, of sorts, in it. But I don't know, and I don't know if you know. And I don't know if even Jeshua knows.

D. How do you perceive it?

B. It's like a pulse. The only thing I could give you a picture of, is that it's like a mother and father energy in one. But it's like a big pulse in it. I don't think you can go into it, but it's like...

D. If you did, you might lose your identity. You would no longer be you.

B. I don't know what it is. First if felt like a mother energy, but when I saw it more, it was like dual.

D. The creative center.

B. Ah, it is, indeed. So, I'm not gonna go in there. My bubble is absolutely NOT gonna go in there. It might just disappear or vanish, and what happens to me then? So I'm not gonna go in there.

D. You'll be absorbed like rain in the ocean.

B. Oh, oh. And if you don't go, and no one goes, there is no way to send in a rescue team, so to speak. So, I'm not gonna go there.

D. So many things you have learned!

B. Ah, ah, yes indeed. And because you add more information all the time it also creates more questions all the time, so I'm constantly in that phase of, you know, asking questions and wondering about things, because the more I see, the more I wonder. So, that's probably it about that. But I'm not afraid to be in the bubble anymore.

Into the Oven (Dec 3, 2017)

Bob finally completed the design of his solar system, which included all the energetic patterns for the plants, animals and atmospheric conditions he wanted to have on his living planet. The model, which he had been keeping in his drawer in my lab, was taken to a tank where the gravity experts, in this case Isaac, came and added a gravity and vacuum field to see if it would float as expected. The test was successful, and then it was taken somewhere to another area of the lab and put in what Bob described as an oven. Exactly what happens in the oven remains a mystery. My guess is that the pattern is infused with light energy, so that when the "seed" is planted in the fish tank, the energetic pattern will unfold and grow with its own internal energy source, eventually manifesting a physical solar system.

Bob, Jeshua, Eli, and Ari describe creation as a very controlled process. Humans see it as randomness that is influenced by quantum and physical laws. Cosmologists and astronomers may be able to write elaborate equations, but reality can never be theoretically modeled. Ari, the most advanced spirit we communicate with, has said our fish tank has been in rotating through this position on the wheel for trillions of (Earth) years. They assure us that gravitational fields are not the same from galaxy to galaxy, and can change over time, depending on the stage of evolution. There are several types of gravity that work in combination with vacuum fields to maintain form and movement. Also, the speed of light is not constant, and black holes do not exist. If any of these statements are true, and I assume they all are, then the accepted models of the Universe are completely invalid, beginning with the theories of relativity and special relativity. It is worth mentioning that the current mathematical models of the Universe would self-destruct, if not for the addition of unknown variables clumped into concepts they call "dark matter" and "dark energy", which they can neither identify nor find. According to the spirits, sound and gravity work together to create a vacuum field that holds objects in place, and may create the appearance of either higher or lower gravity than expected. These primary components of cosmic light, cosmic sound, vacuum, and gravity can be found from the smallest level of atoms and DNA, to massive sheets of galaxies. Current scientific theories only recognize attractive forces on a cosmic scale. They have no knowledge of, or way to measure, the effects of the vacuum field, which manifest as a repulsive force. If the motion of objects around a star, for instance, involves unknown, variable forces, then the estimation of the mass or density of planets becomes unknowable, as do most other conjectures about the principles operating the physical Universe.

B. Ophelia complimented me on my solar system. She said that it became a really good result of my efforts. Huhuh.

D. Are you still working on the finer details?

B. There is something going on with my solar system, with Isaac. So I have left it with Isaac, and I do not see it anymore. It has departed from my drawer, and it is not in my hands now. It's similar like you create a pizza, and now the pizza is in the oven. But the oven isn't open, so I can't see my pizza. That is what's happening here. I have left my pizza with Isaac, and he has stuck it into the oven, and the lid is closed, the door is closed, so I can't go look. So, I'm sure it's cooking, in some way!

D. Pre–hibernation.

B. Maybe that is the hibernation oven! Huhuh. Ophelia sent me a picture of a pizza and said, "This is similar." So it's being cooked! There's a lot of discussion, you and me. We talk about things, and we go over the process of my experience with the solar system, but you also said there was also gonna be lessons ahead about time, the cycles in my solar system. The pizza has no cycles in the same way, when I left it. BUT, when it goes into this oven, this magic oven, it becomes cooked, and it gets an atmosphere. Everything becomes in this magical oven where my pizza is, at this moment.

D. Does Ophelia have any role in cooking it?

B. Ah, she doesn't say, because she's smart enough not to say everything. But in this magical oven, everything becomes, meaning like the trees and everything on my living planet. So if I give you a picture of what is happening here, I created all these patterns for it, you know, but it has to be cooked, and doing so, my atmosphere is the last thing added before you take out the pizza. That's what she said.

In a later session, I followed up on the progress. He said that his solar system had been "cooked" and was being prepared to be launched to its destination, which he had selected. Bob was allowed to pick the location where his solar system would be located, but in order to do so, he had to undergo extensive training to travel in an energetic bubble into the fish tank.

D. Oh, how's your pizza doing?

B. Oh, it's still getting cooked, BUT it's out of the oven, so it's cooling down. I can see it, but it is in like a glass box. It's like a model, and this is later gonna be projected. I have no idea how this is gonna happen. But at the moment, it's cooling down in some sort of glass container. It's kinda big.

D. Does it look nice? Are you proud of your work?

B. Ah, yes. It looks bubbly. It's glowing in there.

D. We'll find a nice spot for it.

B. It's gonna be, it's gonna be in some way placed where it will be like starting from like a bang. Not a big bang, but like a little, like how you create a fire, sshhhhooo, that's how it's gonna just become. Interesting. This is happening all over the place, Isaac said. But you know how you light a match and it appears? It will look similar to what I see here in my glass container. Small in the beginning, but then it will expand and fill out the empty space (*in the Universe*) where it's supposed to be located.

D. I look forward to hearing about how that happens, the process of creation from a human perspective.

B. Well, you might want to write a book about that!

D. I'm trying to.

B. We know! Huhuh.

Bob Travels to View His Solar System (Apr 15, 2018)

He was finally ready to go travel and view the location for his solar system. While it was presented to him as three choices, it seems that Jeshua and Lasaray must have decided where to put it, because it was already there when he arrived. However, it was exactly where he wanted it, so he was quite happy.

B. You and I have been doing a lot of talking, because of the fact of my solar system. It is actually in place, we did depart.

D. We did? In your bubble?

B. Indeed. We did indeed.

D. Tell me about that.

B. First, it was a bit of disappointment, because you made me fall asleep in the bubble. No one told me that. Because of the bubble traveling through several different vibrations, and for some of the vibrations, the bubble was not equipped, you said. But I didn't buy that because it did travel through. So, I think it was I that was not fully equipped. So the bubble travelled through seven different layers, you said. But I only remember traveling through like three or four, three. So the other ones, they didn't come in any sort of order, which you might think they would, like I would be asleep for the first four and then awake, but it was not. Clearly, I was awake at the end, the last one, but I have no idea about the other ones. I asked, "How long have we been travelling?" And you said, "We have traveled through seven vibrational fields to access the location of your choosing." But I was asleep during some of them, and I don't know why. We might talk about that later. You said that I should only focus on the end result.

D. I remember you said that whatever was in the bubble made you slow down.

B. It did. And I didn't spin inside it, but the bubble itself rotated, and it spun in different rotations. It was not always clockwise, from my perspective. I could see the rotation, but I remained still. But, like I said, I was asleep during some, "for my wellbeing", that's what you said.

D. Did you see the three locations we had selected for you to review?

B. Oh, I saw a lot! I saw the Milky Way. I saw another galaxy, and I was like traveling among the stars in a circle, a big circle. And it was just like lights and there were no planets that I could see where I was at, but one location had all this light and it was only stars. And I remember just being like, "Ahh," I was silent in this experience.

D. Was it awe inspiring?

B. Ah, that was one reality and it was completely silent. The bubble just sort of glided through it, and you were also with. It was like being in a vacuum. That's not where my solar system is, but this was one that I experienced, and it was the most MAGICAL experience. I actually asked afterwards if we can go there and maybe not place a solar system, but I would really like to go back. You said, "All realities we travel to carry life forms, in some way. That specific reality is an energetic one, it's not a manifested physical reality." But it was AMAZING!

D. Was it in our fish tank or a different one?

B. Well, you said we were in the same fish tank, so I never left.

D. So there are energetic realities in our Universe?

B. That is true. I was awake, but I was almost in a trance state because I was completely fascinated. And then, I don't know if this was in order, like I said, if I fell asleep, but the second one I came to, that was more like, there was different sounds in them, all these different levels. So the next one, it had like a drumming vibration, this wasn't silent at all. This had like a drumming experience in that one. You said, "This is a very dense reality, and this is not where we will put the Individual, because the Individual needs more light." It had a center star, this galaxy—a huge, big center point. You said that this reality is more dense, but you wanted to show me this—so I did experience this. And it's more like a gravitational stabilizer by itself, almost, this specific star. You wanted to show me a stabilizer galaxy that operates like a stabilizer for other galaxies, so that's why we saw that. And you said that all stabilizers have that in some way, that boom—boom—boom. You said it is similar like a heart in a human body, -that is a stabilizer in a human body-, and every living life form has a stabilizer, whether it's a plant, whether it's an animal or a human, you have the heartbeat which is similar like a stabilizer, it operates similar.

D. These are all locations within our Universe, just different energetic realities?

B. Different energetic realities, but I was still in the same fish tank. But within the fish tank exist levels that you can go through.

D. So, what about the third location, what did you find there?

B. Oh, that's when I got to my location where my solar system is launched. And that is a joyful place! It's a lot of colors, and everyone in this specific galaxy has the ability of progress, and the ability of emotions. Because, like Isaac said, I really want to have an emotional evolution on my place. I was concerned about the mental evolution, I must say. The physical I was fine with, because that's way out of my league. That's all in the Creator's hand, and that will come through the egg and Ia. So I will get a preview, I would think, as to what sort of change, physically, that would happen. BUT, I'm not in favor of this mental evolution all the time, because I have seen firsthand how that can go to SHH—TTT (*he didn't say the "i"*), so I don't want that. BUT Isaac knew that! He knew exactly what I was looking for. So when I went to class with him as my solar system was in the oven, we talked about that. And he said, "Based on what I know about you, Bob, I think you will like an emotional galaxy, similar like where Siah is." So we picked out, or he and you picked out, I did not pick, but I was given this reality, and that's where I'm at. It was singing and the tones here were almost like being at Ophelia's place. It was like harp music and I could sense, as we were traveling in the bubble, that we passed solar systems that maybe students at Ophelia's place had created. It was a very, very happy community, this galaxy. And this was EXACTLY what I wished for my Individual, –to be belonging in an emotional, friendly galaxy.

D. Well, that's wonderful!

B. So I have really nice neighbors, I do indeed. My solar system is, you know, I have my own sun, but all solar systems circle around a central point, a central sun. So my Individual will be happy in this haven where I have placed my solar system. You made it possible for me to observe this because you knew that I would want to see, and you told me that I cannot come here in my bubble all the time. So it's not like I can just take my bubble and shoot off. I don't know the way, and I have to go through levels where I'm not familiar or comfortable with, to get there. It's kind of far away, you said. Because I asked, "Where is it? And have we changed fish tanks?" And you said, "No, we're still in the same area, but you can be a little bit above and a little bit below, and still belong to the vibrational frequency." You said that we put my system a little bit higher up, but I'm still on the same reality.

D. So your system is on a little higher plane?

B. Indeed, indeed. It's a little bit higher. Earth is on this center line and more to nine o'clock. Mine is a little bit above and a little bit further in to the center pole. That's where I am. (*The "more to nine o'clock" is a reference to the vibrational density of the solar system, as it relates to the Wheel of Creation, as shown on page 6. The Earth and our galaxy are fairly dense, although there are other locations that are more dense. The Andromeda galaxy is actually a little less dense than ours.*)

D. Were you involved with placing it there?

B. It was there! I don't know how, it's like it took its own bubble! Huhuh. I don't know, but there it just was. But I recognized it immediately, because I made colors on my planet, my living planet, and I said, "There it is! There it is!" So we went there and my bubble circled around and I could see everything that I created.

D. Was your Individual on it already? Had it been placed?

B. No, no. It was in the making to becoming.

D. So it's in the hibernation phase?

B. Indeed. My living planet simply had vegetation. There was still the fact of evolution to wake everyone up. I have bugs, too.

D. I guess we're going to go back at some point and put your Individual on?

B. The Individual is there, it's just the pattern hasn't been waking up yet.

D. Ah, Okay. Did I say that we could go back sometime?

B. You said that we could observe this from the lab, a little bit, so we don't have to go there all the time. But if there is a need, you said, we can simply make the same journey again. So you gave a window for that, but you said there is no need to always go out, we can do remote teaching and remote adjustments. I don't know how that works, remote adjustments, but maybe it's in that big unknown that I am not supposed to tap into. But I really enjoyed, after we arrived, to go around in my bubble; and you allowed that to take a little while. So I circled all the orbits. I wanted to make sure that everything was in place exactly. I circled out and looked at the stabilizer. I looked at my sun—it was really shiny. It was not, you know, dimmed at all. It was like a brand new, shiny star, mine, and it's a healthy system. Everything was perfectly designed.

D. Ah, well, congratulations!

B. Congratulations to me! Huhuh, I did have great teachers! And then, for the longest time, I was snoozing over my living planet. And I was looking to see my Individual, and I could see, –I mean, it's not there–, but I could see all the vegetation. And you said, "Here is where we're going to wake up the Individual. Here is where your flowers are going to change over to time to become that specific flower you wanted to come later on. Here you can see where the pond is, where there's going to be life forms in the waters. We're going to move in atmospheric shifts as well, so there is going to be a time when there is going to come a lot of rain." After the rain, that's when my Individual is going to wake up. At the moment, it is very sunny. It's not like clouds at the moment. But you're going to put in, or Isaac is gonna put in clouds, so it's gonna rain for a long time. And after the rain, that's when my Individual and all my bugs are waking up. So my system is in hibernation to become, But the system itself was in motion. But everything that I had created was not yet to be found.

D. Wow. That's just wonderful.

B. And you said that from your lab, from where you're going to observe, you said that your concern, or your mission or job, was to make sure that the stabilizer is intact. So that's what you're going to look at, and you said that I can observe my living planet. I guess someone from Ophelia's place will observe the sun.

D. So now that you're finished, did you have any awards or ceremonies? Maybe a graduation?

B. You made me one! Huhuh, you invited all those quiet groups (*the Elahims and others on the sixth, eighth and ninth*), and they actually kinda applauded. You invited all those to come to your study. So everyone was there, and you told them, in your way, what had happened. And you showed on screens my system, where it was. Even though I couldn't really understand everything, some of them I can understand, but I felt like they were congratulating me. So I felt acknowledged by this group of cosmic scientists who are doing the engineering of galaxies. Isaac was there, Zachariah came, Ophelia, all those friends, my family friends, they came and I understood them. And Ophelia said that I did really well. And she gave me an extra plant that I'm gonna launch, a gift. It's like in a glass box at the moment. But it's gonna be launched up there, an additional flower that is gonna be very helpful for the environment, so she gave me an extra one. And Zachariah, he gave me additional information about the evolution and so forth, combined with Isaac. So they gave me more information about the place where my system is.

D. Did Gergen and Ola and Ia come?

B. Nay. I'll tell them later. Gergen said that this was my sunshine, my spot in the sun. Huhuh. But Ophelia said that that specific plant is put into the system (*already*). And I recognize it because it's one of those that really endures and it creates, with its roots, it creates harmony within the soil. So this is a very special plant. I've seen it, but I don't have the pattern for it, so I couldn't make it myself. That was a very special treat.

D. Did she put that on your living planet?

B. Indeed. So, that's what I've been up to.

D. Well, that's a lot!

B. Ah, it's a lot. But there are screens that I can observe this a little bit.

D. There's no need to travel, if you can just look on a screen.

B. Well, you say so, because you probably knew that I was going to ask. So maybe you set up these screens. Huhuh.

D. Did we put your bubble back in the bubble room?

B. The bubble is back. I think it's my bubble, I don't think it is a common bubble for everyone to sort of move around in. It's got my license plate on it! But Jeshua said that I can't just pop in and take off, -and I'm not sure that I want to. And you don't travel in a bubble, so it's not like you and I can take off, which, you know, I would prefer. Anyway, that was that, and I'm really happy because I have all these patterns beginning to take place on my living planet.

D. I'm happy that you got it placed somewhere that you are pleased with.

B. Ah. And there's really nice neighbors, with an emotional well-being. Okay, I'm gonna go now, but we're gonna continue to observe.

D. Well thank you and Ophelia for coming today, it's always a pleasure.

B. Always a pleasure. Okay, bye-bye.

Ophelia's Special Plant (Apr 29, 2018)

Ari had spoken first, and then Ophelia came in to adjust the energies for Bob. Sometimes Bob is prevented from hearing the conversation, as he was this time while Ari was talking. Ophelia occupied his attention by showing him the energetic pattern of the plant that she had given him as a gift.

B. Well, Ophelia is doing really good cleaning. I did not listen. I did not listen. Ophelia said, "We're gonna be over here, Bob. Come and look over here." And I said, "What's happening over here? Shouldn't we be over there?" And she said, "We'll soon go, but look over here." So we've been coloring again. I've been observing and I've been given the pattern of my new plant.

D. Ah, very nice. Is this the one that Ophelia gave to you? Is she teaching you how to make it?

B. Umm humm. Indeed. I was given the secret potion of how to create this plant.

D. It must be kind of complicated.

B. It is indeed, because it's not simply a regular plant. You should know that when you do these (*he looked over towards Ophelia and didn't say anything for a while*), when you create these color maps, which are also in a physical human, then you can add a little extra detail, depending on if that specific creation or being should be able to have or possess a piece from the master mind. My plants, the plants that I created, had less dose of the Master Mind. This plant that Ophelia gave me has a higher portion or percentage of the Master Mind. That is why it is an intelligent plant.

D. How much, compared to a tree?

B. Oh, I don't want say that someone is dumb, but the tree would be considered, most trees here, they might be considered like an awareness of, let's say, like a five to seven–year old. But THIS plant that I was given actually has like the awareness of an adult. And I had not reached that level of learning to create plants that had the awareness from the Master Mind that represents an adult.

D. So what kind of actions does it do in nature?

B. Through its roots, it can create connections with other plants and in some way acts like a battery for them. So even if their awareness is like a seven–year old, due to their extra energy that they receive with root–to–root communication, –it's like a web within the soil underneath the surface–, it might not raise the awareness (*of the seven–year old plant*), but it will become more endurable and it will actually last longer. The life cycle might actually last longer.

D. Does Ophelia's plant pull energy from the atmosphere, the web above?

B. It's like a battery. It's like we taught the sparkles how to become your own light capsule, this flower just does it by itself. It just moves in and out of its own light capsule and it acts like it's generating energy. It acts like a battery for the region where it's placed. One flower might be able to help an area of, let's say, maybe half a football field, and everything within that area will benefit from that flower. But she's not just putting one flower, she said! She puts them out strategically, so it will create no gap between these spots.

D. Do those flowers grow on Earth?

B. Nay, I don't think so. She not answering that (*looks to left towards Ophelia*), but she said that there are some that are similar, indeed. There are similar plants, so this is nothing special. She said there are similar plants acting in the same way here, to create that energetic web and acting like generators of energy and oxygen to a region. So, it's not a brand–new thing. But I don't know if this plant exists here. It's red, when the flower comes, it becomes red.

D. So that's on your planet now?

B. It will become. It's actually in bloom, it's starting to become in bloom, so it's part of the ecosystem that I have. And she said it's going to be highly favorable for my ecosystem. And we have the same thing here (*on Earth*), there are certain plants that act like these generators to improve mainly the soil. So when interactions (*interference from humans*) take place within the soil, then the web that is created to be helpful to optimize the level of growth in that region, it becomes broken. That's why we don't want you to put down bad seeds, because YOU DON'T KNOW! You're not Ophelia. You can't put down seeds that you have no idea what they will do! They're not gonna create a good web! DON'T PUT DOWN STUFF in the soil that you have no idea if it's gonna create a web! It might just clog up the system.

D. If they don't want to do a reboot on the humans, maybe Ophelia will do a reboot on the plants.

B. Ah, and just make those seeds not workable.

D. That would be my goal, if I had any say in the reboots.

B. Ancients knew about this web. And natives also knows about this web, and they operate in harmony with the web in the soil. You can see it as canals, almost. Some are canals with water, and some are with other goodies in order for the region itself to be rich. If someone doesn't understand how to read the energy, they should not disturb. Here it is not considered to be a science, when it is actually the highest science you have—to understand the web and to understand that if you disturb nature then the side effects can be that something happens within the atmosphere. They don't see the correlation between what they put down in the soil to what happens from above, like certain storms and so forth. Because the trees are not singing! The trees are not happy! And if the trees are not radiating and exhaling oxygen and light into the atmosphere, if they are not in resonance, then you see certain weather phenomena that actually takes place. No one thinks, "Ohh, it's because I put down those bad seeds!" Not all are like that, of course, but certain things are. Because if you make the trees not to sing, and the plants are sad, then they don't communicate with the level above, and that creates disharmony.

D. The problem is that scientists can't measure that, can they?

B. No. And because of this filter within you, that you either operate from the mental, the brain, or from the heart. And those two do not communicate as they did before. When an answer is not found in the mental box, then prior civilizations moved into the emotional box or the soul box in order to find the answer. But here, that's not acceptable. It's not acceptable for a scientific person to say, "I feel". They operate in a way of "I think", and "I know", from that way of thinking. Another person will simply operate from the way it feels, and that's how they know. But when these two levels of awareness don't communicate—

D. Then bad things happen?

B. Or nothing at all! It's just like stagnation. So anyway, my planet is not going to be interfered with, like this planet is.

D. Well, you will have a really happy planet.

B. I have a happy planet, I have a happy system and a happy galaxy.

D. That's what you always wanted.

B. Always wanted that.

The Sun is a Jukebox (May 13, 2018)

The next few sections are related to Bob's studies with the foundation of forms (in the fish tanks), which are the melodies and tones resulting from the patterns of interaction between light and sound. The melodies define structure, purpose, and relationships between other forms. A molecule gives off a very simplistic tone, and a planet is a complicated symphony. Gravity, which has many variants, also emits certain tones, and is part of the pattern implemented in all created form. Gravity is also what creates and holds the vacuum field, which is present around things as small as strands of DNA and organs in the body, to large structures like solar systems and galaxies. Again, we want to point out that these are not detectable by humans, but Bob tries to explain the ideas in ways that we can at least comprehend and appreciate.

D. What other ideas did you come in with today?

B. Oh, I came in and wanted to talk more about my own studies, you know, up at the gravitational group. I have entered that area of study.

D. I would like to hear about that.

B. Indeed. And I've actually, I have been appointed one of these highly skilled teachers. So we are now sitting, him and I and you, by a table. I really like him. He's very visual in the way he explains things. He calculates and he draws and he shows me like maps on how to create the different tunes and different patterns, and he makes me listen to different tunes. That's what I've been doing. I've been listening to different realities and the gravitational field that exists there. And from that, I have to, he said, learn to determine what sort of creation exists. That's number one, so I've been going through them and I'm listening. It's almost like being given little headphones, and I sit there and I listen. Then I draw, I draw what creation is supposedly there.

D. How many different variables are there?

B. I have been listening to five different ones at the moment. And then I have been drawing what sort of material, creations, and conditions that I believe exists.

D. Would these all be in our fish tank, or different fish tanks?

B. He hasn't told me yet! He's just giving me five different tunes. He also wants me to tell him the size of this reality, so that's also part of this. He said, "The tune and the melody also determines how big or small that specific region is, not only what exists within in it." So, once you start to change, you simply pick out, like dissecting a frog, you simply pick out—oh, that was not a good image. (*He suddenly looked towards Ophelia.*) You take out like a raisin from the cookie, that's a better way to say it, Ophelia says.

D. She doesn't like the idea of cutting a frog.

B. Nay, I don't either, really. So, you sit there with your cookie and you take out one note, and then you take another raisin and put it in your cookie, and the whole cookie will have a DIFFERENT song all together. So it's like you can delete, if you have like three verses in a song and you put in a forth, the whole changes. The whole condition within that reality will begin to first wobble a little bit, I would assume. But it's actually the foundation for evolution for all. So when the evolution comes in, it actually comes after the adjustment and change within the gravitational song has been looked over (*altered*).

D. Well, here's a question then: Is the song of the gravity programmed in the sun and stars?

B. Ah, from the star, from the star! That's why there's so much singing up at Ophelia's place, because it's from the star! The star is like the, you know how you have an orchestra and you have this dude in front?

D. The conductor.

B. The conductor! The sun is the conductor and the sun is the jukebox, so when you change the melody within the system, you change the center point. When you change the melody within a human being, you change the center point. Everything you do to change a melody, you change the center point! Huhuh. So, if you wanted to change the whole fish tank, then you will have to (*makes sniffing sound*) sniff out the center point, where that is, and then take out one verse or change the verse, so that's how you change the whole system. So the center point, in this case the sun, is the conductor indeed!

D. Huh, wow. That's a good explanation!

B. I knew that.

D. There is a gravity field that comes in from the outside, isn't there? The Creator puts a field in place?

B. Oh, I don't know about that. But now I wonder, now I want to know about this.

D. Well you've said there are two different types of gravity fields, and there might be more than that. But one is internal to the planet, or the sun, and there's another one that is external, and that is the one that is variable?

B. Indeed. BUT there is no limitations where changes can take place. However, that's way over my expertise at the moment. I haven't been singing that song too long, so I don't know that song fully. I'm still learning.

D. Are you going to be changing the melody of the sun on your solar system?

B. Not now. BUT eventually, when I want to change evolution, – because that's when cycles come in–, then all the changes, indeed, start on the sun. You first change the melody within the sun, and then you also change the center point within the living planet. So, like this planet, it also has a song and that song can be heard and felt, mainly felt, not heard with your ears, but from your core.

D. What's your teacher's name, the one you are working with in the gravity area.

B. It's t...r...i...s...t...a...n. Tristan. He shows me the letters.

D. I get a feeling he's going to be around for a while. You really like him?

B. I do indeed.

D. Is he a friend of Isaac?

B. Ah, friends with Isaac. And he's friends with you. I really like him. I'm all by myself here with the two of you. So I have the two of you teaching me, –but I prefer that.

D. I know you do, especially with good friends.

B. And even Jeshua came by, saying, "Oh, what are you doing over here, Bob?" And I said, "I'm learning about gravitational fields and their songs," and he said, "Yes, everything has a song, Bob." Ah, so I'm learning about songs. Ia knows more about this than I do, because she detects and identifies songs all the time, and vibrational frequencies that come with songs. And she knows all about the tunes that come with all the colors, and then when you collectively put them into a map, in a puddle, what sort of song that you create.

D. I guess she would, since she works the energetic egg and DNA, and things like that.

B. Ah. I also took the class, but not to the extent that she did.

D. You're working more with universes and solar systems and bigger forms. Is she familiar with that?

B. Nah, I tell her. We talk about it and I do tell her.

D. So she knows more about the color patterns within living beings, and you're working more with planets?

B. Indeed. And the sun, and what conditions that need to exist in order for creation to even become possible. So I'm gonna report on that. I can sense a great career!

D. You're going to be sharing with the other ones on the council?

B. Ah, I can sense that is going to be my expertise. I might be like the cloud, you know, creating manuals. OH, Ophelia laughed about that, about my need for fame! (*Looking over towards her and laughing.*)

D. Well, it's good to be acknowledged.

B. Something to strive for! Oh, okay, we're going to round this up, Ophelia says. Plenty of information has been passed forward here today.

D. Thank you, and Ophelia.

Bob gets a Suitcase of Elements (May 19, 2018)

B. (*He stepped in and began making faces.*)

D. They let you back in, did they?

B. Seems so. I, I don't know why I couldn't go first then, if it wasn't like the giants were here. Why couldn't I go first? Why do I always have to wait? (*Looks to the left.*) Ophelia says I got a lot of playroom anyway, so I shouldn't complain. And I am not, I'm not complaining. Well, I am, I am indeed, a little bit...I am, yes, I am.

D. You know, you actually get to talk more than anyone else, so that is the truth. You talk nearly every time. Everyone else has to take a turn with whatever is left over.

B. I have things to say!

D. And we appreciate it.

B. Maybe they too have things to say? But, I'm very eager to make my voice heard and to be acknowledged.

D. We love hearing what you have to say, so we are happy about that.

B. I—I've been in training, I've been studying. I've been working more with the elements, with Isaac. I have a suitcase of elements in my possession, that I have been identifying. And he said that I can take this suitcase. So now I have a suitcase instead of a drawer. (*Laughing.*)

D. Do you take it with you?

B. I take it with me—it's mine!

D. Do you put it under your desk?

B. Huhuh, I don't take it to the second, it's not in my office, no, no. My study with the gravitational people doesn't take place in your study, so I don't have a drawer, I have a suitcase, kinda.

And I said, "Is it gonna be bigger, a bigger suitcase?" Because it's like a big lunchbox.

D. So where do you take it?

B. I take it to my studies. Isaac has filled it up with things that I need, he said, on my travels to the gravitational group. So he gave me this, and it looks like a big lunch box.

D. Does it contain materials to study?

B. No. There are like little pipes in there, like glass tubes like you put in a lab.

D. What are you going to do with this stuff?

B. I don't know. I've been given this bag, because Isaac said I'm gonna need this bag in order for me to be able to create color maps for the gravitational field. I'm not creating color maps now for individuals, or beings, or plants. Now they might not manifest in a way that I can see it. They might travel like the wind, this gravitational field. It looks like, –he showed me a big wave. The gravitational field is moving like a big wave, like an ocean. It's like you see it, and then you cannot. All these different elements and materia are consistent. And that makes not only the movement, he said, but the movement itself, the rhythm of this ocean that I see, it is also at play in this reality. (*Other realities affect the Earth, through the wave.*) OH, I see what they are telling me. The gravitational field around this plane has been going faster than it is supposed to, so it wobbles a little bit. Oh, I'm gonna be quiet, I'm gonna see...(*I started to ask a question, but he immediately cut me off, as he was apparently studying something in his own inner vision.*)

D. What—

B. SHHH! (*After a moment of quiet, he continued.*) Oh, you laugh now. You knew this would be coming! I'm looking here on some sort of screen. He showed me different realties, and we're only focusing on the gravitational field and whether the ocean is moving fast or slow. And that affects the whole region and the beings within that region, and the atmosphere surrounding celestial bodies as well, he says. At this point, he showed me how the ocean was around the Milky Way and the solar system here, how it was originally calm, with bigger, longer waves. Now, he says, the waves are faster. The ocean has been blowing up like a, –not a storm, he says, not yet a storm at all–, BUT, it is not that calm ocean anymore. And it is because of the events that take place within the system, like on Earth, for instance.

That's what it means, he says, that everything is connected. Because whatever creates, and whatever is done on certain places, like realities and planets, it effects this ocean, this gravitational field he shows me, like an ocean. Because of that, there is disharmony or imbalance within the system as a whole, like the Milky Way. If the Milky Way, let's say, was going to be like a gentle, friendly ocean, and if that begins to become more like waves that are 3 meters high, and a storm is like 30 meters high, he says, 30 to 50 meters, but even if it starts to be waves that are 3 to 5 meters, it creates problems. The way other realities are hearing it is in the melody, because the melody, the system, is out of tune, he says.

D. So the activities on Earth are causing disturbances?

B. Indeed! That is how everything is connected. That is what you refer to, he said, as the web. But the web is this gravitational ocean that is designed to operate in a specific manner, in a specific melody. The spirit realm sees it as a melody, and hears it as a melody. But he shows me so that I can understand, so that I can see when I look around now. You said that we are gonna look at other places (*in the fish tanks*), so that I can identify what sort of activity might exist. And then, I have my suitcase with the elements, and I am expected to fix the problem with my box of elements! Because the elements are, when I look down in my bag, it's like liquid, so there is nothing that is like a rock or anything. All elements, Isaac said, are melted down into a liquid form, because that is when they are the strongest, actually. You might think that is the strongest when it is like a rock, but it's not! Because it doesn't have the ability to float out and merge with the surrounding area in the same way if you just put in a rock. So all elements who have the conditions of liquid are stronger. That is why, he said, like before, when gold was used as a liquid form on Earth, that is actually the highest form of a fuel on this plane, he said, not in other realities.

We will interrupt for a moment to clarify what Bob is saying about gold. In early 2017, Jeshua gave us some information about the technological achievements of the second civilization (~60,000 to 20,000 BCE). One of their primary fuel sources was produced by combining liquid gold with certain other elements (which we won't mention) to produce a third element. This third element, not found on our periodic chart, could be vaporized and used as a fuel. This technology was harnessed for non–spiritual purposes and explosive accidents occurred. Gold, at that time, could be found in a liquid form at normal temperatures (like liquid mercury). But due to the misuse, the spiritual councils changed the way gold manifests on this reality to prevent a recurrence of that type of explosive power. We deliberately left it out of Wave 1 and Wave 2. However, knowing that the elemental structure of gold is locked, it doesn't seem that risky to put it in print. Another interesting point is that Bob casually references something that was delivered more than a year earlier, showing how deliberate and remarkably precise the spirits are with the words they speak.

D. Even more than as a vapor, a gas?

B. Well, gas is somewhat a residual from the liquid, so indeed, it is still not as intense and strong, he said, as when it is in a liquid form. BUT, you can still use the solid form of the elements in soil that is not feeling well. you can use certain crystals, and even gold and silver; silver you should be a little bit careful with, because it is not always suitable to put in soil. But gold and other minerals, like certain crystals, it is more like a little boost. Whereas a liquid form, if you were to put in, let's say, if we take the gold again and if we put that in liquid form, like I have in a little tube in my bag here, if you want to really have a big effect, it has the ability to heal and transform more than if I put in a golden coin.

D. Huh. It makes me think of when you told (*he mentions a friend in Sweden*) to put crystals into the soil for her little friend.

B. Truls. (*The name of the little gardener from the second dimension, who follows the friend in Sweden.*) But she doesn't have in her possession a melted version.

D. Are there specific types of rocks or crystals that are best for the soil?

B. It varies. It depends on exactly what you want to do with the soil, or what you want to heal. Is it not singing? Is it lacking oxygen or other nutrition? It's not like a McDonald's (*fast food*) type of fix, where you just put one thing down and all problems are solved! Huh huh. Oh, Ophelia said that and Isaac laughed too! There's nothing like one size fits all!

D. I realized that after I asked the question.

B. Ah! That's why I have my bag. And he said it's not like to be poured out, the whole thing. I might take a drop from different ones within my bag of elements. Oh, I don't know how this is going to go, but I'm careful because I don't want to spill. I don't know if there is an endless supply, and if I spill and then I'm not sure if I can get more. I don't know where he got this, but he gave me this and said, "Now you are a big boy. Now you're going to go learn about how to adjust elements and materia within the gravitational fields, and you are going to learn the amount from each potion (*to add*), for the ocean to be as it's intended to be."

D. That's very impressive! So, are you still working with Tristan? (*Studying elements, on the eighth.*) And do you take your bag to his area of study?

B. Indeed. I have my bag. Isaac gave me this bag, because I was gonna go and visit him.

D. So he has given you some melodies, and now you are going to work on how to identify problems and fix them?

B. Ah. I have looked at these melodies and now, he said, "Which one do you feel are out of tune?" And I said, "That's a big responsibility!" You don't want to make a mistake. So I analyze and dissect, and we do that together. It's not like it's in my hands, really. But we're looking at this together, and I'm identifying the melody.

Alone with the Suitcase (May 19, 2018)

D. So you had an idea of how to fix the human with your elements? (*He was contemplating how to fix the human with elements, without calling it a reboot.*)

B. I asked Isaac, because I thought it might be an element issue. Maybe there is too much or too little of something, and I thought that maybe he might be able to fix it. But he's friends with Ophelia. (*Isaac knows not to answer the question.*) So he laughs and shakes his head a little bit and asks, "Oh, so how do you like your suitcase?" And I said, "Oh, my suitcase, I'm so afraid to drop it and the elements." So he diverted my attention with that. So we talked about that, and then he asked if I needed more elements in my suitcase.

D. How are your studies going with the gravity people on the eighth?

B. I'm left alone!

D. Uh–oh. More self–study. Why are you left alone?

B. Because I'm supposed to be in silence. I'm supposed to listen to the songs. If I talk too much and if there is too many influences coming into my chimney and my being, then I don't hear. So he said, "I'm going to leave you a little bit," and then I thought, "OK, so maybe you stay." But you also left. So I'm sitting there with my suitcase, and I'm listening to all these different systems.

D. So, you're listening to the five melodies? (*For his first project, he was given a box with five energetic bodies; a center point, which would be like a sun, and four little planets, each carrying a different melody.*)

B. The five cases, indeed. But it's not like listening one time to a song, and then you're done. I'm trying to identify certain tunes that are high pitched. A high–pitched tone is actually considered very imbalanced, he said, it has a high percentage of an imbalance, it goes faster. So he said, "First of all, try to identify if there is a high pitch that you don't feel like it belongs within the melody," so I'm trying to detect that.

D. It's probably very subtle tones you have to detect.

B. I'm really, really listening to find that, to see if there is a high pitch. There is one that has an opposite, a slow moving, very bass sound. BUT he actually said, "The universe is not constant, things can move around, so you can't just identify one location and say, 'Here is a good one, and there's a high–pitched one over there,' because everything is in motion." And that's when I became a little bit concerned, because what happens with my system if everything is in motion? And what happens if my galaxy suddenly drifts off somewhere else? But you said not to worry about that. You said that's not gonna happen. But that is how evolution occurs, because things float away and interfere and engage with other things and other melodies.

D. Well, the good thing is you know how to make a system now, so you could always start fresh.

B. Ah, but I have all my plants, and I have my Individual. If I can take my living planet and put it somewhere else, that would be better. If everything is in motion, then clearly that can be done. If mine, for some reason, were to float away into another song that I don't recognize, I want to put my living planet somewhere else. Ohh. (*His main concern has always been outside interference.*)

D. I bet we don't have to worry about that. I think we made sure it was in a safe spot.

B. But, it's just when he said that, that everything was in motion, everything changes. So he's gonna switch them around and I'm gonna try to identify them by their melody. He actually said that one of them is this reality, but he's not telling me which one, but that is one of them, and I have to identify it.

D. It's probably squealing like a pig stuck under a gate.

B. It's not like it's very obvious, because you have to carefully listen to a song. It can be a completely good song, but somewhere a tune or a pitch goes up, and that means is out of tune within that region. So it's not like, "Oh, it's out of tune," flof, flof, flof (*meaning an easy fix*), "fixed it!" What is out of tune? What needs to be fixed? Is it the atmosphere, or is it something else? So I'm sitting here in silence, and I'm trying to find out.

D. Did you get any instructions on what to listen for?

B. Indeed, I have a little manual. But I would have preferred that you helped, because I'm pretty sure you took this class. But you took off as well, and you said you were just around the corner. I'm sort of new here, so I don't know where to go.

D. This is like self-study all over again.

B. Ah, and I don't leave this room, because I'm not sure, really, and I don't want to be lost. So, I'm staying here. It's like what you tell children—if you get lost in the forest, you're not supposed to move around. You're supposed to hug a tree and stay put. And that's what I do.

D. You hug your little suitcase.

B. I hug my suitcase and I stay put. Eventually, I'm sure you're gonna come back, because eventually you all want to know what I found, or not found, so I'm pretty positive about that.

D. At least you're not in darkness, are you?

B. Nay, it's light, there's no darkness here. It's colorful, actually, it's very nice here.

D. Nicer than our lab?

B. This is like a round room, a circle. There's like a hole in the ceiling where there is like light coming in, so it's like sitting in a ball, almost. It's really high up. (*He was staring upwards, as if he was looking at the hole in the ceiling.*) Maybe it's supposed to do something, later? But, I am here, and it's such a nice place

I'm pretty sure someone will come by. I hope it's going to be someone familiar, though, because I'm staying put.

D. Well, you know, this is exactly like the self–study, when I left you.

B. Self–study. Then I thought, "Maybe you're just outside the door?"

D. Did you go look?

B. I did indeed, but you were not there. I said, "I'm not falling for that one again! He's probably just outside the door." So I was really convinced and happy because I thought, "He's trying to trick me, but I'm no fool!" So I peeked out, but there was just empty space, and I was like, "Oh, maybe there was haste." So I'm sitting here and I'm trying to identify the shifts in vibration within this tune, to identify, first of all, where the imbalance is, and then we're also going to try to identify what it is, in order for me to open up my suitcase and be helpful.

D. So when you designed your system, you worked with colors, but did you also recognize them as sounds?

B. Well, Isaac did all this for my solar system. He put them in that tank where it floated, he just did that for me. I didn't know what happened, but he came in and said, "Thumbs up, Bob, system floats," and I said, "Oh, okay." Then he said, "I added a melody for your system when it floated. It will next be placed in the gravitational tank where another melody will be added." But I didn't get to hear it or pick the melody

D. Well, you wanted to be like Isaac and come in at the end to fix things, so now you are getting training to do that.

B. Ah. So, all this might be so that later on, I might go and listen to the brain that they have created for the new humanoid, and I will instantly detect if there is like an imbalance, or a mismatch, or something that I could change with my suitcase. Maybe that is the end result of all this.

D. That makes sense, because your primary work is on the second.

B. Indeed. Ophelia said that, that I will come in later on when all the testing has been done.

D. You'll do the final evaluation.

B. So I do similar as Isaac and see if this new brain floats, and then I will give it a melody and I will give them the vacuum field surrounding the brain, which will be like the gravitational field. That's what I think is happening here! (*Bob is talking about evaluating the new model of human that is being planned for Earth.*)

D. Wow, that's really important work!

B. It is indeed. I think I'm gonna get another medal for this!

D. I'm sure you will. If you had to say who is currently your primary mentor—is it Ophelia, is she the one who is directing you now? I know Gergen is still involved.

B. Ah, Gergen and Ophelia, they have meetings, I know they do, and they talk about this project and other projects. But I'm pretty sure they talk about my advancement as well, what to do with me, and where to send me. Ophelia is actually someone, if it has nothing to do with home, then I'm actually talking with Ophelia most. So in that respect, yes, indeed, she would be considered my number one helper. Because she knows things about all places. So when I ask like if I can go places, then she can identify if I can. And sometimes, it has actually been that when I ask to go places, to different fish tanks, then she says I'm not gonna like it there. And I said, "Why is that?" and she said that the melody within that fish tank is not in resonance with my being. So I will feel like physical discomfort, she says, and there's no need to go to those places. And I did ask to go, maybe with her, if she goes to councils. I did say that I was gonna be quiet, that I would just be like a fly on the wall.

D. What did she say?

B. She said, "It's not like every time is going to be helpful. Even if you're there like a fly on the wall, because you cannot understand the melody. So you will just see us sitting there." And I'm not sure about that, if that is true, or if that is somewhat to just put a period to the conversation. But she does actually take me along and I visit a lot of her students, or those who she is training, the younger ones, like Julia—I like her. She's always happy. She's very much like Ia, she's always happy, and she's sharing. And she sometimes sings, and I like that and it makes me comfortable. So when she is reading up on stuff, she has a tendency to sing. So I sit there and I can somewhat, just based on her tone and her voice and the way she communicates, I can understand some of the information in that cookie that she is reading. So, when she learns, she actually sings. Ophelia said that, that Julia, when she learns something, she sings, because that is how it falls into place in her being. So I thought, why don't I sing? Maybe I will learn more!

D. Maybe you'll sing different kind of songs.

B. I have a different kind of tune. I'm more into drumming, you know, like OHHHH! (*Then he sang rather loudly for a while, imitating drums.*) Whereas she sings more like a lullaby. I like her!

Playing the Master Mind (May 28, 2018)

Bob came in after the Elahim Council had been speaking, and as is often the case, he was blocked from seeing or hearing what they were talking about. All he could see was a red fog, so I told him who had been speaking.

D. Those were our friends from the Elahim Council.

B. Is that where we're going?

D. Ah, we might go there sometime.

B. Is that close to where my system is? Because if it is, then we might just swing by. If they are close to my system, then maybe whatever they are doing for here (*Earth*), maybe they can do it for my system too? If they are close by, closer than me, I mean. (*The Elahims travel to our fish tank and manifest in the form of the Anunnaki. They maintain a presence in this Universe, as well as in other fish tanks. As mentioned in Wave 2, the Elahims act as gatekeepers for Earth, preventing certain visitors from interfering. The councils on the fifth dimension are currently responsible for the Earth reality, since most of the souls here are from the fifth.*)

D. Well, they are mostly protecting the Earth. Your solar system doesn't need protection. It's in a nice place.

B. Ah. I asked for that. Are you saying my system doesn't need protection?

D. Not like the Earth does. (*In his answer, which follows, he says "potatoes". He is referring to the people that live at the very edge of our fish tank, in the densest part of the Wheel of Creation. Within the Wheel, the spiritual vibration increases as realities move closer to the center pole, which has no relationship to spacial locations within the Universe. For example, the Andromeda galaxy is at a higher vibration than our galaxy. We know the Earth to be a very dense reality, but there are some locations that are even more inhospitable. Bob was shown one planet that had very high gravity, and it was occupied with "people" that had bodies but almost no neck and very short legs. So, he called them the potatoes. He said they had very little soul energy within. That is what he means by, "if the potatoes come".*)

B. But maybe I can have one of them (*an Anunnaki*) then, and not a whole group. Because it's nice to have somewhat of a, like a virus program! I said that to Ophelia, actually. I thought that we should install like a virus protection wall in the system so that certain things cannot come through. She thought that I meant like certain beings. But I said, "No, I'm simply referring to their consciousness and their way of thinking and acting. So, I have no problems if, let's say, the potatoes come to my planet, or even those with the cone ears. I have no problem, as long as they're right in the head." So I said that to Ophelia, and she laughed. She said, "It's like playing the Master Mind, Bob." Then I said, "Not really," and she said, "Yes, yes, it's exactly what you're trying to do. You're trying to just invite those who are friendly and with a higher consciousness. But that's not how development and evolution moves forward, if everyone is just happy." But I said, "In the spirit realm, everyone is happy, –and we evolve." And she said, "Yes, but you don't have the same challenges. The challenges for souls who incarnate on different realities comes when they leave the spiritual home." Then I said, "I understand that, but if we could only allow in those with the highest consciousness in their backpack or their mental realm." I said, "We are increasing the light within, which is compassion and love and empathy. But because the human has such a strong connection to their mental realm, which is ideas, beliefs, social activities, needs and wants, and so forth, – which are completely in conflict with love, compassion, and empathy, at times. So," I said, "if we just put in like this virus protection when it comes to what is existing within the mental realm. Because I feel like the heart and the light, you know, the soul, those are pure. It just gets colored because there is a mish–mash of signals, and it is connected to the brain." And I said, "What happened with upgrading the brain?" And she says, "I'm not gonna tell you, because you don't work with that."

D. You don't?

B. I don't.

D. I thought you did.

B. Nope. I learned the basics about the human brain and the vehicle. BUT I am diverted at this particular point to other projects, so at the moment I am NOT working with the upgrade of the brain. But, if I were to release other projects, which I am not willing to do, then I'm sure I would be welcomed back. This is being done by a specialist group. But she said I resigned from that group because I wanted to go travel. And I said, "Yes, I did. But I can still maybe have a sneak peek on where they're at." And she said, "If everyone were going to go have a sneak peek everywhere, they would not become specialists, would they?"

D. You enjoy being a specialist in traveling, don't you?

B. I do indeed. And I said that I don't really like if someone who is not trained in my profession would come and sniff around, who doesn't belong, really. At the moment, I am with the council, and I'm also studying the teachings (*associated*) with the gravitational field. She actually said a lot of my teachings, when it comes to the gravitational field, would actually be applicable during the upgrade of the brain. She said, "You will like this, because you will come in at the end of this project." So they are maybe doing like the workshop, checking all the wires and stuff. And then I come in to do something with the gravitational field, which would be like a vacuum, a shield around the brain. So my expertise, she said, will come in at a later point. But I'm not following the brain project of the human. That's why I felt like we could just sort of fix it, you know. Maybe there's just a disconnect or a rewiring needed.

D. Ha. Bad fuse.

B. Bad fuse.

D. Is Gergen working on it?

B. Gergen is. Gergen is, indeed. Because the DNA and light are involved as well.

D. Does Ia help any?

B. I think Ia is there too.

D. You're bringing your own special knowledge to the project.

B. Ah. So, anyway, I asked Ophelia if there would be like different filters put in the human, because she might know those who put in all these filters, like a firewall. I don't know who they are, but I asked her, and she says that is part of manipulating evolution. If you put in those filters, or firewalls, of certain things, like (*preventing*) actions and behaviors, then it's like a reboot. She said that I knew that, I just changed it to another word to make my case heard! She said I'm tricky like that, because I change words. But it's just because I see that it's not going in the way that I hoped for, and I thought we could maybe do something to help.

The Melody in the Boxes (June 3, 2018)

As Bob continues working with Isaac, he is constantly challenged with more difficult assignments. After he sat quietly and learned how to read the melodies from the solar family model in the first box, he was given more boxes to evaluate. The purpose was to demonstrate the differences between realities. In this lesson, he is introduced to cycles. All creations move through cycles, even galaxies and fish tanks. He felt that he was tricked because he was given a box with a solar system that was in hibernation.

B. (*Bob steps in and makes a face.*) You did not tell me everything!

D. What did I not say?

B. There were tricks in my project.

D. The project with your suitcase?

B. Indeed! And in my listening.

D. Is that when we left you alone?

B. Indeed! And there were tricks, because once I had identified and I was done with the first assignment, and I kind of called in some way, sent out a signal for you to come. I thought I was done, and we were going to continue as a group. But then instead of telling me if my answers were right or wrong, you gave me a new group to listen to, to compare to the first group. You said the first group belonged in one fish tank and they had individual patterns. BUT then you brought in five new ones that came from another fish tank. And you said, "Now I want you to ponder about the difference between the fish tanks (*universes*), not the individual differences." Then you gonna leave again, – and I was like, "Are we not gonna talk about my first assignment?" And you said, "No, we're going to do it all together, because it's all connected." And I asked, and you were kind of on your way, and I asked, "Is this second one where my system is?" And you kind of smiled, so I'm thinking it might be, but you did not say. You only said, "It's a new fish tank, Bob. Focus on the difference between the fish tanks, if there is a different melody. See if you can detect whether there is a physical manifestation in that one or not, if there exists physical manifestation in those new five." And I said, "Did there exist physical manifestation in the first ones?" And you said, "That's for you to find out." Then I said, "That's actually on my paper as one of my questions," and you said, "We're going to talk about this, but you have to sit here and identify, and dissect, and ponder." And I said, "How long will that take?" And you said, "How long did your first assignment take?" and I said, "Oh, you know, it took a while." And you said, "Then it probably is going to take a while, again."

D. It's better to learn like this, so then you will know it completely.

B. You said you didn't want to interfere with my thought process, and I said, "Please do, it's fine, I'm not bothered." But you said, "Yes, you will be bothered, because you will not come up with this by yourself." I said, "But what if I come up with something wrong?" And you said, "Then we adjust it after that."

D. Well, if this fish tank is the most dense, can you detect which group of five is resonating with a more dense vibration?

B. The new one is like a lullaby. My feeling is that this one has less solid matter. If I were to say—in this lullaby fish tank—Siah might be here. But I'm trying to identify that.

D. I thought Siah is in our fish tank, just at a higher vibration?

B. No. but they can interfere and overlap. (*Siah's planet, Etena, is in fish tank four, as looked at on the wheel. They have said Etena is on the border of four and five. My question was incorrect, but Bob was not thrown off.*)

D. So the fish tanks interfere with each other?

B. Overlap, you say, sometimes. It's not a constant study, you say. You can't say that everything is identical, because the Master Mind might do shifts and changes. But there is, between all fish tanks, and within each fish tank, there are levels which would be considered little fish tanks, and there are barriers between. So, like Siah's place is on a different frequency, at the edge of this fish tank.

D. As is your solar system.

B. Indeed. And then there is a different fish tank all together. And there is also levels within that one. BUT there is a zone between that is somewhat overlapping, and THAT's an interesting area to explore.

D. It's a remarkable teaching you're giving us.

B. A lot of it, Ophelia says, is for you to start remembering. So, we're having me talk about certain things we do, you and I, to make you remember. And also, to give you information about the second (*dimension*), of course, but also to make you bounce down into your solar plexus point and to remember, Ophelia says. The more we talk, the more you are focusing, cohering, she says, from your center point.

D. It does seem to be forming into a story that I completely understand.

B. That's the point, she said, with all of this, regardless of who's talking. There is a point to this. Everything is designed to come in cups.

D. Back to the cups. Sometimes a spoon.

B. Back to the cups, sometimes a spoon. This one wants a barrel. It's like Tom, you know, you can't bring in a barrel. You can't shoot off a ball, if the receiving end is not ready for the barrel. This reality is not ready for a barrel, it's ready for cups, that's what Ophelia says. It's the same methodology like I'm teaching Tom. There's no difference.

D. It works well, it's a good plan.

B. Provide it in cups, she said, and we provide you information in cups.

D. Well, thank you.

B. Okay, so I'm gonna go.

D. Alright, my friend. I appreciate hearing from you today, and Ophelia as well.

B. Ah. Okay, bye bye.

A Healthy Sleep, or Dead? (June 21, 2018)

While you might be tempted to dismiss Bob's story as an odd tale of his studies, he is actually describing how solar systems are created. Once a solar model has been built, tested, and had other melodies that relate to the elements, such as light and gravity added, it is placed in its designated location in the fish tank, like a seed. This marks the "birth" of a new system, which Bob described like lighting a match. After it grows for a bit, the energetic patterns for the planets divide and separate from the sun and move to their assigned locations. At this point, it goes into hibernation and the density of the vacuum field within the system is increased. The core of the sun holds the pattern for the system, and the other planets "grow" from the center point to become their intended purpose. Since Bob is working with a box, he describes it as he sees it, but the principle is universal to all systems in all fish tanks. Once a system is in place, then it may go through different rebirths, before it eventually ceases to exist.

B. Ohh! I'm waiting and waiting and waiting!

D. That's the story of your life, sitting in the lab waiting, or waiting here.

B. Indeed, and I have questions.

D. Ah, what's your question?

B. The question is about my project in my second box, my assignment—it collapsed.

D. Why did it do that?

B. Because I, I, —it came in similar like the other one, like something for me to investigate and explore. But I had a manual, and the manual indicated I could make adjustments with my suitcase. And I did. And it collapsed.

D. So you poured a few drops into the box, and something happened?

B. It spread out, it was like putting oil in water, it divided. So now everything has divided in my box.

D. It was supposed to do that, wasn't it?

B. I do not know, I don't think so. I'm hoping that you come back before the other one, because I don't want to show him this.

D. Well, did you follow the manual correctly?

B. I think I did.

D. You said it was going to divide.

B. It did, it has divided. The other one was already divided (*the previous project he worked on*), but this one, when I poured in a teeny, tiny dose of, –it was mercury, a little bit of nitrogen, and there was a third one as well, something with a "b—".

D. Can you still hear the melodies from each of them individually?

B. It became silent after it divided! There's no song, it became silent. And I don't know if I killed it. But it divided and moved into silence. BUT Isaac came by and I tried to hide my box. And he said, "Do you need more elements in your suitcase?" And I said, "Ah, ohh," and I think he knew that something was up. So he said, "Can I see the box?" And I said, "I think it's sleeping." And he said, "It's supposed to sleep, it's supposed to be in hibernation. When you create galaxies, they come in as one big energetic cookie. And when you pour in different kinds of tunes, or elements, it will appear as a liquid (*to those observing from the spiritual dimensions*). But the galaxy will receive it as a melody, as a tone, and it will split up and be divided into the hibernation. The trick is to put in the right amount of liquids from the elements, to create this big snooze before something is becoming." And then I said, "It's been quiet a long time in my box."

D. Did he have a look?

B. I, I hid it behind me, and he said, "Can I see?" And I said, "Ohh." (*As he looked down and shrugged his shoulders.*) Then Isaac said, "There's no problem. You haven't done anything harmful," and I said, "Okay." So he said, "Let me have a look and we can establish if it's a healthy sleep, or if it's dead." And I said, "OH! I hope I didn't kill it!" Huhuh. So I brought it forward from behind, and he looked at it. And he was quiet a long time, it appeared to me, and he said, "No, Bob, listen, it's just sleeping." So I bent over and you know, sort of squeezed in an ear a little bit, and I said, "I don't hear anything!" Then he said, "Don't listen like that, you have to listen with your chest, with your center point. Move closer to the box. The box is not dead, it's just sleeping." Ah, so I sat there and he taught me how to connect, –which was completely different and brand new. So I sat there and I listened differently. It was almost like moving into a, –you would consider it like a trance state, that's how I was listening. But he said that box number 2 was actually prepared, –that's why it sounded like a lullaby–, because it was actually preparing to go to sleep! But I didn't know that! So he said, "We tricked you a little bit." And I said, "You tricked me big time, because I thought I killed it!" I don't want to kill anything.

D. Isaac is a great teacher.

B. The other one (*his first project*), it had woken up from its sleep. So the first one I got had gone through the lullaby stage. It was all awake and up and going, you know, like all rotations and all cycles were on–going and everyone was in motion. But the second was prior to my first box, there's no order here. (*The second box was in an earlier part of the cycle than the first box.*) So he said, "We tricked you a little bit. First you got one at the end of its evolution that's ongoing. But then we gave you one that would have come first, if it was in chronological order." So he said, "It was already about to go to sleep, that's why it was a lullaby."

D. What did he say about the elements you put in, was it okay?

B. It was okay, indeed.

D. That's really good. You read up on it and figured it out by yourself.

B. I did, I did it all! But in my box, when I poured in the elements, one was left in the middle, but the other four just shot off into the corners of my box and then it just became still. And I was like, "OOOHHHH!" And first I waited a while, and then I thought maybe if I shake it a little bit, but there was no sign of life. I thought I killed it. But apparently, I put it into hibernation. And he said, "You can't shake the box, because it's not going to wake up like that. It will wake up exactly when it's supposed to." Like a bear, you know, that goes in hibernation for winter; it wakes up when it's supposed to.

D. There seems to be a general order in all of the Universe that follows a similar pattern.

B. Ah. Everything begins like that. He said it is similar like the big bang, it begins as a core of a centralized energy or a puddle of energy, and then interactions of other elements, –or tunes, to make it easy for you–, are blended with that, and it separates. But it's the same with everything. It creates a center point and the other ones are tossed out. (*Once an energetic seed for a solar system is placed in a galaxy, spirits from the eighth add elements to activate it. Then the patterns for the planets move out to their positions, away from the sun, the core of the system, and all enter into a state of hibernation.*)

D. I'm glad Isaac came to visit, since no one else came back.

B. Nay. I'm happy that he came. I was concerned the other one would come and go like, "OHHH!", like I damaged something. And because I can't really talk with him, he might not understand what I did. So I'm glad Isaac came.

D. Well, you weren't given a whole lot of instructions, were you?

B. You gave me a manual, and it was translated into my understanding. But after it fell asleep, I was like, "Oh, they're gonna strip me of all my medals."

D. Busted back to a sparkle.

B. Maybe I'm gonna just be like, you know, "Return to sender."

D. Like the toaster. (*Zachariah once humorously compared the creation of souls to a factory that makes toasters. Souls that don't operate according to their pattern are sometimes returned for repair, so I was teasing Bob about that possibility.*)

B. Like a toaster! Then I'm not gonna be a great scientist, maybe I'm just gonna go back and do something else.

D. Clearly your path is towards great things. Everyone says so.

B. I'm happy that Isaac came, but he teased me a little bit, he did indeed. So, I appreciate that. I should know that by now, that you're all doing that. It's simply to entice my spirit, like I do with Tom. I should be prepared, but I'm constantly thrown back by it.

D. You're afraid you're doing wrong, but you're not. You are doing well.

B. Ah, I was just concerned that I had killed it, which would have been a disaster, cosmic–wise. I don't want to kill anything. They would never let me be in charge of this system, if I'm doing that. I asked if we could maybe put this system (*Earth*) into hibernation, so it wakes up being healthy and friendly. But Isaac said that has been done already, that this system and this planet has gone through several hibernation phases. Now it is you humans who are supposed to understand and are expected to develop from within, by those who occupy the incarnations.

D. You mean this planet here?

B. Indeed. Because I thought if we put this system in a healthy hibernation, and then it can wake up and just remember the good things and how to be kind and remember the first intention we had for the planet. But that's not gonna happen. So, we'll see about that, but that was concerning. But now I have a box that is in hibernation and sleeping, and I have one that is highly active and there is constantly going on things in that one.

D. Like a box full of puppies.

B. Indeed, I see great development, but they are at different stages.

D. Are you supposed to do anything with it?

B. I would like to, but I'm not sure if I'm supposed to meddle. I probably should ask before I meddle. This is like being the Master Mind! I enjoy the idea of being here like the Creator and the Master Mind with my two boxes! I do like that. I want them to get along, and if I make too many changes, maybe they do not get along. One box has highly emotional energetic realities, and you can't just blend energetic realities with physical, because that can create all sorts of confusion. That actually happened here (*on Earth*) as well. There was confusion at one point between energetic beings blending together with those who were manifested fully in flesh. It created somewhat of a conflict where one tried to get the upper hand, saying, "We belong here, and the other ones do not." It's not boding well if someone tries that. (*This is a clear reference to aliens or manifested beings who were mixing with the humans in a previous civilization.*) Anyway, I am compiling my observations of the box.

D. So do you think these might actually be galaxies or solar systems in your box?

B. They are models, he said. They are prototypes of different realities, but I don't know what fish tank they belong in. I tried to ask that, but he said, "Everything in due time, Bob. Now we watch the song, listen to the hibernation melody."

D. I'm still curious how models get from the lab into a fish tank.

B. That's not to be given. It has not been shown. It has not been shown to me how it came from my drawer. It went from my drawer to the oven, and suddenly we left in my bubble. How it exited the oven, and how it was placed in my region of choice in the fish tank—there's a huge gap in my education here.

D. Maybe that will be in a later Wave, Wave 7.

B. Huhuh. Wave 7! Well, I'm not going anywhere, so I'm sticking by for Wave 7. Because I can clearly see that we have teachings here, and there is like a vacuum where no teachings were delivered. (*I assume he means during the past few millennia.*)

D. Does this one (*Christine*) ever come by to help when we are working?

B. Ah, when I was a little bit discouraged with my box, when I thought it died, then this one, he came first, he swung by, but Isaac came quickly thereafter, and made sure that THAT did not happen. But this one, you know—

D. What did he say?

B. "What's happened here, Bob? Are you sad?" Because I'm sure I looked as sad as Tom did. Instead of coming in to encourage me, like Isaac did later, he said, "Do you want to go somewhere?" Similar like you say to a child, like when a child has fallen off his bike, "Do you want to come and have an ice cream?", to divert the sadness. This one, and I appreciate what he was trying to do, because he saw that I was sad, but he didn't know the background of sadness, like you and Isaac did. So he thought that he was just gonna cheer me up.

D. And then here came Isaac.

B. And Isaac came quickly thereafter, and said, "Alright, I'll take over here," it was just briefly, he just popped by a little bit. And then Isaac came. I'm pretty sure you filled in the details with this one, like you put a sign outside of a door, "Do not Disturb, Teaching in Progress", of sorts.

The Moon People (Oct 30, 2018)

Within the spiritual dimensions, work is divided up into specialties, so there are different groups that are experts in each aspect of creation. All spirits who work with form, making the plants, cores of stars, moons, and other celestial objects, are all found on the sixth or ninth dimensions. Bob, being ever–observant, describes the individuals who are responsible for creating moons as being somewhat mysterious and, to him, a little bit scary. There must be something unique about moons, because he discusses them quite often. Perhaps not all moons are specially designed like ours, but many seem to be intentionally placed in orbit around a host planet for a reason, and are often associated with water.

D. (*Bob tried to sneak in without being noticed.*) What's happening, my friend?

B. You found me! Ha ha ha!

D. You're not hard to find!

B. Well, I tried to sneak in behind Ophelia, so that she was creating somewhat of a shield! Oh, maybe we begin new! (*He then tried to sit motionless and not make any of his telltale signs or facial movements, but was unsuccessful.*)

D. No, that's not it.

B. HUH HUH HUH! Oh, you know, dee dee dee da dee. (*He began happily singing.*) I have been given a pause in my secretary assignment! (*Gergen and Ole had assigned him the task of taking notes on everything that was discussed in their council meetings, presumably to make him pay closer attention to the other council members.*)

D. Were you laid off or fired?

B. No, no...was I? (*He looked towards the left, perhaps towards Gergen or Ole, who attend all our sessions.*) Oh, I didn't think of it in those terms! Nay, it came up and they asked if, "Maybe I wanted to take a break?" I might have sighed a little bit. There became a little bit of—I wouldn't say a stressed feeling in the group, but maybe there was. And I might have contributed to that, –so I was given a break.

D. Do you think the objective was accomplished? Are you paying closer attention to what they say now?

B. I had to.

D. Maybe that was the whole point.

B. I did indeed. BUT, I was wondering when it is my turn to deliver my insights, and if this secretary occupation, if that was going to rotate in some way. And I think that is when Gergen, —because there was like a secret meeting between Gergen and Ole, and after that it was like taking a break. They said, "You have an opportunity now to return to your studies up in the sixth." They said they didn't need me; they were gonna have an elaboration of certain ideas and were gonna go through and review. So, I wasn't needed to take notes at that particular point. BUT I was wondering, quietly, a little bit—well, at least I thought it was quietly—, I asked, "When is it my turn? because we have talked about the continents, we have talked about rain, we have talked about moving spines, we have talked about waters," which are FASCINATING subjects, indeed. However, it's not in my box of expertise. (*These are all topics the council is discussing about the present situations on Earth. The spine he mentions is the Andes Mountain, which the second dimension is planning on moving to help the reefs in the Caribbean, which Bob calls "fossils".*)

D. What are you going to tell the other council members?

B. I wanted to tell them about my solar project. I wanted to tell them about my Individual, because they are familiar with the individual, they saw him here. So I wanted to tell them about how you can make the memory awaken. I wanted to tell them that I had awakened a memory somewhere else, –and then I was anticipating, because I'm tricky like that–, I can say something that I know what question is gonna come from my statement. So when I say it like that, that I woke up a memory of my Individual somewhere else. Huh? Beep! (*He uses beep to imply that what he says triggers an expected question.*) Then it's gonna come a question saying, "Where is somewhere else?" Then beep! we are on a roll of introducing different realities and my project. So that was my idea, to somewhat just go from basic talk about my Individual, and then into stuff like that. But then I was—not expelled—but I was given the opportunity to go study somewhere else. Ahuhuh. I guess I'm gonna come back here (*to our lab*).

D. Well that's good, you can work more with me. What are we working on?

B. I am observing a little bit, but there is a model here with something rotating. So I'm looking at that. It's like a model of another planetary constellation or makeup, in another...it's like atoms circling around. You said that I need to understand this in order to get a moon. This is the inside of the moon, you said, it's a different core, you say. So I'm looking here, it's like, one–two–three, and they rotate. One is more still and the other ones are circling like that (*moving* hands). But you say that this is the core in moons. They're different, you say.

D. You've mentioned that before.

B. Different core, you say.

D. Ari said the moon people are a little bit odd. Well, he didn't say odd. Maybe quiet.

B. They're mysterious. They don't seem to want to engage. They don't seem to want to share, and I'm all about sharing, so I get confused when there is no sharing. And I see them, because they belong here in the sixth, and I see them in somewhat of a hallway, and they always walk in groups. They never go by themselves, they always go like a Lucia train (*a Christmas tradition in Sweden, where children have a single-file procession*), that's how they walk. I would assume the first one is the leader of the group, and then it probably goes back down and in the end is the little Santa, but I'm not at all gonna, you know, jump this train!

D. They might go through a secret doorway.

B. And never come back! Nay. There are several doors here, you should know, and I am not familiar with them. What if I suddenly feel encouraged to join this little train, and then we move on out in a space room, and what if you and Ari and everyone else cannot hear me? It's just that they move around differently than the other ones.

D. Do they look the same?

B. Indeed. They wear robes, but they are lighter colored. They are like almost white–bluish, metallic, grayish type color.

D. What color do I wear?

B. You have that dark purple. Eli, he likes red. This one (*Christine's spiritual self*) also likes red, but has blue. This one said, "I like red. I'm taking Eli's red." But you can't just take someone's color, because it resonates to a level of learning, so you can't just shift and move around. It's not like you have a laundry room where you can just grab whatever you like. It doesn't work like that, you say. But I wonder about this train, where they are going. And others they meet, they don't talk with them either. Some sort of do this (*he gives a slow, formal nod*), nod.

D. Polite.

B. Polite. But they have seen me, because I've been in the hallway with you.

D. Maybe they will start chatting with you.

B. But these are not the Evolution Group. These are more similar like you, just quiet. Maybe they don't have that much to say?

D. There's no life on the moon, is there?

B. (*He didn't respond, but looked to the left.*) Ophelia laughs now. Well, there kinda is.

D. Is there life on our moon?

B. Oh, indeed. But they're friendly. It's not like they hold meetings in the hallway, but I would assume this is the council for the moon people. They haven't like a label on them, so I'm free to make up my own mind—and I do. So, there you go. So, I'm here now, in the lab, studying this new core.

D. Is this going to go around your planet? Is that why we are working on a moon?

B. Indeed, indeed. But first I have to understand the core, you say. And I don't, at this point. But I can see it. You are kinda not helping here, you're not helpful. You just sort of put it on the table. And I said, "What is this?" and you said, "It's the moon core. Investigate it." And I said, "How?" You said, "Tune in on it. What sort of melody do you hear? What do you think this is?" So I did, and it has a melody. It sounds like a bee! It's not as quiet as other things.

D. What does your planet sound like?

B. It's a happy sound! Because of the fact of what I created for the surface to have, and it mirrors the inside. I would assume that if you have a sad song inside, that the ones on top would be sad. So I didn't want my Individual to be sad. He's been sad one time (*on Earth*), so that is not gonna repeat.

D. Are they happy?

B. Oh, they're happy! They have become more. Babies came and family units started to create. Certain group activity behaviors developed, both for good and bad, and we had to somewhat look over that. BECAUSE, just because one is a group, doesn't mean that one is friendly. You know all about that here. And here, with my Individual, I did see that. But we interfered.

D. Did you tell them to straighten up and fly right?

B. They don't fly. But they were told to get their act going.

D. Were they competing for something?

B. Territory. Someone wanted the better nest, which is completely unprofessional, that's not what you do—and I told them so.

D. What about the berries?

B. Oh, it was the same thing, because there was a lot more berries around one nest. So one wanted to go to that place, so you can see interference took place. So we made adjustments. I did not go with my bubble there, but we made remote adjustments.

D. That's nice. I'm glad we can do that.

B. Ah, I don't know how that works, but I saw the results. It was almost like shaking hands, –I mean, they don't shake hands. They could if they wanted to, but they do not. But it was a friendly break–up of this nest and the berries, and that's what I wanted. I do not want interference like this, it's not tolerable. I did not design this; I do not want that. So it's better to say it once and for all in the beginning. You set the pace, so to speak. So I did. I said, "This is not a behavior that I'm gonna approve." So you said, "What do you want to do?" And I said, "I want them to get along, I want them to be friendly. There are berries and nests for everyone, so no one needs to be greedy.

D. So what did we have to do?

B. Adjust the color pattern, you did. Isaac came. The only thing that I observed, from the perspective of me, was that a wind came in and from that wind, an understanding took place. It was like a cloud. The Creator came in like a cloud, like a referee.

D. Isaac should run one of those clouds by Earth.

B. That's what we need here. Magic happens with this cloud. It was an instant understanding. No need to remove someone or begin new—simply made the awareness come in in a cloud. So that's what happened there. So, anyway, we're going to make it a little short. But here I am, and everyone is with.

More Self-Study in Lab (Dec 16, 2018)

At this point in Bob's story, he is reflecting back on the experience of building a solar system and what he may have learned about himself in the process. Bob tells how he examines the past from a position of greater knowledge. All souls, when they return home from Earth, engage in an extensive review of their past lives. They replay scenes and discuss how the human could have handled it differently, in a way more in alignment with their soul. Humans, when they ruminate on the past, often do it in unhealthy ways. But there is a healthy type of recapitulation, where thoughts, feelings, and actions are examined for spiritual purity. This type of self-awareness can help someone to alter their future in a positive way.

D. Are you going to have to go back, like Zachariah said, and evaluate all of your thoughts?

B. Ah, evaluate my progress, Zachariah said. And you said so too, that a part of my learning curve here is to evaluate my progress. And if I could go back, what would I have done differently now, looking in rewind, having more information on my plate? What would I have done differently? Would I have added a certain aspect within my being? What hindered my development? And what I could see was my reluctance to self-study. That is a big part on my plate when I am looking in rewind, knowing that I actually enjoyed the silence within my own being, that I would have embraced that opportunity differently. So, when I later introduce self-study to Tom, who probably will react the same way, then I will be able to deliver it in a way that it is a fun experience, and a valuable one, -that it is a treat. Because now I see self-study as a treat. And that will help me to teach others, like Tom, about self-study, to also see it as a treat.

D. Do you think Gergen had the same issues with self-study? Did he ever say he was reluctant to self-study?

B. Not the same, really. He said it was necessary. He didn't seem to like it either, so that's the same. He didn't put it forward as a treat. He said, "It is necessary, Bob." But I'm gonna put forward to Tom that it was the greatest gift, to hear the wisdom within my own being, instead of saying that it is necessary. So, I'm gonna deliver that specific teaching in a different package.

D. That's probably a better way to look at it.

B. It's necessary. How fun can that be? Saying it is necessary to create a bigger foundation doesn't have that same ring to it, than if it is described as a treat to hear my own being within.

D. How did I present it to you?

B. Well, first you didn't present it at all. You said there was haste, and that I was gonna be there (*in our lab*). So, in that sense, there was like no introduction whatsoever. You just placed it there. (*I gave him a book to study.*) But the first thing you placed didn't have anything for me to understand, it was just dots in the book and I didn't DO anything with it. So you came back and you saw that I was probably on the same page where you left me. So you brought in a different way of self–study that was actually more visual teachings. It was probably the same as the dots, but just in a different dish. But, no, you didn't say either way. You said, "While I'm gone, this is what you can occupy your time with. I'll soon be back." And then, instead of questioning why I was there, because I didn't really have the idea to ask that question, I sat there and I did look at things. At first, because you made the book like 3–D, you made it move and that made me intrigued, and I studied up on things.

D. So instead of asking other spirits, you ask yourself questions?

B. Indeed, what comes back. Because it was easier to do that with visual, 3D images. It was more captivating than dots. So you brought in a different way to study, because probably someone told you that dots are not gonna make him excited.

D. I'm sure there were plenty of people observing the situation in our lab, giving advice.

B. Ah. Gergen and others were there. Okay, I'm gonna go now.

D. Thank you for all the information.

B. Ah. Okay. Bye bye.

Moons Resonate with Water (Dec 23, 2018)

After Bob's system was launched and had gone through some early development, we (in the lab on the sixth) began to focus on adding a moon to his living planet. His observation about the dynamic relationship of moons to water is fascinating. We know there are many moons in our own solar system, and, other than Earth, Mars, Uranus, and Neptune are all suspected of having water. In fact, Uranus and Neptune are now considered to be ice–giants, instead of gas giants, with water vapor having been identified in their atmospheres. Like many things the spirits tell us, there is a reason they want us to know about the way moons are made and their relationship to water.

B. Well, I have more post–its, of course!

D. Maybe you can give us a brief one?

B. A brief one. Okay, let's see...(*He looked up and slowly scanned an imaginary wall, left to right, until he stopped on a note.*) Oh, this one is a good one! This is about my advancements in your study (*lab*), as we have now moved into the level of learning on how to create a moon.

D. Oh, I wondered how your moon was coming along.

B. It's coming. It's different than when I created my living planet and the other ones. (*He began to whisper, so he wouldn't disturb his moon.*) This one is more sensitive, and you have to almost whisper when you create it, because it's extremely sensitive. (*He then resumed in his normal boisterous voice.*) And it's in a little bowl and it floats in a liquid, because the moon is actually very much connected to liquid. So even if it's a solid object, you say, it's programmed to resonate with liquid. So, I have my moon in a bowl, in a glass bowl, and it just floats there. Not like a fish, it's still, and it just becomes. It's magical because I can see like electrons and activity in this body of water around my moon. And I'm pretty sure that it might be similar like when Isaac put my system in the oven. It's preparing, you say.

D. So it's taking on the energy from the water or liquid?

B. Indeed.

D. Well, our moon is very much involved with the ocean tides and near–shore currents.

B. It's a communication central, you say, with waters. In many systems that have water worlds, they have more moons. They are communication centrals or receivers to communicate and connect with waters. And now, when I have water, when my lakes and waters have become, then indeed, I can have a moon! But first, because I did not have waters, so I could not have a moon. So the moon comes in, in existence, where there are waters to be found.

D. How long has the moon been around the Earth?

B. It came kinda around when the rains came.

D. So when you first came?

B. I came when there was a big cloud.

D. So the rains came before?

B. Rain came, there was rain going on, but when I came there was actually water there so rain must have been before, indeed. But there was another moon that existed before, here, when there was a lot of water on Mars.

D. Huh, was it around Earth or Mars?

B. No, it was closer to Jupiter and when water disappeared, that one also was dissolved. So it's a direct connection to water existence, water worlds, you say. Even if it's not just like a water planet.

D. Are all the moons like that?

B. Indeed. You said so.

D. So if there are a bunch of moons around Jupiter or somewhere?

B. It's a memory that it has been, at one point, water in the nearby vicinity.

D. That's fascinating.

B. Or, you say, it can actually come before, you say, sometimes, that there is like a...

D. Like a preparation?

B. Indeed. If you want to create, later on, like a reservoir for water, if water is lacking, then you can prepare a host with moons. This is HIGH science. And the moon people, I really don't understand them, so there is a lot of translation here. I watch a lot of documentaries and it's fascinating. But it's not necessarily always in the same order like with Earth, when the moon came after. But sometimes, you say, if we see a reality that is potentially lacking water and in need of water later on, then we can prepare, similar like you have here, a reservoir. Then we have silent moons. They're not active in the same way, they're silent moons. It can be silent or it can sing. There are moons around Jupiter, they're silent, but our moon here, it sings because it's activated, the receiver is on. It's like having an on–off button.

D. The moon wasn't created somewhere else as a solid body and moved in? Was it planted around the Earth and then grew and become?

B. It became, but I don't know if it grew. Like mine now, for instance, it's becoming in my bowl. But when we later on launch it, I think it is sort of stationary in the way it appears. But it could be silent or it could be singing.

D. So it suddenly appears in the night sky over your planet?

B. For some it will appear like "OH! What happened here, something just appeared here."

D. So your Individual will look up and say?

B. "HUH? What's that?" And my moon, you say, is actually gonna be bigger and closer, so the Individual will indeed see it.

D. A nice night light. You said it kind of likes light at night.

B. Indeed. Everyone likes a night light. Ah, um. That's sort of it, and I'm learning about that. At the moment, my moon is in that water bucket.

D. Well, that was a really good post–it too, so thank you for sharing that.

Ari, who you may recall from *Wave 2*, is an Elahim from the tenth dimension. He calls himself an uncle to Lasaray and Seth, which is his way of saying we are part of a small family group at home. In this October 30, 2018 session, he recounts how Bob came to see him with a handful of notes, asking for his help in explaining certain things he didn't understand. Bob was in my lab studying for a long "time" before he ever conversed with Ari.

D. Do you see Bob very often?

A. Oh, yes indeed. I wouldn't say that I trip on him, but it's somewhat—if I say it like this—whenever I visit you in your lab, he's always around.

D. He said he would like to talk to you sometime and peek in your journals.

A. Yes, he already has. He already has provided some sort of scribbles. There are notes, he said, of questions and encounters that he was not sure of, some who he felt were mysterious. He is interested in the moon people, and we have discussed their tendency to appear with privacy, let's just say that. No one really fully understands them.

D. They're not Elahims, are they?

A. No.

D. He said they were mysterious.

A. Huh huh, but yet he wants one! He wants a moon, he said. And he feels that he might need to ask them for the moon. And I said, "We can fix the moon for you, Little One." But he came with some scribbles. There are several in numbers to go through. Not all are questions. Some are basically observations or comments about what he is interested in exploring. But indeed, we will try to accommodate.

D. He's entertaining, though, is he not?

A. He is. Indeed, he is. Never seen such a curious kind. Maybe they all are like that? (*The spirits from the second.*)

D. I don't think so.

A. The moon people are the opposite of that one!

D. Must be shocking for him! He might have a hard time communicating.

A. Oh, he didn't want to go by himself. He said he wanted us to mediate. Well, we'll see. Why don't we just give the Little One a moon—he seemed eager to have one around, circling in his system, he said.

D. It would provide a little night light for his Individual.

A. He has a creature, yes, indeed. There are also new creatures that are waking up. And he planted something, apparently, in the seas, and he thought the shifts of the moon might provide the movements needed for his creatures in the sea. So we will probably have to accommodate this. I don't know why it wasn't there in the first place.

D. It was a future project, something for him to look forward to.

A. Yes, a future project. You told me so. You told me there were steps, some talk about steps. A ladder of learning, introducing certain things to keep him preoccupied in one end, but also focusing on the project at hand on the other side. So I can see the inquisitive mind in that one. Interesting. Funny little one.

D. He provides us a lot of entertainment. (*Ari then went on to give advice, which will be published in Wave 3. He was followed by Ophelia, who adjusted the residual energy before Bob came in.*)

D. Ari said you came by with some notes to show him, some questions and observations?

B. I did indeed. Observations, indeed. And I also had, because I wanted to go to the main guy, I had ideas on how we could improve certain things here.

D. He said he was going to work with you on the moon.

B. Ah! Maybe he will come? He's probably the head of this train (*the moon people*), and if I know him, maybe I can be in the front and don't have to be last.

D. They'll say, "If the Little One is a friend to Ari, we had better treat him nice!"

B. And maybe they will talk, say something, –not just stare. But Jeshua and Isaac, they take me along to places. So who knows who's gonna come?

D. Do you still see Zachariah?

B. I do indeed, sometimes, in the Library. Sometimes I go there to have him help me to verbalize my thoughts. He asks me questions, like, "What is the foundation of your thought, Bob?" And I say something, and then he says, "What is the end result of that thought, Bob?" And sometimes I don't know the end result of my thought. And he says, "You go back and you begin new, and once you have resolved the end of your thought or idea, then come back and we will ponder about it together." Oh, okay, anyway, I'm gonna go now.

D. Well, that's good advice. I'm really happy you stopped by.

B. Well, always present—you can't be left alone, you know.

Let's go Visit the Evolution Group (Feb 23, 2019)

Several months later, after his solar system work had been completed, we found out that Bob had been invited to go and meet with the Evolution Group. He was concerned about certain changes that are allowed to happen. At the time of printing this book, he has yet to go.

B. I didn't need cleaning today, when Ari left.

D. That's pretty impressive. How come?

B. Ari and I are buddies now, so I don't feel like I'm bounced out.

D. You have become accustomed to his energy?

B. Because I have been taking a class with him. Indeed, I have, a short one. Oh, class...I presented my ideas, and he said, "Why don't you and I go and have a silent moment and ponder about this?" So, that was the class.

D. Ah. He mentioned that.

B. So I thought that maybe, indeed, I could just speed things along a little bit. And I had ideas on how to maybe make the species here a little bit more gentle. I said that I have a group in mind. And Ari said, "Who are those?" And I said, "I have been given the opportunity to travel and visit a different civilization in another fish tank. They are highly advanced and friendly, and they care about things that I care about." And he said, "Sometime we can't get too personal, so the things that we care about might be hindering a greater evolution." And I said, "Could you please, Mr. Ari, explain this greater evolution? Then I can adjust my notes. Maybe all my notes are wrong!" Oh, and then you came in. Oh, oh, it's like Gergen is coming in. Then you came.

D. And then what happened?

B. Oh, you said, "We talked about this, Bob, about changing the whole evolution, when we do not know all about the great ideas and intention behind evolution, do we?" And I said, "No. But no one is telling me, so it's really hard for me to do my job if I am cut out of this stream of knowledge and awareness." So I said, "If you tell me, I will stop bothering everyone with upgrades that might not be suitable at this point." And then Ophelia also popped in, and it became like a family meeting, of sorts. Oh, and here came Isaac and Zachariah, and everyone chipped in. And there I sat.

D. Everyone was concerned about your ideas. What was the outcome of all this discussion?

B. That I was indeed gonna go, and I was gonna participate in a hearing with the Evolution Group. But I'm not gonna go there by myself. I'm gonna go there with you. Huh, all of you are gonna come, everyone is gonna go. It's gonna be me, Ari, you, Ophelia, Isaac, and Zachariah. We're all gonna go.

D. Wow, you'll have a whole team surrounding you.

B. I think it's also because I might not fully understand everything, and then everyone is left with questions. And maybe this is what you also would like to do (*talk with the Evolution Group*), so that you can be more helpful.

D. So you're finally going to meet with the Evolution Group?

B. I am indeed. It is scheduled to take place within the nearest future, whatever that means. So I'm gonna have a listen and be able, through some of you, to be able to ask questions. I have risen to the position where I can participate in the greater changes and knowledge of evolution.

D. On this planet?

B. On this planet, only.

D. That's wonderful. Congratulations.

B. I think it's because I have been concerned...there's a lot of my friends, like the gardeners, they ask me all the time because they know that I travel. And I think someone must have felt there was a need for the second to be more involved. Because I get questions all the time, they come to my office and they say, "Oh, Bob, the waters are not feeling well. Can you take that up with someone when you go out traveling?" And I'm like, "OK, I'll make a note," so some of these notes are not mine, they are requests from the second; the water engineers, and those who are about to upgrade certain organs, they also want to know what's going on. I said, "Maybe we should just wait for the manual that comes through the cloud." And they said, "No, maybe you can ask, since you're traveling to the cloud," and I said, "Well, I'm not really going to the cloud, but thank you for trusting me in that respect." So, the Evolution Group is a little bit above, they are like up at nine, ten, but they communicate a lot with Isaac, so I think Isaac is gonna be the one who translates for me. Maybe everyone would be interested in this?

D. I think so. That's a real honor to be able to get some answers to your questions.

B. Ah. I think so. Maybe not all, of course, but if I can get just some, and I can share my concerns and maybe they can rethink whatever they are doing. Because if they think that everything that happens is fine down below, then they might just continue; so I think it is important that they get a voice heard from someone who is very close in that work.

D. I look forward to hearing about your discussions.

B. Ah. If it's allowed to share, Ophelia says. So anyway, I did talk with Ari a little bit, and it was him that said, "Why don't we go to the Evolution Group?" and I was like, "Ohh, I'm not sure!" and you came and said, "But you wanted this, Bob." And I said, "Yes, I did, I really did." So I'm on my way somewhere here.

D. At least we'll all be together. Safety in numbers.

B. Ahh. So everyone who is familiar to me is gonna join, either for translation or for just comfort. It's nice to have friends like that.

D. Well, congratulations on getting to go to the Evolution Group.

B. I am, indeed. And I asked, "Should I prepare anything?" And everyone was like, "No, because you don't know what to prepare." I'm not sure how many opportunities I will get to directly communicate.

D. Maybe they will show you a documentary of what is coming up.

B. Ah. Then I'm gonna have a look-see. Because there are concerns. Every time when I am home, they are like, "What's going on with that? What plans do they, the big ones, have about the waters?"

D. You're the wise elder now.

B. Ha! And I said, "We'll see." And someone suggested that I should have my own seminars about upcoming news from the different councils. That was one of my notes to Ari, if that was possible. I said, "It's not a personal request, it's a question from my friends, if I could be like a spokesperson providing news." You know, it's like saying, "Good evening, everyone. This is the 7 o'clock news from the Council of Nine." Oh, and Ari, he didn't laugh, but YOU laughed. Ari just looked at me like, "Hmm, uhm-hmm." And you said, "Time to go, Bob." And I said, "It wasn't my request. Just passing on information and questions."

D. There probably should be more communication between the dimensions.

B. Oh, I'm sure there are, but not to the ground floor, always.

D. Everyone wants to know that they are contributing in the right way.

B. Ah. So I think I have stirred things up at the second, because it wasn't this much of a commotion when I started traveling. I was very much in the mindset that I had to keep my mouth shut—and that was a struggle! And now, suddenly, probably due to me and my eagerness to share, it has become a little bit of a commotion down here. All fired up. So maybe it's important that more will come. I went first, but maybe more is gonna come, that's what it feels like. And I'm pretty sure that if hadn't been allowed to share all this, then Ole or Gergen, or Ophelia with her harp, someone would have come, -and they haven't. So I'm pretty sure that the next step is that there is gonna be more involvement, not only on site here, but also that more is gonna travel to different locations.

D. You're going to be busy teaching everybody how to do everything that you do.

B. I also need time for myself and my studies.

D. I look forward to hearing what the Evolution Group says.

B. I did ask about that. I hope that they're not going to change my evolution, or be like, "Oh, what is this? This must have gone completely wrong. What have you brought us? This is not how it's supposed to look; we'll fix it right now." Ohhhh.

D. They might send you back to the factory. (*Bob is a little fearful of the Evolution Group, because he knows they have the ability to cause galaxies, solar systems, planets, or specific life forms to very rapidly evolve, and he doesn't want to find himself a subject of their interest.*)

B. So, I did ask that. You all kinda laughed and said, "No, it's not gonna be like that. We're gonna talk, but you're like one of us, so you're going to go and have a listen, but they're not going to do adjustments ON you. We're going to talk about adjustments on the planet, mainly. That's where the limit of your involvement will be." I might sneak in a question or two. Ophelia says I'm just rambling on now, but I might sneak a question or two about the greater concerns that I have about soul evolution in general. What I'm fishing for is to see about that pole and the dissolving business, and then I can maybe calculate where I am before it's time to be dissolved. Ophelia's dragging my arm, but it's clearly interesting.

D. See how far you are from the end of the conveyor belt. Alright my friend, thank you for coming.

Advancements and Rewards

This chapter is a collection of stories Bob told that were not directly related to teaching the sparkles or students, or about building a solar system. As a traveler, his biggest joy comes from exploring new realities, especially out in the universes of form. The first planet he went to, other than the Earth or the learning centers for the second, such as the Greenhouse Planet, was Etena. The planet is a magnificent storehouse of knowledge, and is populated by many other fascinating individuals. In order to get to Etena, he had to undergo some rigorous training, but he was motivated by the images he was shown of Lasaray's pet, Siah. Each of his inspiring tales is woven around a message that the spirits want us to understand. His travel diary to Etena begins when he was first made aware of Siah.

Siah's Planet, Etena (Nov 5, 2017)

This particular planet, Etena, has been the topic of many discussions, not only with Bob, but with other spirits as well. The solar system containing Etena exists in the fourth fish tank, but is on the border area with our Universe, the fifth fish tank. It has plants and animals similar to some on Earth, but they are on a higher vibration. The spirits who live there do not incarnate, they manifest a form and therefore do not die. The Shea occupy this planet as caretakers, but the Elahim also frequently visit because it is a great center of learning. It has many pyramids where knowledge and the energetic patterns of innumerable life forms are stored. Bob has reported that there are spirits coming and going all the time to drop off information, or to meet and discuss different topics. Eli said I found Siah on another planet where he was not being treated well, and his partner had been killed. He said I transported him to this highly evolved planet, where he would be happy and well cared for. The people and most of the animals on this planet are not biological, but are similar to manifestations like the Anunnaki; they have bodies that are more energetic in structure. When a spirit is on that reality, it feels solid, but exists on a higher, less dense frequency than our planet. The Shea are a small group of spirits from the seventh dimension, Ophelia being one, who assist in maintaining the records stored in the center of knowledge on Siah's planet. The spirits who live on Etena are familiar with Earth, since the Elahim and Shea are associated with both planets, and have expressed a desire to share information with us. Since their planet also evolved to its current state from a more primitive condition, we are curious to hear their observations or advice. Bob was given a preview of the planet, because he was going to be traveling there to learn.

B. I saw the show. I saw that creature (*Siah*).

D. How did it look?

B. It looked, not like a pig, but it was really big. His head looked like a hippo head, and his body like a, like a–, he's more like a hippo, in some way, but he moves like a cat. So you can see the dilemma if it was here, it's too big to bounce around like a house cat. And he doesn't understand how big he is, so he's just bouncing around. You have a collar on him, and it's with, it looks like diamonds almost, shiny, and he likes you. His ears are not standing up, they're hanging down, his ears. And he has a big nose, like a dog nose, and he bounces a lot. He's free, he hasn't gone to training, because you don't train here—everyone is left to be who they are, and this is him. He bounces around and he thinks he's the smallest, most tender, and gentle creature, like a housecat. But he's big as a hippo, almost.

D. Maybe you can come and visit him.

B. He looks like a sea cow, he doesn't have horns or claws or big teeth, but he has like sugar cube teeth. I didn't create this! I didn't know he existed. Ohh!

D. It's a nice design idea, though?

B. Yes, and he's extremely friendly. You would think he would be a predator, but he's not. He likes vegetables, he eats plants. No one eats meat there, nothing with meat, because the physical there it's not as dense as a physical human form. So meat will simply make the cells become too heavy within their beings. AND, they honor all life forms. Siah eats, oh, he eats a lot of those greens, something green. Sometimes it looks like there's a berry in it, he eats that. There are two that takes care of him, a couple, a male and female individual that take care of him. They have like a little garden where they grow things, like a greenhouse. But it's not indoors, nothing needs to be indoors here, because the atmosphere is clean and oxygen is enough for everyone; for plants, for people, even for life forms that you can't see, like we talked about the fairies, everything that flies around, you know. So you don't have to have a greenhouse inside because everything is as it should. But they have to have fences to keep him out, because Siah, he doesn't understand, really, that he's not allowed to just walk on the plants. And he's kind of big. He's bigger than them, not taller. But they take care of him, this couple, and they live there and they garden things, and that's what they eat. Different.

D. It must be a big garden to feed him.

B. Ah, ah. He has a little shed thing too, like a little house where he sleeps. So it's like a society. I've never been here—I wanna go! Where is this? Where is this, is this nearby? (*I am always amused when he asks questions like that, forgetting we are not at home.*)

D. Eli said it's behind Sirius.

B. I'm gonna go here, I think, if it's allowed. Maybe this is where we're gonna go, maybe we can pass this way in my bubble?

D. Maybe. It's on the border within a different fish tank, the one at 4 o'clock.

B. I think I wanna talk with them, because they seem really friendly. They are really caring about nature and the plants. The vegetables are different here, it's almost like a carrot plant, but I don't know if it's a carrot underneath. It's different, but they eat that, and they grow things and they are really in harmony with everyone. And if someone has less, a neighbor, they share. There's nothing like, "I have and you don't," and you sit on your treasure and your treats—you share. Even with Siah, because the couple that takes care of him, sometimes they don't have enough green, so neighbors come and feed Siah. But Siah, he can move around, he's free to go, he's not like on a leash, so he's free to go. And he goes every day and sits by a pyramid, and that's where he sits, and when—it doesn't become night really, it's like a sunset, but it doesn't become fully dark here. The darkest it becomes is like a sunset—so when that happens, Siah goes back.

D. Eli said he sits by the pyramid, waiting for me to come back; he misses me.

B. Ah, ah, maybe we should go. I think I wanna go here because I don't feel uncomfortable coming here, because this seems like a really friendly place.

D. What do they look like, the ones who tend to Siah?

B. I wouldn't mind having my Individual taken care of by these people. They have big eyes, big eyes; look like human eyes, but they're bigger. They're not like ET eyes, like you say, like black. So they're like human eyes but a little bit more egg shaped and go up on the sides, upwards. And they don't have hair. They have like a big smile, big smile and little nose. Big head, like whitish in color, light grey, beige whitish color. Fingers, let's see, one, two, three, four, ah, four fingers here.

D. Just like us then, with a thumb?

B. Nay, nay, that's including the thumb, not the same. But Siah's feet are not like a hippo, they're more like a dog. Huhuh.

D. Are there a number of creatures like Siah, or is he all alone?

B. I only see him! I tried to look around to see if there's more, but I can't see. There seems to be only Siah, but he's friendly and he moves around. He likes to be scratched behind his ears. They live in family units here, so that's what they do. He moves around freely. There are only smaller animals here, and they seem to be a little bit, hehe, like, "OOHH," and run off when he comes. Normally he doesn't run, he can just walk, too, walking gently. But when he gets excited, –he likes butterflies, so when he sees that, like things that fly–, then he bounces around, and sometimes he tips things and they fall, because of his nature and size. So that's what happened here. Huh huhuhuh. Siah doesn't seem to live in a couple unit, he seems to be by himself, like a lonely individual. But I didn't know about this individual. If I did, I might have put it on my living planet; but then again, my Individual bounces and loses track of its feet when it's happy, when they play—but this one gets like that just if a butterfly flies by and he sees that. Then he bounces around and he tries to catch it, and the ears fly a little bit and he bounces around and loses all sense of direction, it seems. Huhuh.

D. He seems happy.

B. He is happy. Oh, that was interesting, that was interesting to see that, so I think I wanna go here. Ophelia laughs about that.

She says I do like different animals, and this one is friendly. She looks after it sometimes, she said. Ophelia knows this place, Ophelia has been here, she said. I, I haven't been here, I don't know why, but I think I'm gonna go. But she said, "If we give you all the treats first, what's to aspire for if you know everything in advance?" So she said I'm definitely gonna be able to project myself here, –with you, probably. Huhuhuh. So she said she has things up her sleeve for me, too.

D. Maybe she's making you a saddle, so you can ride him.

B. Uhuhuhuh, ride on Ia—Siah, not Ia, of course. But Siah is almost the same, need to watch my tongue here. But Ophelia knows, because Ophelia's people (*the Shea*), they are very much involved with the way the civilization here became. So people with light, and they honor the light. She said they honor the sunlight, and they get exactly the right amount that they're supposed to have. And the atmosphere—it's something that is within the atmosphere, it almost looks like gold, I would say. It sparkles, and it creates the exact conditions for everyone to be at peace, and to have exactly the amount they need. They never take more than they need. And sometimes, she said, they can use somewhat of a solar panel thing, she said. But it's not like those big ones. It almost looks like a little plate, because they only take exactly what they need. I would assume, because of Siah eating so much, if there is a lack of growth in one area of the garden, then they can put a little plate there and just add a little extra energy. I don't know about this sun, how big it is. I can't see it, because the atmosphere is in a bubble, it's almost like seeing this planet floating around in a soap bubble, completely intact. The sun is quite big, I think the sun might be bigger than the one here. It's protected, so that's why it can be closer. Interesting. I don't know what the purpose was for designing it like this, like a soap bubble, but it's completely protected. It looks like a soap bubble, like a glass bubble. (*The atmosphere is perfectly designed to protect and nurture the planet.*)

D. So what do I do on that planet?

B. You meet your friends here. And there are these pyramids, but I can't see inside them. It's like a community where there's a lot of discussions about sunlight and energy. This is not traveling energy; it is to increase and help growth within this reality. This would clearly be of help here, to know exactly how much to use so the soil is correct, and the growth becomes exactly what it is supposed to. But as long as individuals here (*on Earth*) are not up to speed with that understanding, then it's not gonna be the same atmospheric opportunities. What you do here (*on Etena*), Ophelia says, this is a place of rest, and a place to just be happy and meet friends. And they're really interested in hearing about your journeys because they don't really leave, it seems. So you come here and tell them. They're interested in Earth, because it's somewhat similar, with the plant growth and so forth. And some of them are really trying to be helpful and to give advice, asking if they can pass on a note to someone here on how to do things right. And there's a little council here that just makes, – I wouldn't say laws, because laws has such a bad ring to it, that it's something bad that someone decides over you–, but it is a council here that decides what's best for the community. But everyone can pitch in, everyone can have a listen. So it's not in a closed room where some old dudes sit and decide things over the other ones, everyone can be heard. There is one here that wants to be more helpful. And when you're there, they pitch in with notes that they want to be delivered here, how to do things better. They feel like Earth is a little bit left behind, and they want to help and make it more in harmony.

D. Maybe they'll be able to pass some notes through you later on during this project?

B. Ah, a note to man on how to be. But the key thing is, this society is completely different than the society here, because there is no difference, everyone is together and helping. Here (*on Earth*) you have all these separations, not only between like what would be considered race, but it's also even between the sexes. It's a combat sometimes. It's like everyone is trying to protect themselves all the time, always on high alert that there should be an ambush or something. That's not at all the way it is there. They don't understand that, they don't understand why there is this feeling of being attacked, because this society never had that. This is a very, I would say, a very nice destination to go to.

D. Good place to vacation.

B. Good place to vacation, ah. They want to pass on notes, they say.

D. Well good. Since you can see them so clearly, maybe you can pick them up.

B. I don't see the notes. Maybe I will, maybe I will indeed, if they let me. Ophelia says we will see about that. But she is in favor of this. She says the meeting of this planet and Siah was one of her little treats she had up her sleeve. It's a treat for all of us, and I think I'm gonna go, in some way. And if I can't go, then I'm sure I'm gonna be able to pitch in. When Isaac and this other tall individual, your brother person, Eli, (*go there*), I might try to go with him. I don't know what he's doing, he didn't really say to me, but he seems to be—

D. He's my older brother, and I think he studied with Isaac before he went up to the tenth.

B. Ah, I'm WAY behind here, I feel. Well, I'm gonna go here, if I'm allowed. And I will be happy to tend to Siah, to talk with him, because I think he would like that. He's very friendly, he's like, you know how certain dogs here, they bond with only one human? Even if they are in a family with several humans, they only bond with one, that is a little bit like him. He's not unfriendly with the other ones, it just that he bonds with one. He's your personal companion. He's still fine with his like adoptive parents here, but he's still more bonded to you. So you might need to go here and just spend some time with him.

D. So he goes and sits by the pyramid, waiting for me to show up?

B. There's an entrance into the pyramid, I don't know what that is, maybe we will explore. Oh! "Not today!" Ophelia says. (*He suddenly looked left towards Ophelia.*) She detected that I saw it! I saw the entrance into the pyramid where he was sitting, and she said, "Not today, Bob. All good things come to those who wait." Ah, ah, if you say so. This is going to be a fascinating place to go in to. I know in one of the pyramids the council exists, so maybe we will go in there. There's also a library here, one of the pyramids I see here is a library. She said we will get access to it.

D. Oh, nice. Are there trees and things like that on this planet? Is it a green planet?

B. Umm, it's really odd. I see all this green that they grow, but there's not very much trees around, so I can't see them around where I am now, but they have a lot of growth. I would assume that outside of this city-like center that there is more green, and they have some sort of fruits here too. So they grow things. But we don't explore more here than the city center.

D. Are the pyramids being used on this planet?

B. (*He talked about the pyramids briefly, which was presented in Wave 2*). I don't know about this planet because they have the same ones. But we haven't gone in because we're supposed to wait. But I know one of them is a library. If I give you a picture of this place, it's like I'm on a big, middle street that is somewhat wide. It's not like dirt, or it's not like cement, it's just very—I mean, it's soft, or not soft, but it's not like cement. It's almost like cobblestone but it's a little bit softer and white. And on each side, the left side, it's like a row of pyramids, and it's the same on the other side. And way up there is where Siah goes and sits, next to one of them. From my standpoint, here, this place has like at least twelve, fifteen. And some are bigger and some are a little bit smaller, so they're not like the Giza ones, every one of them.

D. Do the people use them, do the ones in white use them for anything?

B. Ah, like one is a library here, and I can't see into the other ones, and we're not supposed to today. But there's something inside, –it's not just for show! Huhuh. I think I'm gonna go here. Ophelia is really happy about this, that we discovered this place today. And Siah is gonna be happy when we come here. I will be able to send him messages from you, because I will be able to go, –if you don't go when you sleep. And I can scratch his head—it's a big head, but I don't know if I'm gonna reach. He's friendly, but when he opens his mouth, if you don't know that he's friendly, you might think, "Oh, it's gonna eat me!" But he just sort of licks.

D. Well, you can probably move pretty fast, can't you?

B. I can indeed. I might play with him, I might run around and hide behind the pyramids and play with him, and he can find me and I can go, "BOO." And he's gonna be all excited like with the butterflies, Hehehe. "We'll see about that," Ophelia says, because sometime he loses track of his feet, and we don't want him to make something tip. But he has been taken care of. Well, anyway, this was a joy, this was happy. I think I'm gonna go here. I like these people. They're friendly and they're curious.

D. Sounds like a very peaceful place. I can see why we go there to rest.

B. Ah, you go there, sometimes just to chit–chat a little bit with them, too. To catch up and talk with them, see what they're up to. A friendly community, like friends, family, like what you want to have. And that's also why you felt a little bit disconnected (*as a human*), because you know how it feels when there is a genuine care. And for you here, it sometimes doesn't seem to exist. But it does exist, you just have to find it. Here, it's more like everywhere. But on Earth, it's like, "Why do people say certain things to make others feel bad?", for instance. Here, that's not what they do.

D. Eli said I manifest a body on Etena.

B. Ah, well I can't see you here. But the little community, they look the same, but I don't think they leave. I think they are locals, of sorts. And Siah doesn't leave.

D. So they must not be incarnated there?

B. They're there, but they don't leave. You seem to come and go. And you have this couple that takes care of Siah for you. We should probably go here. And we should go into the pyramids. Oh, Ophelia said we're all sorts of ahead of ourselves here. Hahaha.

D. All in due time.

B. All in due time, whatever that means. Oh, she laughs about that. She says this is a treat. Oh, okay, okay. Well, that will probably be it. We explored something new today, new for everyone. And I'm happy to not be excluded, because I wouldn't want to miss this. There's plenty of places to go here. "We'll see about that," Ophelia says.

Jungle Bob (Oct 7, 2018)

Bob had tried to trick me by sending Ia in first, but she just smiled and didn't make any of the telling facial expressions that I have come to expect every time Bob takes over control. I knew it wasn't him, even though she didn't say anything, so we had a little laugh. After Ia stepped out and Bob came in, he began his talk by telling how the spiritual world is always communicating with the humans via the chimney (the energy field above the brain). Even though we are consciously oblivious to the little second dimensional spirits who are protecting their creations, on some level we hear them, loud and clear.

B. HUH HUH AH! That was a surprise, wasn't it? You thought it was me, but it was not!

D. I knew it wasn't you. I assumed you were coming, but I knew it was Ia before she spoke.

B. Ah.

D. She didn't replicate your expressions, let's just say.

B. Ah. I might need to work on that. I might need to go to disguise school. I might, actually, take up theater! Oh huhuhuh. Ah. I'm gonna take theater class, maybe with Ophelia and Julia, and just try to see how one can be disguised. I might do that.

D. Why would you want to be disguised?

B. Just to sniff around on other places, maybe. You know, I think it might be fun. I think there might be those sort of interactive classes, like at Ophelia's place, because they are very much with singing and, you know, plays.

D. Not so much in our lab.

B. I have never actually seen you in a play, in your lab. And the other ones are also kinda serious. But, in this great play (*Earth*), then I might indeed too like to portray myself, similar like you do when you take on a physical body here, –you dress to the occasion. This one is constantly trying to act the part, like theater, saying "What is this role demanding? What are the demands on me? Oh, I'm gonna dress like this, and I'm gonna take on this personality," similar like that. I never get a chance to be someone else, like you do. I think that might be fun. This one talks a lot about that, so that's why I think that I might wanna do that.

D. Maybe you can act like a little gardener.

B. I think I would like to have the leading role as an explorer, like one who crossed the ocean here to find a new continent. I might actually like to be like that one in the movie, an Indiana Jones kind of guy.

D. Well, you are like that, because not too many on the second travel like you do. You just need a hat and a whip!

B. Ahahaha! I'll be Jungle Bob! Huhuhuh. Ah, I might actually write a little story about that—what would I do if I were to pick an incarnation? First, I would like to be Jungle Bob! I might actually write about that, because the sparkles, they don't go into bodies. They only blend with trees and animals and so forth, and they might think this would be like a great teaching, as well as a great novel of amusement! Uhuhuh.

D. That's a good way to teach.

B. It's an excellent way to teach. And I am full of ideas of how to teach, and I think this will be great.

D. A lot of the sparkles never observe or interact with humans, do they?

B. Well, they observe if a human pass by, when they are in a tree. And like we said before about making fire, if it's not advisable, then the sparkles are supposed to send out their own thought bubbles to that species that is doing that. So, you know, the humanoid actually can detect thought bubbles from sparkles in trees.

D. Really?

B. Indeed.

D. Can we detect the thought bubbles from the little sparkles in our plant? (*We have a little plant in our home that is growing extraordinarily well, and Ophelia said there were sparkles from the second who had come to blend with the plant, as a gift to us.*)

B. Indeed. This one does.

D. What do they say?

B. It's like a kindergarten, she says. Ophelia says it sounds like a kindergarten. It's a lot of talking, so it's like a big mumble. This one hasn't yet detected the different bubbles, or the different tones in it, just the collective tone. But this one can tune in and listen to them. They're like little me's.

D. Little you's?

B. Indeed. So, oh, but I am indeed, I am indeed gonna write myself a fictive story of me in the jungle.

D. You might decide you like being a writer and fill your little library full of books.

B. Ah. Gergen and Ole, they have a lot of volumes.

D. Oh, like teachings and stories?

B. Indeed. Teachings and also journals from different locations where he (*Ole*) has been traveling to. This is the one I'm HIGHLY interested in, and I'm trying to get a peek and somewhat set up a meeting in his office. But every time I try to do that, Gergen shows up. So, I'm not sure if it is allowed.

D. He probably just wants to monitor what happens.

B. Oh, I don't know. I'm a bit sneaky, but it's also because I feel that there are greater mysteries that have yet to be revealed. And I'm eager to listen to what others also has experienced when they were like Jungle Bob, somewhere. I am indeed still very highly interested in going to Siah. And I have actually been told, after several complaints on my part, that we are actually gonna go.

D. Well, good! You and I? That will be—

B. And this one. This one has friends up there (*on Etena*), in the library up there, and probably your friends too. But this one says, "I like to go there."

D. It's a place of relaxation for us, isn't it?

B. Maybe it's like a spa.

D. Do we send a lot of our energy there?

B. Bigger, more. It's a place where they store records, that's what you said. And since I'm all about knowledge, I am eager to go. This is a place where there is a storage unit of knowledge, when it comes to stellar traveling, this one says, and different destinations. So it's like a big library. That's why we're gonna go, Ophelia says, that's where we're gonna go next. It has shelves upon shelves upon shelves on different destinations and travels. There are different libraries or storage units where knowledge is kept. Not only underneath the big Library in the vaults (*on the fifth*), but there are, spread out on other realities in other fish tanks, different locations or centers where certain knowledge is stored. And here it has to do with travels and different destinations. So we're gonna go, this one said and you said, and we're gonna go visit Siah, and go and visit the library. It's not a library, Ophelia says it's more like a center, that's what she calls all these places. And there are several centers in all fish tanks that have reports of different activities. And the Creator can tap into that center and get all information needed from that specific action or location, if that is a center of geographic interest.

D. So who maintains the library on that location? (*We have learned it is a small group of spirits from the seventh, the Shea.*)

B. At Siah's place? Siah likes to sit outside, he doesn't go in, so Siah sits outside. But there are those dressed in white, and they have like gold adornments or somewhat of a necklace, but it's bigger than a regular necklace. It covers the chest and it carries different gold medallions based on, probably, your access within this center. They are in charge of organizing the records.

D. Well, once you go there, do you think you'll be able to go back whenever you want? What does Ophelia say?

B. It's part of the unknown, but it's a treat, she said.

D. It would be nice if you could go visit Siah whenever you wanted.

B. But I'm not travelling by myself, so, you know, whenever you have time.

D. When we decide to go somewhere, how do we actually move from place to place?

B. First, you made me fall asleep. My first travels, it was just like I went into my own place, my space in the second, and sort of went into like a little bit of a sleep or trance state. And from that state of being, I transformed my energy and I was assisted, in the beginning by Ophelia, to her place. And similar like you did with me, I don't remember going through a door, in the beginning. I was somewhat picked up and brought. After that...

D. You must leave a part of yourself, a passive particle, so you can pull yourself back and forth.

B. Indeed. But I don't have a passive particle at Siah's place. But once I do, I would be able to go, similar like I can go to your vault. But I cannot go there unless you invite me. You still have to have an invitation. Even if you leave a passive particle, you still need that approval and invitation to come. So, it's not like you can go everywhere, and I cannot travel just freely. I have not left a passive particle where my solar system is, so I can't go there. But I can look on the screens in your lab.

D. What about somewhere like the 4–H Farm.

B. I can go there, of course. It's manifested within our own reality, if you like. It's in the second dimension. But if you think of each spiritual reality is also like a fish tank, and the Greenhouse Planet is within that fish tank. So you cannot go there, because you don't have a passive particle. So it's not a planet similar like Earth. It's a "*planet*" or a destination that exists within the second dimensional vibrational field.

D. I understand that.

B. So I can go there whenever I want. I don't need to go to sleep or wait for someone to invite me, because it's my reality. But if you were to go there, you would have to be invited. And you would not go to the spiritual aspect of that reality. But when I go to your lab, it's somewhat of a manifested part of your reality, and

I can be invited there. Isaac, he seems to travel without invitation—that is my goal!

D. He has a keycard everywhere.

B. He has a keycard to everywhere, so he doesn't have to have an invitation.

D. What about Ophelia, she must travel a lot?

B. She has probably endless accessibility. Meaning, it's the same thing that I have in my second dimensional vibrational reality, that once you reach a certain level, I'm sure you can just go anywhere.

Advanced Bubble Training (Dec 10, 2018)

When Bob went to explore the location where we had installed his solar system, he traveled in a protective, energetic shield that Jeshua created for him. It was like a big sphere around him, a bubble filled with some vaporous material. The next step in his training is to actually merge his own energetic field with the protective bubble around him. Eventually, he will generate a protective layer out of his own light capsule. The purpose is to shield his being from the waves of energy he must pass through while traveling to different realities. He was encouraged to master this technique because it was the only way he would be able to go visit my pet, Siah. Ophelia dangled a carrot when she gave him a detailed preview of the planet Etena and its inhabitants.

D. Gergen mentioned you are going back into bubble training?

B. Ah.

D. Where are you going to go?

B. I'm gonna go to meet Siah.

D. Finally!

B. FINALLY! That took a long time, too. Different bubble training, going differently.

D. Is it a different type of bubble?

B. No, it's the same. It's just that it is created differently. Not a different bubble, same bubble, but it maneuvers differently. But I'm gonna go and I'm gonna collect data from the library, and I'm also gonna play and tend to Siah as well.

D. So when you are in your bubble, will you travel in your bubble, and get out when you get there?

B. At Siah's place, I'm gonna get out of the bubble, you say. You say, "You're not gonna float around in the bubble when you're there. It's just the transportation device to get through the energetic barriers." I'm gonna go talk with your friends up there. They are like record keepers, you say, and we're gonna go and look into certain scriptures that exists over this fish tank (*five*), in particular. But they have scrolls of all sorts of things, I imagine. So, I'm gonna go. There's a friend there I'm gonna meet, you say. One of your friends that's gonna take care of me. But I'm thinking that you might want to go too, so that I behave.

D. I probably need to go visit with Siah.

B. So I'm thinking that we are both gonna go. In the meantime, I am training to transform my energetic being in a different way, so that my bubble transforms. You are careful with this word, but you say in some way the bubble—it doesn't dissolve, because you are careful with that word—it constricts. It's like I go in the bubble and then I become the bubble, so it's gonna be different. That's how you travel, you say, "Everyone comes in somewhat of a bubble." It's just that now I will become the bubble. I was floating the first time inside the bubble and sort of moved around freely within (*when he went to view his solar system*). Now you say, "Where we're going now, you don't have to just float around in the bubble." The next level of learning is that I become the bubble, it just sort of sucks around my being. And that's what you do.

D. Wow, you are going to be proficient at traveling. Will you be able to do that anytime you want?

B. That has not been given! But I'm gonna ask!

D. I would assume so, once you learn how to do it. You'll be floating around with this one before long.

B. Ahh! This one is like, "Okay, now you're ready for the big trips, Bob." And I was like, "Where are those?" And he said, "First you learn how to constrict and become the bubble, then there is no bubble anymore." And I was like, "A life without a bubble, how's that gonna play out?" But he said, "You wondered why we didn't travel in our bubble, but we're just making it shrink around our soul energy and we become the bubble, and we learn how that specific shield can be controlled and adjusted," he said, "and it's different depending on where you want to go. You have your bubble and you sort of make it encase you. But you adjust the components and the makeup based on where you want to go."

So he said, "If you want to go to the other side of the center pole," and I was like, "Sure! I can come. If everyone else are going, I want to come." And he said, "That's a completely different shield." First of all, now I'm learning to not be afraid when the bubble shrinks around my being, because that was scary, I must say.

D. The first time it happened?

B. Ah. I went in the bubble, and Jeshua said, first time he said, "I'm gonna make it spin a little bit, Bob, but you inside are not gonna spin," and I was like, "Okay." Then he said, "We're gonna make it shrink a little bit, Bob, it's not like you're gonna suffocate in there, but it's gonna feel like the bubble is closing in. It's because it's gonna become like a second skin on you." OOHHHH! So, that's where we're at.

D. Have you done that already?

B. A little bit, but it hasn't come all the way in. It's a little bit like feeling trapped. But he said, "It's the same thing, the same procedure. You can still come in and out as you please. This is how you transform and travel. This is the only way, Bob, that you can visit Siah." (*He then made a sucking sound, like he was building up courage.*) So, that's what I do, and I'm in that phase of training. It hasn't completely encased me yet.

D. Are you doing this in our lab, or in the bubble room, or where are you doing it?

B. It's in the sphere room, where the bubble is parked. But it was my bubble, I didn't expect it to change, at all! I thought this was going to be my bubble for all sorts of travels. But I was also confused, because you don't have a bubble. But you did, at one point. It's just that now your bubble is like a second skin. This is going to be discussed more, Ophelia says, because this is how you travel here and there, moving around. This specific technique.

D. Humans can't do that, can they?

B. No, you have your skin.

D. But if they are outside the body, like with an OBE or a near-death experience?

B. Not the same. So, anyway, that's what I'm doing now. Training with Jeshua, and you are present, of course, as well. And this one laughs, because I'm sort of hanging upside down. And I don't know if I'm supposed to be upside down. Then you came in and you said, "Why is he upside down?" And this one was like, "We're playing a little bit." And I was like, "Am I not supposed to be upside down?" And you said, "No, you don't have to be in any shape or form. This is not about being either horizontal, vertical, or upside down." So I don't know who played tricks on me and made me be upside down.

D. I'm pretty sure it was this one.

B. Ah. Anyway, I'm gonna go now, but this is where I'm at.

D. That's wonderful, I look forward to hearing about Siah and your travels.

B. Ah, I'm gonna go soon, after I master this. So, I'll go now. So long, and I'm gonna continue my training. But at least now I know I don't need to be upside down.

D. Seth is a trouble maker. Always teasing.

B. He's a player. A player on all sorts of levels. Teasing. I'm kind of the same, so I had it coming.

D. You're kind of a player too, because you tricked me last week when you had Ia come in (*during the session*) and act like you.

B. I'm tricky too. So he and I are kinda the same, so I don't get mad. When you come in and say, "Oh, why is he upside down? Why is he hanging there?" HUHUHUH, this one was laughing, that's what he did, he laughed. And I was like, "OH! I fell for it again. I didn't need to be upside down."

D. At least we have fun together.

Shrink–Fitting the Bubble (Dec 16, 2018)

A few weeks later, Bob continued with the story of his training practices. At home in the lab, Seth often plays around with him, to make him laugh or feel less anxious, like when he had hung Bob upside down as he was practicing to generate an energetic layer around his spirit energy. All spirits who travel must learn how to do this, and seeking the silence within may have some application to those who are doing out–of–body explorations within our fish tank.

B. So I am indeed, and I am currently progressing in my bubble training, because I am eager to depart. I wanna go and see Siah, and in order for me to do that, I have to power through this sensation of being trapped within my bubble, which is gonna shrink around my being and become the second skin.

D. This one isn't still making you hang upside down, is he?

B. Nooo! No, that was tricky. When I got down, I poked him a little bit and said, "You trick me all the time!" And this one says, "It's just to create a little bit more fun in your training. It's to make you relax, to make you not be so stressed or hyped about things, to make you in a more relaxed state of mind." He knows I learn better when I'm a little bit happy and laughing, because it disarms me, he says. So, he had an agenda.

D. Do you appreciate it, or does it bother you?

B. No, it doesn't bother me, because I know the agenda is to preoccupy my sensation of fear, in this case. So he was playing with me.

D. We laugh about your interactions with this one.

B. It's because this one knows and understands my nature, but I also understand why I can't be with him. Because of the fact that if I did, if I always was cheerful and didn't focus, then I would miss the greater teachings and stillness. You said that in order for me to be a great cosmic engineer, I have to understand the still point that exists in all matters. And that has been tricky on my path through development. Not only with you, but it is that fact of silence, like I said with the egg, how to be silent. BUT this one comes in sometimes to poke me and play with me because he sees that I get a little bit stressed about certain things. So he just tries to preoccupy me by playing.

D. So we sort of work as a team?

B. Indeed. This one doesn't stick around all the time, busy. He's always on the move, always going places. So he comes by quickly and hangs me upside down and laughs and then leaves. So he's more like coming in and doing a quick thing, then you are left with all the details and questions to help me persevere. And then this one is gone. So it's more like, if I were to compare, he's like the wind that just sweeps by and then is on its way again, and you don't know when he's gonna come back. Then, when you least expect it, whoosh, he comes again and says something or does something or just briefly drops something in my lap. So he's always on the move.

D. Kind of like that here, too.

B. Always going places. And then I try to ask, "Where are you going? Can I come?" And he says, "No, I'm just on my way, and you're going to be here." And I say, "What are you working on?"

and he says, "I'm working on my maps, I have travels to do." "Travels to where?" I say. "Different places," –so he's very vague. It is a fact that you told him, at one point, to not be a full display of everything, because of the fact that you are left with the questions. Sometimes when I ask you, "So, what is he doing? What are all those maps for?" then you try to distract me, "Oh, look over here, Bob. Today we're gonna create a moon!" And then I'm like, "Oh, are we gonna do a moon?" and then I forget all about it. But then I remember again. I'm a little bit like that, it doesn't stick.

D. So how is your bubble training progressing?

B. It's actually proceeding well. I have allowed it to almost encase me now. The problem is—when that happens, you are left alone—and I said, "Why?" You said, "Because you are, similar like when you move into your light capsule, you are supposed to learn how to navigate and generate energy within this encased bubble before departure." So it's not just (*makes a slurping sound*), making it shrink and then we go. I have to learn how to radiate my energy so it fills up correctly. So I'm not supposed to be in hibernation, at all, in here.

D. You said we all have a little bubble around us, like that, when we travel?

B. Indeed, it was a bubble like mine at one point, I'm pretty sure.

D. So, what's the exact purpose of this bubble?

B. It doesn't affect me when I go through different layers, you say.

D. So your being doesn't interact with these fields?

B. No, but I'm perfectly awake. In the bubble, the bubble took the hit of different vibrational fields as we transitioned. But now I'm gonna be constantly awake, so it's not gonna be deflected and I'm gonna be fully in the experience.

D. That probably takes a little bit of training.

B. Indeed. So what happens is that I am left alone now when this shield has encased me, and then it is modified differently for the occurrences that can come my way, you say. So you put in different events into the sphere room, you put in not only the sensations, but the visual as well, for what I will experience as I travel to Siah (*the planet Etena*). So, I am training now for what will occur, so I don't freak out, because there is no rescue team, like it was with my bubble. Because the bubble was in some way remotely adjusted and controlled from somewhere. But now, I AM the one who maneuvers my own case.

D. So you are like your own little spacecraft?

B. I am my own spacecraft, indeed.

D. I'll travel with you, won't I?

B. Indeed, indeed. But now I'm training to learn how it will be felt as we move, but also what I would experience and see. And you said, "It's not just a visual excursion, you're also here to do good." So as I travel, if I sense a place where the melody is out of tune, I need to take notes, so as I return, adjustments can be made. And that's how you travel, you say. You're not just on a road trip.

D. Is that why a lot of spirits travel through these different realities, to look for problems?

B. Indeed. And a lot of souls here have a sensation of just floating, like in meditations and so forth, how they are just floating in space. And that is a memory of how these specific souls have been navigating and experiencing certain occurrences around in different fish tanks, normally this one (*our Universe*), how they feel very familiar with floating around and reporting. But it's not just like a visual road trip, it's to also be on alert for problems. That's why there's always these little capsules out and about in the fish tanks.

D. That's fascinating! So when you get to somewhere like Siah's place, can you get out of your bubble?

B. Indeed. When you reach your destination where you have decided or are allowed to go, then indeed. You don't get out of it, it's simply a way of being and a way of existing. You say, "When you later travel to another place or when you want to go back, then you just move into the vibration, you transform your mental capacity and from your center point you recreate," you say, "this shield."

D. Is that the way that we travel, like when the Elahim came to Earth as the Anunnaki?

B. Indeed, indeed. So, inside your shield at that time, you had your shape of preference. So you came and as long as the shield was on, it would appear that you were half-and-half. As soon as the shield was de-activated, you came into the form that existed within your capsule, which looked like the Anunnaki. That's not so tricky, you said. So, in my case, I will be the way I am, as I exit or deactivate. It's easier to say it like that, –you activate and you deactivate your travel capsule.

D. Are you still in bubble training?

B. Well, not training, I'm mainly learning how to shift my energetic self. Jeshua said that I'm supposed to somewhat be asleep inside the bubble. So I'm not gonna travel fully like this, like on high alert. He said it's better for me, because if you're on high alert, then you think you remember everything. BUT you actually are more like a sponge of knowledge and impression if your mind goes into a little bit of a meditation state. So he said I'm gonna be in that, –I'm not gonna be asleep–, but I'm gonna be in somewhat of a passive state within my mind, but not sleeping, he said. And that is because I have to detach my mind in order for all the impressions to come in correctly. And when the mind is detached from its normal day-to-day activities, that's when it has the ability to completely fill up. So you have to be like that. And it's the same with a human mind, because your mind is constantly on alert with all these signals coming in from like internet, phones, and all around you there is noises, so your mind is never asleep, it's never silent. Once the mind becomes a little bit silent, and not necessarily that you sleep, then you have the ability to simply receive signals correctly, and the images around you. And that is what I'm gonna do in the bubble, he said.

D. Well, that's wonderful. I was thinking about that while you were talking, how that relates to a human and meditation, or going into the dark void.

B. You have to make your mind silent, and when the mind is silent, then it has the ability to understand the signals. It's like the signals are not going as fast and you have the ability to see them for what they are. And signals can be verbal or noise, but they can also be images or impressions that you have around you. But if you are on high alert, then they just come in and they're like missiles, almost, which can damage. Because the mind is not as big and as grand as it can be, it cannot deal with missiles. SO, if you still your mind, if you go into a silence within you, and have your eyes wide open so you can see everything, you will be able to understand what signal is true, and which signals only create confusion, that are only missiles. Once you see that, then you have the option, by choice, to not invite that (*disturbance*) into your system. But if you don't recognize the difference, then they're all gonna fall in, both of them. The missile creates more of a crater than the ones that are purely sent, and the craters will NOT be undetected.

D. This is exactly what Ari was talking about.

Jeshua Instructs Bob on Traveling (Jan 6, 2019)

As part of his training to go to Etena, Bob took an introductory class with some other students who were also preparing to travel somewhere. Jeshua had them in an auditorium with screens like a planetarium. Once Bob had established his suit, he thought he looked like a peanut, so he forever after calls his protective shield his peanut suit.

D. So, what notes did you have to give us today for your book?

B. I'm not sure if this is gonna be in the book, but I have actually completed my bubble training, into becoming my being.

D. Oh? How did that feel?

B. Oh. I would assume this is how it feels to be a peanut. I kinda look like a peanut in my suit, so I said, "Am I supposed to be like this? Do you look like a peanut when you travel?" And you said, "No, I'm more like an oval, like a cylinder form." And I said, "Why did you give me the shape of a peanut?" And you said, "It depends on the inner being, the melody. It's not like we give you a shell, your being will create the shell." And I said, "Are you indicating that I am looking like a peanut?"

D. So, it's kind of bulgy on the ends and thinner in the middle?

B. Indeed! Indeed!

D. I'm surprised you don't look more like a pine cone.

B. I look more like a peanut. So this is how I will appear, apparently. I don't know if this is how the Master Mind looks at me, like a peanut. But, it's comfortable in this suit. I have been going through lectures on travel experiences as you move through different vibrational fields. Like my peanut (*suit*) is not gonna be bothered as much, but in order for ME to not be bothered, I have to face them head on. It's like conquering your fears. And it is more in my face as being a peanut than it was in the bubble, because the bubble was a sphere that was sort of taking the hit.

D. And you kind of fell asleep sometimes, didn't you?

B. You made me fall asleep in there. I don't know how I fell asleep otherwise. But I did, indeed, so I didn't need to conquer any sort of intense experiences.

D. Who's giving the lectures?

B. Jeshua.

D. He's a good one to do that.

B. He's a good one. There are several here, but they don't look like peanuts. One is kinda round, –I don't know where the other ones come from–, but he's like red, round. I look like a brown peanut. But we are sitting here, it's like us sitting here and I have you behind me, and everyone else has their person behind them. So we're sitting here, and then Jeshua is there (*nodding to the front*). It's like an auditorium with a huge screen behind him. And he said he was going to show us different levels where we could travel. I don't think that everyone is gonna travel to the same place, so I think this is kinda the basics. So we're sitting here and he said, "What I want you to do, in your suit, is that you remain awake and open and that you face the visual and sensational experiences that come your way. You will have your tutor or helper behind you, so you will not be left alone. You can still communicate," he said, "with your helper."

D. So, in this auditorium, does it simulate the energy waves and everything, and what you'll see?

B. Indeed, see and feel. I talked with this one before entering this training, and he said, "You will see a lot of how I feel and see, when I travel on the light waves." And then you came and said, "Let him experience by himself."

D. Well, once you figure it out, it must be pleasurable to travel.

B. So, I see visually on this big screen—the screen isn't flat, it's vaulted up.

D. Like a planetarium?

B. Indeed. So Jeshua said, "Here we go." And then stepped aside, and first nothing happened, and I thought, "This is easy," but then it started to come a lot of colors and was like traveling in a tunnel, and at the same time it started to vibrate in my being. "You can use certain tools to visualize this transition as you travel," you said, "you can use birds, like you are traveling on a bird. So, you will experience the transition as you travel through certain barriers, but you will feel less alone if you visualize that you travel on a bird." Maybe the other ones have something else, because they're not from the second dimension, so they might not even know what a bird is! But I know what a bird is, so I picture like a big, white albatross, and that's what I'm traveling on here. And you said, "You can be on this big bird for a long time. But eventually, when you feel comfortable, you say goodbye to the bird, and the bird will just descend, and then we will continue." It is having like those rockets that you have on your spaceship that takes it off, and then they fall down. It's the same thing here.

D. So, in some way, you have to intend, or control, how you travel, don't you? (*I was thinking in terms of actually traveling, not sitting in the simulator, so my question was not very useful.*)

B. Ah, I'm in control of the experience, but I'm not in control of the environment, and that is the scary part, because I don't know what environment I'm traveling to. It's going kind of fast. It begins kinda slow, on the bird, but after a while when the bird has disappeared, you encounter everything by yourself and you have to be maneuvering. You actually rotate when you travel, you don't travel just like this, steady, head-on, you rotate as you travel through certain barriers, then you become still again and travel kind of flat, like this. But as soon as you come and enter a new barrier you have to, like a drill, rotate through. And that is the sensation of you don't know how long that spinning will take place. Certain barriers are wider than others, and that is when you have to conquer your fear and sort of power through, you said.

D. So are these barriers between fish tanks, or are they also within the fish tanks?

B. We're just in this little one, at the moment, before I can conquer the big barrier. My spinning experience through that one is gonna be more intense. Here, I'm just sort of, to give you a sensation, if the first barrier that I ploughed through, which is entering different galaxies, would be considered ten seconds, so you gradually build it up. The next one would be like, okay, I have to go through thirty seconds, and so forth. But you say when you travel between fish tanks, the big barriers, you have no idea how long you will spin, or rotate, before you eventually come out in the new fish tank. No one knows, you said. That is why you have to navigate from within and trust your inner map and your inner navigation, your inner compass.

D. If you ever get concerned, you could always call out and you would be assisted?

B. I would assume so. You say so. But the experiences is still my own, and you have to trust that there is an opening at the other end. Depending on different conditions, normally established from the Creator, then the border between can be wider. And you might not know that the first time you travel between. Eventually, you will find different entrances and exits that will resonate with you. The first time, you don't. The first time you have to navigate from your inner compass. But I ask you, "When you travel, don't you know the barrier? Don't you know how long you're gonna spin in between?" And you said, "Yes, I do now, because I go through familiar locations—entrances and exits." And I say, "Maybe I can use yours, if that is familiar, if that is already open and established?" And you said, "No, you create your own by numerous travels through. You create your own path. I cannot help you create your path." And I said, "That's unfortunate, because I wouldn't mind using yours, if that is a lit-up tunnel." You said, "You're going to create a tunnel." Then I said, "Ohh...ohh." So, that's the difference, that's why you also have to be granted certain things. You said, "Once you have traveled numerous times into a certain fish tank, then you will feel comfortable, because you will just go through your tunnel. And your tunnel, at that point, would be lit up." I said, "I don't have a tunnel." And you said, "No, and I can't give you one. This is what you need to do if want to explore the beyond." And I do want that, I do want to explore the beyond.

D. But when you're done with your training, you'll be able to go and visit Siah?

B. Ah, yes indeed. I'm wondering where the other ones are gonna go. You said, "Don't focus on the other ones, try to pay attention, Bob, on your own travel. They're going to create their own tunnel, their own hole. They might not even go to Siah, we don't know that." And I said, "Why are we sitting here all together?" and you said, "Because this is a general lecture, from Jeshua." I said, "As I enter the big barrier between, will someone meet me on the other side? Or am I supposed to navigate again, by myself?" And you said, "No, I'll be there." Then I said, "I still want to kinda go in your tunnel. I'll be completely quiet; you will not even notice me. I'll be like a shadow, like a teeny, tiny fly on your back. A peanut fly." But you said, "You will not pass through, neither of us would, because it's adaptable to my capsule and my energetic being. If I changed, then my tunnel would also change and be closed."

D. No one would send you somewhere where you would be in danger.

B. Nay. No. But the thing is you have to somewhat conquer your concerns, and just trust that you are creating a tunnel, a passage. That's what I do.

D. Jeshua and I would never mislead you.

B. No. No—no, you would not, and I'm excited to go. I fulfilled this training and now it is time, actually, to go.

D. Well, that's wonderful.

B. Mmm. So, I'm gonna go soon here to visit Siah, and I'm gonna create a tunnel, a passage.

D. That will be fun.

B. It will be extremely fun. And the thing is, you gave me the image of Siah and everything in advance. So I know what to look forward to, as I might feel distressed in my being as I create a passage.

D. Yes, that's the next treat at the end of the tunnel. I'm sure there are a lot of places in this universe you can travel to and explore?

B. Indeed. After this training with Jeshua, I will be able to move into different galaxies and realities within this fish tank. I'm actually interested in the one next to here.

D. This galaxy?

B. The next one, Andromeda. There's a lot of activity there.

D. Is it a different vibration?

B. Different vibration. Same fish tank.

D. A little bit higher?

B. Ah, a little bit. Not much, but a little bit. If I were to give you a picture of the levels, it looks almost like wide steps, like stairs. Not like teeny, tiny stairs, but long. It's a little bit higher up, and I would like to go there. (*I'm guessing he means there are broad areas of similar frequency, adjacent to other areas with a slightly higher or lower vibration. The Milky Way galaxy might be one stair, for example.*)

D. Have any visitors come here from Andromeda?

B. Indeed, indeed. There are friends there. We're gonna talk more about that, but now, my time is up.

Traveling to Siah's World (Jan 8, 2019)

At long last, Bob was able to master the creation of a protective bubble around his energetic being, and we traveled together to Etena. Bob describes the movement from the spiritual dimension where we started, through the barrier and into to universe of fish tank four. He perceived the boundary as a thick fog that he had to courageously penetrate. His achievement was honored by those on Etena, and he was very happy to finally get to meet Siah and the spirits who travel to or live on this wonderfully pleasant planet.

B. Huhuhuuuu. Ahhhhh!

D. Hello, Bob.

B. I got a diploma!

D. Gergen said you went somewhere. Where did you go?

B. I made it through!

D. To where?

B. To Siah! I'm through the barrier.

D. Excellent. Tell me about it, because I'm curious.

B. The beginning was a little bit intimidating, because it was that big, grey fog, and you were standing next to me.

D. Where did you start from?

B. I started first from your space. Then we together, you and I, we drifted off into, it looked like a platform, but it wasn't like a planet or like a room, it was just a circular platform in front of this big mist. And I said, "Where are we on the wheel? Are we on the other side of the pole?" And you said, "No, no, Bob, we're not. We're just going to go next door." So I said, "Where is this next door?" And you said, "This is to 4 o'clock, this is where we're at." Because I was wondering if Siah's place is just on the other side of this wall, or is it all the way across, all the way up to 3 o'clock, and you said, "No, no, no, Siah is really close." And you said occasionally, because of this mobile barrier that moves back and forth between 5 and 4, sometimes, you say, that Siah is actually moving into the fifth reality (*our fish tank*). And that is what is coming, because of the interaction from the species that exists here, they are highly welcomed to come and participate and teach those who exist in the fifth box.

D. I remember they said Siah's reality is between four and five.

B. Indeed, but you said that sometimes, because of this mobility and this movement between the boxes and the barrier, then, you said, sometimes Siah's reality is actually almost moving into the fifth, so they are blending. And I said "What determines that? Why is it moving back and forth like a jellyfish, or like a squeeze box?" And you said, "It is like a squeeze box." And I said, "Who is the one who decides when it goes in and out?"

D. I think you know that.

B. You said that! You said, "You know that. It's the big boss upstairs, inside the pole." But I was wondering why and how that is determined. I asked, "Is four o'clock moving into five, occasionally?" And you said, "Yes, indeed. The first time we were down here, when we didn't incarnate, then indeed the barrier wasn't as thick as it is now. It was merely like a threshold." So, at that time, four and five was almost like one, you say. But then, because of the events that took place, the big mist in between developed and came about.

D. So had you put your suit on at this time?

B. I am in my peanut suit. I still look like a peanut, it was not just a one-time thing, it remained and I have my peanut suit on. I have blown up my self-esteem, inside.

D. Feeling bold?

B. I am a bold peanut, ready for departure, even though I do appreciate that we're doing this together. So we were on this platform and it's a little bit intimidating. You tried to help me, and you said, "My entrance and exit is just going to be parallel with yours, so even if you don't see me you can know that I will be on your left side." You said you would send out like little tiny Morris code signals so I could hear you, even though I still navigate in this mist in blind. So that was a treat, because that was not given to me in the training room. So we took off.

D. So you jumped into the mist?

B. I thought I was going to just sort of jump into it, but you said, "Now you welcome the mist, from the platform. You welcome the mist and let the mist become you. And you let the mist sort of encase you and take you along." So we stood there, and then you said, "Are you ready, Bob? I'm going to invite the mist." And I said, "Okay. I am ready. Do you have your beeper on?" and you said, "Yes, the beeper is on." I said, "Do I have a beeper?"

and you said, "I know where you are, I will be able to detect you. You don't necessarily have a beeper, but I will sense your energy differently. Because I have traveled here numerous times, I always know if there are others traveling." But for me, I did not know. So I said, "Do you have on your beeper?" and you said, "Yes, the beeper is on, and let's invite the mist." And so you did. It was like you kinda made a, you made a somewhat of a sound. You invited the sound and then the mist came forward, and the mist had the same sound. So you mirrored, I guess, the sound, and it was like...(*he made very faint*) bum bum bum bum bum bum bum bum, and the mist responded to that. And you said, "This is how you have the clearance, because you can imitate the tune. It's not my tune, it's the mist's tune. So I know I can call on it, because I know the melody it carries and the pattern that it holds." Then you said, "If I stand here and just made sounds like, plinky plonk plinky plonk, the mist would never come. So that's how you get granted access," you say.

D. So did you have to make the sound too?

B. I kinda imitated you a little bit, but you helped, so I didn't need to fully do that. But I tried to imitate you. But the mist, as it came, it was like you and the mist had the same chanting, or the same melody, and we were just sort of absorbed in that. During my whole experience, as I was rotating through, I heard this bum bum bum bum bum (*gradually spacing out the sounds*), but I also listened for your beeper, which was different. I had pictured it to be silent, but it was not.

D. So as we went along, what eventually happened? Did you pop out in the universe, or did you end up at Siah's place?

B. The mist changed color, so first it was grey for a long time, and you said that before, that the beginning is the trickiest part, and after a while it will change colors that will be more to my liking, you said. So at the very end, I came out, and it was like sunshine mist. And at that point I started to see a silhouette of you, so I knew we kinda had arrived. You are aware when you travel, but you move into a different perspective. So, you are awake, but you are acting in somewhat of a trance state. It's like the peanut is in the trance state, but me inside is alert. Something like that. And when I got out, it was sunshine. And then, not only did I see your silhouette, but there were like birds that came, a whole line of birds came. And they were just there, like another barrier, just sort of flying in this sunshine mist.

"These birds," you said, "they are like the guardians for the atmosphere around, they are protecting the first level." (*The first level of protection.*) They are like keepers or guards. If someone were to come through that did not belong, then the birds, I'm pretty sure, will guide them kindly back. They are the first, it's like coming to a door and knocking on a door and someone opens it. But on this reality, it was a long line of birds. (*I can only assume this is some type of spiritual manifestation that takes on the form of a bird.*)

D. Did they welcome you and let you pass?

B. They let me pass, and then we were just floating in this sunshine mist, and then I could see the place, Siah's place, way over there. And the birds, some of them joined and followed, but most of them remained. Nothing bad is gonna come in here with the birds, they're a protecting group of entities. I think I would like to have that here, now when I've seen it.

D. Put them around your planet with the Individual?

B. Ah, and here (*around Earth*), to make sure. Because it's a completely different feeling and harmony here. And then I saw the planet over there. We were together and there were some birds around. And you laughed and said, "It wasn't that bad, was it?" and I said, "No, it wasn't. Is it harder to get back?" And you said, "Sometimes it is. It depends on what experiences you had at the location where you went. If you feel a little bit homesick, then indeed it can be a little bit more difficult. It will feel differently when you go the other way, because you go back into an environment where it is a little bit more dense. But it has to do with the experience." You said, "The barrier is what it is, but depending on what you feel and what you have experienced on the other side determines, a little bit, how you transition."

D. When a soul dies on Earth and they leave, do they cross through the same barrier?

B. It's more happy to go from Earth to the spirit realm through the fourth, than it is to go from the spirit realm through the same barrier. It's the same thing here. It depends on the other side where you're going.

D. So you saw Siah's planet?

B. I saw Siah's planet, and I saw them, friendly. I came there and there was this friend of yours who gave me the diploma. You signed it, and he signed it, and there was a little welcome committee that welcomed me. And it is just sunshine and everyone is just happy and everyone is just in...ahh. (*He drifted off into a pleasant stare as he was re–experiencing being there.*) First, the welcoming committee saluted my journey, my virgin journey! Huhuhuh. It was very overwhelming to feel so welcomed and to be so appreciated, and have a sensation of belonging. And you said, "Now we're going to go visit Siah." And Siah is with a couple that takes care of him. So we went there, and they have like gardens, and there was Siah. Siah was like on his back, feet sticking up, and there was somewhat of a butterfly on the nose, and he was just lying there with his big paws up. You made like a whistle sound, and because he turned so quickly, all the grass and the plants were rattling. And then he came at a full gallop, and you said, "Here he comes! Here is Siah!" And Siah came and he just sort of jumped, and he was so happy! He is curious about me, he sniffs me. I don't look like a peanut any more, I look more like myself now. I don't have to be in my peanut suit, apparently, all the time, which I'm happy about.

D. What color robe did you have on?

B. I have a travel robe.

D. What's that, red?

B. No, it's light blue, because I remember that everyone here has light colors. There is no red here, and I wanted to blend in. I didn't want to be the odd one out, even though I kinda am!

D. Are they about the same height, or taller or shorter than you?

B. They're shorter than you, but they're taller than me. They are very human-like.

D. How many came to greet you, when you first showed up?

B. At least twenty or thirty. They came out from their work space. Some are like a pyramid, but it looks like they are in metal. But, I'm tired after my travel, so we're not gonna go inside and look, you say.

D. Into the library?

B. Library. But we're gonna communicate and engage with those who live here. Siah didn't leave at all. But, more to come. Ah...just so friendly. And they have so much knowledge here, and they keep records. There is so much activity in the atmosphere. There's just coming in new individuals all the time, leaving things. Flying in and leaving things, to this civilization.

D. Ophelia said this is where they store a lot of information about this reality and others in this fish tank, and other fish tanks.

B. Ah. Because there is constantly a lot of activity of coming and going here. It's like you think of a place where they have all those trucks that depart with fruits, to stores, like a central hub, but they don't leave fruit.

D. Dropping off data?

B. Dropping of data, just a quick chit chat and then leave. I see there's a lot of things coming in here. I was wondering if I'm gonna leave my notes, if that is the intention here. But you said, "Not today. Today is just a celebration that you mastered to go through the barrier. And now we're just going to play with Siah."

D. That was nice.

B. Siah gives like healing energy, so when you pet him, he sort of radiates an energy. It's like the two of you dock together and share energy, and then everything that you wanted to say, everything that has been missed, is just instantly transmitted between the two of you. More is gonna come, so I'm gonna go now. But I'm not gonna go through the barrier at this time. I'm gonna remain here for a while.

D. Next time, you'll have to tell us how you returned.

B. I'm not sure I want to, I might wanna stay here for a while. I might want to see what this is about. But it's not up to me.

D. Maybe you'll want to bring your Individual there and turn him loose, so he can play with Siah?

B. Ah, but the Individual is not tame, so I don't want to bring something that is going to be considered disruptive. He's not mean, he's just not tame. And everyone here is tame and organized and friendly, but the Individual is more free. I'm not saying that these are not free, they're just more controlled. So anyway, I'm gonna go now.

D. Congratulations, my friend.

B. Congratulations to me! I got my diploma, another one to put in my...

D. You're going to need a bigger wall.

B. I need a bigger office! I might need my own palace! That's what I need. Oh, Gergen laughs. Oh, okay, I'm gonna go now. This was fun.

D. Alright, my friend. We'll talk soon.

Return to Siah (Feb 12, 2019)

B. So, I have indeed been back to Siah's. Like I say, I'm a busy person.

D. Did we go together?

B. Indeed. I don't go by myself.

D. Did we look around any? Maybe visit the library?

B. Ah. I'll take you. It's huge, it almost looks like a huge cathedral, this one that you took me to. It's like grey marble, that's how it looks—I'm giving you a picture here—and it's really high in the ceiling. There's a corridor, and on each side, there are openings and pillars that goes to different vaults. In the far end, we never went to the far end, but it's very beautifully decorated. This one (*Christine*) has seen it, this one has been there. It's like the grandest university that you can go to, and you can come here to learn. Like I said, It's almost like a university, this marble building.

D. In what way is it different from the Library on the fifth?

B. It's very much about the–the–the different fish tanks. I mean it's kinda similar, but I haven't seen all the topics. In some way, the Library on the fifth and this one are very much alike, but it's more hands–on, here.

D. I thought you had said it's more of a physical place?

B. It's a physical place, indeed. But everyone looks so different here, it's not like everyone looks like the ones taking care of Siah. I get confused. It's like when I went to Ophelia's classroom that first time, when there were all these different individuals. And like I said, they are physical. They are not energetic here, no one is energetic. You transform into who you are. I don't look like a peanut anymore. I said, "If everyone is gonna show their true identity here, I have to have something else. I don't want to be looking like a peanut in my suit." So, I picked a shape and a presence. Everyone is indeed physical here, but they look so different—there's so much commotion here. Everyone is moving back and forth, and they're attending classes here. So, in some way, it is like the Library on the fifth.

D. Is it more advanced, like for specific studies?

B. Indeed. A lot of it has to do with cosmologic teachings, astronomy. It has to do with connections. A lot of it has to do with connections, because they seem happy to meet here, like representatives of different fish tanks and different physical realities that come here.

D. Can you understand what they talk about?

B. It's like, ah, –it's so much noise. In the Library on the fifth, it's not noisy. But here it's like everyone is meeting old friends and catching up, but it's moving kind of fast. You're not there that long, you come and share information and you take some sort of class, you leave things off and you learn something. The teachers look like those who look after Siah. But those who come here, they look like grown–ups, but they look different. They look very different. But maybe they think I look different. Maybe they look at me and think, "Oh, what an odd thing!" But I am not, I'm just Bob. And I'm there with you, and we go around and there are meetings here—you say we are gonna meet some of your friends from another fish tank. You call them Tallock. They're here, there's like seven here that you meet and just catch up with. You talk about different things that happens on Earth, and they kinda laugh, because they think it's a little bit primitive! Huhuh. And they kinda pat you on the back, saying, "It is really good that you go there."

D. Everyone says that Earth is primitive.

B. At this point, it's about raising the consciousness here. And that is what you're telling them, that you are trying to increase the light within the consciousness, the brain, in order for higher advanced knowledge to be accessed in the future. So you are working on the behalf of creating better conditions and bodies for those three, for instance, who are going. (*There are three little Elahims going to Earth, which will be discussed in the next chapter.*) You are preparing the consciousness and the light within the brain to be in a different way so it matches when others are gonna come in. Ophelia and Isaac will work on the DNA and the light within DNA, because certain strings within the physical has been shut down. So you explain this, it's a whole biological and physiological change that will take place. The upgrade of the human depends on that certain adjustments within has taken place beforehand. Like adjustments in the mental, as well as navigating from your center point more frequently. And to see beyond certain illusions that, at this time, humans are trapped within. There seems to be somewhat of an urgency, because you know that there are gonna come in different souls that will be demanding a highly different brain and body. So you have an agenda here, and you talk about the agenda and the upgrading of the vehicle.

D. The Tallock have actually spoken through this one before.

B. Ah. I'm–I'm–I'm here too! I'm here too, I have not been ignored. I stand next to you and I'm curious. They seem friendly. They look different, I must say, but at this point I don't judge. I've seen so many things, you should know, that at this point, I do not get surprised. I don't even raise an eyebrow anymore. I thought, "Okay, that's how you look, that's how you want to present yourself. I am Bob, this is me. I come from beyond."

D. What color do you wear?

B. Light blue.

D. Do you have any stones or anything like that on?

B. I have, indeed. I have a belt around my belly, with crystal stones.

D. What color are your stones?

B. They are white and light blue. I also have a little bit of a necklace, you can see (*he leaned forward to show me*), also with matching crystals. I look like, ah—a great merchant! Coming from beyond! And this is how I look. I have my fancy travel suit on. I said I did not want to look like a peanut.

D. What color am I wearing?

B. It's like dark purple.

D. Do I have any stones on or anything?

B. Indeed, you have one that connects the cape, kinda. It is the thing that you all carry, the dark blue. Elahim all have that one, connecting. It's the color that connects you.

D. So, did you make any contributions to the discussion with the Tallock?

B. After you told them about what you were doing, then you introduced me. You said that I was highly involved with maintaining your mission, to keep it as long and intact as possible. You actually gave me credit, saying that I was very helpful, and that we were working on this together. And then they kind of wanted to know about you, from my perspective. So, that was kind of funny.

D. So what did you tell them?

B. I told them that, "Sometimes, because of the fact that Lasaray is so involved with the mission, that he sometimes forgets the personal journey of coming here." So I told them about what a personal journey can look like. And I told them about this one, because they're familiar with this one, so I said, "When Seth goes, he takes on all sorts of different characters. He goes into different human personalities, almost like a show. But he's there with a different agenda than Lasaray." So I told them about the difference, a little bit. But then I asked, "So where are you coming from, great spirits? What are you doing?" Huhuhuh, so they told me a little bit, but then we had to rush off. And I said, "They seemed so friendly, maybe we should meet them later?"

D. Which fish tank are they coming from?

B. Eighth. Eight, nine (*on the wheel, corresponding to the locations of the hours on a clock face.*) Mainly eight. Eight is very—

D. I think that's one that Ophelia likes, isn't it?

B. Ah. But Ophelia is also in one of the upper ones, like one or two, she likes it there. There is one there that I struggle with the tones in it. It has such an intense vibration in it, so it's disturbing to my being. But I haven't been there, clearly. I have listened to a lot of tones, as you are aware, in different fish tanks. And I can detect whether it's suited for my being, if it is something I would like to engage in, or if it might be something that I will wait to visit, later. And if it is like I believe it is, that you have to cycle through a couple before you dissolve, then I am in no hurry.

D. Which one do you like the best, outside of this one?

B. Oh, I like the fourth. I like being here (*Siah's planet*). I said, "Maybe we can go here more. If you're not gonna go to Earth that much, because it seems like you are not, then maybe we can just hang around here?" Everyone is friendly and there is great studying going on here, but no one looks like me! I look around to see if there is some familiar faces, maybe Ole or someone, but I haven't seen anyone. They're all so tall!

D. I bet Ole has been there.

B. Ah. I'm gonna ask, when I return to Council studies, if I'm allowed to talk about this place. Then I'm gonna ask Ole. But Gergen has probably been here, too, because Gergen sends me off to things that he has already investigated. He doesn't send me off randomly. So he investigates everywhere that I set foot, so I'm pretty sure he has been here before. Ophelia comes here, but she mainly hangs with the teachers. But the other ones, they come with—it's very much about communication between fish tanks, and communications are the transmitting of information, but it's also how to travel between. So it's very much the...oh, there it went blank. You took away what I was gonna say. That's interesting. Sometimes you do that, you know, you erase a thought. Sometimes you even erase a question! I can begin, "Oh, Lasaray, what about—", then I pause and it's like I'm frozen in time, and then the wind passes. And then I'm like, "Okay, let's go and continue talking about my Individual." (*Lasaray is always present during our sessions. Sometimes when I ask a question, my higher self will answer Bob, who then tells me. Bob said it often like I am talking to myself, with him as the middleman.*) Sometimes I think that you do that. But it is a great hall of teachings here, and I have been privileged to join you. But I haven't gone to any classes. I'm simply here in the center, in the corridor between the pillars. On the sides are where you leave off different information. And there are those who are involved in storing this information, also. There are classes going on, and it's also like a meeting place, a physical meeting place, for several different fish tanks and entities, beings, to come here. I wonder how they travel here? They must travel similar like I do.

D. Well, you said that you have seen them coming and leaving, so how did they go?

B. Some looks like a star fall, just shoo–shoo–shoo, and I have actually seen somewhat of a craft coming, but I don't know what that's all about. This is a physical place, but everyone comes and goes, so it doesn't seem like you remain here a long time.

D. That's all fascinating. Well, since this one is going to Sweden, I'm going to be working on your book the next few weeks. I was wondering if you had any direction you would like to give me, specific instructions on what you would like discussed?

B. I would like to create a big platform about the care for nature and for animal life, and to be aware of the impact that you all have around you, that no one is an island, that everything that you do creates somewhat of a ripple effect in many different energetic vibrations. It could be like an emotional ripple, or it could be mental, and so forth. But the physical can also be affected by disturbances within your atmosphere. I want people to appreciate the land that is around you. We also want you to care for yourself. As long as you don't care for yourself, you have not the ability to care for anything else. The first step is to appreciate your center point, your soul, to welcome all sides of yourself, and to see it in the light that you learn. As you do so, as you are more connected and loving—and also not blind to what you are feeling and doing—then you have the possibility to transfer that love and compassion to the physical realities and to nature. It is very hard to be lacking empathy for the environment if you love yourself, because you indeed are a replica, in many ways, a mirror of the environment that you are in. And if the environment is suffering, then it is hard to love yourself, because YOU are, indeed, the same as your environment. So the first step to change an environment is to start to change yourself.

D. Wow. That's really good advice. Do you think we should talk much about your travels to the sixth, and working on your solar system?

B. Absolutely! Because it's a way of progressing, as all souls do. So all souls have the ability to travel to the manifested side within the spiritual reality. But I cannot go and fully stay in the sixth. All souls have the ability to travel to other spiritual realities and learn. And some will recognize working in different environments that creates stars and so forth. Not all will understand. But I think it's important that it creates a platform of what a soul is doing when not in physical. So this is like an extended life-between-lives regression, if you like.

D. It's a really interesting story, so I hope that I can present it well.

B. Ah, we'll help. So anyway, I think that will be it.

D. I'm going to miss you while she's gone.

B. I'm gonna be here, looking over your shoulder to see that you don't trip.

D. Haha. I appreciate that.

B. Oh, I'm gonna go now.

D. Alright, my friend, thank you for coming.

B. Ah. Okay, bye bye.

Bob Joins the Council (Feb 10, 2018)

B. HUUUHHHOOOO!! Le le le le le le le le le la. Huh huh. (*Then he started singing again*) We had a like a little party with Gergen and everyone!

D. Oh, you did? When was this?

B. Oh, just around the corner, you know. There's no time really, so it was just recently.

D. What were you celebrating?

B. Oh, it's just the fact that everyone is really happy. There is a cycle going on, there are several cycles, I must say, because there is the cycle of teachers rotating into learning, and there is also a rotation of students who are given specific assignments to follow up on. They get really excited about that, to get their own personal assignment. They are gonna report back to Gergen and other older teachers and such, so that's what they're gonna do. So there's a lot of rotation going on, and there's a celebration of that because everyone feels like they have bounced up a step, a little bit.

D. Did you or Ia get any assignments, or have any changes?

B. Ia works with, ah, another new egg. But the egg has actually started to dissolve, and they are becoming like dots. They are like...

D. Pre–sparkles?

B. Ah, HUH HUH, pre–sparkles! They–they–they sing now. That's one of the first things they learn, because singing is like rhythm, and that's what they do, and they like that. So they are actually in a lot of music classes, if you like, these little pre–sparkles. Huhuh. I'm working with my volumes, my books, and so forth. So that's what I do.

D. Do you work in the library, or in your study?

B. I've been a lot in our library. I've also, actually, –and I don't want to blow my own horn here, but this is part of my cycle–, and I have actually been participating in the council with Ole and Gergen. I've been participating in a way, like I'm a, I'm not an apprentice, but I am...

D. An advisor?

B. I am! Because I have knowledge and information to share about my communication with humans, like this, and also about what you and I fibble around with in your lab, so to speak. So, we talk about that. It's a very grown-up assignment. It's a lot of me listening, because I'm sort of the youngest here. But I have been given a seat at this council. So, again, I don't want to blow my own horn, but I have actually got my own seat.

D. Oh, I'm very proud of you! Congratulations!

B. Ah, Ohh. Ia is probably gonna get one too, because we work together a lot. But she's not into that part of fame. (*He snorts and laughs rather loudly.*) And I am, sometimes! I get really proud.

D. Well, that's okay. It's probably a lot of work.

B. Ah, well, it's a lot of listening. I guess that is also why they wanted me to do that reflection first (*the self-study*), so that I would be able to absorb information that would come. Gergen said that, that I got somewhat of a, —he called it a medal. And I think he called it that because he's been calling that since I was a sparkle, that I've been given medals. I think it is because he knows that I like to be promoted, and I like to be acknowledged, and I like to have, you know, a little bit of a present thing that states I have advanced.

D. A diploma, of sorts.

B. Of sorts. And so he said that one of the criteria for me to get this seat was that I had paid attention and listened, and I was acknowledging the wisdom that came within the silence of the wind. (*His success at self-study.*) So! Huhuh.

D. Does Ole talk a lot in the council meetings, or does he mostly listen?

B. Nah. He also listens. So he's on the other end, and he is like the oldest listening, and I'm the youngest listening. And then we have all these uncles in here in the middle who somewhat try to collect data from all sorts of different places. There's a lot of collecting data, I must say. Ole is like a chairman in this council; he can see if something is important or not. But he's very patient and kind. Because there are some that comes and wants to provide data to these meetings, and Ole says, "Maybe we should wait about that." But he says it in a way so that the one who provides it doesn't feel like he is put down or anything. And I want to provide my data from the solar system I built, or what I find when I'm out traveling; so that's gonna be my contribution to this council. But Gergen says that I should wait a little bit, because some of the other members have not been traveling, and I don't want to sound like I'm blowing my own horn and that I'm somewhat special, –even if Gergen says that it IS special. He doesn't take that away from me, and Ole said the same thing. But it is the fact that if someone has not, you know, done the same thing, you have to say it in a way that doesn't make them feel left out. And if you can't say it in a way that is not very charming, then you should be quiet. So, I'm waiting to see how I should put it into words. But, that's gonna be my contribution here. So other people have collected data differently.

D. Well, that's wonderful. I'm proud of your hard work.

B. Ah. There's a lot of growing up here, it's that whole rotation that goes on. And that is the celebration, because they try to make, I mean, there are smaller rotations and circulations and advancements that goes on all the time, but sometime they have all these big gatherings, and everyone takes a bit of a spin into a new level of learning or something. And that's when we have a little festivity of sorts, where we dance and we sing and there's a lot of colors. It probably looks like fireworks from your point of view, but it's like energy flames with different colors, so it creates a very merry, happy, big festivity. Ahh. So what have you been up to?

D. Mostly nothing. I didn't think we were going to have a chance to talk before this one took off. (*Christine was leaving to work in Sweden for a couple of months.*) So, I'm glad to once again hear your voice.

B. Well, I'm gonna be here, you know, –make sure you're OK and don't trip on stuff, because you have kinda big feet. So I'm gonna make sure of that, that you don't trip on things, and that you eat correctly. And if you sleep too much, I'm gonna poke you! That's what Jeshua said! Huhuh. I can tickle you if you sleep too much! He wants you to be persistent and to persevere and do your best.

Several months later, Bob told how he was introduced to the method used by the council to join together and share ideas. This was just as we were finishing the editing of Wave 2, and I was reminding him that we were preparing to compile his thoughts into a separate series of books, which he was quite happy to hear. We have come to expect that he will express ideas with words that sound a bit odd to the ear, such as, "We are group activity," meaning the spirits on second dimension operate in groups and seem to prefer company. We could change the wording, of course, but we feel that would detract from the integrity of the process of passing on the messages from the spirits. Therefore, we often leave his statements unmodified, adding them to the growing list of unique expressions from Bob.

D. We're going to work on your book next. What do you think about that?

B. Oh, I'm in favor!

D. Maybe Ophelia will let you come a little closer when we work on that one, and whisper in my ears. (*During the editing of Wave 2, Ophelia had instructed Bob to not push too many ideas into my chimney.*)

B. I'll whisper. I'm gonna talk about the process of development among groups, because we are group activity, so how one evolves in groups as well as independently, we're gonna talk about that. And also, how you later evolve when you come into councils. And one might say, "What if the council is out of tune?"

D. What if there are people who just leave passive particles? (*I was poking him a little bit, because he had admitted to withdrawing a lot of his energy from the council meetings, leaving behind what Gergen called a passive particle.*)

B. Ahh, oh, I did that. It wasn't intended to be detected.

D. We laugh about that. Maybe you've seen us laughing, but we do cardboard cutout poses of how you might look to the other council members.

B. Oh, Gergen said, "That's not how we operate, Bob." And then he said, "Maybe you don't want to be a part of the council? Maybe it was too early." And I said, "No, it's not too early, I want to be a part of decision making." This was a private conversation with Gergen–, and I said, "It's just that I felt that nothing was happening. There were a lot of times we were just sitting in silence." And I didn't understand why. I was like, "Are we meditating about a topic here?" And Gergen said, "Shh, wait, Bob." We were sitting there in silence, and he said, "This is how we establish thought bubbles, quietly, before we engage our thought bubbles with others in the group. Because if we just shoot off thoughts," he said, "then we're not going to get anywhere." And I said, "I don't feel like we are getting that far ahead!" And then he said, "We are compiling our thoughts, and that's what we do in silence." And I know how to compile my thoughts. Zachariah talks about that a lot. (*He then mimics Zachariah, like a dry professor lecturing students.*) "Compile your thoughts, Bob. Put them in the right box and then decide—should this box be forwarded at all? Or should it maybe be stored?" So, I know about compiling thoughts. BUT because we are a group of nine, ten, no, we're eleven now...

D. Eleven? Are you still the youngest?

B. Nay, it's someone else here, a gardener that joined. Gardeners, you should know, are better in compiling their thought bubbles.

D. That's because they always work in silence.

B. They work in silence. I'm more like, "Let's toss ideas and see whether it has a possibility to become." BUT when you and I work, you also are a little bit in that mode of compiling thoughts in silence. I wanted to talk about it because I didn't know how to compile the thoughts, because I didn't have any thoughts. I didn't know what thoughts I should have, because I was brand-new into the field of cosmic engineering. So I didn't know what to think. Then Gergen said, "Pay attention." So I did. But you were more accommodating, because of the fact that we were just two, then you adapted your teaching quite rapidly to my way of ticking. So we moved in a way that was suitable to my being. But when I joined the council, Gergen said, "Now, everything is not just about you! Now, you have to allow others to pop ideas." Mine were kinda rapidly established, but others took their time. And one of the teachings was to sit and wait until all lights ignited in the room.

D. I did have a question, since you're talking about passing thought bubbles around. I have wondered this—when you are communicating with a group of spirits, sitting in a council like that, can you talk to all of them simultaneously?

B. Umm. I decide who I want to invite into my bubbles of thoughts, and if I had not invited that individual to engage in that specific communication, then another one would not hear it. So let's say we eleven sit there, and a twelfth was standing in the door, but the twelfth is not invited fully, it will simply see, even though he–she–it might be on the same level, but if it's not invited in the group discussion, will not hear because I have not sent my thoughts to twelve, I have sent it to eleven.

D. If you are sitting there and think everybody is quiet, is it possible they are talking to each other without you knowing it? Or can you tell when someone is talking?

B. Ah, you're not supposed to do that, it's kind of rude. You're not supposed to do that. In this group of eleven, then everyone in this group are engaging. It's not like ten talk and one is left out, because that's not what you do, that's bullying. That's not what you do when you reach this level. You're supposed to not bully anyone. You're not supposed to do that anywhere, but sometimes indeed, when you are in sparkle school...not bullying, that's the wrong word, but we tease each other a little bit.

D. Can you tell when other spirits are communicating?

B. Indeed, and I can detect when there is communication going on. If I pass two individuals on the second dimension, and if they are talking freely, so that anyone can hear, then I will also hear as I pass. But even though we speak the same language, if I pass by, I will not hear it if I'm not invited. So you choose. With all telepathic communication, it's not like just turning on the radio and everyone in that vicinity of hearing will hear it.

D. So you can have private thoughts and communication?

B. Indeed, if you tune in on that one.

D. And when you are sitting in your study having thoughts?

B. They can be private and no one would hear, not even Gergen.

D. That's nice.

B. So what we did, we were sitting there (*in the council meeting*), decreasing the volume in our radios, silently sitting there collecting and creating our thoughts. And once they were established, then each of us increased the volume on our radio. And what took a while was that, you know, not everyone increased their radio at the same time, huh, let's just say that.

D. You just cranked yours right up! Does your council ever get information passed down from higher councils, while you are sitting there?

B. Ah, it appears almost like a cloud.

D. Is that also on the second, or do you know where it comes from?

B. No. (*He sounded kind of sad.*)

D. So the cloud moves in and you get information?

B. Information in it. Some can detect it better, like Ole. I don't hear it, fully. And some say, "If you're quiet, you will." Hehehe, it was like a tease. So, I'm saying that, it's not like bullying, but it's a tease.

D. Do you and I tease each other?

B. Ah.

D. Does this one tease you?

B. Oh, this one teases me. Pokes me and says, "Later you will go here, Bob. Do you want to do that?" And you say, "You know that he can't go." And this one says, "Of course you can go, you can go with me, Bob." And then you say, "You have to have certain training first, like swimming in gravitational fields. It's not like swimming in the ocean."

D. That's not very nice.

B. Well, this one is similar in his soul personality, in some way, like I am. Likes to take off and do things, and knows that I am the same. So he says, "Do you want to go somewhere, Bob? Do you want to do things?" And lot of times I also sit and listen to his stories. I like that.

D. He must have a lot of them.

B. Plenty! And you know, sometimes I say, "Oh, I did see that episode. It didn't really end correctly, did it?" And he said, "No, it was like not having money to finish the movie, it ended early." (*Christine has a history of picking male lives that are flamboyant and dangerous, and they sometimes end before they were supposed to.*)

D. Low budget.

B. Low budget, not being able to fully finish the movie.

D. He got called home early. So from your perspective, and I've always wondered this: say you are split up between studying with the eighth, with the gravity people, part of you is in the vault, part of you is with Ia, and part of you is in the council. Are you simultaneously aware of everything that is going on, or do you shift your focus from one to the other?

B. Indeed. It's like looking through different windows. I sort of left a little bit in the council, but I kinda closed that window. It's still open, but it's a little bit closed. From my center point, I can choose to go look at different things.

D. But you don't look at them one at a time, you can kind of look at them all together?

B. I can do both. I can look at it one at a time, and that's what Gergen tried to get me to do here. He wants me to focus on one window at a time, a little bit. But I can indeed split up so I am present and aware (*of all the anchor points*). He actually found me somewhat asleep in my study. I had withdrawn plenty of energies and I was sitting in my study, and I said, "I'm practicing my light capsule." And he said, "No you're not. You're having a snooze!" HUH HUH HUH. Ah, but I am aware of everything, and if there is something going on of importance, then I will feel that as a sensation within my being. Even if I'm at the council and I feel like there is something going on, let's say, in the gravitational class, I can move more awareness there. Gergen says that's not really true, because he says that nothing goes on that would interfere with my work at the council. So I can't play that card, he said. But in general, I can sense if there is a specific window that is in demanding more of my attention.

D. So as you move your energy from one place to the next, is your awareness based on how much energy you are putting on a certain place?

B. Indeed. My awareness is always constant, but not as alert.

D. I see. That makes a lot of sense, actually.

B. That's what I said, that I'm present. But he said, "You're present but you're passive, and we want you to be active. We want you to listen." Then I said that I was active in the gravitational class, but he said that the class was over and I should have come back. Hehe. So that's KINDA how it works, so you have a picture, a little bit. I just shift my awareness and my sensation of belonging, but I constantly absorb information on every reality that I am allowed to travel to. So anyway, it's gonna be a short one today, but Ophelia says we're gonna talk more about groups and stuff.

D. Thank you for the information. We're really happy with everything you gave us for the book, and we're pleased to continue on with the next volume.

B. Ah. Okay, I'm gonna go. Saving energy. Bye bye.

Ole, the Wise Listener (Apr 29, 2018)

D. Since we're talking about councils, I was wondering, if Ole is the most learned one in the council, why doesn't he just make the decision?

B. Because he wants us to come to a solution by ourselves. He's not there to act like a principle and say, "This goes. This goes not." This is how group dynamics should work, and how everyone should be on the same agenda and be on the same level. This is how a group evolves. In many ways, you evolve individually. You have your own soul evolution, if you like, and you have your own progress. But then, there is also group evolvement, evolution, and development. And that is what all the councils are all about. You develop in the same way you do as an individual, but you do it in a group. The groups start out with, let's say, around ten. Eventually, these councils will grow, and then it might be a hundred that has to evolve in the same pace. So once you come up into those, it is different than when you are a little baby sparkle. The sparkles are in a group setting already, but they are working on becoming individuals.

D. They are developing their individual talents?

B. Indeed. So you can see the progress here, to not make a big story out of this, but once you come into the level of councils, then you are expected to evolve, progress, develop—as a group. At this point, I have only been progressing and focusing on my own development. This is new to me, and I understand that is why Ole just doesn't go in and say, "Okay, let's take this idea, let's move forward," because he is training us to evolve as a group. And we are like eleven, with Gergen and Ole and me. Some are a little bit more shy, they are conservative. But there is one here that I like, and he's very like a happy go–round kind of fellow, so I like him. But then again, it has nothing to do with personality here. Some are fast, like me, and some are conservative and take their time. BUT nothing will leave the room as a ready idea until all have agreed and reached the same solution and same level of development. So, councils are about that, in many ways, I have been told.

D. Can you give me an example of a project you're working on?

B. We are assisting those who work with atmosphere, and we are concerned about the spread of desert areas, –the lack of rain in certain areas. So we are looking into that, combined with other councils. There are actually those who come from the eighth that come in and talk about the atmospheric shifts needed in order for us to make the correct adjustments in those areas where there is too much desert. It expands and stretches because of the lack of rain. At this point, we are looking into whether it is favorable or not to put that specific region into somewhat of a hibernation for a little bit. Or if adjustments need to be made to change the shifts of climates and the shifts of how the stream of clouds are moving, in order for it to benefit those areas. There are certain places, like in Africa and the Middle East, that are of a concern, and it also contains the unfortunate behavior in those individuals present. All living beings, you should know, even dogs act a little bit different there. If you were to observe a dog in this area of heat, and you would observe a dog in in the area of Canada or somewhere north, then you will see the dog is more aggressive in the area of heat and lack of shade, and the abundance of sunshine. So we are looking into that. Everyone in our council has to understand, so we are analyzing a lot here, I must say. I came in in the middle of the project. I did not come in in the beginning, so I asked, "Where are we? You started here, here is the end result, where are we now when I come in?" There's a bit left yet, because you can't just make things start to rain and don't expect there not to be certain side effects. Not all side effects are beneficial. If it rains too much, there could be movement of, let's say, animal life, that will encounter the leading mammal, and that will create disharmony as well on a continent. So there is not just like a decision saying, "OK, let's put in more rain, let's make it work," because there can be side effects. So we are looking into that, and this is what is taking time. I'm kind of wondering where we are on this decision-making timeline. And Gergen says that I should not focus on timelines so much. I should simply focus on getting results and hearing everyone's thoughts and everyone's concerns.

D. Because Ole is the head of this council, do you think he's still individually learning and growing in that way?

B. He's in charge of group evolution and group development, but if he didn't have his own, then I'm sure he would be dissolved! So he must have something that is beyond my comprehension. (*Bob uses "dissolved" to describe a spirit making the final ascension and merging back with the Creator.*)

D. Do you ever hang out with him?

B. I do indeed try to, you know, stay behind class kind of thing to talk with him, because I find him fascinating, and I know that he's been operating on so many different realities. He's not only been to Earth, so he has knowledge about several realities when it comes to creation of what is manifested. HE is the one you should go and talk to if you want to talk to someone about like the half-and-half, you know, those who are not fully manifested, those realities. He actually has knowledge about creation and what sort of manifestation is available in several different fish tanks, both planets and realities. So I'm interested in hearing from him, to simply sit and have a listen, like having someone read a story to you. I'm in that phase where I feel like, –because I'm so passive at the moment–, that, "Why don't you just read me a story of something interesting?" Not just having the same thought going back and forth about whether to make it rain, or something. But I volunteered to come and have a listen when he reads out loud from his journal! HEE HEE. Oh, Gergen laughed about that, and Ole laughed! Maybe he wants to go down memory lane, and I would be happy to just listen to that!

D. You might learn a lot!

B. Gergen said, "You have to ask for permission to listen to someone's journals," and I said, "I just did!" And Ole, he didn't say no, but he laughed. He smiled and diverted me by asking about my journals, and what I've been writing about. And the discussion simply changed in a way that I started to talk about my journals, and after a while I understood, like, "What happened to the discussion with your journals?" Then it was like, "Okay, time for a break!" so I sort of trotted off to my study. Then it hit me that he exercised a mysterious maneuver to make me think of something else.

D. That's a good lesson to use with Tom.

B. Oh, I have tricks when it comes to Tom, because Tom needs to be, not like put in a box, but he's kind of a wild child! Gergen said, when I talked to him (*about Tom*), he said, "You were simply the same. You had all these ideas about doing things at the 4–H Farm. You wanted to bring these happy animals and establish them on places where they were not suited to go to." And apparently, I said in my early days that I wanted, because there is no death in the 4–H Farm, they are simply healthy and live. So I said, –because I saw misery both with animals and other entities–, I said, "Why don't we make them to just be, just live?" But Gergen said, "No, we're introducing cycles, like reincarnation cycles, and in order for that to be, someone has to go in order for someone else to come in." And I said, "What's wrong with the first one that seems friendly? Why make them die and have someone less friendly come in?" So I never understood that. And he said, "It's part of a greater plan from the Master Mind." He tends to say that when I ask a question, and it's to somewhat put a period after it. He will say, "This is the intention of the Master Mind," because I can't counter that!

D. Having never spoken to it.

B. Indeed. And I'm not sure I really want to at this point, because that means that I have to go into that center pole, and I'm not sure I can get back out. No one seems to have gone in to have a listen—and come out.

D. Maybe they come back out as a sparkle.

B. I don't want to begin new. I don't want to be an egg. I don't want to be sung to. It's a long process to be sang to. But every time I ask Ole, "Did you ever go into the center pole, the Master Mind, for a little chat, so that you can improve your work?" And he said, "No." And I asked you, "Did you ever get additional information from the Master Mind?" And you said, "No." So I did ask. And Ophelia, I asked her, of course, I ask her the most.

D. She's standing right beside you, what does she say?

B. Ah, she laughs. She said I'm so curious. Sometimes I need to focus and look down on my feet, where I am at this point. But, it's just that, why not answer that one time and the questions will be over? Why not just answer, "Are you allowed to go into the center pole, have a quick recap of something you wonder, say thank you, and then return to where you're at, and never bring up that thing again?" Just move evolution and development forward, like (*makes a whooshing sound*) spin!

D. If you think about it, though, that would defeat the point of the Creator creating little minds to learn and grow.

B. Ah, if you can tap into that big google, or that big library of knowledge, then indeed, the little individual mind will not progress. I see that. BUT, certain things sometimes, –like here, we have this endless discussion about something I feel could be resolved quite quickly. Then we could just say, "Why don't we go and see what the Master Mind wants to do with this specific problem with the desert and the rain?" But then Gergen said, "The group will not evolve, it will simply mirror and repeat the Master Mind, and that is not development." (*He looks towards Ophelia.*) That's what Ophelia says, "That is not development, at all."

D. I can understand that.

B. I do, I can indeed. I'm, I'm mainly a bit tricky. What I really wanted was just to sit and listen to some stories. So, anyway, it sort of occupies my time.

D. So you and Ophelia have been working on the seventh? Is that where you are doing your studies with the color patterns?

B. I've actually been on the fifth. I've been on the fifth, in their gardens. We're working with the new bugs, and they belong in a greenhouse setting, a jungle setting, and that can be found on the fifth. So I've been there and Ophelia has been coming. Ophelia has really nice assistants, too. There are two of them. I really like them, they're much younger, but they're so friendly, and they never say no. Ophelia sometimes says like, "Nope." But these two, hehehe, they like me. I think they almost see me like, not a pet, but someone who is a funny little friend. But Ophelia always lurks behind a palm tree kind of thing and comes forward and she says, "Nope," just when you think she can't see anything and you're trying to make these younger ones give information. But just behind a leaf or behind a palm tree—there she is.

D. You can't get away with anything.

B. Ah, but we have really a lot of fun. I like them and they like me.

D. Are these little Ophelia's in the making?

B. Ah. They're like, if you were to see age, they would be like 16 to 18 years old, so they carry a lot of knowledge already.

D. You're like their funny Uncle.

B. I'm like their funny friend. Ah, we have a lot of fun, because we're creating things and there's a lot of laughter. And Ophelia's not really always engaging, but when she detects that there is something going on, out of nowhere she seems to emerge. But I'm actually working with these two lovely assistants of hers, I really like them. Julia is one of them.

D. Are you building a prototype of this insect, since it has already existed?

B. Indeed, indeed. It flies, we have several, actually. The one that I'm working on is like a mixture of a dragonfly and a beetle, but it flies. It carries a lot of light, it spits out...uh (*he was struggling to describe the process*). Where it lands, and if it creates a nest, then that specific area will become more cleaned. So, it's almost like a spider web, but it's more like a cocoon where they live in, like how the wasps and bees live, so they create that and that's how they live, in those cocoons. It's a way to generate light in (*flora*), not only from the bottom, because that's from the worms and other entities, but it also needs to be from above, so the tree can absorb fully the light, sunlight, and oxygen that comes in, and also other waves of, ah...(*he was looking for the right words.*)

D. Sometimes it's hard to find the human words.

B. Ah, because if I say light and oxygen, that's only like five percent, Ophelia says, of what the trees actually absorb from above.

D. Is there some energetic field that they are drawing from?

B. Tapping into, so they help the trees to access this from above, and other entities and helpers are doing the same from below. So that's what they do, and if they create a nest then that specific area is helped. So, anyway, I think that's gonna be it about that, but that's what I've been doing.

D. But it will help you to create new creatures?

B. I'm learning things here, so I can apply it back home. So it's not just me out doing space travels, I actually have to use the information. Because I don't belong in the sixth, I don't belong in the ninth, or the seventh, or with Isaac, so everything I learn has to be applied in some way at home, or shared with the council. So, you take off to learn different things, —like Ia, she is going a lot with Ophelia, and even Isaac, to seven and eight, and she learns a lot about light, because that is the foundation of not only the light capsule, but also how the DNA strings are operating correctly, the wires. So she is absolutely involved in this, the details within the light wires.

D. Yes, the group here before you were talking about how sound varies, but light is constant.

B. I think I'm more of a sound guy. I'm listening to things, but I'm taking all different kinds of classes, I do indeed. But eventually it will all have to connect and combine and be applied at home in the second, in some way. Ophelia said that I can't be everywhere, but I can absolutely have a little bit of my input (*to the new human vehicle*). Like with a painting, you come in a paint a little corner, and I can absolutely do that. So I'm going to paint a corner when it comes to the brain, by adding the gravitational field, or the vacuum field around it, and I will probably provide it a melody. Maybe not by myself, because I'm sure the council will have to be involved. Ohh, it's going to be a long discussion about that, what song (*pattern*) we should put in. Oh, everyone has a different preference when it comes to songs. I have to prepare correctly here. Anyway, I was thinking that maybe I should say to the council, "There are five songs to choose from," so I don't bring in a whole CD collection! HUH HUH HUH. Oh, that's gonna take all sorts of time (*he is talking about the pattern for the new human, and how it is going to involve extensive conversations with the other council members if he brings in too many options.*) Oh, Ophelia said I'm way ahead of study here. It's not a juke box! she says. Huhuhuh!

Training for Earth

No soul is sent to Earth without a lot of preparation, and that includes the spirit guides who follow and assist the incarnated person. In this final chapter, we get a completely unfiltered view of how the spirits work together and practice for the different roles they are assigned. After Bob became a companion of mine at home on the sixth, he became a mentor to a few of the younger Elahims. They are destined to have lives on Earth, but have yet to begin the cycle. Spirit guides play an important role in the grand play on Earth, because they have so much influence over human activities. But spirit guides also benefit from the relationship, as they are evolving hand-in-hand with their companion. Bob, for instance, has been able to collect data on how the soul interacts with the Coat of Karma and the energetic connections within the vehicle. He then reports back to groups on the second, who use this information to make adjustments in the design of upcoming vehicles. He is given rewards and medals for the contributions he made to a successful life. Because of his experience, he is also a magnificent teacher in the spiritual realms for those who travel to our planet.

Elahims who are predestined to travel to Earth are usually paired up with a spirit guide from the second dimension. They become friends and build a strong relationship long before the first incarnation, and stay together through the entire reincarnation cycle, and beyond. (*The spirits from the second never incarnate.*) Bob and I were paired up millions of Earth-years before I first came down in "the ape shape", as he called the early versions of a humanoid. He has been my companion during each of the 1200 bodies he said I have occupied on this plane. There are usually less than one hundred Elahims on Earth at any given time, and the three young Elahims are about to come down for their first incarnation. Since each of them needed a companion from the second dimension, Bob was asked to recruit and prepare three spirit guides. His remarkable enthusiasm is evident later in the book, when he goes into great detail about how he devised entire training schools to educate the young Elahims and their companions from the second about the challenges, difficulties, and confusing situations that both the incarnating soul and the spirit guide must face.

In this chapter, we have included talks by Gergen, Bob's mentor, and Ia, his closest companion at home on the second. Bob has been the leading voice in this Volume 1, but Gergen and Ia have both made significant contributions to our understanding of the second dimension and how they interact with the plant and animal life on Earth. *Notes from the Second Dimension* would be incomplete if some of their talks were not included.

Guiding and Guarding the Soul (Jan 8, 2017)

Bob has followed me through countless incarnations, always watching, guiding, protecting, and taking notes. Some of the notes are for his own use, but he also collects notes that we compare after each life. Spirit guides gain valuable knowledge about the environment where their human travels, along with observing how humans interact with each other and the Earth.

D. So, the notebook you carry around, does that have all the notes that you've ever written, or do you periodically put them in a box?

B. I file them, so I begin new. I have one that I begin new when I follow you. Those I give you afterwards for you to review, because you tend to lose your memory a little bit, because you don't bring a lot of big notebooks in your computer. You say, "I have to strip myself in my computer." So, in many ways, because you lack the ability to see everything, hmm, you see it in a spirit way, of course, but experiencing it here, you tend to miss certain things. So I follow you and I take notes for you. Some things that I take notes on is for your benefit, so you can add it when you come back. Because of what you say, "I want to explore this—and this—and this," so I follow you and I help you. I record and I keep track on certain things that might be helpful for you when you return, to put in your own book. So, that book I change every time, of course. So, it's an extra addition to your own experience that you already have within you. But I actually follow you and take notes, because mainly, when you have lives where the computer isn't that big, I want to be helpful.

D. What did I ask you to take notes on this time?

B. Oh, there was a lot of notes in your, around the age of nine to fourteen, fifteen, because you said you wanted to rest for a while. So a lot of things you didn't experience in your own soul energy, so it was never stored in your own soul, necessarily. You wanted to do something else, you said, so you kind of left a little bit. So I picked up your experience and recorded for you, what the physical creature experienced, because you had somewhere to go, you said. That was kind of odd, you had to go somewhere, so I think you left. So, a lot of things that occurred in that time frame, nine to fourteen, are in a fog for you, – because I have the notes! Hahaha. You will get them later, because you said you had to go somewhere. I wonder where you went? Well, you know, I saw you, I followed you. You seemed a bit different. You were quieter, you were more introverted and reflective, in some way. I couldn't reach you in the same manner as I did before, either. (*The spirits said I brought in seven percent, but reduced it to about two percent during certain times.*)

D. Were you there when I had a near–death experience, as a young boy?

B. I called, yes indeed, I called for Ophelia. Ophelia was there, Ophelia helped you, Ophelia is always around you. So we all protected and guarded your physical vehicle when you left. Ophelia had the discussion with you. I only saw the physique. Ophelia communicated with the soul, with you. So Ophelia was the one who encouraged you. It was a meeting between the two of you, –you will remember if you ever chose to go to that path to remember that experience more deeply. You will communicate with her again, similar like you did then. Me and Zachariah were more outside.

D. I also had an experience when I was in my early twenties that completely altered my way of perceiving life—

B. YOU CAME UPON THE RIP! You were in that space where everything was still, and you understood. So, you remember that sensation that you had. You actually both have had a near encounter, let's say, with that rip. You can remember how that felt, because that will give you a signal if you once again stumble into that rip. But you were in that rip, and you came across where space and time sort of meet, where there is complete clarity; and it is also soundless, because everything is just from within. External noises almost disappears, and it's a way to just be in your own voice and hear your own spirit. This was a time, also, when you wanted to leave (*the physical*) again, but you were stopped that time. You had the clarity of (*a NDE*). But it was also because Ophelia was there, so you didn't leave again. Because she knows you do that sometimes, you want to leave. (*The experience was a turning point in my life. I had absolute and complete awareness of how my perception of life was inverted. I was looking outwards for validation of an artificial human identity. I understood that my true identity does not depend on the external world. I saw the world for what it is, and that moment marked the beginning of my journey as a spiritual researcher.*)

D. Are we going to stumble on that rip again?

B. That is something you can explore, if you wish. But that is what happened with you. So you go back and remember the feeling of how everything felt around you, the stillness around you, the silence, and almost the same vacuum–feeling, like the other experience, just more joyful. And it's more of like turning on the light, -and that is it. So, a lot of the experience in the rip and when you move into those frequencies is that first, it's stillness, and you can experience somewhat of a fear. But as you adapt in that reality, it's like turning on the light. That's how I can explain it. So, I think you have a lot of information that you can work with when it comes to that, and a lot of it is personal. It will be very helpful for you as you move into the next phase. So, that will be it.

D. I appreciate you following me around and taking care of me, taking notes.

B. Well, someone had to take notes! You said, "I have to go, can you just keep taking notes?" And I said, "Okay. When will you be back?" And you said, "I'll be back later." Who knows when? So I just followed you around a little bit. You were a little bit sad, you know, but I documented that too, because that was an experience the physical in some way experienced, because the soul energy was asleep a little bit. You did come back, but you actually slept a little bit up to the age of 25, and then you continued to sleep to 30. You came and went a little a bit, and I didn't know exactly when, so I kept journaling, just to give you that afterwards.

D. Well, thank you for that. You've been a good friend, you and Ophelia and Zachariah.

B. Ah, because you know, you had places to go, that's what you said. I don't know where, but I met you sometimes. But during that time, we (*Lasaray and Bob*) didn't go that much to the lab, because I worked taking notes on the physical experience. So there was a lot of that that took place from the time of nine, ten, and forward. From 30 you came back more, like a boom, more came back. We continued our work in the lab and in the vault a little bit more, and you said, "I can journal myself now, a little bit." I said, "OK." We change and we communicate how we want to work. So, that is a little bit of what took place. You didn't like the snow, it felt cold, so you said, "Maybe you can experience it." I said, "No!" So we laughed a little bit about that. In some way, because you did come and go a little bit for several years, when you came back you were somewhat detached from experiences, didn't really involve yourself with individuals and locations that much.

D. That's true. Well, I guess I'm mostly back now?

B. Yes, you are indeed. You're not sleeping now. Now it's time to explore and be awake.

D. So, once again, thank you for coming, and Ophelia and Jeshua and Zachariah. I appreciate all the information.

B. Ah, okay, Bye bye.

Gloriously Colorful (Apr 16, 2017)

No matter what task Bob has to master, he always puts his entire heart and soul into doing it well. He has said on a number of occasions that he doesn't want to let anyone down. When it comes to leaving a footprint here on Earth, he wants to be acknowledged and appreciated for the beautiful wisdom he shares. Since he has never experienced being a human, he had to learn a little about human emotions and humor. And he also had to figure out how to blend with Christine and manipulate her vocal cords, read her mental dictionary, and convert his ideas into human language. I think the first few times, Ophelia must have joined with him to guide his energy to the right spots. Since she used to incarnate, her soul is well practiced at the art. Admittedly, it was a learning process, but one he mastered after a few months. When I listen to early recordings, his personality was always present, but he seemed a bit timid at times. As he got more comfortable, he came fully into his personality as the lovable friend we know today.

D. Before we came down, when you were in the meeting with Ophelia, planning for this mission, did you know you were going to be doing this? (*Talking through Christine.*)

B. Ah, because I was taking notes and we discussed about the blending part. But I didn't really know exactly how that would play out. I did know that I was told to blend, but not in our way, —differently than blending with a tree, but to provide more of the energies to the vocals. So, when you blend with a tree, you put all the energy sort of spread out, or you center it in a specific region in the tree where you want to be seen. So, even though you can't see, for instance, in a tree, you can't see a face, that means the second dimensional creatures inside it have spread out. If you see a face in the tree, that means that it's centered, it has put all its energy in one spot. So, when I was told to do this specific mission, to communicate, I was told to put all my energy from the throat area and up, so it would be more easier to communicate. So, it would be a blend with the mind and throat.

D. I've also been curious about this: part of you is in the vault, and part is in the lab, and part is on the second dimension. Which part comes to us?

B. Oh, I'm not that much at all, in the second dimension, at all. I do tend to remain in the vault a lot of times, so the energy that moves to your lab, or to Ophelia's classrooms, that is the part of me that comes here. So that is a traveling energy.

D. That's kind of what I thought. Your traveling self.

B. My traveling self, the one that has the passport! Huhuhuh. (*Laughing loudly.*)

D. You've got a lot of stamps in it now!

B. I've got a lot of stamps in my passport. I do seek more stamps.

D. Maybe you'll get an Isaac stamp pretty soon?

B. I'm gonna get an Isaac stamp really, really soon! I'm gonna ask about that, when I'm going to work with him more closely, if there is a way for me to get clearance to go there. So, I'm ready.

D. When you blend, do you put all your energy that you brought inside her, or is there a part that sort of stands beside?

B. Mostly it's like I move into her energetic field, like a mask, if you like. That is why you can see me in her face. Also, I put all the effort of that energy mainly in the head, throat and mind, because that is the most important part if I choose to communicate. If I choose to move around, like I initially wanted to, I would have to put some of my energy into the rest of the vehicle, which will make the communication and blend with the mind a little bit less strong. So if I spread out, the communication link becomes weaker, and that is not really a good option—that's what Ophelia said. I only have a certain amount of energy to my disposal, and in order for it to be successful, it is suggested that I put it over the face and throat box, the voice box, and blend with the mind. I can see now how I would become weaker if I spread out.

D. You'll be as weak in the head as me!

B. Hehehehe! I don't want to make judgements about that. But it is the traveling energy that moves around from certain places, out and about.

D. Did you have any way to prepare before we started doing this, the first time?

B. I did. And it was mainly, –this has nothing to do with the process–, the preparations involved was actually mainly to understand my different energetic layers. So it was like going into a hibernation for a while. It was the part of me that was in the vault, and the traveling energy, those two. Because I do have about, I would say, about ten to twelve percent left in the second dimension that is sort of like an anchor that I can return to, –and that never changes. The other part I can move around. I have about thirty in the vault, and the rest I'm trying to use it at the disposal of traveling. So, when I prepared, I used the energy from the vault, as well as the traveling energy, mainly the traveling energy, and I went into a hibernation, where I prepared my energy in a...how can I say? This isn't really something of importance, but I filled myself up with different colors, because color carries different vibrations of certain places you wish to go. So, in this specific place, I actually added a lot of red into my energetic being, because red is somewhat related to this plane. Red and green and blue. I added those.

D. What about the personality?

B. That's yellow. (*All soul personalities resonate with yellow, but the spirit can have other colors that show its primary mission and level of development.*)

D. You have such a wonderful personality, is that directly a reflection of who you are?

B. I already had my personality, so I didn't need to add that! I needed to understand the human aspects of certain things, and the human experiences a soul carries when it incarnates. So, I learned different colors. I needed to understand, for instance, that I can't move (*Christine's body*) around as I would choose to. That is related to the red, because it's physical. And then I also needed to move into green and blue. Blue is communication, so I needed to understand how to blend in a way that a human expresses itself. I needed to tune in on a human vehicle as it communicates, I needed to understand that. In some way, green is like a link between the two. It is where the personality can come in and blend with the emotional and empathic nature. This isn't important for you to know, but you asked about how I prepared. So, I went into somewhat of a color spectra where I tuned in on certain colors that are resonating mainly on this plane, so I could understand them. The yellow is the personality that you always carry with you. Like I said, you are little bit stiff, and that is in your color yellow; and this one is also a little bit more stiff, so her color is also yellow, because it resonates with the personality. However, when this one goes into a body, she shuts down a little bit of the yellow and moves into more of the human emotions, which are more related to the green.

D. That's fascinating!

B. So, I did do that. But the core being of who you are as a personality resonates with the color yellow, and that is why it is also located in the solar plexus area. It's an ancient remain, huhuh, wisdom from ancient times, because it relates to where the soul particles enters. (*The association of yellow with the solar plexus was known in ancient times, but the meaning was forgotten.*)

D. So, do you have a natural yellow color?

B. Indeed, that is my personality, that is also in my center. My center is my personality. Soul to soul communicates through yellow, because that is how you recognize the other one, the personality that you are.

D. Well, you have such a good sense of humor. Did you have to learn what humans think is funny, or is that universally funny?

B. Nay! You know, a lot of it, because I was allowed to bring a lot of my own personality, my own yellow into the green, the human personality. So, see it like this; the green is somewhat related to the human personality. When you travel, for instance, you bring your whole yellow into the green, so it sort of blends up so you can't really see the difference. Whereas this one brings less of her yellow into the green, and she almost becomes like a human expression, so that is the disguise. When I travel in, I was allowed to bring a lot of my personality into this green, which is related to the human expression of emotions.

D. That's a very good description. Thank you.

B. Yellow is what you really, truly are. Fortunately, it seems like it's working! I–I think, I kinda like that.

D. Well, we are really happy that you are able to communicate with us this lifetime.

B. I want to participate, and I have all these notes on my wall, and what if we don't have time, in your sense of thinking, to go through my notes? Who knows when this opportunity will come again? I don't know if you're going to come down, the two of you, like this again, if we're gonna continue in a hundred years. I don't know that, no one tells me. So, I have all these notes and I'm eager to make sure we introduce them in some way. I do not think that you plan on doing this more than once, neither of you, so in some way it's a little bit like a grand finale of leaving something as a treat for humanity.

D. I hope we do a good job, then.

B. Well, we're all hoping, because we're all a part of this. If one falls, everyone falls! Huh huh. Ah, I don't want to be remembered as someone who did a bad job either; because this is my first time, and I want to be remembered like someone, mmm, glorious (*he said very quietly*), –but, you know.

D. Well, you've done more than your part. You've really brought a lot of wisdom to the conversations—so thank you.

Shooting off Balls of Knowledge (June 3, 2018)

Bob talks about how his young friend, Tom, comes to his office and showers him with questions. He said Tom will ask a question and then take off on a line of inquiry into areas where he has yet to be trained. So Bob compared the questioning to a disorganized form of baseball. Anytime in the future that Bob mentions baseball, this is probably what he is referring to.

B. So I've also been in my study. I do, too, need to reflect and recharge and work on my own light capsule. And I do that very well and easily in my area of study, where I can ponder about things. But Tom is on the loose. I don't know if he's on holiday or some sort of break here, but he has been popping by when I'm trying to ponder and reflect on my decisions and my choices and my findings, really, and he comes in and talks about his findings. So I'm also being a counselor.

D. Are his questions getting a little tougher?

B. Indeed! But he is getting way ahead of the questions. So there are questions, but he is like ten to twenty–five questions ahead of the current question. So I have to take him back and say, "What is your original idea over here, before we look over here?" (*He nodded to the left and then the right.*) And he said, "I think like—" and then sort of tells the story of something that potentially, POTENTIALLY could happen. I'm not saying it will not, but we don't know that yet. So we are focusing on questions that have not yet been raised.

D. So he takes an idea and just runs off with it?

B. Runs off with it! And it's my job in some way to collect it back. It's like baseball. He shoots off an idea and then just takes off after it like a ball, exactly like baseball. And here I stand, you know, on the home base waiting for him to maybe come back around. So, that's kinda how it goes.

D. Are you his primary mentor?

B. Well, not for the Water World, of course, because I'm not fully qualified. I only took like the beginner's class, so he has tutors there as well. But I am, let's say, in charge of his personal development.

D. Is that like how Gergen is to you?

B. Indeed. I'm helping him to create a plan, or a schedule, for his learning process. And when I see that there is baseball, that he shoots a ball off, and you know, that's fine, I did that too, but he takes off after it!

D. And then he tosses it again?

B. He tosses it again, and here I stand. I don't remember if I did like that? (*Bob paused as Gergen sent him a message. He, and many other spirits, always listen to our trance conversations.*)

Gergen said that indeed, I had my bat and kind of shot off the balls, but I didn't take off in all directions. But I'm not gonna run after him (*Tom*). I'm gonna make him drop the bat and we're gonna analyze the ball instead of shooting it off. And when we have analyzed the ball fully, then together, we can lift up the bat and we can shoot it off in the direction it is supposed to go. And then we can both go to that specific zone, and from there we advance step–by–step.

D. He'll figure that out, eventually.

B. Indeed, because he gets frustrated because there are balls all over, and he's running after them, and I said, "We have to work zone to zone," and that's what we're gonna do.

D. Well, you certainly know how he feels.

B. Indeed, I know all about that, and I'm trying to be encouraging, because this is a very positive aspect of his being, because he's constantly going to explore and feel limitless in his being and in his way of thinking and learning, and I AM NOT putting a stop on that. I simply withdraw the pace a little bit. I said, "We ARE gonna play baseball. We are both gonna take off, and we're gonna explore all these different zones where the ball lands. But first we have to understand the ball itself, what sort of knowledge exists in it, and should it go to the right, left, or somewhere else, or should the ball perhaps EVEN be dropped and picked upped at a later time? And should we pick up another ball that is more up to date and more correct for the level of learning, for the zone, or platform, that we are at?

D. Well, he's still very young, he'll figure it out.

B. Ah, but he likes the games, he doesn't like to be still. I said, "We are gonna play the game—we ARE gonna play the game. We just need to understand and know what ball we should shoot off with our bat."

D. He's like you were, "What's beyond, what's beyond?"

B. Ah. So eventually I will go to that platform over there, that would be considered beyond.

D. Well, if you just think of how patient and kind Gergen was to you, he was very accommodating.

B. Ah, he understood my unique nature, and that's why he took me aside and we had a lot of individual discussions. And then he gave me all these treats of me going to all these places and explore. Because I'm an explorer, I'm a traveler. I'm not sure if

Tom is that, –Tom is an inventor, but he needs to understand if he shoots off an idea and it lands on that platform out at sea, what sort of reception will that idea have, if it's ready to become something. So he's gonna shoot ideas off in all sorts of directions, but based on the receiving end, he needs to understand where the idea belongs, what platform it should land on. If you see it like we're standing on the shore with all our balls and a bat, and out at sea there are like ten different platforms where the ball can land, we need to identify exactly where this specific ball should land, on number one to ten, because if it lands on the wrong one it's simply going to disappear and vaporize.

D. So he's just tossing them out there in any directions?

B. Indeed, in all directions. And I said we're still gonna play the game, but we need to identify, first of all, the ball we have, and also, where it's supposed to go, what platform out at sea it should land on, –and if the platform is ready for that specific ball, it's the same thing.

D. So you have to analyze the receiving end as well.

B. Indeed. It's like here on Earth. We can't bombard you with consciousness from the Master Mind, because the receiving end, the platform, is not equipped. It's the same thing. Do you understand?

D. I do. That's a really good picture, a good description.

B. Ah, so we're trying to analyze, we're not gonna just shoot off and have all these great ideas land on platforms where, first of all, they don't belong, and secondly, that might not be ready for that specific knowledge and wisdom and upgrade. So, we're looking into that, but we are going to play the game. Whereas, for me, I was an explorer. I was constantly asking, because it came in during our studies. I overheard things and I stopped and said, "Who are they? Where are they? I haven't seen them." And then Gergen and other teachers tried to just continue the class, and I said, "I've never seen them, I've never created them, I haven't seen them, none have been talking about these individuals. Where are they?" So that's why, at one point, someone said, "That's beyond." And I said, "Beyond what?" And they said, "Beyond here. Let's continue the class." Then I said, "Beyond this classroom? Beyond where? Beyond where?" And that's when Gergen sort of stepped in and said, "It's a different location, where they also have classrooms and also have studies. And they might view us as 'beyond'." So I said, "Oh, so we're beyond also for someone?" Then I said, "Then there might be friends, or I might want to go there." And he said, "It's later," and I didn't know what "later" meant, so I kept asking about that. And that's when we went, me and Gergen. And that's also when I was removed from that specific group, and I was working a lot with Gergen for a while, and then you and I met.

D. So they yanked you out of class, because you are clearly designed for something other than whatever they were talking about?

B. It was identified, yes indeed, that I was designed, in my makeup, to explore the beyond. Whereas the class had, first of all, probably no interest, and it was not a class to explore the beyond.

D. Like Ia said, "We'll do it when it's time."

B. Well, it was an alarm clock that went off inside me when I heard that, and I wanted to explore. I was wondering, who are they who view us as beyond?

D. Your little color pattern was all lit up.

B. It lit up, indeed. It was like a little amusement park starting to ling–ling–ling, like colors and all sorts of things. It was completely activated, indeed. So I'm working with Tom on that, trying to make him see that the platforms out at sea from our beach are still there. And I said, "Can you, from this perspective where we're at, can you identify where this specific ball belongs, one to ten?" And that's when he became confused. And I said, "Here we have a point. You don't know really, from this perspective, because you can't identify from this distance what platform out at sea this specific ball should land on. Perhaps we need to establish more information from this ball. What do you think, Tom?" And he said, "Yes, I think I want to know more about this ball." I said, "Let's do that," so we took that ball (*the idea*) and we turned and flipped and analyzed it. So that's what we did.

D. Well, that's a really good teaching. You're a good teacher.

B. I am, indeed.

D. You knew exactly how to address his concerns.

B. I address it, but I also entice his spirit, because I don't want him to feel like we're never gonna play, that we're never gonna shoot them off. We simply don't want the idea to be vaporized on the wrong platform out at sea. So, it's like sending out, you know, higher consciousness in your computer. It's like, "Okay, let's shoot it off into that person down there," and it just goes phfft. That's the same thing.

D. So when Tom is not coming around asking questions, you said you were doing a lot of contemplation. What are you thinking about?

B. I'm trying to indeed. I'm journaling. If questions come up, I'm writing them down. That's what I do, I have new questions since my first assignment was done. I had questions lined up, but they were put aside as another assignment came in.

D. So you're working in that study area on the eighth, but then, when you were done with that you pull your energy back?

B. Indeed, I withdraw and I also need to reflect and to recharge. I'm not sleeping, but I need the rest.

D. Gergen said you were sleeping.

B. I'm resting! Ah, it can appear so, indeed.

D. Do you ever sleep, or like shut all your windows down?

B. Indeed, but mainly if there is something major that I feel like I need to reboot, then it's like a big sleep. Oh, Ophelia says we are saving energy here, so I'm probably out of time.

D. That was a really good talk. I appreciate the info.

Working with Fossils (July 8, 2018)

D. What ideas would you like to share with us today?

B. I would like to share the progress of Tom.

D. What's Tom been doing?

B. Tom has settled down. Tom first moved into a sensation of sadness, and it was because he felt like his ideas were not heard; and I resonated with that, because I, too, went into a similar phase before I got to receive the first level of exit from the second dimension and to go to meet with Ophelia. So I told him, "This is just a preparation for you, before you are moved into greatness!" And he said, "What greatness is that?" And I said, "It can be very different, depending on your journey. So we're not gonna reveal this greatness in advance, because we don't know fully, do we? Because it's gonna be a treat, so that you're not fully prepared on the treats that are gonna come to you." So I had a lot of pep talks with Tom. Tom is also concerned about the waters and the mammals in the waters. He wants to go and talk with the fish, and he can do that, I said. He wants to reassure them that help is coming. He said, "I don't know if they can hear that." And I said, "There are great powers operating around the seas and around the fish, so I'm sure they are in some way notified that help is on the way." But he is indeed about to travel with others. The area around south of Japan is their first mission. But he also planned a visit, it appears, to the region around the Caribbean islands and the fossils in the ocean that needs to be tended to.

D. What in the ocean?

B. Ah, the ah...

D. It sounded like you said the fossils?

B. Indeed.

D. Oh, the reefs! I'm with you now.

B. It's a fossil.

D. That didn't occur to me, but it does now.

B. They need to be also tended to. But we had pep talks, because I told him that before each upgrade there is a sensation of being in some way forgotten or left behind. And it is to reflect on how far you have come to that point, and to be in stillness to appreciate the next level. But he didn't know that, so we sat down and we talked, and I told a lot about my stories.

D. That probably helped.

B. It was helpful, indeed. (*Then he began aggressively rubbing Christine's face and nose, as he often does during the sessions.*)

D. I tease this one that she bothers you back home, so that's why you rub her nose. What do you think about that?

B. He does tease me a little bit, he does do that, but in a playful way. You get a little bit mad sometimes, because you see that he comes in and tries to distract me, asking, "Do you want to come and play, Bob? Do you want to do something fun? Do you want to go and look at the showroom? Do you want to go to the bubble? Do you want to go see my bubble?" (*He gave a really boisterous laugh as he was imitating Christine at home.*) And then you say, "No, he's supposed to sit and ponder." Like I do with Tom, telling him to sit in stillness and reflect before an upgrade. I too am in that phase where I'm sitting still and reflecting, in order for me to level up a little bit. But this one comes sometimes, swings by, and says, "What are you doing,

Bob? Do you want to go somewhere? Are you bored?" And I say, "Maybe a little bit bored, but I'm not sure I'm supposed to leave." And then you come by, –you must always sense what is going on–, so you come in and say, "No, he's reflecting." And he says, "Do you want to reflect later, Bob? Do you want to go somewhere? Do you want to see what I do? Do you want to go and look how you travel? I can show you a model of how you travel, do you want to see that? Do you want to go see the maps? Huh huh huh." (*Christine often comes by my lab to tease Bob, but it is usually just to make him feel happy.*)

Several weeks later, Bob continued discussing his work with Tom, again mentioning the spirits' concern about the condition of the oceans. Most of the spirits that were created in the same bubble with Tom share a pattern that resonates with water, so many of them will work with the waters of the Earth, in one area of expertise or another.

D. Do you listen to Tom, or do you do most of the talking?

B. I listen to Tom, but I also tell stories to cheer him up, because he is, indeed, ready for departure and to go and be useful with the seas.

D. So he's finished his training at the Water World?

B. Ah, ah. There is a concern in that region with the little fishes, the plankton fishes in the area outside of Japan, because those are in the food chain for the bigger fishes. There is a concern with the fossils over here. (*He nods to the left, indicating the Caribbean.*) Then there is a concern with the plankton in that region, (*nods to the right*) because it has a lot of mercury, actually, and it creates a bad chain for others. So they need to get to the root of the problem over there in the Japan area. They have to reduce the level of mercury within the plankton and the little fishy. And over here they need to increase the light in the fossil. It's sad, he said it is sad. And then he becomes sad, because he sees that it's breaking down, the eco–chain is breaking down. He wants to rush to it, like an emergency ambulance kind of thing. So I said, "You have to do it in somewhat of an order, everything follows an order." But he is like I was, he instantly wants to go and fix it. So he feels like my stories in some way are slowing him down. He's happy about the stories, but he also feels like it's taking a little bit of time, and his ambulance is ready to go.

D. I guess when he goes to Earth the first time, then he will be splitting his soul energy, his traveling energy he's going with?

B. Indeed. There are these two regions, so I'm not sure if he's gonna split, or if he's gonna go to one of them.

D. I mean from leaving the second.

B. Oh, yes, indeed. So this is something we have also talked about, but he had that training, so he knows that.

D. I guess he had to split to go to the Water World?

B. In some way, yes, indeed.

What is the End Result? (Nov 6, 2018)

Zachariah and Bob still work together in the Library on the fifth, and as a next stage of his development, Zachariah told him he had to go back and review all the major ideas or intentions he had when he made various decisions, and then identify what steps needed to be taken to reach a certain end result. If there were other end results which he had not pursued, then he had to map out the paths required to reach each one. It sounded like a tremendous undertaking, but I think it the purpose of this exercise is to show how certain choices we make have the potential to alter the direction of our life. Our life, after all, is a series of decisions and subsequent experiences, so Zachariah was pointing out the importance of making wise choices.

Bob tries all the time to trick me in some way before he starts to talk, either trying to hide and see if I notice him, or fool me into thinking he is someone else. His efforts were futile until he enlisted the help of Ia, who mimicked some of his facial expressions, and I mistakenly assumed it was him. When it was his turn to speak, his glee was uncontained as he boisterously teased me.

B. HAHAHAHA—This is Ophelia!! HAHAHA—This is Jeshua!! Huhuhuh.

D. (*Laughing with him.*) Oh, you fooled me. But that's not how Jeshua looks (*Bob was gleeful because he tricked me.*)

B. A little bit more stoic! I am not. We have one of those in the council who has that personality. Stands with his arms crossed, ponders a little bit, takes an extra ponder pause on everything.

D. Dramatic.

B. Dramatic. Let's not go into haste. So I think about what you said, "Oh, there's haste I must attend to," and I wonder how it will be adapted on a level where there is constant haste. I don't know if there is constant haste where you are at, or if it is, indeed, simply a way for you to excuse yourself.

D. I think there are things that go on that need attention. There's a lot of balls in the air, so to speak.

B. Lot of marshmallows in the fire, need to tend to them. I guess I understand. So, you know, huhuh.

D. What's been going on?

B. Oh, I've been journaling; I've been collecting my thoughts. You know, there's a lot of thoughts that have randomly left its home base. And one needs, sometimes, to collect one's thoughts and to retrieve them, like Zachariah said. He made me think of that. I have all these thoughts, BUT do I have an end result of that thought? And that made me think. So I retreated myself, I excused myself, and I returned to the area of my study. And I sat down, and I tried to write down all my thoughts that were sort of flying around that had not landed correctly or that were not in place. So I tried to go back.

D. How far back did you go? There must have been an immense amount of thoughts.

B. It took a while. Zachariah said this is part of progress, to not toss away all your thoughts; to understand that you do not simply toss away a thought that you can follow up on, or that you have a full intention with. Meaning, the intention is the starting point and how it travels. And as that intention travels, you are supposed to calculate what could happen to this idea as it moves along here on my timeline. Then, I have an imaginary end result. And I have to calculate, Zachariah said, how long this specific idea, idea A, from the creation of it to the goal, how long is that specific idea gonna need to travel in order for it to reach that solution or goal. And what could possibly happen on the way with that specific idea A; idea B could be a completely different journey. So he said, "Go back and put them in numbers," I didn't have letters enough for my thoughts, like A to W, so he said I could use either numbers, or I could use colors.

D. Can you give me an example of one that's not too complicated, that I would understand?

B. Of my ideas?

D. Yes.

B. That I have been pondering about?

D. Yes.

B. Umm. So, I have this idea about my personal development. So, from the state of mind where I was when I created this foundation of my ladder—and I, like all of us, we create an idea and we create it in blind, because we don't know where it will lead. So we have to, first of all, identify, if this specific idea is coming from the brain, so to speak, if it is a need, or is it a drive, or an empathy, to evolve not only myself, but (evolve) with others. Is it a selfish or a collective idea?

D. Huh, I didn't think spirits would have selfish motives.

B. Well, you know, it's still a part of progress. You can have selfish goals; selfish is not bad. Selfish simply means it is an individual thought. So it doesn't have to be bad, just because it's like a selfish idea doesn't mean it's bad.

D. I was thinking in human terms.

B. You always do, when you're here. You're so stupid! Huhuh. Think bigger—think Lasaray, he understands. So, I will change my words. We have a collective idea, or we have an individual or an independent idea. And this specific idea was, first of all, independently, what is it that I would like become and evolve within? And I established that I wanted to become a great traveler. This was before you and I even met, –or we had met, but we hadn't met in your lab. BUT my intention was, because I was fascinated by you, that you came from somewhere else. So, I thought, there must be more of him somewhere that looks differently, maybe. So I wanted to become a great traveler and find them all, I wanted to find EVERY ONE that is available for me to explore. That was my first level of idea in this specific idea. And then I thought, what could I possibly need for this travel? What do I need to develop within my own being? And I quickly understood that I, –because of the fact that I am, in my core being, group activity–, I had to establish somewhat of an independence within my being. I knew that I would have to do this by myself. This was not gonna be like a tour thing with all of us. So that was the first parts when I created this idea. Then next I thought, "Okay, I need to probably learn how to adapt if I'm gonna pick this path, I have to adapt, because the other ones are not gonna follow."

D. That makes sense.

B. And then I thought, "Where could I find these beings?" And I created different scenarios. And I didn't have that much to compare with, except from Earth, so I kinda created an idea that some will be like in winter, cold, and some will be in water. I'm not really in favor of water, but if I find a creature in water, I will have to dive into the water—so what do I need for that, and so forth, and so on? So in this line that I had created, I didn't have an end result. I couldn't create it all the way, because I hadn't fully experienced it at that point. But now, I'm sitting here and I have this loose end on my independent path that I created way back, and my end result is that I want to be known as a great traveler. And that I have collected encounters with all kinds of visitors, so that everyone could benefit to understand WHO lives WHERE. (*I think this is the loose end. He didn't pinpoint where he made the decision to start collecting information to share with others.*)

D. With your line, it doesn't really end, though, because there are still places to travel to, or was it just related to the spirits you had met at that time?

B. When the idea came about, I only had you. I had met Ophelia, but that was in her lab. (*Bob's desire to travel was a result of meeting me, after I had manifested in the forest and then just vanished. That triggered his interest in knowing where I went.*)

We will interrupt the conversation to clarify what Bob says next. In this session, Eli had come in first and talked about karma and how we can visualize the soul coming to earth and walking the same path over and over across a field from birth to death. When we do things that are not spiritual, it is like digging up the soil and throwing it off to the side of our path. Bigger mistakes can be seen as bigger shovelfuls of dirt. If we keep making blunders lifetime after lifetime, we will eventually find ourselves walking in a trench of our own digging. It is a beautiful teaching and will be part of Wave 3, but we will duplicate it here, so that Bob's observations make sense. After Eli had finished talking, Bob came in and offered his own version of the story.

E. Everything encased here encounters evolution. Evolution is part of where karma lies. You have to walk over certain karma—or see that field again—you have the field where you have plowed your own path. You still, on each side of your path, could have soil that you have accumulated, put on each side, once you plow the field, so to speak. The meaning is that when you have ended your journey, when you look back on your path, meaning numerous existences, lives, then you should have put back whatever you have dug up. The field should be flat, even, again. So you come in in your first life and begin to plow your path, like a mole, you can see it and you can see how the dirt goes to each side, creates a little wall. When you learn, you understand that you can go back and forth in this lane, in this lane on your field that you have plowed, and you can eventually look back with great satisfaction, (*knowing*) that when you look back, you do not see your path anymore. As long as you look in rewind and see this line and soil on each side, there is still things to go back and re–do, look into. So, everyone who sets foot here plows their own path; even animals in some way. They don't necessarily work through karma in that respect, but they learn through the Creator. The Creator creates the path through the animal and the Creator looks for the same result with that animal. Different. I wish I could give you the picture, better. The Master Mind interacts in other creatures, creating paths, their own plowed field, learning how to operate within a third vehicle, if you like, slightly different, though. But still the same idea—that when you have reached the end of your destination, your journey, you feel tired, but when you look back, the first glimpse the soul is looking for is to see whether the ditch is still there.

We will now resume Bob's discussion of his goals and paths. Bob takes the example of people plowing karmic trenches to an extreme, describing humans digging a ditch so deep that only their heads can be seen moving back and forth across the field, like heads of cabbage or lettuce; a description we found very amusing.

D. I completely understand what you are saying. That's a remarkably fine goal. (*Reviewing his intentions and end results.*)

B. So that's one of them. (*His goal to be a traveler.*) But Zachariah said that is part of soul evolution when you are not here. (*It's a goal when you are home, in spirit.*) We don't demand that from you here (*while incarnated on Earth*). Here you just go in your karma path. (*He snorted and laughed.*) I heard Eli! Huhuh. Some, you should know, when they walk in this ditch where they have plowed through like a mole, the ditch goes to the ankle, which is good. But if someone has a ditch that reaches to their shoulders, then you just see heads moving across this field and you know that's gonna take a while for that one to throw it back in! Huhuhuh!

D. That's a really good analogy, I can see that picture!

B. If you see a big field, you can just see all these big heads, like salad heads, just walking back and forth!

D. That's a really funny description! So going back to your desire to travel, why didn't others, like Ophelia, spark the same interest?

B. Ophelia, I had met at home. I didn't meet her behind a tree! Ophelia never changed. When we are in your lab, you don't dissolve. You don't come and go and dissolve like you did in the beginning when I met you here on Earth. You don't do that at home. You don't have that magic power! Huhuhuh. Maybe you do, but you don't do that at home. Ophelia never does that. If she does, I would say she's a ghost!

D. The only time you disappear is if you wander too close to the center pole (*the Creator*).

B. Uhh, I'm not doing that. I'm trying to talk with Zachariah, because he has all these books in his possession, all these volumes from all sorts of places. I ask him, "Do you have like scriptures or volumes that explain the process of dissolving?" And he smiled a little bit, but he didn't say anything, he was quiet. So I asked again, just to make sure he heard me. And he said, "Yes, there are, Bob. There are."

D. Oh, that's interesting. But he didn't show you where they were?

B. Nay. He did not. He said there are records of everything. But, he said, "Go back and focus on your thoughts and ideas and see where they went. And some," he said, "you might not have the same intention anymore, like you had way back, but they still might be active, you know, like a little light dot. So you can make a ceremony for it, and you can make it go to rest—you don't kill it. Everything that you have created in the spirit realm is of pure light, and it is of the purest intent, so there is no need to be that dramatic that you kill it, so you just make it go to sleep."

D. But not everything has a deep meaning like your intention to go traveling? That was a pretty intense thought, so do you have to address all the minor thoughts?

B. Ah, for instance, I had a thought, at one point, to learn how to appreciate to be a fish—but I did not want to be a fish. That specific idea had existed, but it hadn't gone anywhere and I didn't want to develop it further. But because I created it and it was an active creation from my being, then I made a ceremony, similar like you put something in the soil, or you burn it. So, I made a ceremony and I thanked it for the experience. That's what you do, you thank the Creator for the experience of having that idea and the opportunity to follow it. You should appreciate that the Creator gives you the ability to pop all these ideas. So you thank the Creator for the ability to have that intention or idea in the first place. You thank the Creator and you put it back into the soil, so to speak, so that someone else might be able to use it. So, it's all about the intention that you are not killing it. (*I think this is a particularly poignant idea; that we be thankful for our individuality, the ability to be like the Creator and have thoughts, but also, to be the receiver of thoughts sent to us by the Creator and our spirit guides.*)

D. That's a really beautiful teaching. What about all the little thought bubbles you pop when you're sitting in classrooms?

B. Ah, there's a lot of those. I need to collect them, I need to look at them. Not all, it's not like I go back to all the thoughts that I had, I have to go back and simply focus on the major ones. But also, the major ones that I discarded. That is the one that you say "thank you" to; that you had the pleasure of acknowledging that idea, but, "it is not for me". Maybe it's for someone else, so you don't want to kill it, you just bury it and make a ceremony and thank the Creator for the opportunity to have that sent to you. Because he–she–it is the one who made it possible for me, and everyone, to even have ideas.

D. That's such a wonderful teaching, so thank you.

B. AH, so that's what I've been doing. So I'm probably gonna go now. A lot of things to look into.

D. I guess everyone has to do that?

B. Indeed. Everyone does that. I have avoided doing it, and Zachariah knows that.

D. Is this similar to journaling?

B. Ummuum, similar. And you should be appreciating the opportunity that you stumble upon a certain lesson, because the Creator gave that to you as a gift, for you to explore. And because you had it in your possession, the Creator thought you worthy of that specific thought. But he–she–it never gets upset if you don't take it fully into your arms, so to speak.

D. So, like the compulsion you had to travel, which I guess was part of your pattern, you just recognized it and acted on that impulse?

B. Indeed. I recognized the impulse. So there you go.

D. Thank you.

B. You're welcome. So, I'm gonna go now.

D. Alright, my friend, thank you for coming. And we thank Ia, and everyone else, and Ophelia.

B. Ah, always present. Ah, okay, I'm going. Bye bye.

Gergen Makes Himself Known (Dec 10, 2018)

Gergen, Ole, Ia, and the other council members from the second come to every session and listen to Bob chat with us, although Ia is the only one who has occasionally spoken. On this day, Gergen must have decided to prove that he was perfectly capable of talking, since I had tossed out a comment that maybe he didn't know how. We were glad he did, because he gave an impressive lecture, displaying his brilliance on a variety of topics. Bob talks about Gergen, his mentor, all the time, so the influence of his guiding hand is evident throughout this book. It is not only a handful of Elahim who have a guide from the second, but nearly ten percent of the humans in certain regions, mostly in the Americas and the colder climates of Europe, also have a companion from the realm closest to nature.

B. Ahh! Gergen is here!

D. Well, hello Gergen.

B. Oh, let's see if he might want to have a word.

D. That would be nice.

B. Ah, let's see. He says, "I don't want to take your sunshine," but I say this is a stage to be shared. Ia is also here, and everyone in the council is here. I don't know if everyone plans on taking the stage though.

D. Maybe Gergen doesn't know how to talk through somebody?

G. Oh, uh uh huh huh huh huh. I do indeed! Just because I do not interfere, it doesn't mean that I have nothing to say and cannot speak. Huh huh.

D. It's such a pleasure to finally hear you!

G. We do travel together, this little firecracker friend of ours! He is a firecracker, indeed! Huh huh. So he has been progressing and evolving as well in the council, and he provides, finally, a couple of notes. Huh. It is of importance, however, that everyone feels they are engaging and participating. And yes, indeed, even you, Bob (*as he looks to the left*). So we have what you would consider an open speech meeting, where everyone shares briefly—briefly, Bob—what one has as their expertise. We have shared some already, and Bob has talked about his Individual and how the Individual is now brought to life again. And that might be it, before we continue with the discussion of the bubble training, which is somewhat of a mystery for the other ones (*in his council*). It has to come in cups, and he is familiar with that. Doesn't only apply on this reality, but on all levels. Providing something in cups is a way to, little by little, open up your crowd, to let them come and sip your tea, instead of bringing in the whole pot. It's also to try to figure out what sort of tea is suitable for your guests. Not all teas in your cup is going to be appreciated. So, think of that you are creating a tea party, if you like, and you provide different herbs in your teas based on who you are engaging with. The softer ones, the more sweeter scents, might be provided to a more female inclined audience. Whereas a more scientific, or male, or a more logic crowd, might need a little bit of spice in their tea. Think of providing a little teeny, tiny drop of whiskey in it, to spice it up! Some will indeed be needed that little extra spice of whiskey, to make it more like a bang, powerful, in many ways, because they expect that from you. Look at your audience and see what cup to provide at your tea party. It's a way to engage and to read your setting, to at best be welcomed and heard. This is what we talked about, Bob! Think about your cups, don't bring in all cups, Bob. One at a time. Look at your council, –do you think they can have all cups? No. Think of the cups we talked about, not all have whiskey in them. (*He is using whiskey to represent a more logical energy.*) We did talk about these things, but he is a joy, he is an amusement and a fire within all realms that he sets foot. The councils are little–by–little warming up to his fire, and we are happy to have him on board.

D. I'm happy to have him following me as I go from life to life.

G. He has talked about that a lot, how he has a person to follow, and what his person is doing on Earth. He likes to chit–chat, this one, and he brings all sorts of stories, all sorts of spices in his teas. So I am well familiar with the two of you and your journeys. And he has progressed in this remote teaching, as well. At one point he did fall asleep, early on, and it did not bode well for your physical. There was a bonfire that reached out of control, not just affecting you, my friend. (*Several others must have died.*) He felt really bad about it because he said, "I did fall asleep. I excused myself and I went elsewhere." This was early on, in the beginning. He said you were kind of clumsy, but he recognized the fact that, due to that, he should have been more present. But he had found nearby a plant and a berry that caught his attention. Meaning the bonfire was neglected.

D. Which lifetime was this?

G. Early on, probably the second or third time around.

D. Did you have any involvement in picking me to work with Bob?

G. I did indeed, indeed. It was a joined conversation with Ophelia and Jeshua. Jeshua was concerned about the family (*the Elahims*) traveling here, and wanted to make sure the best support system was available when the family, like he said, traveled. You were interested in upgrading the brain. And it was suggested that was done from within, meaning you had to be part of the incarnation program. Doing so, number one, a helper was needed, –clearly it was needed, because of the bonfire. It only happened once. After that, he was like glue on a piece of bark as he follows you. But indeed, we did discuss the project where Bob had reached a level of inquisitee on the second dimension, and needed to be enticed. His star started to dim a little.

D. He needed something to focus his attention on?

G. Indeed. It was a treat, of course, for both of you. His star needed to be lit up a little bit, he needed to have a new project. He was constantly seeking projects. Zachariah was also present in discussions before the introduction meeting between the two of you took place. And it was suggested, on your part, that you needed a little bit of amusement when you came here, that it should not only be work.

D. How many people have someone from the second who follow them, as a percentage?

G. About ten to twelve percent.

D. Oh, really? That's a pretty sizable number.

G. But they are not leveled out on all areas. Mainly, our presence is known in the Americas, Australia, and of course in the cooler climates. So when I say ten or twelve percent, that might not be correct for the whole population. But in those regions where we are more...also, don't forget the seas, but there are none of you (*humans*) there. So if you ask about the seas, then the percentage is much higher.

D. So you assist the Master Mind when it is in different creatures in the sea?

G. Yes, indeed. Okay, Bob, you have waited long enough, and I have indeed taken a piece of the stage.

D. Well, it's wonderful to finally get to speak with you. We are writing a book on the second dimension, so anything you want to get across or share, we would really appreciate hearing.

G. I would like to have acknowledged the sensitivity between species. Meaning not only between your own species, but also that you are here as a chain of helpers to this plane. You are co-creators, and you are visiting with others. Don't claim land for yourself, think of other species, and be helpful to them. See where they need to be in order for your whole environment to flourish. You are not here to proclaim space, because you are sharing space. Before, when this behavior took place, a big wave came in. Landmass disappeared. This was south of the equator.

D. Was this Atlantis, of which you speak?

G. Among others. The region was in waters west of Africa, but also in the region around South Japan. Two great civilizations that took too much space. These didn't move like you do, in airplanes and so forth, but energetically they took too much space. They had other abilities to access the web above, connecting to the center core within your planet, within your host. They created teleportation's between these two zones and there was an overuse of energies. Two civilizations trying to connect to the fourth reality, practiced teleportation between the two. They didn't stop proclaiming territory as theirs, especially the one in the Japanese region. The landmass existed there—now it's water, sank.

D. How long ago was this, in Earth years?

G. The first time it happened was before the more recent cycles you discuss with your family (*the Elahims*). When you go further back, this occurrence took place around 600,000 years ago (*around the time of the first civilizations. However, the spirits have also discussed earlier groups of beings that were here before the dinosaurs were placed here, so to call any society the "first" is probably misleading*). So you see, the story continues to unfold. But it happened again. Water disappeared, continents rose, returning to its original intent. The wave that you refer to as Atlantis was later, but same location. The Japanese location never reemerged to the surface again. What was your question? Did I drift off? I tend to do that. I tend to, indeed, to drift off. It's a habit.

D. No, I was listening, and you answered my question.

G. Oh, did I? Well, there you go. Okay, Bob, I will indeed step aside for you to return to the platform. There you go, lovely to meet you.

D. It was lovely to meet you as well, Gergen. Thank you.

G. Oh, you are much welcome. I'll probably see you again!

D. I hope so. Goodbye, my friend.

G. Goodbye.

B. SEE! SEE!

D. So, he does exist!

B. He does exist! You didn't think he would talk, did ya?

D. I did not. I had hoped to hear from him.

B. Ah. He's busy, he's like Zachariah, busy. His office is really messy because he has all these scrolls. When you come in there, it looks like there's no order. But he says there is order in the disorder, which kind of contradicts, but he always knows exactly where things are. He's busy, so I do appreciate his attention. He's like Zachariah.

D. I'm surprised he doesn't assign you some of his work.

B. (*Looking to the right.*) Oh, he laughs about that. "Maybe that's to come, when you can organize your thoughts," he said. I can indeed, I can have order in disorder as well, –in my being! My office is clean, but his is not. But I can also have disorder in other places. So, that was him, that was my mentor and role model on the second dimension.

D. It sounded like he was giving you a hard time about the cups.

B. Ah, but it's because I have no reference of volume. First of all, how big is this cup supposed to be? Who says that your cup is better than my cup? Should I have one of those teeny, tiny British tea cups, or should I have like a big beer glass from Germany? Maybe that is my cup, because it has an ear as well, it's not a glass, it has an ear. So I said, "Who knows what sort of cup I should have?" and it's also because I didn't know where to start my...(*looks to the left, at Gergen*) "rambling," he said.

D. There's a lot of stuff to cover, so you never know where to start.

B. It is a lot of stuff; I did not know where to start. It was similar like here, but Ophelia, when it came to the conversations like this (*channeling*), then Ophelia gave me a whole manual and outline. You begin here and you talk like this, and you refer to this, and here we go. So I had somewhat of an outline, before I was freestyling by myself.

D. Yes. Gergen mentioned that you've been with me and let something burn up. He talked about a bonfire?

B. Ah, that one, yeah. Well, it was a gathering and you were sitting around the fire with the other ones in your tribe. It seemed perfectly harmless and there seemed to be happy activities. There was a—I did see a teeny, tiny plant that I had been looking for, for a long time. And I thought, "Oh, he seems to be doing okay over here, so I'm just gonna go and fetch it." So I took my eyes away, BRIEFLY, from you. But it's like you say about children, you're not supposed to leave them by the stove and go off to the toilet or something, because you never know what will happen. It's the same thing. You were not really accustomed to certain things. And the bonfire, because it was a happy occasion and someone put in more wood in the fire so it started to burn, and it kinda spread to your huts. It was an oops, and when I got back, you know, you and I were about to leave.

D. You mean I was dead?

B. Ah. So you said, "Look what happened, Bob," and I said, "Oh? What did you do?" And you said, "It became out of control and it spread." And I said, "Well, that was stupid!" Then you said, "Why didn't you tell me about that? You should have sent your alarm images into my chimney. Where did you go?" And I said, "I just took my eyes briefly away from you," and you said, "Well, you know that I'm not accustomed yet to this place, so you can't take your eyes away from me." And I said, "Clearly! You do tend to be tended to." So, after that, I did nurse you more closely.

D. Thank you for that. What about other humans that don't have someone from the second; does their spirit guide kind of do the same thing?

B. Indeed. We get training. But it seemed harmless that you were sitting there with your friends having fun. And because of this plant that I wanted to fetch, in my mind, it was just a brief departure on my part and I was gonna come right back! But when I came back, disaster had struck.

D. Oh, well, that's all right. They come and they go.

B. Ah, you said that. You said, "Next time, especially when there is fire and you know I'm not that accustomed to it yet here, just try to pay attention." And I said, "Well, maybe you should try to listen better also." So we laughed about that. There was no hard feelings, really.

D. Of course not.

B. But indeed, I learned how to navigate with you, because clearly you were clumsy, and I didn't really know that you were gonna be so extremely clumsy. I thought you were gonna be a little bit more in control. But you said, "I'm trying to operate the brain, I'm not here to operate the physical as much, so I'm not watching where I'm going." That's exactly what happened.

D. Am I still like that?

B. No. But there were other times when you were like that. You were operating within, with the brain, so the body was secondary. It sort of moved independently from your soul being, in many ways.

Ia Tells Secrets about the Planet (Dec 23, 2018)

Several weeks later, Ia came to discuss her work with plants and soil on Earth. Ia has several specialties where her talents are put to use. Just like all spirits, she splits her energy up and does many things at once. She has part of her energy working with the latest energy bundle and the brand-new souls on the second, another part is teaching the little sparkles in a big classroom, a third part is working with Gergen on the foundation of DNA, and yet another is actively engaged with Ophelia and Isaac to figure out new ways to improve the transmission of light energy into plants and soil. She has a very soft personality, much like a shy version of Ophelia, but has incredible knowledge about her areas of expertise, so we are always glad when she decides to talk.

Ia. Hehehe. Ah, Bob has been extremely impatient the last cycle here (*since the previous session*).

D. He didn't want to be left out?

Ia. No, he did not. He did discuss, with us all, over and over again, about his desire to participate, and due to that, there was actually given somewhat of a little holiday break in council work. We all took a break, because why should only he be allowed to take off to his private, secret project—that he would gladly share, if it was allowed. This is what he calls it, his secret project.

D. We're working on your book about the second dimension, so I'm glad you decided to come today.

Ia. Ah, always popping by, did not know if I was allowed to come first, but he is in the Christmas spirit of sharing (*we both laugh*). So, indeed, the agenda for not only me and Bob, but also the council, is to make ourselves known to man. Some already sense our presence in nature, and we are introducing a new wave of sparkles, making it even easier for humanity to connect to the level just below their feet. These sparkles are sent to create harmony within your atmosphere. Your atmosphere is suffocating in many ways, similar like a lake full of algae, where you need to give it a little extra assistance.

D. Oxygen?

Ia. Oxygen providing light, indeed. The amount of eruptions that occur within the soil, underneath the surface, is a similar effect as thunder and lightning has within your atmosphere. It is to create the balance from within, to the levels just above your head. The eruptions, such as within volcanos and such, will have a possibility to increase, due to the connection that needs to take place with the higher atmospheric surrounding. The sparkles simply operate as little helpers to create this bridge. How can I give you the picture? The center point within your host, your planet, it is that heart, the engine that provides all conditions that you see around you. But it also has the ability to operate as a conductor to assist its atmosphere. It's similar like your heart versus your skin, where your skin would be considered the atmosphere. If the heart and inside is not working correctly, then indeed you will see certain phenomena on your skin. In your case, my friend, you have taken on a body that is more receptive. Because of the fact that you have certain imbalances within your center, you are more sensitive to the intake of food, similar like the planet itself being sensitive to what occurs, not only within, but on top of its surface. The effect is what you see in your atmosphere. You have taken on a vehicle as a gauge stick on what the intake of food will do to your skin. This one did similar before, but not in the same modality where it was a reflection of her intake. (*In Christine's last life, she had a serious skin problem, which made her feel like a prisoner in her body.*) It was a different lesson that she took on, when she wanted to experience how one felt with less self-esteem. Your connection is to understand the intake of food versus your skin, similar like the planet. You operate similar as your host.

D. I've always had trouble with a lot of the foods that I eat. (*That's the primary reason I began eating organic foods four decades ago, before GMOs, pesticides, and herbicides became such a common and pervasive problem within the food chain controlled by the mega–corporations.*)

Ia. But you are also sensitive to your surroundings, so it's not only what you eat, but where you are located. You operate similar as your planet, your host. Can you see what I am trying to tell you?

D. Yes.

Ia. So as a human, you are taking on the sensations and feelings that your host is experiencing at this time. Your breathing is similar like the planet feels; it can't breathe. It can't communicate with the other celestial bodies around it. You take on the same; you operate similar as your host. Do you understand?

D. I do.

Ia. This is how the planet feels, the way you feel, that it can't breathe, that it can't communicate, that it feels trapped within its physique and its vehicle, limited, not fully blossomed. You take on the same sensation as your host. You have the ability, both of you, to fully connect with celestial bodies in your physical appearance here, and you can connect and feel how that planet experiences its reality. That is one of the teachings, Bob said, that you carry from the sixth and the ninth, the Elahims. There you go.

D. Wow, that's truly amazing.

Ia. Do you wish to ask a question?

D. I'm always interested to hear anything you might like to add to your book, and your own personal observations about things.

Ia. What I would wish you to share then, is that there are other humanoids that experience what you do. They experience exactly what the planet at this time experiences. Those who are more connected, certain souls who do not understand why they feel certain ways, why they feel limited within their being. Even though everything seems to be fine, they feel and sense the experience of your host. You are not that many, but you and others do exist. Share that.

D. Are they mostly from the sixth, or other dimensions?

Ia. Some come from the seventh, those who are bordering into the eight. Eighth, there are certain souls here, not that many, but who actually operate directly from the eighth. They are not so visible, mostly working with environmental tasks. Some, as marine biologists, others as geologists, understanding the movement of landmass and how it creates a connection to their own being, seeing a pattern that is hard to prove to your science community, that there is a connection about how your planet feels and the way you feel. If you knew, I'm sure you would tend to your host much better, wouldn't you?

D. Indeed. You said something about the volcanic eruptions?

Ia. Indeed, it has the same ability to clear ions, and make a balance between positive and negative. It creates a connection within to without.

D. I know a lot of times the volcanic eruptions produce a tremendous amount of lightning.

Ia. It is a connection and a bridge to clear the atmosphere. Bob, my friend here, would probably call it a reboot from the second dimension! The second dimension versus the eighth.

D. Is that something that will be occurring more frequently, volcanic eruptions?

Ia. Yes. Due to certain places where there needs to be a clearing within your atmosphere. The atmosphere is not constant around your planet. It moves, and the holes that we see, or the eighth observes, when they see a hole, they communicate directly to the second, in a way for volcanic eruptions or similar activities to take place. It's a communication between us both. There you go. Okay, "Time's up!" he says.

D. Huh, he's not that generous with his Christmas spirit.

Ia. "Wrap it up!" he says.

D. Well, I'm so glad you came to join us today. Thank you for sharing.

Ia. I would like to stay longer, but it is indeed a time for sharing.

D. So happy you could join us. Goodbye.

B. Huhuhuh! (*Bob came in and began laughing.*)

D. That was nice of you to share.

B. Ah.

D. Did you bring a note today?

B. I have several. It's like several post–its, just to make sure that certain things are covered. But you saw them, when we talked about this, and you said, "Uh–oh, you have a whole wall of post–its. What is this?" And I said, "These are ideas I would like to pop in and share, for my volumes." (*We named this book, Volume 1, because Bob has advised there will be more volumes to come.*) And you said, "Oh, okay," when we stood there in my office. But then I brought some to yours. (*The lab on the sixth, where we work together.*) So we now have a post–it wall, both in your office and in mine. You said, "You can bring certain post–its that we can investigate, and we can see whether they fit into the story." And I said, "I think all of them fit!" and you said, "We need to ponder about this, because we need to make sure it comes in the right order, don't we? And that the end result is what we intended it to be." So I'm moving my post–its around a little bit, you know, changing the order here.

D. We're going to have more than one volume, I'm pretty sure.

B. Ah, you said that. And you started to re–organize my notes, here, on my wall. You said, "This doesn't belong. This is more like you and me, so this doesn't belong." And I said, "I think it belongs, it's a nice story, when you were moving around in different ways on Earth." And you said, "Some of them are kind of personal," and I said, "People here are personal, they like personal." So I have different notes indeed, and we are re–organizing, together. It's not like you take them away and toss them in a basket. But you take a note and you say, "Okay, what's the end result you want to achieve if we launch this note?" and at the moment, I have mainly put up a lot of notes. I haven't really reflected on all of them. But it seems like that you pick the ones I haven't reflected on. So I wonder why you don't take the other ones, but I think you are trying to teach me something here. There's probably at least a hundred notes on my wall.

D. What do you think this first volume of yours should cover? We've talked about it, I guess, so what are the objectives?

B. I would like there to be a notion of the existence of entities, like myself and the sparkles. That there is an existence, even if one can't see and touch it. That they have to return to that sensation they had as children, like for Christmas, when everything was magical. Once you move into a sensation that you feel like magic can actually occur, then you are indeed, in a teeny tiny way, connecting to our reality. Those who have a sensation of excitement and magic and to be together with others and just feel a sensation of pure happiness about something, they will detect the entities that exist within the second dimension. So, it's all about a shift within your limited brain, to somewhat embrace what cannot be seen. A thought cannot be seen, it cannot be touched, but it exists. And most people recognize a thought as somewhat of an occurrence, –and we are the same. We can exist similar like a thought. If you focus and tune in on that sensation of excitement and magic, then it's the same. So if someone says, "You can't prove that they exist," then you can say, "You can't prove that you have thoughts, because I can't see them. I can only see your actions."

D. (*Laughing.*) That's a really good analogy.

B. Just say that. And we actually have the ability to manifest and show ourselves; whereas a thought only manifests within your fourth dimension, or in your own reality on your path, as a crater or a pebble.

D. That's excellent. Was that on one of your notes?

B. Oh, you know, you say that. One of my post–its is to embrace magic into one's awareness. Because when you do so, the other illusions that you are trapped under, they will start to dissolve, because you are moving into a sensation of sunshine. Like the sparkles, the sparkles always believe in magic, because we are taught from the very beginning when we start to move, that there are no limits of what can appear and what you can achieve when you are in the sensation of excitement and sunshine. But because your species tend to be drawn to more gloomy events, and you forget how it was when you were a child, like for Christmas, that sensation of running down the stairs and see, "OH, how many gifts are under the tree?" It's the same thing. You can create within your own being the sensation of your own tree, which will indicate and mean the tree of knowledge, and how many gifts are under this tree. So you can visualize a Christmas tree, if that is helpful for you, and as you do, you can sense that there is indeed activity and life within this Christmas tree, and that is the sparkles. And you have all seen cartoons where there is like squirrels in the tree, "OH, magic!" So it's the same thing, you move into the sensation that ANYTHING is possible, and when you do so, it's kinda hard to be gloomy.

D. When I was young and walked in the woods, I always felt like there were a lot of unseen creatures around.

B. Well, you know, they were, because we were observing you, and we were like putting things in front of you, and stuff like that. I activated my friends, too. And I was there, of course, so I trotted along. You sensed that, but you are, like Ia said, you are like the planet, you feel exactly what the planet feels, which is kinda unique. There are others, of course, that have the same ability. We're talking soul evolution here, in incarnations. But there is also soul evolution when you are in your home, and one stage of development is the ability to tune in and actually feel a celestial entity, like a planet or even a dimension. When you reach that level, then you can just tune in and exactly feel the planet or reality. Then you don't have to travel there to make remote adjustments. You just tune in and instantly feel and sense where adjustments need to be made. So, in this case here, you, you do feel strongly about the atmosphere, because that is similar like your skin and your ability to breath.

D. That's probably why I get so upset about all the chemicals they are spraying in the atmosphere and on the soil.

B. Indeed, because you feel like you can't breathe. But what you are actually feeling is that the planet cannot breathe.

D. That's a good note.

B. That's a good post–it. Another post–it, the last post–it of today, is to be a community, like we are, to reach out to those who you might sense lack a community. To invite those around you to your magic, to your tree. The more you invite and the more you connect with others, creating a little friend circle or a community, then when you come down to your Christmas tree, the day after, another gift is gonna be there. So as you invite and share, you yourself will get a reward and somewhat of a treat as well. As you do so, you grow in numbers in the connection of the light. And that's how you will be able to conquer the illusion of fear and feeling belittled.

D. That's a good note too. Is that one of yours?

B. Oh, Ia's probably involved. She's very diplomatic and all about big groups. I'm kinda like a one (*of a*) kind satellite guy, my own satellite. But I come from, I originate from, the memory of group activity. So, in my core being, I do want to belong. I don't want to float around by myself in space, I do not at all want to do that. I am in favor of group activity. So, with that, it is to create the community where you bond on a topic or a sensation that will conquer the veil of fear. And to invite those who you feel might stumble around in loneliness, because no one likes to be alone. It's worse to be not seen. So if you acknowledge someone, and it could be just briefly, –it's not like you have to join hands and sing, "Kumbaya"–, but if you meet someone, you can just give them a smile. Or if you see that someone might be a little bit low in energy—especially around this time, more people feel lonely (*around the Christmas season*)—so if you can't bring them into your cabana, then you can, at least, you know, connect with them with a smile.

D. That's really good advice, my friend.

B. Ah, we'll talk more about it, but that was a couple of notes for you. Bring in a little bit of sensation of magic, and that you are not just necessarily alone...just because you can't see it at first doesn't mean that you will NEVER see it, or that it doesn't exist.

D. I remember you said one time the natives could see those on the second, because they believed they could.

B. Indeed, indeed. First you believe, then we show you, and that's a treat.

D. It would be nice if you could show yourself to me.

B. I do! All the time. Anyway, I'll go now.

D. It's kind of a short session today, is no one else going to talk?

B. No...(*looks to the left*) No. Ophelia says we're saving energy.

Bob Brings a Bag of Notes (Dec 31, 2018)

Bob made a casual comment about how he sees our sessions, and I found his description a little perplexing, but also very thought–provoking. As a human, we see our activities progressing along a time–line, day after day. But Bob said that he just comes back to us and delivers messages, or notes, as if he is stacking them one atop another, and not spread out at distinct locations in space–time. He sees quite clearly what he has given us in the "past", and just adds his latest notes to the pile. Perhaps to the spirits, we don't appear to move, and our life experiences and memories are ever–present around us. While it doesn't really explain "time", it does give a better way to visualize how the Coat of Karma stores all our memories.

B. You have your journal sometimes on the desk, but I'm not allowed to look into it. You share and we look together, so you do share. And I bring mine, so we share notes. I say, "So what do you have in your journal?" and then you say. And then I say, "Okay, I have something similar here," and then we discuss a topic and then we fill in each other's blanks. You also need help with journaling your life when you come here, because you tend to miss certain things. So you say, "Okay, I was here. I was a farmer and did some writing." And I say, "Ohh, but you missed all these details!" So I go through my notes and we fill in the blanks, that's what we do. That's a big part of how we occupy our time, is to just sit and chit–chat and fill out different blanks in our history book, in our journals.

D. I'm glad you're with me all the time and taking good notes. You're a good friend.

B. Ah. So are you!

D. Did you bring any notes today?

B. I have a bag of notes. Ophelia said when I came, "You can't provide all of these notes, Bob." And I said, "Oh, I didn't know which one to take, so I just took them all, –just in case!" So I have been, indeed, occupying myself with trying to have an end result with my notes. It's a lot of preparation because I'm putting the ready notes in my bag. BUT the bag just kept on adding up. And then I thought, maybe I should just begin new and make a smaller bag, but then I thought, "Nay, I'll just wait for that. I'll bring this bag, because I put so much effort into, you know, putting them all in." There's no order, really. As I pondered about the note, and I pondered about the outcome, I put it in the bag of "delivering". Then I took another one, and it kept adding up. And I couldn't really put that many in the pile because they were not supposed to be delivered, at this point. So it actually became almost like ninety–five percent are in the bag of delivering!

D. (*Laughing.*) Well, I'm sure they're all good notes. Do we discuss which you should deliver?

B. From your lab, from our different encounters, yes, we do indeed. But there's also notes from home, and you don't meddle with those.

D. Ah, from the second? From your council?

B. Ah. Council people. And I do ask if they have any notes they want to deliver to the giants. There is one here, he is really curious. He hasn't traveled (*other than to the Earth*). He's like a geologist, and he's HIGHLY connected to the activity in the mountain regions near Tibet and Nepal. He's fascinated to understand more about the creatures that put certain things in his mountains, he said. And he said, "I did observe that, that there were someone coming and putting things in my mountains. They kinda just flew in." And I said, "I didn't observe anyone flying in." But he said that he did, and he has always pondered about that. So when I came in to this council, and I said that I have friends that write things down and have stored knowledge here on this plane, then he got really attentive. He thought maybe that you were the ones flying into his mountains and putting things there.

D. So these were visitors to Earth?

B. Visitors indeed. I did ask you, because he's really inquisitive, and I like him. He comes into my office sometimes, and he asks, "Where do you go, Bob, when you're not in council work?" He's older than me, but he has never left. But he said, "I have seen activities." He mainly occupies mountains and he observes the curves (*waves of energy in the planet*), the seismic activity there in the mountains. He is the one who can give an idea if a mountain should be moved. If an energetic area is out of control, then he is the one that moves the spines (*mountain ranges*), so to speak.

D. Huh. Is he involved in moving the South American spine?

B. He has, that is in his group of scholars, because of the fact that there is a...oh, I should have known this, because I took notes about this when I was a secretary. But due to the disturbances in the seabed, especially around the Caribbean region and in the fossils, they actually want to increase oxygen a little bit in the waters there. But they feel like the vibration in general below the landmass, which is South America, is not helping the surrounding area. So they want to create a little bit of change. It's not like you move the spine from the west coast to the east coast, that would be confusing. "But you can make certain canyons within this mountain range change," he said, "and some canyons are not visible on the surface." So he said, "We can make shifts and move things simply by creating canyons underneath."

D. Huh. So it changes the energy flow within the planet?

B. Indeed. So sometimes the mountain chain itself, or the mountain itself, looks the same, but the roots of the mountains are different. So some have deeper roots, like deeper canyons and sometimes, he said, we shove it up, so it just becomes like a tooth, you know. (*He said this he leaned forward and was touching Christine's tongue to her front teeth, to emphasize what he meant.*) You have roots, and sometimes with a tooth, it's like, "Oh, we just want this one to be for show," then you can cut the roots. It still looks like a tooth, like this (*he again made a dramatic show of pointing out the tooth with his tongue, indicating a fake tooth*). That's what happens, he says. But he's really interested in knowing about visitors. And I said, "You and me both!" So I said, "I do have a friend who might know these things. So if you like, I can put in a note and ask him." So that's what I do, I ask if there were certain visitors besides you that went into that region. He didn't say they messed up the mountains, he said they put things IN the mountains.

D. I wonder what they put in? Did he describe it?

B. One time, he said it looked like a box.

D. So they were hiding something in there?

B. Indeed. He said it's like a box, it's not a big one. But the box came in and it was sleeping. But then he said it started to make like, "Beep beep beep, beep beep beep, beep beep beep." Then, he got alarmed, because he is like the mountain keeper. So he rushed to that and saw this interference within. It's like a receiver, he said, that's how it looks, so he wanted to know about what sort of receiver was put into his mountain in Tibet. So, I have that on my note. So if you have anything you would like to say, then, HUH HUH HUH HUH, I'll be listening and I'll pass the information forward! I said I would ask during this session and see if certain information comes! (*He was laughing while he said that, knowing that my human self is clueless.*)

D. (*I was laughing with him.*) I'm sure, within the group that's gathered, there must be someone who knows!

B. Ah. Ophelia says that we are moving into a territory of knowledge that is about to come, about visitors.

D. That will be fascinating. A lot of people are interested in that.

B. Ah. So am I! And so is my friend here, –what I will call him is Joel.

D. Joel.

B. Joel. It sort of rhymes with geology.

D. So, with all these notes that you brought, do you think we are going to have a chance to talk about them all? Are you going to be able to deliver them all?

B. During MY lifetime (*snorts and laughs*), or yours? HEHEHE.

D. Yours, probably—mine, maybe not.

B. Nay. I do need to tend to you, so you don't go up in smoke, you know. I do need to tend to that, because you do tend to be a little bit clumsy. It's because sometimes you don't fully maneuver the physical because you are so preoccupied with the activity in the brain. It's like you're up there and you're moving things around and you're fixing things, so the physical is sometimes just independent from the soul being, –and that's why you need me! Because I make sure, "Oops!" I push you back up on the sidewalk again, so you don't get hit, because you're like looking up in the head, "Hmm, hmm, hmm." And then whoops! there you go. So I push you back up. There's certain places where I'm extra cautious. I'm cautious when you walk on sidewalks now. Not before, because there was nothing really that could interfere that quickly. (*Before the 20th century.*) But I'm also cautious if you would go like on a bridge near water, because you tend to be...if you think of yourself inside, instead of looking straight forward, you are, YOU, is like this, up! (*As he looks towards ceiling.*) So you can see that you miss what your feet are doing, and that's why you need me. So I'm kinda paying attention to your feet, because I do know that you are sometimes like a professor inside, occupied with understanding the signals within the brain, so that you can report back to the councils where you belong.

D. Are all my lifetimes like that?

B. A lot of them have been like that. You take on certain physical things sometimes, but you are mainly interested in understanding the mental connections, the communication between species here in this dense environment, and how the atmosphere and the web affects the being, meaning the humanoid, and the ability to communicate and receive. So you put in this brain, which is the receiver for all sorts of information. But currently the receiver is just taking in non-important signals, so it misses things. And there is all this noise that interferes, and that is on my note here—we can talk about that note. I do see, because of the extreme commotion and noise and disturbances, that the receiver, the brain, doesn't fully connect to the true signals it's supposed to receive, in order for you to have even a possibility to start to communicate telepathically. So even those who are more intuitive struggle with having clear signals when there is this commotion of energetic messages floating around in space, so to speak.

D. What about radio waves, microwaves, and electromagnetic pollution in the atmosphere; does that mess with people, too?

B. Indeed, indeed. The receivers, the brain, –we can call it the receiver, so when I say that, know what I mean. Well, there is also the receiver in the center point where the soul is, but what we are talking about today is the receiver in the brain. And you are very interested in how this brain is operating, as the amount of signals and waves from different sources interfere with the humanoid. So, your soul perspective from within is like this (*as he looks upward*), and that is why sometimes you trip and you fall. So we do not want you to trip and fall. But the amount of energetic influence in the atmosphere are not only manmade, but because of the field around the atmosphere, the web, has dissolved a little bit. So even outer influences, that you are not supposed to ever hear, starts to come in and creates a mishmash in the receiver. When they are combined with the active waves that you have created here, like radio waves and electromagnetic frequencies and so forth, the receiver, your brain, it can't handle all these different influences. And some (*influences*) are not from here. Certain individuals who appear with mental illnesses, they actually get confused because they receive signals that don't belong here.

D. That makes a lot of sense.

B. So that's why it becomes too much of a mishmash within the receiver, the brain, and people who have these problems of different mental diseases or psychological problems, they actually—it's like they tune in on a radio frequency a little bit higher up that they're not supposed to hear, because they can't dissect those signals, because the brain isn't equipped. There's a lot going on to try to figure out how to upgrade the receiver in the head.

D. Well, I'm glad you're tending to my body and where I walk.

B. You do tend to be taken care of. It didn't go that well in the beginning! I–I–I–I was a little bit concerned that you didn't want me to stick around anymore, after the bonfire, that you didn't feel me to be qualified enough. So I promised that I would pay better attention—and I have! And sometime, when you left early, I said, "I did not do that! You did that by yourself." And then you said, "Well, my mission was kinda done," and I said, "I thought we were gonna stick around longer." Sometimes I don't know the actual end result of the life you picked. I know kind of little details, but I'm not always filled in on the detail of departure. That's why it's important for me to stick around closely.

D. You are a good and loyal friend, indeed.

B. There are a lot of things to be discussed, of course. But I am also here today to talk about the activity in the mountains of Tibet. So, what you said was that there are, in certain places, these receivers from extraterrestrial visitors from other systems. And most of them belong in the same fish tank, you say, they're just in a different frequency band, but they are in the fifth fish tank.

D. So what are those receivers for? Do they communicate with the Earth itself, or with these visitors?

B. With these visitors. And they read the activity within the planet. That's why a lot of them are in mountains. Some, you say, are also up on the poles, in the eyes, because they want to monitor the big fork.

The fork was described in *Wave 2*. It is the energetic field that runs from pole to pole, creating a web that communicates with all life forms. This is what Bob refers to as a tuning fork, a harmonic melody the planet itself emits. This melody resonates and communicates with all life forms on land and in the seas. Humans have interfered with this energy field due to the misuse of microwave transmissions, GMOs, poisons, and pollution. Our activities cause confusion and degradation within plants and animals everywhere on the planet. The Earth project has been ongoing for billions of years, long before humans were even contemplated. The boxes that Joel saw being installed by visitors were placed about 100 million years ago. They also put receivers on the rotational axis to monitor the poles, which are referred to as "eyes", by Bob. As the crust moves, the boxes are relocated to maintain positions near the poles. The information is collected by the visitors and passed on to the councils in the ninth and fifth.

Another interesting statement is about the stone cones, the pyramids, being installed to stabilize the energy in that area. While they may have had other uses, the spirits have always said the stone cones collected energy from the web above and pulled it into the structure, where it was either stored or discharged into the Earth. The alien travelers who assisted in the construction were here to benefit the Earth project. Just because we do not understand the reasoning or the technology involved does not mean that the explanations given by the spirits are inaccurate. Bob said that boxes, or receivers, were put beneath most of the oldest pyramids. The stone cones on the Giza Plateau do not have receivers, but the ones that are hidden probably do.

D. So, the visitors are being helpful, I guess?

B. Indeed. So these were left here WAY back (*in time*), and it is to read the activity. It's not so much to read the activity of squabbles between the humanoids, which is pathetic from their standpoint, you say. They don't engage in that sort of squabble, but they are interested in understanding the inside of your planet. So there are a lot of receivers on the poles, especially on the north pole, and eyes that are observing. It's almost like a circle around the fork to maneuver and follow up on the activity within this tuning fork. And then there are a couple in the mountains, to make sure that the stabilizing force, -because mountains are stabilizers, as well as the stone cones-, so they make sure that they are working. There are little receivers actually, you should know, underneath each stone cone. And some of the receivers are more active, and some of them are asleep. But if you try to dig under the ones in Egypt, you will not find a box. But there are pyramids that are hidden, in some way, by trees and vegetation, and under there, there are actually little receivers or boxes to be found. But the visitors are looking into these energetic zones, and how the stone cones and mountains are providing that stability over energetic circulations. And then the ones at the poles, they are trying to detect the wellbeing of the fork—that's what you say. And those are placed by visitors. And then I asked, "Who were those? Who were the visitors?" And you said, "Well—" and you smiled. And then Ophelia came and said, "Come on, Bob, time to go!" So we will talk about that, maybe later. But it hasn't been said, "Maybe later," but you smiled and then Ophelia came and said, "Class over! Come, Bob, let's go over here." So I said, "I would like to report back to Joel, because he would like to know about the Tibetan mountains and the receiver box that he saw was placed there at one point." So you said, "You can tell him, you can confirm that it is a receiver about the wellbeing of the energetic circulation underneath the mountains, and that he doesn't have to be concerned because it's not going to affect his work at all," because Joel was concerned.

D. That's good to know.

B. So Joel and I, we sit a lot in my study and we talk. And he's like, "Tell me about those big beings." And I said, "Ah, I go and I visit them and I learn all sorts of magic." (*He whispered in a secretive way.*) And sometime Gergen comes by and says, "Ohh, times up! Time to go. Break is over, time to go and continue council studies." And I say, "Well, let's continue this talk another time," and Gergen says, "We'll see about that."

D. Maybe Gergen doesn't want you to get him all wound up. That might make the other council members feel like they aren't learning as much as you are.

B. But Joel, he came because he did see that activity at one point. Okay, Ophelia says, "Times up!" Oh, oh, oh, I might give away too much information here, she says. This is what happens when we talk about things, she says. I get too excited and then I fire you up, and then all sorts of things can fly around. And she says we still have an agenda to follow.

D. Did we sort of drift off-topic today?

B. No, she said not. She says that we're like pals sitting around a bonfire, just sharing, and that can be different here than sharing at home. When we share at home she doesn't really interfere, unless I ask about visitors, because clearly, she came by. I wonder how she knew I was even there?

D. She's like Isaac.

B. She just pops in. Maybe she knows exactly where I am. Maybe I have a receiver somewhere inside! Ah, anyway, I'll go, but I'll be back with my bag. So, there we go.

D. Alright, well I look forward to it, my friend. Thank you so much for coming and sharing with us today.

B. Okay. Bye bye.

Bob Becomes Tom's Mentor (Jan 6, 2019)

Bob's retelling of his life story has compacted many cycles of growth into a few short descriptions. Only a few pages ago, Tom was a student in Ia's classroom, but is now practicing to be a water engineer on Earth. There is no way to correlate the learning cycles in the spirit world to "time", but I'm quite sure there is a considerable gap between when Tom was a sparkle and his current level of development. Along the way, Bob became more and more involved in helping to educate Tom, and was eventually assigned to be his mentor. Unlike on Earth, where a mentor may be involved for a few months or years, in the spirit realm, it seems to be a relationship that lasts indefinitely, although many other teachers may step in and help with certain subjects.

B. I have been given the opportunity to mentor and tend to Tom.

D. Oh, that's a surprise! (*Not really. As his story has unfolded, all indications were that Tom and Bob would be working together.*)

B. Tom has developed into a fine young man, I must say!

D. Oh, what's he doing now?

B. He has been extremely busy with journaling his adventures, so he has a collection of notes. I wonder where he got that idea, to take notes? Huhuh. But he has his own collection. And he's been in a group, the water engineers, so he's been trying to develop different new prototypes that will not only exist in the ocean, but also to be on a secret mission to radiate light! Some, he said, are gonna appear on the seabed at certain locations that are not feeling well. They will never be shown to fishermen, they will never be captured in the net. They're gonna be way down in the dark, but they are there to clean. They look like kind of a jellyfish, but they will hover over the seabed and create light within the foundation of the seas in certain regions. Some of them are going to be over in the Japan region, in that region, so a brand-new species is under development and will be designed to clean up the seabed. And the seabed carries events, not only from the last, you know, your hundred years or two hundred years—there are certain events that has been kept down there that are intended, from our council on the second, to be deleted. Similar like you delete certain memories from your atmosphere, like certain events in the fourth. You can also delete certain events that are physically manifested at one point on this plane. And he (*Tom*) is looking into deleting certain events, which is interactions of certain minerals that were not in favor. But it's still there. It's still there until you delete it in some way. And that cannot be done by a fisherman or a person going down in a scuba outfit or a submarine, that has to be deleted by us. So, he's working on that. He has grown, I must say.

D. So you have been assigned to take care of him?

B. Indeed, because he has so much training under his belt, so to speak, that he is indeed ready to hear about certain things that I do.

D. What are you going to teach him, specifically?

B. I'm gonna talk about different travels, and I'm gonna talk about and teach him how you yourself can travel differently once you master your different vibrations. And how you can learn...he's in that phase where I was when started to move and travel into the fifth and to later meet with Ophelia. Ophelia actually came and met me the first time in the fifth, I didn't go to the seventh. She met me in garden, sitting on a bench, very friendly, sitting there radiating love and knowledge. So, he is ready now to depart and take his next level as a traveler.

D. So are you going to be the one who helps him divide his energy?

B. I'm gonna teach him how you master and how you divide, and how you constantly remain here. As well as he will have a huge percentage—like I had a huge percentage of my being in the library for a long time—he will have a huge percentage present in the water engineer group, because of the high profile of that mission.

D. Where will that be located, that group?

B. The group itself is in the second dimension, but they operate in direct contact, through different councils of course, but operate directly through these new individuals created on the seabed. So, it's like remote teaching, but through, not a human, but these creatures on the seabed. So they might go in and blend with them, he's not gonna blend with a tree.

Gergen says to Appreciate the Small Things (Jan 8, 2019)

Gergen begins with an informative talk on those souls who are here with folded Coats. Many spirits do continue to come to Earth once their ladder of learning has been satisfied, but they do it because they want to help in some way. Gergen says that those who come always leave a footprint, even if it is a minor contribution. Later, he tells us to be aware of and appreciate the small things that come our way. He said that our spirit helpers are always observing and intervening to give us these small gifts. A few minutes of peace during a busy day. The smells from nature; a beautiful sky; a kind word from a friend; the warmth of a blanket—there are so many things that we should be grateful for, if we only pay attention. One of the keys to happiness is to recognize the many small gifts we receive each day.

D. How do you and your Council feel about our work here?

G. It has been an interesting development for us to follow this journey, through Bob. And also directly, to see the information that you are revealing about the second dimension. To also make people aware of the little things, the life and the magic that exists even in an ant, to not only focus on ascended masters, archangels, and so forth—nothing bad of course about those friends in higher realities, but for some it's a struggle to wrap their minds around an ascended master, what that potentially could be. An ascended master exists in all realities, and it simply means you have risen through the levels of knowledge either in that specific fish tank or spiritual reality. So, in that respect, a human, or the bottle with a soul in it, once the Coat is folded, that specific soul is an ascended human being! Huh huh, if it makes sense to you. (*The Coat of Karma was discussed in Wave 1. When a soul has learned the main lessons it was predestined to experience on this plane, the spirits say, "the Coat is folded". Souls can continue to come here for various reasons, but karma is not normally associated with the activities recorded during the lifetime.*)

D. That's a fairly low bar.

G. But it's still a bar, it's still a bar, and you should know it is tricky. We see that, since we do not tap into the bottles in the same way like you do. However, we observe the footprints that you make, that we have to clean up. So in that respect, knowing that all souls are pure, but seeing the events that take place, makes us stumble a bit and think, "How did it even become like that, with such an intelligence inside?" Considering that we never tap into a human, we can only analyze and decipher your footprints. With that said, knowing the inside is highly intelligent and pure, but the footprints you make might not reflect the soul intelligence, indicates that it is a struggle to be here. Meaning that once the Coat has been folded, then one could actually see that as quite an impressive bar.

D. Alright, well said!

G. Then you make different footprints that do not remain for others either to fall into, or that are not visible for the spiritual realities to investigate.

D. Once the Coat is folded?

G. Indeed. So, the footsteps are invisible.

D. Huh, so like when I travel, I don't leave any footprints?

G. You do not leave footprints for us to clean, but you can make a mark, that's different. And normally, souls whose Coats are folded, leave even the teeniest, smallest contribution. It is still part of the development that, even if you have folded Coat, that you are here to somewhat assist and to leave a mark. But your footsteps, meaning what we need to investigate and clean, are not there.

D. Interesting. Perhaps you don't know, but what percentage of humans are coming here with a folded Coat?

G. Ah, that would probably be a question for Ophelia and Isaac, I would assume, who monitor the development of Coats. You should know that it's not advisable to have too many folded Coats here, because of the intention of lessons. If you have only folded Coats who come here, then the events the Master Mind wishes to investigate will never take place. But then again, this is a project, and one of the projects is the footprints you leave behind, so that different levels (*dimensions*) learn from them. If you make footprints, let's say, that are related to nature and agriculture and environment, then councils from the second, including myself, will investigate and make notes and indeed, pass that information further along to Jeshua and Isaac and Ophelia; and we discuss—in our Monday meetings! Huh huh. That's what I told Bob we have, and it sort of stuck.

D. Yes, he mentioned that, as you know.

G. Ah, I do monitor, because he is tricky. He tries to zig–zag his way forward.

D. He's been really good; once he learned the rules, he hasn't been divulging too much information, I assume, that he shouldn't?

G. Nay. Just the fact of rules was something that we avoided teaching him. We actually changed the word "rules" in our development and study, before this even happened. When he was young, we called it cycles of suggestions—that is what we call it, we do not call it rules—they are cycles of suggestions. And indeed, he cycles through them and makes remarks about these suggestions.

D. Ways to improve.

G. Improvement, indeed. And he's very eager to improve. Well, anyway, here he stands with his diploma, and I'm sure he has things to say. What we wish to transmit is that people should pay attention to the smallest activity in life, not only, like I said, a small ant, but the smallest activity during one's day; to appreciate the silence of simply not having your phone ringing, or simply not having an e–mail coming in, to rest in the knowledge that you are in your own space and in your own environment of rest once in a while; to appreciate the sun, if one has experienced a lot of rain for a while—the little things, to not simply gaze into the future for the big events. The big events will come or cycle through your life, regardless, but the little things are the ones that you will look upon when you return into your spiritual reality; to investigate how you welcomed the smallest gifts, not only the biggest package of all. This is what we talked about, Bob (*looking to the left*), to embrace the smallest present, not just go to the biggest one under the tree. So, it's the same thing, that you try to see during your day, and maybe, in the end of the day, to pay gratitude to at least one or two things during your day. And when you go to bed, to be in a sensation of gratitude, to think of at least one thing or two that made you happy or felt blessed, or felt relaxed, if you are in a life that is very stressful. Let's say that you were given a break during your day because someone cancelled their appointment, and you were given (*time to relax with*) an extra cup of coffee. Just the teeniest, tiniest things, not the biggest things. To pay gratitude at the end of the day, before you go to bed; to appreciate what has been given to you, some perhaps from a spiritual helper, observing you and seeing what you might need.

D. That's a beautiful teaching, Gergen.

G. You are much welcome. No one wants to go to bed and feel stressed and feel a discontent. So try to find something and be grateful for that, and say it out loud or within yourself, before you go to bed. And start your day with the intention that you are gonna find something to be grateful for, when you go to bed.

D. That's really wonderful. Thank you for that.

G There we go, there we go, there we go. Okay, thank you for your time.

D. Alright my friend, thank you!

G. There we go.

Three Small Elahims Looking In (Jan 13, 2019)

Bob is actually very sensitive, and while his personality is quite happy and outgoing, he does experience sensations of sadness, frustration, nervousness and other emotions that are quite human in some ways. This story of his encounters with the other spiritual beings on the sixth is a good example of how he interacts within strange surroundings. After Bob began coming to the sixth dimension, he and I were alone together in my lab and office area most of the time. The spirits on each dimension transmit thought bubbles on different frequencies, Lasaray learned to send thought bubbles and emotional waves to Bob, so we understood each other perfectly. But when he went out to different areas on the sixth, the others were not trained to communicate with him, so he felt left out. The young students on the sixth, the little Elahims, seemed frightened and ran away. So that made him quite sad. Just as I learned how to "speak" Bob's language, the little Elahims eventually learned as well, and then bonds of friendship formed among them. But initially, Bob felt very isolated and rejected by the other spirits on the sixth, as he laments in the following session.

B. You said that sometimes when I move around, like up in the sixth, some were sort of like—I don't know if they were afraid of me, or if they were just curious about me—but some of the younger ones didn't really know what I was. But I tried to make friends, like I always do. I went forward, but I went kind of rapidly to one of the little ones at your place. I sort of ran over there, –and this was way back (*when he first came to the sixth*), but I ran over there and was like, "Hi! What are you doing? What do you learn? I'm Bob. I come from beyond. Do you know about beyond? Because this is beyond for me, so do you want to know about beyond for you?" And he just disappeared! He just took off. Then I saw another one, and I ran off to that one and I said, "Hey! Hello, I'm Bob. I'm from beyond. You are beyond to me. What do you learn? Are you interested in knowing about beyond?" And he ran away, too. So no one seemed to want to listen. And then you came and you said, "They've never seen anyone like you. But you can talk about the beyond with some other friends." And I was like, "Who are they gonna be?" We didn't have any friends at that moment, so Zachariah came. And Zachariah said, "Why don't you tell me about beyond, Bob." And I said, "Oh, I'm gonna tell you about beyond from your perspective." I was eager to share about my home environment.

D. Was Zachariah receptive?

B. Indeed. But I think he was brought in, because no one else was receptive and you saw that I was a little bit sad that no one was curious about me. So you brought in Zachariah, who clearly has no judgement of strange entities and beings, because he knows them all.

D. I'm sure he was well aware of the second.

B. He's probably well aware. I later heard that Gergen and you decided, combined with Zachariah, to let me introduce my reality to Zachariah. But I was a little bit sad, you know. I didn't know why they just ran away.

D. They're a little reclusive, up on the sixth.

B. They were kind of quiet, and maybe it's because of my personality? Because they don't run. Neither of you move very fast. I can move very fast if I want to, and I think that was a little bit disturbing to them, because they didn't know what I was. Then I ask, "Maybe if I tiptoe? Maybe if I just drag myself around, will that give me some friends?" And you said, "We can try that." So I actually did. I went to the museum, where I knew there were gonna be little students, and I just sort of dragged my feet, kinda. But then I said to you, "Do you think they see me as a ghost? Like I'm sort of uuuuhhhhh" (*He made a long, low moaning sound, imitating a ghost.*) And you said, "It's all about blending in, Bob." So, I tried that. I came forward and said, "Heellloooo, I...am...Bob." And there was one there that was a little bit interested in who I was.

D. Some marginal success.

B. I don't know if it was success, but I changed my approach to blend in better. And that's also why, like when a soul comes in here, and it's not used to human activities and responses and personality outbursts like that, then one can just think that, "Okay. Here, I might have to change my whole appearance and my whole perception to somewhat blend in, to not be the odd one out." And then you have to somewhat figure out, –like in my case, I had a much more vibrant frequency than the other ones, so I had to somewhat dim mine. But it could be the opposite. If you come in here, and you are dimmed already, then you might need to focus on colors. Colors are movement, colors are to make things go faster. And colors are the first level before it becomes a tune. So from the Creator, it's not just white light in there, it's different colors, and from that color a melody or a tune is created. So someone who feels, "Oh, maybe I'm a little bit slow, maybe my surroundings are quicker than me," then they can start to try to fill themselves up, visualize how they fill themselves up with different colors, and that will reflect on the surface. They're not gonna become green! But they will indeed blend in better. So, in my case, I came in with a whole rainbow color to your place, because I wanted to express myself from the best way possible. But they (*the students on the sixth*) were more like in one color, so they were confused with me coming in with all sorts of colors.

D. What color do you think they represented?

B. They were like light blue. And I tried to make friends, radiating my red and purple, and they didn't understand that. And because of the fact I moved a little bit faster—I didn't chase them—but you said I kinda did. And I said, "Why did they run away from me?" And you said, "We don't run, necessarily, here. So when you started to run, they took off."

D. It's like if the moon people all looked at you and then started running towards you.

B. Ooohhhh! Nay! Nay! Ooohhh! But they're scary! So that's different.

D. It's all matter of perspective.

B. You think they were scared of me?

D. No, they just didn't understand you. But since you've been in our lab a long time, have you made friends with any of the little ones?

B. Ah, ah. I have like three. After I stopped running and went back into your room and I sat down there, you said, "Why are you so sad, Bob? Why are you so sad?" And I said, "They just run away from me. I don't think they like me up here." And then Zachariah came, and I got to tell him. But after a while, when you and I were sitting there, suddenly, in the doorway, I saw three little heads looking in. So, now I do have three little friends. But they came with their person, so there were three little heads and three big ones. And you said, "Look, Bob, we have visitors." And I said, "I'm gonna sit still then. I'm not gonna do anything," And you said, "No, just sit still. Let them come to you, instead of you going to them." That was a great teaching by itself, to let something come to me, to not go to someone or somewhere to get the information. So it was all about me being passive, –and this was before self-study. This was the whole thing, that lesson of being passive. So, I sat there on my chair, and eventually these six came in and sat down around. And you sent me thought bubbles, like, "Just be quiet, Bob. Just be quiet and let them look at you, because you are different. They don't know who you are. It's like when I came down to your place, the sparkles didn't know what I was, so it's the same thing." And I said, "What do you think they think I am?" You said, "You probably appear to them like the cone ears did to you, because they have never seen anyone like you, but they are curious. They are like travelers in the making, here, so they are curious about what they can encounter." So, their person, their tutors, brought three little travelers, who will later encounter and work with someone like me. So like you and I work, these three are gonna work with someone from the second, eventually. I'm not gonna say that to Tom, because Tom is at the very top to get one of these. But I'm not gonna say because it's not already decided. But that is the whole thing; eventually these three, when they become in the level of learning and age of you, then they will get someone like me, if they're gonna travel here.

D. That's a real blessing for them, then.

B. Ah. So as I understood that, a new friendship was born, and we could talk about what can happen when they come to Earth and meet their person for the first time. So I told them about certain things, like, "We don't touch everything we see." And sometime later, "When you're gonna go and be in a humanoid, then someone like me will help you," and they were really interested in that. They had no idea about incarnation, so I kind of squealed, you know, gave away a secret! Huh huh. So we talked about that, and they asked, "What's that gonna mean? What's that mean?" And you said, "Sometimes when I go there, I don't go like this. I go and—," and then you showed on the screens, "this is what I looked like." And you showed some of your different lives on the screens; you showed the furry one, and then another one, and they were like, "Aaahhh." So it was like a whole lecture and discussion, a talk, a presentation, of what was gonna come and what was gonna happen. And they were really excited. And they were like, "I also want to have a little friend, like this one," because you showed like a film; the film was you in physical, but the film also showed me! I was not invisible, so when we look back and we go through life reviews and so on, we also see ME! I'm manifested in these little films and documentaries that we can look at. So we can see, like with the fire thing, we saw that my manifestation was not in the picture. (*He gave a little nervous laugh*). But we didn't show that, uuuhhh, we didn't want them to feel like, "Oh, you're gonna go down, and this is what you're gonna be—burnt up! You're gonna be burnt up! And your person is outside of the picture!" So, we didn't show that. We showed, similar like we do with the sparkles (*on the second*), we showed sunshine stories, so they are enticed by the journey itself. We showed different screens of different lives you had and my contribution to that life. That was a fun time!

D. We've had some interesting lives together, haven't we?

B. Ah, I've been really helpful. After that fire, I paid much more attention.

D. It's nice you are so involved in this life, and being able to talk like this is a wonderful experience.

B. We didn't show this to them, because it's not very common that you and I sit and talk like this. But we showed like, "You're gonna be in something like that (*a human body*), and your helper—someone like me—is gonna help you with certain things." And we showed that certain things could be just avoiding disasters, but also to feel that you have a friend when you're far away from home.

D. When you are watching these films, do the other spirit helpers, like Ophelia, do they show up in them sometimes?

B. Ah, but mainly when I look at our films, it's you and I. But if something happens where another one was needed, then they will also show up. But when everyone comes back and does a life review and looks at their movies, they see all spirit guides that were present during a specific time. But we don't want to confuse these little ones, so we're showing a film where only I appear as a helper.

D. A starring role.

B. Well, you're kind of the leading actor, and I'm sort of the assistant. But when someone comes back and they look at these life reviews, they can actually see certain events and how a spirit guide helped, because it would be manifested in that film that they look at, how they tried to intervene and in what way. That's how they can learn to, next time around, to somewhat adjust. If they maybe didn't allow themselves to feel—let's say that they saw their spirit guide, someone like Isaac or Ophelia was sending tremendous support and assistance to the center point and the chest, and they didn't hear that, then they will know that there are different things to adjust next time around. So they will see the interactions from their spirit guide, they will see themselves, and they will see their spirit guides and how they tried to assist and help.

D. That's a really good thing for people to know, how they are always cared for. I had a question. This one doesn't have anyone from the second to help, does she?

B. Gergen actually. Gergen, because of the fact that this one didn't want to come in the beginning. But Gergen doesn't follow, like I follow you. But maybe it's because this one says, "I'm not so clumsy!" Huhuhuh! That's what this one said, "I don't need to have a babysitter all the time!" (*Laughing.*) That's what this one said. But I'm not a babysitter. Well, I kinda am. But this one said, "I don't need a babysitter all the time." But he actually kinda does, because he tends to come home early.

D. So like in past lives as well?

B. Gergen has been present in a couple of past lives, indeed. But mainly Isaac and Ophelia watch this one.

D. They don't want something to happen that would interfere with our project.

B. At certain times, Gergen actually follow this one. But it's not like us—I follow you always. I kinda want that too, I don't want to miss an opportunity to learn. And I said, because you said, "Maybe you don't have to follow every time," then I said, "Look what happens if you are by yourself!" So I kinda introduced the importance of my presence. I showed a lot of lives where it went well! So I really pushed my importance to come, because I also want to learn.

D. I'm really grateful for all your help.

B. Ah, I kinda want to join. I said, "It's better to have a friend and not need one, than to not have a friend and really want one." Because I might not be able to come when you call if you had said, "Oh, I don't need you," then I would have said, "Well, if you don't need me, you're all by yourself!" So I said, "Isn't it better if you just have me tag along, just in case?" Then I said, "Why don't we shake hands on it?" and we kinda did. So you don't go by yourself, even if you don't always need me.

D. I'm sure I do. You've been a huge help.

B. Well, sometimes it's just the fact, like when you observe the brain, that you sort of want someone to monitor the physical, the body. So a lot of lives have been like that, that I just take care of the physical, to make sure that it doesn't take harm, and so on. So, that's what we do. But these three are really interested in this when they see our movies. And I said, "You're gonna get someone like me, someone who's gonna take care of you and join." And we showed different scenarios that can take place as you tap into a human. So, they're in the beginning of coming in. And curious as I am, or I tend to be, I asked, "What is your mission gonna be? Why are you going down? My person goes down and investigates the brain and group dynamics. What are you gonna go down and do?"

D. They probably didn't know, did they?

B. No. And then their people said, "Okay, meetings up," and then they left.

D. And you could hear them going out the door saying, "What did he mean by that?" –and their person was left with the questions!

B. Indeed! Hehehehe. But they have come back. This was like the first time, and now when I move around freely, I don't run, I don't drag around, I wander like this, "Good afternoon." (*He nodding slowly and formally to each side, showing how he addresses those on the sixth*)

D. To the moon people?

B. To the moon people– "Good evening to you, Great Spirit!" and I nod. And I'm very authoritative and dignified.

D. How is your communication with them, the little ones?

B. Ah, I thought you meant the moon people, and I was gonna say, –it's non–existent! HUHUHUH. Oh, the little ones, the three ones, they now communicate easily with me. There were translations, of course, in the beginning from you and from their people. But now I am allowed to talk with them, because I've been instructed on what I can say and what I cannot say. There is like one or two from this group that ask a lot of questions. *(He dropped his voice and began to speak in a secretive whisper.*) One time when I was sitting and doing self–study, that one came in and the other one came right after, and they came in and they said, "Can you tell more about the Earth and what to expect there?" And instantly, you came. And I was like (*he put his hands up*), "I'm self–studying! I didn't do this. I didn't say anything!" So they're curious. But at the moment we only have discussions when there is a person present, like you, or someone from them. So we are not left alone, and I'm not sure we will ever be.

D. It's kind of like you and me right here, I'm sure Ophelia would never leave us alone to chat.

B. Probably the same thing.

D. Because I'm curious.

B. Ahh, and they're curious. But because they're curious and I'm eager to share, we have actually set up a schedule of meetings to talk about Earth activities and incarnations and what to expect.

D. How old will they be when they start incarnating? (*Spiritual age relative to human years.*)

B. Oh, at the moment I would say that they are like twelve–year olds, kinda. And they will start to travel when they are like sixteen. All souls begin when they're around similar to what you would consider a sixteen year–old, that's when you start to really work. That's when the demands come. Now you're an adult, now you have to go out and fulfill your color pattern or your blueprint, now you have to go and do whatever you were intended to do.

D. The Elahim Council was talking before you came in and said there are about one hundred Elahim here at the moment. Two just returned home.

B. And that's also part of this, and I don't know if they understand that, that they are not gonna come down in this little three unit. They're gonna be spread out. That's why they need to have a friend. So we're talking about that. And they were like, "Ohh, going all by yourself?" I would assume it might feel for them like being tossed out into space with no lifejacket. And I said, "We will be your lifejacket, that's why you will have someone like from my friends." So eventually we will...(*Bob was suddenly shown that he would be helping to introduce and train the young ones on his dimension to be companions for the three little Elahims.*) Ah! That's a treat! I'm gonna be the one taking them down and meet their people they're gonna work with at my place! Oh, that's gonna come up! That's why they're sniffing around me, because they're gonna go with me and I'm gonna be the one showing them around. Ohh, and I'm gonna do interviews now, you said, with certain students from the second dimension, to see which one will be best matched with someone from your group. Oh, that's a great responsibility that I take very seriously, and I'm hugely and greatly honored! Huhuh, that's a treat!

D. That's will be a long commitment for them, since you're signing them up for the whole cycle of incarnations on Earth.

B. I kinda think, though, Tom is on the top of the list. Tom will be disappointed, to say the least, if this gets out that I didn't offer him the same opportunity to grow. BUT, I'm gonna tell him, "There's a big treat coming your way, Tom, but first you have to do certain things." "What treat?" he will say, similar like I did, "What's a treat, what's a treat?" and I will say, "Just think of it as one of the BIGGEST treats that you can receive at this particular point, and just navigate and operate from that understanding, that the greatest treat is on your way. But I'm not gonna tell you what the treat is. No one tells you."

D. It gives you motivation.

B. Ah. But he has certain different things that he also needs to work on before he is given a person. So, what I'm doing is interviews, and I'm going to do some sort of selections. But you can't take one that already has one. They asked if I could come and join them. And I was like, "That's not necessarily how it works. You will get someone LIKE me, but you will have your own individual contact. We don't have several."

D. I don't think there is anyone like you.

B. Nay, nay. They are similar like the sparkles when they wanted Ia to go (*to Earth and merge with trees or rocks*), they said, "Can you come, can you come?" And she said, "No, I'm taking care of the new little ones that come." And all these three wanted me to come, and I said, "That's a huge honor, but we are only assigned one of you."

D. Do the gardeners ever get somebody?

B. Sometimes gardeners can follow, but never souls from here (*the sixth*). They will follow a soul that can be from the fifth.

D. Well, like S— (*a friend in Sweden*), she has a little gardener?

B. Indeed, she has someone, but it's a different characteristic in the gardeners than it is in me. Someone from your home base will get someone like me or someone like Tom. I probably need to pick Tom. I would have been extremely upset if it had come out that Gergen hadn't picked me. I think that's why I was given Tom, to potentially just pass the torch forward of what I do.

D. It seems like there is an intention behind everything that happens.

B. There is always an intention, and you said that (*he imitates me, speaking slowly like a stuffy professor*), "There's always an intention, Bob. Try to find that intention. If there is no intention, then you missed something. So you go back to the drawing board and you find the intention." That's what you said. So, it's a great responsibility, of course, to find a companion for them.

D. Well, congratulations for that.

B. Congratulations to me. Congratulations to them. So that's gonna be, ohh, oh oh, I'm happy! That was a great thing, though, but okay, that probably will be it for today. Maybe I need to rush down and start my interview selection!?

D. You can't tell them, though, can you?

B. I cannot! It's a secret interview. They might wonder, "Why are you asking all these questions?" I'm gonna put up, on the board, that there is assignments coming up relating to Earth and remote teachings, and those who have certain qualifications are welcome to send in an application of interest.

D. I'm sure you'll get plenty.

B. Ah, I'll probably get plenty, and then the selection begins. So, that's fun! Oh, oh, okay, I'll go. But that's happy.

D. Thank you so much for all the wise words today. I really appreciate it.

B. And thank you for giving me the honor of picking friends for your friends, your baby friends. So, okay, they're gonna go into training now about incarnations and study up more on that, and when they are ready at the age of sixteen, then they will go down. So I have a little bit of time, here.

D. To teach them how to hear the walkie–talkie?

B. Indeed, and how it's not like traveling like who they are. They're gonna go through the training now of incarnating, and I'm gonna find the best helper that I can provide. They're gonna have other helpers, too, but these three are gonna have someone following them like I follow you.

D. They're lucky.

Let the Interviews Begin (Jan 28, 2019)

Bob was given the task to go back to the second and find suitable companions for the three little Elahims. He was to select a few good candidates and then evaluate their interest and potential as spirit guides. It seems his strategy was a bit more expansive. He let it be known to large groups of students that he was looking for some volunteers for a secret mission. Then he became inundated with interest. This led to interventions by Ophelia, Ia, Gergen, and Zachariah, to figure out how to not disappoint the students. Most of the volunteers were assigned to act as helpers or guides to other groups from the fifth and seventh.

D. (*After a discussion on other subjects, Bob began telling about his progress with finding companions for the three little Elahims.*) Did you have any notes you wanted to pass along?

B. Ah, I have several, of course, that I have been investigating. But I thought I might share the progress of my interviews! Ahh, it became a huge success!

D. Did you have a lot of interest in the program?

B. Ah, it's a huge line. And I was like, "Everyone will come in, all in due order."

D. Did you let the cat out of the bag, and everybody found out?

B. I kinda put up a note, like you would do in the cafeteria, I put out a note that there was...

D. Did you say, "Bob, the great traveler, is conducting interviews for a secret mission?"

B. A secret mission to assist beings from beyond, who are looking for a friend.

D. Did you actually put that up?

B. Ah, in small letters, but it still was there, and it seemed like everyone saw that. My friends saw it and asked, "Who are we assisting from beyond?" And I said, "That's not to be given at this point, but you're going to be like a tour guide for some who are not familiar with Earth." I had to say that. Before the interviews, Gergen actually came in.

D. Did he lend a hand?

B. Ah, ah. We're actually, at this point, the first selection of interviews was to invite them to the training. It's like a boot camp. You are given a counterpart, so you're working in pairs of two, where you switch, –one is the incarnation and one is a spirit helper; then you switch. In this facility (*Bob made his own school for the interviews and training*), I have been creating different events that can take place (*during an incarnation*). And I have actually used certain experiences in my own knowledge bank from our travels. The final test, that they don't know, is about the fire! First, they are paired up in the school where they're gonna be taking turns and so forth, and then there is me—as the great evaluator. But I didn't think that so many would apply.

D. How many did you get?

B. Oh, it was like eighty to a hundred and twenty, and they just kept on coming. And I was like, "You in the back! Don't spread the word further! So we have a stop after you back there." Tom was in the middle somewhere.

D. Did they have to become like guides, were you trying to get them to communicate with one another?

B. Indeed. And I staged events that could take place. So, at this point, I have selected students for the first round. Because no one wants to feel like they failed, so at the first roundup, I cut the group in half, so they were like forty.

D. That's still a lot, since you only needed three.

B. I only need three, and I have forty at the moment. But I began with one–twenty, eighty to one hundred and twenty. And then I had to say, "We cannot take in everyone. But there might come more later on, and then others can join." So the ones that didn't make the first cut, they are gonna be in the first runner up for the next level, so I'm hoping that I get more. Maybe Julia, or someone from Ophelia's place, can come, so I can continue this. I feel a little bit bad. I didn't expect that there would be such a high interest in assisting someone they didn't know.

D. Well, maybe they're enthusiastic about what you do and they just want to be part of it.

B. It appeared like that, because they said, "We have heard so many of your stories!" And I was like, "Huh, ah." And they said, "We also want to do that, because your stories, there was just so many adventures you seem to have gone on. So we also want to have one of those." And I was like, "Oh, we'll see about that." So sometimes talking too much can backfire, –and it kinda did. So, I learned my lesson here, that I should probably not have blown my horn so frequently. Huhuh. Anyway, so I had interviews and I asked questions, like, "What would you do if your person went missing?" And they were like, "Where would the person have gone?" And I said, "That is the question! If you don't know where the person has gone, what would you do to find them? What tricks would you use to find your person?"

D. Did you ever lose your person?

B. I did. I lost you a couple of times.

D. Really? You couldn't tune in on me? (*Within the mental realm, the level of the fourth dimension, your soul is always conversing with your spirit guides, a fact of which we are generally oblivious.*)

B. Well, from my perspective, you lost me. You disappeared out of my radar zone. But you said that I disappeared, and I said, "No, I'm pretty sure you disappeared, because I was right here all along, on my spot." And you said, "No, because your spot changed. It's not the same spot." And I said, "I'm still in my spot." So we had to understand that when you are in charge of helping an individual, then you have to think as the individual. Where is this person gonna go? Because it's different, it's like, ohh—

D. Well, when I'm wandering around on Earth, you can find me anywhere, can't you?

B. I can indeed, now, of course. But in the beginning, I kinda found that you sort of trotted off.

D. So what's the correct answer to your quiz?

B. My quiz, the answer to the question, "How can I find my person when my person is missing?" The trick is to not run around like a chicken, but to remain centered and to listen for that melody that the two of you will have established, and that is how I found you. The first time I ran around calling, "La–Sa–Ray! Lasaray! Lasaray!" and I probably missed you a lot of times, because I was just hearing my own voice saying, "La–Sa–Ray! Lasaray! Lasaray!" And then, I said, "Nope! Let Lasaray come to me. I'm gonna stay put and I'm gonna listen and I'm gonna send out my signal and my song to Lasaray, and he will find ME."

D. Did that work?

B. It did, most times. So, there were interviews about certain topics, and some were just curious, they just came to have a listen. And I said, "You don't really have the qualifications yet, do ya'? You're still in sparkle school." And they were like, "Well, you told such a funny story one time, so I'm interested!" and I said, "I'm sure you are, and we're gonna talk about this more, but this is like a hands–on project." So I said, "You all are gonna go into a separate school, where you're gonna see the documentaries of what everyone else are doing." So, I don't want them to feel like they are left out. So they're gonna watch the documentary of this bootcamp training! That might make them want to wait a while.

D. You'll have to change the questions, later.

B. I'm gonna change my questions.

D. What else are you going to do to them to weed some out?

B. Well, I have to weed them out because I only need three! They're in this remote teaching school, where they're observing different activities that can happen, and it has to be up–to–date. You can't have like a wooden ship, if there's not any wooden ships to be found. And here comes the expertise of Ole and those in the higher councils, because they know what's gonna come when it is time for high action. So I know what's gonna come for you, what you do. But your little students and mine are gonna be training over here, but when it's time for high action, who knows what the world is gonna look like then?

D. Did Gergen have any idea what the world would look like when the three come down?

B. Ah, but I was not allowed to be participating.

D. That's too bad, because I was going to ask you.

B. Huhuh, I'm pretty sure that's why I'm not invited! But, it's not like they tell the students and not tell me. But they create scenarios that's gonna be mirroring, somewhat, the reality at that point. I sneaked peeked.

D. Can you give me an example?

B. Ah, it's different vehicles (*human bodies*), absolutely. Everything is more quiet, and things are flying more. Everyone looks more the same.

D. Is it still a human-looking vehicle?

B. Ah, but the atmosphere has changed, so the humanoid, yes, indeed they are, but they look different, they're slimmer. No one is fat, it seems, or overweight. (*He said this delicately, but he was clearly making fun of how sensitive people are.*) Everyone seems slimmer. But there is something with the atmosphere, so they have to protect themselves. The skin is sensitive. Everyone looks the same, they're wearing somewhat of a suit thing.

D. Are there still a lot of Caucasians, white people?

B. Ah. But thin. More thin. Taller, thin.

D. This must be after the upgrade?

B. Ah. This is way ahead. Anyway, so I'm doing that, I'm working with my training school and I have to weed them out.

D. Do you think Tom is going to make the cut? Is he qualified?

B. Ah. He is highly qualified, and he comes after class every day to make sure that he is qualified, and wants to know if there is anything he should do to become more qualified, if he's not.

D. It's good he's enthusiastic. He's a little star.

B. He's enthusiastic. He is a star indeed, in his mind. But I kinda feel a little bit bad about weeding them out. So actually, one of my notes were if I could have more from you?

D. Did you ask Gergen?

B. I asked you. I asked if I could have more than the three, because I have forty! Huhuh. And you said, "You have forty?" and I said, "Yeah, it sort of became like that." You said, "How did it become forty? You were just going to look around for ten, tops, and then quietly proceed." And I said, "I was kinda quiet," and you said,

"Tell me exactly what happened here." And I said, "Well, I put up a note and said there was gonna be a high mission of helping individuals from beyond that are going to Earth. And there were people very interested in that. And then word spread, and it just kept spreading. And suddenly they were all over the place, and then it became like that." And then you said, "Well, I gave you three, and now you want forty?" And I said, "Well, maybe we can meet in the middle somewhere, and I can get like thirty-five?" And you said, "That's not in the middle!" and I said, "Well, from eighty, it is." So we kinda laughed about that. But I see that I made a little bit of a problem.

D. You'll have to think of something to make them feel not too bad about getting cut.

B. Nay. I'm thinking about that. Anyway, that was my note for today, that I am in the middle of training and selection and so forth.

D. What does Ia think about all this?

B. Oh, Ia, she just shook her head and said, "What's going on over here, Bob?" And I said, "I have interviews." And she said, "This almost looks like a rock concert. Why are they all here?" And I said, "I had a note," and she said, "Yes, I saw your note, but it almost felt like anyone could come." I said, "That was not my intention." And she said, "Now you have to solve this."

D. You had everybody from the fifteen–year olds down to the sparkles.

B. Well, like down to the seven–year olds. I said, "This is not like going to the 4–H Farm, it's not the same at all." So anyway, we're saving energy now, Ophelia says, but I wanted to pop by and just share.

D. We had a separate session because we wanted to hear your ideas.

B. Separate session—my stage.

D. We knew you wanted to talk.

B. I kinda did. And we will have to continue this talk about my recruiting business. Because I don't want to fail, I want to do this again. But at the moment, you said, "You have three. This is what you learn, Bob. You have to learn how to do with what you have."

D. Manage the crowd.

B. Manage the crowd. Maybe I can offer them something else? We'll see.

D. They can be backups.

B. I kinda thought that they could be like those who are in the background.

D. Gergen said about ten to twelve percent of the people here have someone from the second following them.

B. But I am selecting for the three from the sixth, and that's different. It's different criteria. But I did ask if I could have more from you, and it didn't seem like I could. So I'm now going to Ophelia, and I'm seeing if I can maybe have someone from there.

D. I bet there will be a few that come down.

B. Indeed. So I'm probably gonna do that, because Ophelia, she can see the end result of the commotion here, that it would be a sadness, and no one wants sadness. So we might pick someone from her place. Or Zachariah, he is always very helpful, he also came by and said, "There are actually those ready from the factory to come down to the Earth." Zachariah was helpful indeed. He said, "If you feel like someone is doing good, then we will give them someone from here." (*Zachariah specializes in training souls who have advanced technical or scientific missions. Most of the souls on Earth now are from the fifth, but only a handful are in Zachariah's programs.*)

D. I would think a lot of the training is similar?

B. Ah. I have all the gardeners also here. They are here with their shovels, and they want to help too. So Zachariah came, and Ophelia; so you, Zachariah and Ophelia are all here to help. Initially I was only gonna interview for the three. But it became such a merry occasion, so now we are creating a school for more. And then they don't have to feel so discouraged, because they will also get one, but they will not get one of the three.

D. You can make it a more general education for everyone else?

B. Indeed. I will see if they might be better suited for someone from Ophelia's realm. So I might be more like a puppet master at that. Now, when I have more at my disposal to use, then I might invite the other forty that I cut off.

D. You might become the headmaster of a school for spirit guides and incarnations.

B. Ah, because I did have eighty to a hundred and twenty.

D. You've had a lot of experience being a guide, so maybe this is something you're going to take on—training sparkles to become guides.

B. So, that's what we're gonna go. But Zachariah, he came by and said, "If there is anyone who feels like they're left out, I will gladly oblige and provide some from my factory." And Ophelia, she doesn't call it a factory, she says, "We have lights that can be sent." And you were like, "You got three from me, that's what you got." So you're more stiff. We'll see about that. Oh, I'm gonna go now, but it became more of an involved project.

D. Well, live and learn.

B. Ah. Hehehe. Oh, anyway, I go now, but okay, see you soon.

D. Alright, my friend, thank you for coming.

B. Ah. Okay. Bye bye.

A Training Camp for Guides (Feb 3, 2019)

D. So there was never a formal class on the second to teach people how to work with their person?

B. Ah, the classes were about remote teaching.

D. So when you were training you didn't really have a school to go to?

B. Nay, I was taught to work with transmission and communication, but I didn't have my person there. You were not on the other end, so I was just, like when you are going out in space and you sit in those...

D. Simulator?

B. Simulator, indeed. So, I felt like it was important that you had someone to train on. We did have friends to train on in class, so indeed, it was in that sense a class, but I now have different obstacles in my training school, because we had different experiences. And this training school that I set up is actually gonna be for those from the sixth. I went to a general school, like a public school, and this is gonna be like a specialist school, because the three that are coming down from you are a little bit different.

D. How many people are you training for this?

B. We are now about twenty.

D. Oh, you cut it in half, again?

B. Ah, I send the other ones to the regular, the public school, but this is the specialist school that I am conducting. To go here, then you have to have personal experience in guiding someone from the sixth, someone like you, because they are the same as you. Not everyone is the same in the different realities. Like on my reality, it would be like saying that everyone would be gardeners—and we're not. It's the same thing on all realities, so everyone on the sixth are not the same. So I'm training for those who are like the two of you.

D. Did Tom make the cut?

B. Tom is still in, he's working here. It's different, because it's different in your physique when you come in. They have to look at different signs and signals than like the gardeners, when they get someone from Zachariah's factory, they're gonna observe things differently.

D. Can you give me an example?

B. Like the physical, for instance. When the two of you have traveled here, it's been different, you report different things about the physical. Like in your case here with the skin, and this one did that before. But your personality, the personality that you travel with is different, normally, so there is a different need from you from the caretaker (*the spirit guide*) than those from like the fifth, for instance. Because the fifth, they are more at home here, so there is not happening that much within their inner experiences in the same way. So the physical might look the same, but the inner experience is different, and we address the inner, the soul, differently with you. Because you are in some way separated within from the physical experience, where the other ones are more merged. It's like guiding two—I guide the soul in the car and then I also take care of the car itself, like I'm a mechanic. So I have to be a mechanic as well as a therapist, if it makes sense to you.

D. It does, it does indeed.

B. So there you go, that's what I do. So these can not only tend to the car, they have to also be observant about what could go on inside, because the three that are coming, they are gonna be sometimes operating like you did with the brain, and then you have to measure and balance when you need to tend to the vehicle more closely, so it doesn't happen like it burns up. The other ones (*from the fifth*) are easier to reach, because they are like one, they are connected in some way, so you send your full information and your full attention directly to that being that you are following. But with the Elahim, you might need to adjust, similar like talking human language, or talking spiritual language, and then you have to also know the spiritual language that your person inside understands. Whereas when you communicate with the other ones, you simply remote teach and it's instantly heard in different ways, or not heard at all, in some cases. It's hard to give a picture, really, it's just that it is dual, the job, when you have someone from your area of the sixth. Like I said, not everyone from the sixth are the same.

D. Okay, I follow that, that's a really good explanation. If Ophelia sends a soul from the seventh to incarnate, could any of your students help work as a guide?

B. If they have the training, indeed they can. Probably someone that Ia selected. Ia has different criteria.

D. Was she helping you out a little bit?

B. A little bit. I asked her, –because we're all family, so she knew some of them–, so I did ask for a background check on some of them.

D. Are there any gardeners in the group?

B. No, they're gonna go with Zachariah, and I told them that. (*He then spoke slowly, in a loud, clear voice, as if he were addressing a large crowd*) "There is a great opportunity coming up. I just heard word that there are an abundance of souls from my friend Zachariah that is coming in to assist the planet and the environment." And I said, "They specifically asked for someone who is familiar, closely, with the environment. Who in this vast group feel like they are encouraged to assist pioneers coming to Earth to assist the environment?" And then all shovels came up. (*Meaning all the gardeners in his group raised their hands.*) And I said, "Great! Please leave your name and you will be contacted as soon as I have heard word from this hub of departing souls that are coming down. You will be going into separate training, because there are different criteria for those specific souls. Thank you." And then there was still too many. So I said, "I have also been given word that there is gonna come down souls from beyond, another level, that is gonna help with healing certain emotional disasters (*problems*) within this humanoid. They're gonna take on certain emotional experiences, and they are in need of a guiding hand that is very empathic and have a great ability to listen and who will be able to radiate warmth to their friends."

D. And a lot of little hands came up?

B. A lot of little hands came up. And this is also when Ia came, and she said, "I have a lot of them who really wants to help with souls coming in, assisting on the emotional level, and to work with certain things like loneliness. There's gonna be souls coming in that are gonna take on lives where they feel like they are in solitude and lonely, and they might need two (*guides*)," she said, "coming down for those missions. So, who here feels like they want to be like a big nanny?" And there were several, because some of them have already been in the nursery with Ia. So there were several raising their little hands for that. Mine is gonna be more in charge of changing, there's gonna be a shift of scientific and energetic knowledge, resources of the energy, so it's gonna be different with these three.

D. Which time frame do you think they are coming down in?

B. Well, I'm not sure if they are gonna be in that slim version I mentioned earlier. Like you came down furry one time, before you came down in this (*nodding towards me*), so I'm thinking we're not that far ahead, it's somewhat of an urgency. So I'm pretty sure that these three will begin to come down, Ophelia says, in about a hundred and fifty to two hundred years. So it's not that far off. But then again, I don't know if that would be similar like you coming down in the ape shape. But they still need someone to take care of them. The first time it's rough; you feel lost, and they're not gonna travel together—the Elahim never do, normally. Like the two of you coming like this, it's not very common. And that is also a different teaching, because they will have to know that their main person is gonna travel with someone or souls from other locations (*other dimensions*), to Earth. So they might feel a little bit like they operate independently. I'm not sure that my people from second would like to go by themselves like that, like a solo artist.

D. Like you? You're kind of a solo artist.

B. Ah, but I mean going to Earth as a solo artist. Those from the factory, they go together in a big group from the same area of the fifth. (*The souls from the fifth often incarnate in big groups, and are surrounded by friends from home.*)

D. This one and I have shared a few lives together, haven't we?

B. Ah, a few, some, indeed. One with a boat.

D. What about in Scotland? (*Christine has vivid memories of this lifetime when we were together.*)

B. Ah, in Scotland, too. This was around 823, 825 AD. 800 to 900 there. But you were, you know, this one tried to help you with, –there was an emotional distress that took place in your family, because the little one died. And you shut off the whole world, and this one tried to help you connect with healing energies. You wanted to see how great loss would be experienced in a human vehicle. So there was a soul, a friend from Ophelia (*the seventh dimension*), that took on a short life as a child. And when it left, you really had a struggle to send your soul awareness into the heart center and brain to calm this sadness that took place. But you were, again, monitoring behavior. And in that life, one of the things you wanted to explore and to investigate was how loss and sadness can take over all realities within you. And how it's like all centers within just shut down; and how one could assist that being, oneself that is, to understand that growth comes from loss. This one helped you, and eventually, with different techniques and assistance, and myself included, you did start to see the light within the darkness. Because you created more darkness, instead of seeing the little light that existed, and then you saw that this is very common for a humanoid, that when sadness strikes, or loss, that everything becomes very dark and black—black and white. The mission was how to create, from within a world that appears to be black and white, how to create it in color again. And one of the things you investigated was the assistance that one got in nature, –and I was there. So this one helped you and said you should go out and listen to nature. So you were out on your horse a lot, and your horse was also helping—I communicated there too, so you felt the warmth and tremendous compassion from your horse and within nature. You sat down by a creek. There was water, and you started to see the fairies. And in that experience, you felt the greatest gratitude for having, for being given, even if short, that experience and time with your daughter who disappeared. And when that took place, that you felt gratitude for even having her in your presence, then everything started to look in color again. And you started, from that point, to see that you could communicate within you directly to her. And you said, "Even if she's not here in physical, she's here in every other aspect of her being. And even if I can't touch her, she's still as real to me now as when she was in physical." Then, with that understanding, the world took color again. Others thought you were a little bit crazy, but this one, who was your wife, she encouraged that. She said, "You just have your relationship directly with her." And you did. And in that sense, you were different because you were detached from the human experience of the loss. And others were coming to you saying, "Oh, I'm so sorry for your loss," And then, at that point in the story, you had healed, because you said, "No, she's not lost, she's still here, and I communicate with her in the same way." And then others came and said, "But you can't hug her in the same way, it must be devastating." And you said, "No, I hug her inside, I hug her in my dreams. I can hug her all the time. When she was in physical, I didn't sit and hug her all the time. Now I can."

D. Wow. That's a really good story.

B. Anyway, so I'm gonna go now.

Bob Brings a Catalogue to Zachariah (Feb 8, 2019)

After Bob began training his students from the second to become guides, he started to worry about who they might be paired up with. He was concerned that they might be disappointed with their partner, especially when it came to new souls from the fifth who are fresh from the factory, so to speak. So Bob made a catalogue with a detailed analysis of each of his young friends and began searching for compatible spirits in the fifth, sixth, and seventh. Pairing of souls has been going on since incarnations began on Earth, but it has usually been done by councils and mentors. Bob brought his catalogue to Zachariah, who was mildly amused. But he appreciated Bob's methodology, and the dedication and concern he had for his students.

Z. Good evening to you. This is Zachariah.

D. Zachariah! Well, well—welcome my friend.

Z. Well, there is a little bit of an issue we need to address. Issue might be the wrong word, but a matter at hand that has been put forward. Issue indeed, because there isn't enough to go around for the journey ahead for our Little Friend's friends from the second.

D. Meaning what?

Z. Friends to assist other friends! Bob pointed out, he said, "Isn't it a factory, indeed?" And I said, "Well, it's not a factory in that respect, that we just go and create randomly, –it's not an ice cream store. When ice cream runs out because of the nice weather, you just put an extra effort and more ice creams will come. It's a little bit more preparation behind creating souls from the factory, than an ice cream." And then he (*Bob*) indicated also that he had demands on these factory–made ice creams, indeed! So he came not only with a box of notes for his friends to be happy with the one they will be paired up with, but he also came with a whole catalogue of identifications on these students. He came in and said, "This one will not do good with someone who has too much temper, because this specific student is very gentle. So for this one I would like to have a soul that is more tender in its persona." He put that note down and then took another note, "This one however, would need a little bit more of an excitement character." So, he came with this whole catalogue into the office, and he had put in great effort indeed in detailing and categorizing these sparkle friends, making sure I knew exactly what ice cream to create in the factory.

D. Well, he took it very seriously, his assignment.

Z. He still does.

D. He's trying very hard to do his job well.

Z. So here we sit with a catalogue of students and all their criteria, personality traits, needs and wishes—not all are their own, I would assume. Then he said, "I would also like to see your catalogue of what is coming from the factory." And I said, "We don't really have a catalogue, it is, like I said, not like an ice cream factory. It's not like we have a poster of different souls, and it is way beyond the level of, I wouldn't say, expertise, but what I am allowed to do. I am not the one manufacturing the new ice cream brand." But he wanted to make sure it was a good match, so he said, "I might take this catalogue elsewhere." And he smiled about that. So I said, "Where are you going to go then, Bob?" and he said, "I might go to Ophelia's place." And I'm pretty sure he's already been there with his catalogue. So, he's trying indeed, he's like a matchmaker, I would say.

D. We started with a need for three, and he has well in excess of a hundred young ones that are interested.

Z. He has indeed become a matchmaker for destination Earth. He had a little bit of, it's not a poster, but it's a little bit of a business card, almost, where he calls himself a messenger and matchmaker, a travel agency. This is what he has designed, a complete experience travel agency, destination Earth. So he has become, on his own design, a tour guide for all these sparkles. And indeed, matchmaking, because of the fact he wants to make sure of the compatibility—and I do appreciate the idea and intent behind it. However, even the most melted ice cream needs assistance. Even if it's only a plain vanilla ice cream that is headed for its purpose, it is still, based on all karmic laws and ideas of development and evolution, it still is granted a spirit friend.

D. Not everyone gets a spirit from the second. How, in the past, has it been handled? Who does the matching?

Z. It's council work, between the second and seventh, mainly. Fifth has progressively been taking over. More coming from the fifth needs assistance from the second. Due to the fact that destination Earth needs more attention, and we wish there to be a presence from the second as a spirit helper, remotely teaching this new ice cream. But indeed, amusement indeed, where we sit and go through this catalogue.

D. Are you going to try and supply a few souls for him?

Z. Absolutely. I already have some friends, they're not brand-new from the factory, of course, but still ready for departure. So I asked, "Who do you feel, in this vast catalogue, will be ready for high action and to go and help? I have some who are in training; geologists, biologists, marine biologists, -not marine like you think, not the army. And he did, he flipped to the very end in his catalogue and he did have five that he felt was more progressed and ready for departure. So I said, "Let's just begin with these five, and I will bring you five. Then we will mix and match these ten. So we will begin there with the easier ones who are ready for departure.

D. What does Gergen think about this?

Z. Gergen didn't see how this could spiral outward the way it did. He came and did have some concerns about the wave of activity. But he did indeed applaud his spirit of taking on the project. He said, "I haven't seen him so excited down here in a long time. He's not as excited in council work, but this really fired him up." So, he is grateful for this opportunity for Bob. He said, "He is unique in that way that he works best if he is excited about something. If he feels like it is moving too slow or if he doesn't feel engaged fully, then he tends to drift." Gergen had the intention of making him more excited by bringing him the three, to start interviews. He did not, however, foresee the outcome of placing a note in the study area about all these opportunities. Created somewhat of a commotion down there. Well, there you go.

D. Sometimes that can be a good thing. I've really missed talking with you. You kind of disappeared after the first wave.

Z. Not really disappeared. I have archiving to do. I'm moving archives around; some will go to the destination that you call Siah's place (*Etena*). So indeed, there are different ideas and memories that will be removed from this location and stored in that vast library where Siah is.

D. I'm really happy that you're helping. He assumed you would step in and fill the void.

Z. Oh, yes, he assumed. He assumed both me and Ophelia and everyone else would chip in. He said, "Maybe if you run out of souls, maybe someone from Ari's place can join?" And I said, "So, you want us to give you someone from the tenth, who don't even come to Earth anymore?" And he said, "Well, they might want to come if they have a good friend like I'm gonna train this friend to be—the kindest, best friend they could ever want. So maybe they'll want to come if I have someone like that providing a guidance for them?" He has an interesting view of the way things work.

D. Well, it's precious.

Z. So it is. There you go. I'm pretty sure we have someone here who will continue the discussion.

D. It's truly a pleasure to hear from you again. I hope you come back soon, because we miss talking with you.

Z. Oh, I'm always on standby, especially now. There you go. I'll see you, my friend.

D. Okay. Goodbye.

B. (*Bob came right in, popping his lips.*) Ahh! Huhuhuhhuh! Deet–de–deet–de deet. Thank you, Zachariah, for coming today and providing your views.

D. Did you listen?

B. Half and half.

D. Did you appreciate what was saying?

B. Ah. It is a joined effort, and I have been a little bit concerned about giving all these precious friends to someone who is not gonna appreciate them. So suddenly I felt like my enthusiasm came to a stop, because I was like, "Who are you matching my friends with, and what are they gonna do?" So I didn't want to make my friends all excited after training them in all these different manners, and then have someone who clearly might not do good. So I said, "I want to have someone who is gonna do good." And then Ophelia came, and Isaac came, and Jeshua came, everyone came and they said, "This is like bypassing evolution again." And I said, "I'm not bypassing evolution. I simply say that it's appreciated if my friends will get someone who is gonna do something good, or be nice." And they said, "Well, you're not casting for Siah's world, you're casting for Earth and the lessons are different there." And then I said, "Maybe I should instead cast for Siah's world. Because then mine are friendly, and they are friendly."

D. There's hardly any need for someone to guide on that planet.

B. Bhah! Bhah! (*He then made a spitting sound.*) You sound exactly like Zachariah! He said, "There's no need to go through all this work and training, if you're just going to send them to Siah's place." And I said, "Well, maybe so, but..." Then Isaac came. Isaac is the one that comes when I get a little bit winded up (*wound up*) by evolution. So Isaac came and said, "Why don't you and I go for a walk, Bob?" and I said, "Where are we gonna go?" And he said, "You and I are just going to stroll here a little bit." It was in like a forest kind of thing here on the fifth, where we met, and he said, "Why don't you tell me exactly what your concerns are?" And I said, "That's very kind that you asked about my concerns." And he said, "Well, go back and think when you first joined with Lasaray." And I said, "Well, he didn't fully understand how to navigate on Earth," and he said, "Look how good the relationship has become." And I said, "It is a really good relationship. But he listened. What if I get someone for my friend who's not gonna listen?" And then so we walked and we talked about that, and I said, "I just don't want there to be disappointment." But he said, "You can go back and remember certain lives with Lasaray, when he came back, he understood everything that he had done on Earth that might appear from the spirit realm as a disappointment. But when you met again as friends, then you were as tight as ever in your friend–couple unit. So you have to differentiate, separate, the Earth visit and the friend. So, tell your students they are going to get a nice friend who might appear differently when they leave (*the spirit realm*), and how they can assist that friend to remember the real individual that they are."

D. That was good advice.

B. So he said, "Evolution is to let this friend go into an environment and to grow from that experience, and to repeatedly go back, and more and more they can take credit for that. And he said, "You took credit for a lot of Lasaray's advancement, didn't you?" I said, "Yes, indeed. I did indeed. I took absolutely credit for certain advancements. Like when he did a wheel thing one time that was to create, like in the water, to create energy, and I actually popped that idea into his head. So I took credit for that." And he said, "And they can do that." So as we walked though this little forest, I became more calm. And he said, "Don't you want your friends to have an amazing friendship and experiences like you've had with Lasaray?" And I said, "Yes, indeed," and he said, "Think of certain lives that Lasaray had, were they all very charming?" And I said, "Nooo!" and he said, "Look at this one, what if I abandoned this one just because of certain lives that were like, uh–oh, what is going on over there? But I am a friend and I'm assisting the soul," he said, "and it's almost like being a parent to the incarnation. You're a friend to the soul, but you're like a parent to the incarnation." That's what he said.

D. That's really profound. He's very wise.

B. He's intelligent and he always makes me calm. So he said, "That is evolution, to separate, to understand that the soul is maybe equal and on your own level, so you are friends, but the incarnation is a child. As a spirit guide," he said, "you shift and turn friendship versus being a parent. So that's when you step into the role of being a spirit guide when you start to remote teach, is that you have to sometimes lose the grip of being a friend, that you are instead being a parent or a teacher." So that's what he said. So, when I heard that, then I said, "Maybe I will move that forward to my students." And he said, "You can use this as your idea, if you want to." And I said, "I might actually do that." And I did. I said (*then he began repeating what he said to his students, as if he were on stage in a big lecture hall, loudly enunciating the speech*), "Once you move into remote teaching, first you will become and build up a friendship with this soul that you are given. Are you ready for this assignment? Can I hear a HOO–HA?" So I did. This is this group of five that's gonna go with Zachariah first, because the other ones are still in training, and that cannot be rushed, because there's specific things they're gonna do that I'm not fully up to speed with yet, so we're not releasing them yet. BUT there are a certain five that are ready to go. So I said, "Can I hear a HOO–HA for those who are ready to meet their friend from the level of five, which is beyond?" And some of them (*his students*) have been to five (*the fifth*), so they're no rookies. Then we're gonna sit down and pair them up. And I said, "You're gonna first be friends and learn and enjoy this new friend of yours. Let them know about where you come from as much as you learn about where they come from. So after that, they are gonna take on a different persona and then you are no longer friends, you are more a parent in the beginning. The more this soul comes back to Earth, then they are not gonna need a parent anymore, so you will become a friend on both locations. But in the beginning, Isaac said, then you are supposed to, when there is the departure, you are supposed to enter the role of a parent. But as you do this more and more you become a friend." That's what I told my students. But like when you go, I'm not a parent anymore, I'm a friend, – the same both here and at home. But in the beginning, since you were so clumsy, then indeed it was like taking care of an infant. So this is how Isaac said, the first couple of lives, the parent they have to transform into will take care of an infant. Later they will take care of a five–year–old, and so forth. Once they reach somewhat of an adulthood, then you can drop the parent part and just become friends. Your partner or friend might still go, like you do, but it's not like taking care of an infant anymore.

D. Have you met the other souls on five?

B. I have, indeed.

D. What are they going to be working on?

B. One is gonna go and work with the curve. He's gonna come down and assist in some sort of engineering to monitor the curves underground. And he's gonna invent an instrument that will balance, or first of all, find the imbalances. It's gonna be an interesting journey with that one! ("*Curves*" *are Bob's way of describing the vibrations or natural fields emitted by the Earth.*)

D. That's a good one. Tom and his friends, the ones you are joining up with the sixth, they're not ready yet, are they?

B. Tom is not going with these. Tom is in special training to get one of yours, because they're gonna work on more of an energetic level. They're gonna be working on communication. They're gonna go down and they're gonna be working with telepathic communication skills, and they're gonna be progressing in that field. Maybe we should go too! That sounds interesting; I don't want to miss that. It will be like Tom comes and tells me, and I feel completely left out—if you're not gonna go.

D. Well, it's like with Gergen and you, you work together, so doesn't Gergen help sometimes with Lasaray's issues?

B. He helps if I have an issue with Lasaray, then I go to Gergen and Gergen and I talk, and then I adjust.

D. I'm sure you'll have the same responsibility.

B. Ah, that's true. I might not be hands on.

D. You'll have 20 of them coming to you, asking for advice.

B. Ah, it became more than expected. And some of them are over with Ia and they're singing, so those are gonna go with Ophelia. She kinda took them back and she's working with creating energy. They're gonna work with transmitting light energies in different regions, so they're gonna get someone from Ophelia's place.

D. That's good. How many did Ophelia offer you?

B. Thirty.

D. I gave you three, and she gave you thirty?

B. I got five from Zachariah. I'm almost up to my forty here!

D. He's going to give you more, though, he said.

B. I guess he will, because I put in great effort into categorizing their skills that I have found, so far.

D. That's what he said. He said you've done a remarkable job on that.

B. But then I said, "Are all necessarily needed on Earth?"

D. Where did you want them to go?

B. I offered my—not my best, necessarily, and I wouldn't say that anyone is at this point better than anyone else—but I said, because some of them are a little bit tender, so I said, "I have a group here of like (*mumbles as he is counting*), fourteen. And I thought they could go to Siah's place and help someone who goes there. Maybe be of assistance to take care of Siah and just be of assistance to...(*he fades to quiet as he is thinking*).

D. How was that received?

B. He said that there is not the same evolution over there. It would be like them going to visit someone on the fifth or on the seventh. And then I said, "Well, maybe we can begin like that." And he said, "No one from Siah's place is going to, at this point, incarnate on Earth. They might later, but they have already done that lesson." Then I said, "Why did I get like the crap destination?" And he said, "Don't call it a crap destination. It is the one that is evolving to become like Siah's place." And I said, "Okay. How far away is that, before it's evolved into becoming like Siah's place?" and then he said, "Now you're trying to bypass evolution again, Bob." And I said, "No, I don't think so, I just need a little bit of a gauge stick, to somewhat know what to prepare them for." Then he said, "You're not allowed to fully prepare them, because there is a joint development on both sides." So, we talked about that.

D. Earth is a pretty rough place sometimes.

B. But it's also, like he said, "Don't forget about all the beauty that exists here, and all the beautiful souls that come here. Observe the beauty and the kindness and you will see that there are several places that are similar like Siah's place." And then he brought me to a place where we watched sort of a documentary. And I could see certain things that I had indeed neglected to notice, that I had kind of overlooked. And just to see, and I think that is a sadness amongst you humans that you are sometimes forgetting, like I did, the beauty and kindness and empathy that exists among you and around you. So, find those, because when you find a light, your light increases. If you find darkness, then your light will dim.

D. That's really good advice. Pick your friends wisely.

B. And your light will increase. Do wrongly and yours will dim. And that's no good. So, if you feel like your light is dimming, meaning that you might be drawn to negativity, like negative thoughts and actions and so forth, it might be that something in your surrounding is actually dimming your light. It could be a person, it could an event, it could be a setting that you are in.

So you need to be aware of that. Is this person, is this environment, is this event, is this location, is it increasing my light or is it dimming it?

D. That's really good advice.

B. So, that's part of the training. I'm not gonna be too long in the tooth here. (*We talked about OBEs for a little bit, before he left, but that information will be included in Wave 3.*)

Where Did They Go? (Feb 12, 2019)

This session is interesting because it gives a glimpse into the organization of the classes and activities in the spiritual realms. Bob had lost track of some of his students and ran around looking for them.

O. I will go first. This is Ophelia. Bob is on high action today. He's been running around with notes and calculating the students. Apparently, some had gone missing and his notes did not match the original list he had. So he came up to me to see if someone was lost and had navigated up to my class, where we were having the musical or the instrumental classes. Then he burst in, wondering if some of his students had potentially gone missing and ended up here. And I said, "How would that happen, Bob? You know that they cannot travel without companionship." And he said, "I have a lost a couple, and I don't know where they are," and I said, "They are not here at the moment, Bob." And he excused himself, and I'm pretty sure that you were next. So he took off and he ran around, and Zachariah also reported a visit indeed, looking for these lost little students.

D. He might have had better luck asking Ia.

O. Probably, or Gergen.

D. It's kind of hard to lose sparkles, isn't it?

O. You would think so.

D. Did you ever lose yours?

O. No. But his list did not match the reality, and this is where confusion hit. Then he started to run around looking for them, wanting to know if he had put them in another classroom, because they are indeed, at the moment, in different classrooms, gathering and connecting with the different souls that they are supposedly to be paired up with. And he has been given a huge amount from me and Julia.

D. That's nice of you.

O. So Julia indeed is in charge of, from our level (*the seventh*), this group of twenty–eight or twenty–nine.

D. That's about thirty, so Zachariah must have offered a few up.

O. It's still not enough, he declared. But I did say that not everyone might necessarily feel that they are ready for departure, even though it might sound interesting. It's similar when you read up on an adventure or a journey you might wish to engage in or to take on, BUT when the date approaches, one can hesitate and have different concerns or even fears. It could be anything, it could be the travel equipment, airplanes, in this case (*as a human*), or it could be something else that the soul or the human would not feel ready to engage in. "So, even though," I said to him, "you have a hundred and twenty, if that is the case—". "And rising," he said. And I said, "No. No, no, no. It's not going to be rising anymore, Bob. We will have to be selective."

D. Ah, he doesn't know how to say no.

O. He doesn't know how to say no, and that's also one of his new teachings. He had never been in that situation where he had to say no. So, that is a whole new teaching coming his way, that he has to be selective as well. And he has to set an example to see where and whether someone is ready for this kind of adventure. But, like I said, it's similar to a human who might say, "Oh, I wish to jump out of a plane," or, "I would like to climb a mountain." When the date or occasion arrives, one can have second thoughts. And it's the same for all souls. It doesn't matter if it's a sparkle from the second dimension, or if it's someone from our reality and our schools. Reading up on something is very different, but once you are set to take on that adventure, there are hesitations; and it's the same on all levels. So I told him, even though you have a hundred and twenty, "and rising," he said, I said that some will still fall off, because not everyone will feel that they are ready, or they might have other engagements. But he is running around a little bit.

D. In the past, have most of the sparkles been assigned someone to take care of?

O. If they feel like they are ready. It's the same thing with all souls, –nothing is pushed. When a soul feels the calling of travel, the spirit helpers and coaches assist that travel to take place. But even to the last second, if a soul doesn't feel ready to do so, it is not pushed. However, the intention of his training program, that he was assigned, was to indeed have a specific purpose, similar like a bootcamp, for those three he was given. And those do not have the same option. They are trained to jump out of that airplane, if you like. It's not like having options, to give you similarity for your training, your army—if someone is just trained to watch a fire or be a chef, then no one is expecting him to jump out of a plane. But if you are trained to jump out of a plane, it is not acceptable to simply say, "I would prefer to just watch the fire." So great effort is taking place in teaching those three and others from sixth dimension as well as the seventh, for future travels. So that will be a little bit different. However, those who will come from Zachariah's...

D. Factory?

O. That's what you call it.

D. That's what he called it.

O. Those have a little bit more options to potentially not go, if they are not ready. They don't have the same training, as they might not go down, all of them, with the same agenda.

D. Is there a difference in how souls are guided? I know Bob follows me very closely, and you also follow me, along with Jeshua, Eli, and others, but is the day–to–day stuff left to Bob?

O. I would say so. After you grew up (*in this life, as Dave*), a lot of the day–to–day guidance Bob covers, and he discusses it with me and Jeshua. When you were younger, I tended to you more frequently, together with Bob. Not Jeshua, really, he let you be.

D. Well, I'm glad you were there. (*She then gave some information about the future work, before taking her leave.*) Very good. Thank you for that.

O. Oh, you are much welcome. And yes, Bob, it is your turn.

D. Oh, he finally showed up?

O. Oh, he has been here all along. But he doesn't run around, at least. So, there you go.

D. Thank you, Ophelia. It's always nice to hear your voice.

O. Until next time. Thank you.

B. (*Bob came in making a gagging sound.*)

D. Popped right in, eh?

B. Ahh. Ha lalalalalalala. I've been out and about, you know?

D. I heard you lost your students.

B. They kinda disappeared on me. They were moving around and I had not been fully informed of their whereabouts, and how some were moving around.

D. Where did they go?

B. Some that I had on my list, that were supposed to be with Ia, when I came there to talk to them, they were not there, and others were there that I did not have on my list. And then I got confused, and I had my catalogue and I said, "I'm looking for this and this and this—where are they?" And Ia said, "Maybe they are with Ophelia." And I said, "They can't just shuffle off and go places without me knowing, because we are missing classes here. Who gave them permission to go there?" And she said, "I thought you did," and I said, "No, because I'm working on those who are going to go with Lasaray, so I can't be everywhere!" Then I went up to Ophelia and I was just sort of quietly looking around to see if they were in her class, well, not fully quietly.

D. I heard she had a class going on and you just barged in.

B. I didn't know that they had a class, but I did indeed enter, and I kinda peeked around. But my lists are indeed getting smaller, it was just that there were three or four that had gone missing that I couldn't locate. Then I felt like, "What if they are in a setting or a classroom where they don't belong, and they might be either confused, or overly excited, which might be even worse, and then are taken off the program?"

D. So where did you find them

B. I did find them with Zachariah.

D. That's a good place to be.

B. Ah. Zachariah is hosting a big class about Earth, so they were there. They were there and they were curious, and I don't know how that happened, but Zachariah said that he had invited those that he felt, from my catalogue, that would do great with working with someone who simply will travel to Earth, that they will not necessarily explore other realities than just going to Earth and going to the fifth. So he had a really big class now.

D. He probably has a pretty good eye for that?

B. Indeed. I thought I had a good eye, but I tried to make a game out of it first. Like, you put someone on a chair and then let's say that there are thirty sparkles, but you only have like twenty-eight chairs. And then you walk around these, you put the chairs in a circle and you walk around with the music, and then when the music stops, you're supposed to sit down. And I thought maybe that's a good way of selecting; so if you snooze you lose, kind of thing, if you're not fast enough. But THEN Gergen came in and Ophelia came in and I said, "This is happy, this is a game!" And then she said, "Yes, but what happens with the ones that don't get a chair?" And then I had to rethink the whole thing and make different plays and different games. But now, indeed, I am grateful for that. I am working at the moment with twelve for the sixth dimension. So from the twenty I had, they have actually split up, so some are going with Ophelia and some are probably in this big hearing with Zachariah. Zachariah is a great teacher. You should see, it's VERY different than going to Ophelia's. No one says a peep at Zachariah's class!

D. Is that because he's intimidating?

B. Might be. They sit completely quiet and take notes. But at Ophelia's place, you are allowed to move around. Zachariah doesn't move around, he doesn't dance, there's no music there. Very different teaching. But at the moment, he was teaching them about the movement of the landmass. It's like a history class, so you are going back in time so they know how certain things looked before. A trip down memory lane a little bit, just to see what sort of individuals existed. But then, they're also gonna have not just documentaries that go in rewind, but documentaries going forward.

D. Oh, I'd like to hear about that.

B. Ahh. They're looking into environmental changes, so they know what sort of environment they will be in. And they can indeed make some requests. It's not a given that they will go there, but they can make requests if they want to be in a cooler climate, for instance, or if they want to be assisting someone who is gonna be more connected to water. So, Zachariah, he already has my background check, which I did a great job detailing their skills and qualifications and needs and personality traits. For instance, like me, I'm a traveler, and that would be on my resume. So I'm helping them to create a resume, so that they later on will be matched with someone who not only will enjoy their company, but also that my friend, my sparkle, will be in the best way suited to assist.

D. Yes, everyone said you did a really nice job with your catalogue.

B. Ah, umm. I put great effort into categorizing and to just make sure that it was a great match. But NOW we are entering the theater classes!

D. What does that involve?

B. That means that when you have been paired up, and now I'm talking about mine. Zachariah's, they're gonna be sitting there for a while, you know, he can TALK. I've been in his class and you don't leave, not even to go pee! (*He was laughing at his joke, since spirits don't have bodily functions.*) You learn, but it's very different, –like when I'm with Ophelia, in her classes, I can dance and I can move around and I can touch things.

D. That's what you like.

B. But it's good they have different training. BUT, the twelve that I'm working with, all are gonna be assigned someone from the sixth. My three is gonna be a little bit different, so three from these twelve will move into special training in the end, but they're all having similar training here.

D. So you have twelve from the sixth coming down, but three from our group?

B. They're gonna be paired up with more from the sixth, but they're not gonna be the same.

D. So the little Elahims?

B. Those are the three, the ones that came into your office, popped in their heads. I'm friends with them, so I'm talking with them a little bit, asking, "What criteria are you looking for in a tour guide?" And they say, "We would like someone like you." And I said, "Well, there is some that are similar, but we're all very different. But I have a full background check on all of them."

D. Like with Tom, because he is your student, are you giving him special priority, or are you trying to be impartial?

B. I'm trying to be neutral, but because of the assignment that's gonna come where these three, at least, will be working with communication. One will be working with communication underwater; I'm thinking Tom would be a great match to that one. But I'm also looking into personalities aspects as well. I want them to learn similar like you and I did. Like I learned from you, you learned from me, so I don't want there to just be a party trip. I want the Creator to later maybe give me a little gold star or a diploma, and to say, "Wow, look what a great match! Who were responsible for creating these excellent teams going down to Earth?" –and there I am. Then maybe I can be promoted or something.

D. The Creator probably passes out really nice medals.

B. Ah, so I'm aiming for somewhat of an acknowledgement. And I'm telling them both that I expect greatness. I expect changes within the consciousness, and also how to care for the planet, and those who are there (*incarnated*) to be great leaders. And then you come, and everyone comes in here and says, "You're bypassing evolution again. You don't know the mission, really." And I said, "But I can indeed set the intention! It's like creating—" and then you said, "It's not like you are creating a superman. There are still conditions on Earth that you can't bypass." And I said, "Why can't you come more like you are? These three in the future, maybe they can come more like they are? And that would be like James Bond, and they will just fix things." So that's what I'm hoping and that's what I'm training them for. But there's a lot of involvement here. I'm not by myself, I'm not allowed to just be by myself and plant a seed of things, because they have their own tutors on standby. But what is happening now is that I have twelve sparkles. There are those three, plus other students who have not decided yet, from the sixth, whether they should go or not. But all together we are twenty–four, twelve on each team, and we are doing role–plays. So, I'm creating like a drama here of certain things, and everyone is involved in this, it's not like just two in a game. I'm creating a whole village and a whole lifetime of events here for what can happen.

D. That's probably a lot of fun for them.

B. Ah. But I'm not creating it in a future setting, because I don't know at this point about that, so we're using, the model that I'm using now, and we're gonna use different time zones, but I'm beginning now in before BC. So I'm dressing someone out like to be like a goddess, and we're working on different things and we have things that happens. There are merchandises on ships coming in, and we are creating...it's hard to give you a picture really, but it's like a stage, a Hollywood stage, but it's 3D and I can change and shift.

D. So the people that you're showing, are you creating those?

B. No, they dress up. I'm making them dress up, because otherwise they'll just sit there passive and listen. I'm different than Zachariah, I want them to engage, I want them to not just observe. They're gonna be the goddess, they're gonna be the merchant person and the captain. I got help from Isaac. I said, "Now, I'm kinda redoing the Minoan times, so I'm creating different things. It's not gonna be the same big wave, it's gonna be a little bit of a smaller wave." BUT I'm creating, with the help of Isaac, different atmospheric or weather phenomena's. —I have so many plays that I can use!

D. You mentioned a big wave. Was that what wiped out the Minoans?

B. Ah, a wave came one time.

D. About what time was that?

B. There were several. There were two or three, –there was a big one about 1500 BC, but there was an even bigger thing that happened about 3000 BC in the same region. But I'm not doing the big one. And this one (*Seth*) comes in, because he saw this role play, and he was like, "Oh, I've been there, I can dress up and I can be the captain on the boat!" And I said, "We are full, actually, here. But you can observe." And then everyone got so excited when he came in. They were like, "Oh, did you go there?" then everyone moved towards him, leaving their positions. So then I was like, "You! Go back and stand there by the boat; and here is the house and there is where you should be with the dog." When he came in, he started to talk about that he was a great ship–man, and how he mastered those waves. And I said, "I don't know if that was the case, really. I saw the show and I'm not really sure." And he said, "You don't see all my shows, do you?" And I said, "Well, I kinda think I did. But, okay." (*Bob said he watched the recordings of all Seth's lives, like a TV series.*) So, he came in and everyone got so excited, but there's a big role play here and I'm dressing them up. I mean, I'm dressing yours up, because mine are gonna be helpers and they're not gonna know everything that's gonna happen. So when the wave came they did not know that. But, I told my trainees (*the second dimension spirits who will be guides*), "There was gonna happen somewhat of a disaster, and you are gonna have to guide your person into safety." So, I'm doing that. And now I have a new catalogue and I'm collecting a lot of data from prior visits. I have several that I'm gonna stage here, and then I asked you and those other three (*the older Elahims who are mentors to the younger three Elahim trainees*) that have those little sparkles, I asked, "What do you think that we should work on?" And I'm kind of fishing a little bit to see what's gonna come, but I asked, "What would you like me to prepare them for?" Huhuhhuh!

D. Did it work?

B. Not fully. But you all said something like, "They have to work with and learn how to navigate certain weather disasters, because there is going to be different occurrences ahead that might need a sensation of finding safety." And then there's gonna be regular plays where they have to learn how to bond, relationship–wise. They don't know that really, fully. And some of them are gonna go by themselves, not all of them, but the three are gonna go very much by themselves.

D. The three little Elahims?

B. Ah, the three from your place. But the other ones from your place (the sixth) that are not these three, they need to know a little bit about how you behave when you travel with others, because they might be paired up with someone over there in Zachariah's class. They're gonna be given family members from other places that are not from the Elahim, probably. (*The Elahims often go solo. The others from the sixth will sometimes be given companions from the fifth and seventh who are going to be incarnating on Earth.*) So I'm doing that, I'm creating different scenes and I'm dressing them up. I have a huge closet at my disposal, and I just dress them up in different things. And then I say, "One, two, three, ACTION!" And then comes the wave, and I'm monitoring and assisting the sparkles so they know what to do when they realize, "Where is my person?", because the person might have gone missing in the wave. Then I tell them, "What do we do then? We send out a signal and we try to locate the person, and then we assist." And then I go, "CUT! What did we learn from this experience?" And then everyone gathered around, and I said, "How did you feel when you were overwhelmed and surprised by this wave? And how did you experience that your person heard you and felt comforted by this experience, even though there was danger? How did you and your advice get through?" And then we begin new, and I say, "Okay, we will do it all again, but we will do it differently. Now, those who are the actors will have a sensation of being more confused and hopeless. And what do we do if our person becomes confused?" So I'm giving them different ways to handle problems, if you see what I'm saying?

D. I do. That's really interesting!

B. So next scene, I say, "One, two, three, ACTION!" and then those are gonna be acting confused and sort of wanting to surrender, "But how do we respond if it's not meant for your person to surrender, as your person is not supposed to go home—what do you do?" And we (*the instructors*) watch what happens, and then, "CUT!" And then we evaluate. And that's what we do. And we have different scenes coming up here, but this is one.

D. Do you think that is the way all spirit guides are trained?

B. I didn't get this training, I made this up. But I didn't get this training, I was just free–styling with you. I mean, I got a little bit of training. We talked about what you were gonna do, and so forth, and you said, "I'm going to look like that." I got training on the communication, but we didn't have role–play, like this.

D. You're giving them a lot better chance to succeed.

B. I'm adding my own style to the training program. I'm gonna share more, but today we had training about certain weather phenomena, after Isaac came in, helpful as he is. And over there in Zachariah's classroom, they're still sitting and they're taking notes. We're doing differently.

D. Your class is probably a lot of fun.

B. Ah. We have these, and I'm pretty sure that all twelve from each side are gonna go. And in these twelve, of course, are the three that will break out later on. But this is like an introduction class on what can happen on Earth, and they seem to enjoy it. And then we take turns, because you get familiar to being with one person, but at this point a person hasn't been given. So we rotate, not everyone understands each other because there are different signals between. So, at this point, since it's just the introduction class, we are rotating a little bit, just to make it a little bit more tricky on both sides. Not only to hear the advice and the guidance, but also to transmit and do remote teaching.

D. It must be more difficult on Earth, because once you are in a human body, then you have all sorts of strange behaviors and lessons?

B. Ah. So we're doing that so they can really get a sense of what can happen.

D. Did I listen to you pretty well when we first started working together on Earth?

B. Indeed, but you had a different receiver within. We had a little, almost like a radio within you, because we didn't want you to wander off, clumsy as you are. We didn't have this kind of training, since you were not a sparkle when I met you, so you were more ready to go and just informed me of what you were gonna do, and then I just learned as I went along.

D. Did Gergen or anyone come around to help?

B. In the beginning, I had Gergen as an assistant as well, when I felt like, phut, phut phut, (*blowing into his imaginary walkie-talkie*) "Come in, come in, come in—Lasaray, come in," and it didn't really always work, then Gergen assisted. So in the beginning a lot of times we were two. But these are different, they're not gonna have two.

D. Well, they'll have you.

B. Ah, indeed. But I'm not sure I'm invited to participate when it's high action.

D. Who better to call than you?

B. Well, we're gonna discuss it, of course, when everyone is home. But I'm not sure I'm gonna be able to engage like Gergen did with you. But like I said, they have different training than I had. We just started, you and me. You came in and were like, "I'm going to do this, and I'm going to look like that," and I said, "Oh, okay." And you said, "This is my color, and this is my tone." And then I said, "I don't really hear your tone, can we have like a little bit of a button installed to increase it a little bit?" And that is what we implemented in you, so that I can adjust your signals remotely if I can't hear you that well. That's different. Don't get confused. I'm not saying this to them because they will be like, "Oh, where is the button? Where is the button?" and there might not be a button. It's different. But with you, because you were all grown up, we did differently. So, that's what I wanted to say today. I'm gonna leave now, Ophelia says class is over, and I still have a couple of scenes to observe in this drama, and make sure that everyone is learning.

D. I'm glad you found your students, and it sounds like you have a really nice program going on.

B. Ah. This is my kinda style.

Training Camp is a Great Success (Feb 12, 2019)

D. (Bob moved in and he spent a few moments settling in.) Didn't feel like cleaning up today?

B. Nay. Nay, I don't know why I couldn't just...oh, Ia is here. Ah, Ia, oh, okay, okay. (*Ia asked to speak, and Bob let her come in.*)

Ia. Humm.

D. Hello, Ia.

Ia. Oh, good morning.

D. He just stepped aside?

Ia. Just a brief little comment about the progress of the sparkles and all the different classes that presently are on–going on the second dimension. There has been a huge success with Bob's training camp, and I thought that I would give the feedback, so that not everything comes from himself. He said he didn't want to blow his own horn, and asked that I give the feedback of how I perceive this process of training. It has been a huge joy and a huge success, and more are indeed applying to this specific way of moving forward in their own development.

D. His plays and acting?

Ia. Play acting, as well as the opportunity to join someone who will take a human form. There is a huge interest to participate on Earth, to move forward with certain environmental projects. Zachariah, indeed, had revealed that there will be more souls coming in who will be more inclined to improve the way that you perceive your host. There are many different lessons coming in at this particular time. However, the environment and atmosphere needs a huge spotlight. Meaning, that there is a great opportunity for us from the second to participate more closely. Depending on different lessons that have taken place within the Earth's evolution, the amount of participants or helpers from different realities shifts. At this time, we have been granted a future amount of souls to join, and more will be accommodated by someone from the second. So there.

D. So they enjoyed his classes?

Ia. Oh, yes, indeed they did. I participated as somewhat of ah—I didn't have an acting role, but Bob said I could absolutely be there as support, because we entered different teachings that Bob thought might be bothersome. So there were actually me and some other teachers present on the helpers' side. So, we are lining up for different events. He dresses them up very similar to how they will appear on Earth.

D. That's probably a lot of fun for everybody.

Ia. Oh, indeed it is.

D. Better than the musical chairs as a way of selection.

Ia. That was maybe not the best way, but it is the fact he was overwhelmed by all the interest that had arrived and felt bad about the selection. And he talked with Ophelia, and he talked with Zachariah, and he talked with me and Gergen, and I'm sure he talked even with you, how to solve this problem. And you all sort of took a step back, saying, "This is a great lesson for you, how to solve it." The opportunity to solve problems are always nearby, regardless if you are in spirit or if you are in a fish tank. So, this first solution of the chairs and the game, perhaps not the best way. He tried to avoid, indeed, the responsibility he had placed on himself. He said, "I did not do that." And I said, "Yes you did. And now you have to work with diplomacy, with care, and with compassion, and maybe the chairs don't represent all three."

D. He came up with a very good solution after that, so I'm very proud of him.

Ia. The acting, the role plays, are hugely appreciated. And more are actually going to participate, from both Zachariah's as well as Ophelia's classes. So, it's not just for those who will accompany those students from the sixth.

D. That's really good training.

Ia. He is proud of that indeed. So, I wanted to congratulate him on this amazing project and training program that he has now developed, and the gold star is indeed for him. So there.

D. You deserve one as well, my friend.

Ia. Oh, thank you so much. So there.

D. Thank you for coming.

Ia. Always a pleasure. Talk soon. (*Bob immediately stepped in.*)

D. Congratulations to you!

B. Congratulations to me! It's been a huge success, indeed, and I have now several acting classes ongoing. Meaning, I have to engage assistants, like Ia, to observe different things, because I cannot be fully, a hundred percent, attentive to all different plays. It's like having five movies in creation. I'm working here with different things, so we begin easy and then we gradually add more. We are actually, with your group, having them act in more like a drama. Sometimes the scenes will mirror like a comedy, and sometimes, from their perspective, appear like a thriller. But it's not intended to scare, it's intended to be realistic. But when we are moving into drama, then we are working on behaviors. Instead of dressing them in costumes, they are dressing up in different personalities. Some are dressing up as a narrow-minded executive. I had one of those. Then we have those who are overly emotional, who cry a lot. And we have all these and I staged this, because I wanted all these personalities to be together; so first I thought, "Should they be maybe in a family?" But it's highly unlikely that all these different characters will be in a big family, like cousins and so forth. So instead, indeed, I created a company. So I have a company now, it's aaaaaahhhhhh, like a tall building, several floors. So, we have those who are like secretaries; we have those who work with the copy machines and the coffee machines; and then we have different levels as we are moving up. The ones on the top, I gave them narrow-minded personalities, like with greed and to step over others. So I have all these different qualities, personalities. But also, in each level, there is a mole who is very different. So even in this CEO board meeting, I actually have those who are working for change, but in a realistic and friendly manner. So, for my helpers, I'm trying to make them see if they can detect that even if there is a group of those who are acting immature, or with a lack of empathy, but within that group there is also one who is different, the opposite. And they will have to try to, first of all, find the different vibrations from these, and then ask themselves, "How do I send information to, let's say, one who is narrow-minded? Do I channel my teachings through this one light-being, the mole, or to the one who doesn't listen? Or do I try to go directly to that soul?" So sometimes a spirit guide can actually not go directly to his person, but he navigates THROUGH another one who carries the qualities of the teachings and the messages that the spirit helper tries to relate.

D. Huh. I never thought about it like that, but it makes sense.

B. Oh, we do it all the time. If I can't be heard, then I might try to poke this one to tell you something. So, it's similar like that. And this is how we teach. I said (*he then delivered this upcoming speech as if he were lecturing in a classroom, quite loudly and pausing to emphasis words*), "When they move into different characters, you will see that some will be less receptive to your teachings, to your little walkie–talkie. They all have a walkie–talkie, but you can see some hold it in their hands, whereas others simply have it in their pockets. If it's in the pockets, then they will not hear you! Try instead to navigate and identify one who has their walkie–talkie available in their hands. You try to do that, you try to see, 'Is my person holding his walkie–talkie, the receiver, or is it in the pocket, or is it perhaps left at home?' If it is, then you have to find different ways to reach your person. First of all, identify if the walkie–talkie is present in his hand. If not, what do we do? And in general, it tends to be that those who have, from a human standpoint, a higher position, their walkie–talkie can be in a drawer. And those who are more connected to the little things, and it could be to simply operate the copy machine, or providing mail in this huge building I have created, their walkie–talkies can be more on. So you try to identify those, and sometimes you navigate and you choose to, let's say, use the mailman going up all these levels, and you use the mailman to deliver, not only the physical envelopes and the mail, but also an emotion or a sensation to get your person to stop and look around and to change, perhaps, what they are currently doing." (*He delivered all of this in his teaching voice.*)

D. I guess there's a lot of coordination then?

B. It is indeed. I'm staging and I'm writing all these plays, and then I'm dressing them up, –and it's not only from the sixth now, because it became such a huge interest and project, so we are now including people from the sixth and from the fifth. So it has become a very merry occasion, because they might not have met before. It's like connecting all spiritual realities in some way, in my office building. But I only work with the helpers that are from the second, but I approved that anyone could be participating in any of my shows.

D. Are the ones that are participating, have some of them been to Earth before and know the different personalities?

B. Some have been a few times.

D. Do they just watch screens and see how people act, and try to impersonate it?

B. No. It's put in them, it's similar like a suit. You transform your soul being and you become almost human. It's similar to taking on a dress or a suit or like pants and so forth, it's the same thing, you become the person that I assign you. And then you can, just to make the play more amusing, you can dress them up in costumes as well. But it's the same thing, this is like almost being incarnated, you take on human characteristics and human events, but you have not tapped into a body. It's like being 50/50.

D. That would certainly help them to understand a lot of things.

B. Indeed. And at the end of the day, they're really tired and they're happy to get out of the suit and to get out of certain personalities that they feel, "Whoa! That was tricky! I'm not sure I'm gonna take that one." And I said, "You probably will, if your gonna evolve not only as a soul, but also as a soul within a human, then you have to go through all these different characteristics and personalities."

D. They might get scared to come down here.

B. But they are encouraged to continue, because everyone wants to evolve. BUT I don't tell them that they will dissolve, I'm not saying that that is the end result, that we will all dissolve. We did have a class about fire, then there was a sensation of dissolving, and not everyone was happy and not everyone enjoyed the lesson learned. But I said, "It's important—you don't want this to happen, you want to have a mechanism within you that, instead of going into a fire, you're trying to escape and you're trying to find solutions. So, it's important lessons. But we're not gonna talk about dissolving.

King Henry VIII Rides Again (Apr 14, 2019)

The spirits are always thinking of ways to pass on messages that are useful to us, and these stories of how Bob teaches his students are filled with good advice. Bob captures the essence of all the trappings of vanity within a single portrait of himself, as he portrays a King of England going to war with France. We should understand the portrait is meant to represent all the symbols of grandeur we surround ourselves with—cars, homes, jewelry, clothes, titles, positions, and so forth. Bob summarized it for the modern human in one word—selfies, which is self-aggrandizing at a most simplistic level. Humans seem to have a need for others to view them as special, or better than others. In this story about a king, and the next one about Robin Hood and the Green Rebels, we are told, in no uncertain terms, how the spirit world and our guides view many of our commonly accepted behaviors.

B. Deet–da–da–deet–da–deeeet! I have a trumpet in my class.

D. It sounded like the announcement that the king is coming.

B. Hehehe. It is to summon the actors of this grand drama that I am staging at this time. So, I have my trumpet going deet–da–deet–da–deet–da–deet, "Everyone in their positions, and this grand drama will take place!" I did show myself to this one, you know, with my outfit.

D. It was very royal, I hear. (*Christine often hears short phrases or sees images flash into her mind that he projects to her. Since he is my guide, he is always around as we go about our day. He showed himself wearing royal clothing and a fine hat, and he also looked a little plump.*)

B. And because I also wanted to make an effect. I am not as chubby as this one saw me as. I actually put a little pillow underneath my outfit, so I would look even more pompous and grand.

D. Well fed.

B. Well fed, indeed. So I had that, and that's why this one said I had a belly. I had a belly indeed, it was a pillow underneath my outfit, and then I had my hat and my accessories, to make a full effect of what I'm trying to stage.

D. What was the play about?

B. The play is about group behaviors, and your person (*the incarnated spirit who is being guided*) might take on lives in groups where they are sent to create that change of consciousness. So here again I'm trying to mirror what took place in a conflict between England and France. I'm England. I sent these groups off on ships, and some didn't really want to go on ships because of the fact of the earlier play with the wave. (*His re–enactment of the huge wave that rolled over Crete around 1500 BCE.*) And I said, "It's not gonna be the same wave here." So there was a lot of discussion about that to make them even enter a boat. And this was the ones from the sixth, because now I'm operating only with those from the sixth. So, I have my three little Elahims, but I also have three that are not Elahims. They are from the same reality, so they are friends; they probably go way back in their classroom. But I have my six, that's what I have. And at this point, that's the only ones I'm allowed to train, fully.

D. So you have six from the sixth?

B. Six from the sixth. Easy to remember, don't you think?

D. Is Tom among your group?

B. He is, he is actually now been given one of the three Elahims, so now they are paired up. They are paired up, and at the moment, all six are operating within the same play, and they see the other ones. So they are incarnating in this play as brothers, or family members. But what I'm not saying at this particular point is that they will, especially these three Elahims, that they will not come down in a group together, they will be by themselves. But at this point in their learning program, we are all together. However, due to the fact of the grand wave that we encountered in my last play, some of them have been resistant to enter boats, because of the fact that some of them did not make it, in that play. So we have a little bit of encouragement going on. And then, one in the Elahim group here, he is very bold, I must say. He is like, "I'll go, I'll go."

D. This sounds familiar.

B. Ah. He says, "If Seth did it, I'm gonna go. I'm gonna go." It's a little one with a personality similar like this one (*Seth*). Oh, god, it's gonna be a repeat! We'll see about that, because Seth might not have had someone like me in the background during his training. Who knows what sort of training he had! I'm gonna ask, because I do not necessarily think it is beneficial, if everything just repeats with this Elahim sparkle here. But one said, "Oh, I'll take the ship. I'll go on the ship." And then there was one here, of the other three, that was like, "Okay, I'll think I'll try it. I'll also go." But the other four are gonna be the foot people. And they were like, "Maybe we can get a horse?" And I said, "Nope, you will be on foot." And they said, "We did see that we could get horses." I said, "Nope, not this time around. You're gonna be on foot and we're gonna march, and I'm gonna be there with my trumpet. I'm gonna have a horse." I didn't really have a horse, it's like a mule. It's bigger than a donkey. And they said, "Why do you get to sit on one?" and I said, "Don't just question the teacher all the time, we will never get anywhere in this play." Deet–da–da–deet! (*as he imitates a trumpet*) "Silence in the group!" And then we were gonna march through France, and the two on the boat, they were probably gonna come earlier because they had a vehicle. So that's also something I pointed out, "They were bold enough to take on the sea again. There's still gonna be struggles on the sea, but there's not gonna be that big wave, they're actually gonna experience—because there were like diseases going on, on the ships—so they will experience a different disaster." And I said, "You will feel differently, because you're gonna be on foot, but you're also gonna experience different things. BUT, the important lesson here, all different details aside, is whether to follow this madness coming behind you with a trumpet." That is the thing, because what is gonna happen here is similar, they're gonna feel like they are shushed forward by a force that will appear for the soul like a trumpet. And here, because of the fact that as soon as this leader, meaning me, saw that there were diversions and consciousness moving in a more spiritual direction, then the leaders were there, you know, with the trumpets. So, noise creates bad decisions! And if there are too many disturbances, –and it can be white noise, which is probably what's gonna happen in the future when there really is high action for them, but they are gonna be exposed to disturbances that the soul and the brain and the being will receive similar as a disturbance from my trumpet! So I asked, "How do you operate if there are disturbances?" So here I am, on my mule, and my pillow on my belly—it was a struggle to get up, I must say, but it's all for the effect—and I'm dressed in my finest.

D. You're grand!

B. I am indeed! I have all sorts of tingle–tangle on me. Huhuh, and my hat! It's not a crown, it's reddish with stones sewed into it...see? (*He turned to give a side view of his hat, which he forgot was invisible to me.*)

D. That's nice.

B. And I also said, "You will also encounter vanity, which also comes when you have power. What you will experience, in somewhat of a vanity expression from someone with a trumpet, whether it is a real trumpet or not, is that they will be extremely self–absorbed. So, I had my portrait (*which he pronounces as "poe–tret"*) with me as we were marching. I said, "This is vanity!" It's similar like all these selfies!

D. You carried your portrait with you?

B. I carried my portrait with me as we were marching to France. And I said, "This is similar to what you will see." I'm just trying to make the idea move forward. So, I had little helpers carrying my picture next to me, and here I am on my mule, with my trumpet and my spear, and we are moving forward. (*The students were marching in front, and he rode behind.*) And I said, "What do you think of this person behind you? Do you think this person behind you is knowledgeable about what is coming? Do you think this person behind you with the trumpet is looking out for your best interest, or not?" So we stopped the scene—those on the boats, they are still on their way—but to the foot people, I said, "STOP!" And there I sat on my mule with my portrait next to me, and I said, "What impression do you get? Do you think I am a person that will look after you, that has a mission that is gonna generate benefits for all...or just for me and my portrait?" And they were like, "We don't recognize you, you're never this pompous." And I said, "Nope. Exactly, but this is what you might encounter—someone who is trying to be a leader over you. Someone who is extremely self-absorbed, like I am, here with my portrait. Someone who is just thinking of themselves." This was the general idea of me bringing the portrait, it was to make the impression of being self-absorbed. So I said, "What would you do if you feel like this is not the right thing to do and you are surrounded by a group that might not even say out loud how they feel? But within you, if you four here think the same, what is the possibility that the rest of these five hundred (*referring to the king's army*) feel the same, but are not saying?" So I said, "Think for a while, and then we're gonna see if you have the same idea about me, the portrait, and the mission." And all of them said they didn't feel that I was looking after them, because I was just trumpeting behind them, pushing them on. And they said, "Why aren't you in the front? We don't know what's coming in the front, so why aren't you first, with your portrait?" And I said, "I get a better view back here." So that's an indication; if someone says, "I'm gonna be behind here, but you're gonna go out and you're gonna fulfill my mission for me. I'm getting a better objective view from my helicopter," as someone would say in this time, –but I said it from my mule. So I said, "There you go, that's a good indication something might be wrong. I'm not engaging, sitting here behind with my trumpet." So all these four had the same sensation of not being fully taken care of. The sparkles (*the second dimension companions who will be acting as guides to those from the sixth*), at this time in the scene, are on standby. Those out at sea, they have their sparkle with them just to make sure they understand what's going on, because they have to meet a different kind of dilemma on the boat. But, these four and the four sparkles here, they are on standby as we go through the details before we move forward. And I said, "Okay, so the four of you, without talking to each other, had the same sensation, the same idea. What do you think is the possibility that all five hundred feels the same?" And they said, "We think that if the four of us feel the same, at least seventy–five to eighty percent feels the same." And—this is good, because one said, "I think that there are some who don't engage, who feel that they are so let down by life that they don't care." And I said, "That is correct. So they don't CARE what they are being told to do. At this particular time there could be, in a different setting that you will encounter on Earth, that you will meet a larger percentage who don't care, that simply want to be moved around like cattle. That is the whole agenda, the whole idea with this exercise. SO, what do you do when you feel this?"

D. That's a good question. In a situation like that, if say they decided to not participate, the king would usually have soldiers that would kill the one trying to run away.

B. Indeed.

D. So is that the correct path?

B. What they always put in is, "Mutiny! Mutiny!" Now they don't say mutiny, they say "danger to the country", or "Traitors! Traitors! Traitors!" So again, that is a simple word, similar like a trumpet, that you put into the rest of the group consciousness, that if you don't do exactly as this leader with the portrait, or the selfie, is asking of you, then you are a traitor. But who are you a traitor to—this person with the portrait, or are you a traitor to the Creator? What is worse, one might wonder? A traitor to a soul of the Creator and your spirit friend who is eagerly standing there ready to help you, or to this person on the mule with the portrait? And then I said, "What would be the worst thing to do, to be a traitor to me, or to yourself?" Then they said, "I don't want to be a traitor to myself, because I'm 99 percent myself, I'm only 1 percent here." So I said, "It's worse to be traitor to yourself, than to the incarnation and to the game. The game might not be fully real, it might be staged, like this. You will encounter events that are staged, just to see if you listen to that inner being and your spirit friends and what is ringing true to you, or if you follow that teeny–tiny trumpet voice that says, 'Traitor! Traitor! Mutiny! Mutiny!'" So now four of them decided not to participate in this, and that is actually what I wanted to see. So I'm bringing the boats back, and the spirit friends are guiding these four out of this scenery into a parallel event. SO, that was my class!

D. That was an incredibly wise teaching you gave to them, and to me!

B. It is a fact that there is a huge percentage, a huge group, that don't care, and that is the same here. What if you come across those who don't care? That means the surface is passive, the inside is trying to make itself heard, connected with a spirit friend. But if you don't feel like you can contribute to the grander design and the greater benefit, then one can become passive. It's a struggle with the passive ones. It's easier to navigate for those who do wrong; you can either bring them home, or put a lot of effort into transforming that drive. Because at least they have drive, they just channel their drive in a wrong direction. But someone who lacks drive at all, who is just passive, who doesn't care, that's harder to ignite. That's a teaching here for the sparkles. Among these four who will incarnate, some are gonna be passive, and some are gonna be receptive and have a lot of drive, just in the wrong direction. And the sparkles said, "It's harder for me to be heard by the ones who don't care, than the one who is marching really fast, trying to make good, even if it's a bad good. It's easier to transform that one, than it is for the one who sleeps."

D. Clearly the ruling powers are aware of that, because they invest great effort into intimidating people to be submissive.

B. Traitors! Traitors! If you don't think like we do—Traitors! But the inside and the connection to the Creator and to the source, that is what you are supposed to align with. You know, everything else is just mish-mash, it's just staged to see if you fall under the spell of the trumpet, especially if someone comes as dynamic and impressive as me, here. I have all my finest on; I also have a vehicle, my mule; and I also have this grand portrait of me, so I must be someone highly skilled and highly advanced, and potentially similar like a god! So how someone portrays themselves is a little bit key whether they have followers or not. And the ones like me—the me I'm portraying here, the king—are actually in favor of that group, the passive ones, because they don't question, they're just gonna follow the trumpet. That one, the eager one, even if he's like, "Oh, I'm ready to go into the battle," but that one, I know, could easily be persuaded otherwise. So those who are like me, in this scene, want the followers to be passive, but the spirit realm wants you to be active. So there you have the dilemma. So that is what the scene was all about, and I think I made my point. When the other ones came back on the ship, I asked, "How did you guys do?" and they were like, "We didn't feel that well at sea." I said, "The teachings for you was to be locked in a position where you could not leave, like on the boat." These on foot could leave, they could run away, but those on the boat also encountered problems, but they were stuck. Different teachings.

D. On Earth today, the media and politicians attack people all the time for expressing the truth about the dangers presented by different religions, GMO's, pesticides, vaccinations, microwave radiation, and government corruption, which makes people passive and afraid to speak out.

B. That is again the thing, this pompous one in the background with trumpet is setting the rules of what goes, and what goes not. But the one inside, when worse comes to worst, you become passive and you don't care. But the other ones might feel like, "I know that everything streams from light, so it is a manufactured fear in many ways." So that's what I've been doing, a little bit. Ia comes by also and looks at this, and says, "What a grand scene you made here!" I said, "I did indeed!" And she said, "What do you have on?" and I said, "I have my finest on. I'm portraying King Henry. I'm Henry the Eighth."

D. You might want to incarnate, if you enjoy this so much.

B. If I decide to do that, if it's possible—Ophelia is not giving a green light on that—but if it is possible, then I would like to be somewhat of an explorer. I would like to go around in jungles and I would like to go to Egypt and I would like to expose all the secrets that I KNOW are hidden on different locations! (*Looks to the left.*) Ohh, Ophelia is not gonna allow that to happen.

D. They'll make you forget like they make the rest of us forget. You'll come in just as bad off as everyone else.

B. Ohh, oh, hmm. I will fall under the spell of forgetting and of karma. I am not really under the spell of karma, in that sense.

D. You'll be stuck on the wheel of incarnations.

B. And I might get one of those vehicles that don't respond. Nay! I'm not gonna get one of those bodies. I don't think I'm gonna get like the one with the trumpet here the first time around. Because if you're brand-new in the game, you're not supposed to dress up in all these shiny things, because you're not trained to be a leader over a grand group. That is also one of the things we see, that certain souls coming in are not fit for the part that they are playing, like being a leader like a king with a trumpet.

D. We have a bunch of those.

B. Indeed. We're trying to balance with more increasing light within in other fields, so it sort of balances. The thing is, even me here on my mule with my portrait, I will fall flat if this whole group of five hundred, instead of having their back to me and moving forward, if all these five hundred would turn and move towards me—I, mule, portrait, trumpet—would fall flat. And that is the whole teaching of this, that the group in large have the possibility, as they organize themselves from the source of their soul particle, they have the ability to remove ideas and fears, either individuals or ideas that flies around uncontrolled. You are more powerful than you think, this group. You just need to make those who are passive to become more alert and to be willing to engage. And that is a little bit of your work, to make people enticed by having someone on the inside (*their soul*), who is clearly here on a secret mission, to radiate bubbles of light into the grand design and into the grand web.

D. That's a brilliant teaching, my friend.

B. Ah. So, I've been doing that, and I'm still preparing a little bit for the Evolution Group.

D. Well, congratulations on your wonderful play, that was a good teaching, I like that. It's going to your Volume 1. How do you like it?

B. Ah, it's good. I like my book, I did well. Everyone did well, not just me, even though I might be the grand talker. Everyone participates, and some of what I say actually comes forward from Ia, or the council, or Gergen or Ole, you know, so it's everyone. So even though I'm the spokesperson in many ways, it's all a joined effort.

D. We'll make a note of that, so people understand that you're a spokesperson.

B. I am a spokesperson, from the second dimension.

D. You're a good one.

B. I take my job very seriously.

D. I'm sure they're proud of you.

B. I'm also a little bit proud.

D. You should be.

B. Even though being proud might be considered like pompous. But that is also something! Some say, "Don't say that you're proud of your achievements." "WHY NOT?", I say. Everyone is good at something. You should, as a human, even applaud yourself sometimes, saying, "I'm really grateful I did so well on this test." Or, "I really helped that person growing, I think I did really well." There's nothing wrong about saying you actually do well, because if you're only thinking, "Oh, I did that thing bad. I did not engage there. I didn't do well." But then the scale will be completely out of balance. In the spirit realm, we are allowed to say what we did well. And if it's wrong, someone will correct us, and we will stand corrected.

D. That's a better way to be. It's more honest.

B. Ah, well I'm gonna return to my play. I have a sequel scene! Part two in this grand drama where we're gonna go to France.

D. Alright, my friend, thank you for coming.

B. Thanks for joining me! DEET da da DEET! Bye bye.

Robin Hood Teaches the Rich (May 11, 2019)

We were going to end this book with Bob's portraying himself as a pompous King. But then he gave another wonderful talk about human behavior, so we are including his epic tale of Robin Hood and the Green Rebels as a little bonus for you. Bob has followed me through many medieval lives, so he is very well qualified to reenact the behaviors he observed. This talk was about class distinctions between the rich and poor, and how human behaviors are often contradictory to the will of the soul. The main lesson is about greed, which is a pervasive problem in society. It is not only money, but it is also about ideas, information, and control over others.

D. What have you been working on?

B. I'm working on teaching the students about charity. Because of the fact that once you come down here, after a while you have to be more of a charitable person. You have to be in a place where you give more than you receive. I'm mirroring that in a way that you take something and you give it to someone else, but you don't take credit for that invention or that experience.

You're passing something forward. To be in a position of charity, then you grow as a soul in the human, because you are in some way objectively observing the human experience, but the soul is independently working on a larger mission. It is to enlighten or even share light with others who lack it, who are dimmed on the inside. So, as I am mirroring this way of taking something from someone who might not appreciate it, or might not even be a charitable person, I have put on a new hat. (*He is portraying a human characteristic.*)

D. What kind of hat is that?

B. It's green. Moss green. And it has a little feather. (*He turns to the side so I can see.*) It's also a little bit green–brownish. I also have in the front a little red button, it has no purpose, the button, but it is to make it a little bit more nice.

D. So what sort of play are you putting on now?

B. I'm putting on a play where we have the six students, and we have the six sparkle guides. The six students from the sixth, three are gonna be acting like they have a lot of knowledge, but they don't share. The other three have been given a little bit more soul awareness. I have dimmed the three who are a little bit greedy, so they might not even understand that they are greedy. I have dimmed the soul awareness within them, and I have increased the soul energy and the enlightenment and understanding in the other three. The spirit guides know exactly what has happened, and they are here to in some way direct this play. How do you penetrate a group, a person, or an organization that proclaims to have the possession of a knowledge or an idea? Meaning those three that I have dimmed over there. They have all these treasures, but they are sitting on them, and they don't share. The other three here knows that there are treasures indeed to be found. But how do you penetrate stagnation when someone is not in the understanding and in the presence of having a willingness to share? SO, I am similar like Robin Hood.

D. (*Laughing*) Is that what the green hat represents?

B. Indeed! I am somewhat of a Robin Hood. So I said, "Let's just penetrate the fort, and we're gonna take these treasures and we're gonna share it with the public." So we are in disguise. Me, I'm with the three I have lit up a little bit, so we're gonna, you know, attack the fort and try to, –in a gentle way, when we come into the fort–, make them understand that their light is dimmed. Because they're not happy in the fort. They're just so eager to sit on an idea or a belief, and they are not in the mindset of sharing. They are in the mindset of being entitled. That's a word I do not like, –entitled. Who said that, that you are entitled? Who said that you know best? Who said that you have the right to sit with your pompous butt on the coffin of treasures? Who said that? YOU (*meaning the entitled*) said that. The Creator did not say that. The Creator said, "We have given you a treasure, we have given you access to ideas, even monetary treasures, but you are supposed to share it." If we dim your being, then you will have less access to the sensation of sharing; but sharing will actually increase your light.

D. That's a good lesson.

B. So, as we are now moving into this fort, I gave them the same hats, but I have a button on mine, so that's how they can see that I'm the leader in the group.

D. I thought you had a feather.

B. And a button. I have my feather in the back of my hat, but in the front, I have a red button. They don't have that. So I gave them the hats, because they like to dress up, they like to be in character, like they say. The other ones (*with the dimmed light*) are also dressed up. They're dressed up like Lords, Dukes, Sir, you know, they have titles. And that's also a thing, all these titles: Doctor, PhD, Sir, Duke, Duchess, Lord, there are all these titles, and you really don't need them, because it just separates you. It's like putting yourself on a pedestal a little bit. And it is, in some way, to say, "My portrait is much nicer than your portrait." But who said that one portrait is better than the other? So, there's nothing wrong with having a portrait, but how you paint your portrait and how you display it is key. So, up there (*in the fort*), we have Lords, Duchesses, Dukes, and so forth. And we here (*in the green hats*), we are equals—except me. I have a button, but it's just to show that I'm the teacher. So we went into the fort—I created this whole medieval drama with ropes hanging down, so they could climb up. I was already up, I just remotely put myself there; no need for all this physical mumbo–jumbo. But they were in character, so I said, "You can go up the rope here on the wall, and I'll meet you up there." And as we came in there, there was a huge medieval festivity going on. And these other three were dressed up to be like three Lords, coming from different territories, and they were comparing these treasures they had; and they were like, "Look at my shiny golden cup," and, "Look at my shiny golden sword." And they were sitting there comparing, not even noticing that we came in. And as we did, they were a little bit surprised, and they started to call for guards, but I made the guards go away, so there were no guards. I said to my group in the green hats, the rebels, I said, "It's sometimes good to be a rebel, because a rebel, in its core being, is good." Those who use the word rebels in a bad way, they have sort of hijacked the word, because rebels are actually indicating to in some way penetrate stagnation in a system, or in a belief, or in an organization of sorts. So, we are rebels—huhuh, Rebel Greens!

D. That's funny!

B. And here we come, and there are no guards, and they are sort of baffled. The spirit guides, they are present but they observe at this point, so they are also here. And I said, "This is where mediation comes in, when we start listening to each other. What do you think is the end result of you having all these shiny cups and swords? What do you think that will say about you, your progress, and your soul within?" And because they are dimmed, they don't really feel like they have a soul within them. So, first of all, you have to ignite the fact that there is an inner being within that might want the surface to do differently. So, what I do here, with some sort of magic, I increase the light gradually in those who are dimmed. And as I do so, there is a presence of a higher being in the room. The green rebels, at this point, are just sitting and radiating this to the other three, which are friends, –at home all are friends. So, I have instructed Rebel Greens to, in some way, radiate and ignite the light in those who are dimmed. That's why I have three and three, working in pair. So, they are sitting here, and the ones that are dimmed, they are somewhat confused at first, and they are in some way trying to fight this. And that's what you're gonna see; that even if someone tries to ignite a light within someone else, they might resist and even attack and fight it. But it's simply the human, the ego, primarily the mental, where fear strikes. Fear is not that often detected within the heart area, and NEVER detected in the center point. But what they are trying to do here, and this is what you do when you light someone up from the inside, you try to dim the mind. You try to move that (*mental*) light into hibernation, so that they simply experience everything from the heart and HOPEFULLY from the center point. I don't like the word "attack", so I will say "we address" the mental, because the mental is the one connected to fear and to greed, and to have all these sensations of being entitled to certain things. Once you are lit up in your center point and in your heart, then the mental will in some way surrender. So, what I'm having these rebel greens do, is to send out an energetic link to the center point and the heart, making that lit up more. That is when the mental, and the brain, will somewhat start to surrender. And as that happened, these three, in the presence of their friends here who tried to ignite them, and did so, they started to cry, and they were extremely shameful of their behaviors. And they said, "Why don't you take it all?" And Rebel Greens, they were like, "We're not here to take it. We're not interested in your golden cup and sword. We are interested in you. We don't care about what you have. We don't care that you might own more than we do. We care about you. We care about your wellbeing and the fact that you are dimmed. We are here to make sure that you feel the sensation of love and connection to your source and to others."

D. That's a really beautiful teaching.

B. Ah. So that was that play. And I was really proud of my greens. And after that we sat down and there was a lot of comforting and encouragement of the other ones. They said, "It was almost like I was asleep. I couldn't hear the inner calling. Why did I act like that? I don't recognize myself." And I said, "This is similar to what sometimes is gonna happen when you come down into a human body. You might not recognize, really, why you are acting, behaving and feeling in a specific way. You might start to think, "Why do I react like that? Why do I feel these things? Why am I drawn to negativity? Why can't I see the light in others? Why am I so afraid to surrender?" Surrender, here (*on Earth*), in many ways indicates defeat. Surrender in the spirit realm indicates growth and learning. So those who are in that phase of attacking, or putting themselves on top of the coffin (*their treasures or beliefs*), then they are in that mindset of fear. To them, surrender indicates somewhat of a death. Instead, it is actually a sensation of rebirth.

D. That's a very profound teaching, my friend.

B. Ah. So, we're teaching that, because you cannot always fully direct the scenes when you are in a human. You can't direct what others are doing. It's not like me here, I have full ability to direct this scene. But when you come into a human experience, you don't have that ability to be in charge of what others are doing. You can only be centered within your being, to not be afraid of surrendering, and to acknowledge that you might have been wrong. To be in that mindset of explaining, or acknowledging, that you have been wrong, –that is a way to surrender. And when you surrender, you don't lose; you win. You always win. It doesn't mean that if someone comes and tries to put their thoughts on you, that you should just say, "Oh, I surrender, I grow!" But if you are in a mindset that you are not feeling content, let's say, that's a sign that something is dimmed, and something is wrong. And then someone comes and tries to ignite you, or be friendly, and they might not say, "Oh, I'm here to ignite you, I have come to lift you up." But they are there in some way to assist you.

D. That's really good. I'd like to put that in our current book, but it's already pretty long.

B. Ah. I don't know. Ophelia says, "It's up to you." But I want my book to just go on and on. I don't mind. It's important, but, you know...

D. I can type that up and add it to the end?

B. Ah, that might be good. Maybe put it there. So anyway, that's what I've been doing. And Tom, Tom is with his person and they are really getting along. His person from the sixth has a GREAT sense of humor, but he's more calm than Seth Junior. Tom's person was actually in the rebel group.

D. What about Seth Junior?

B. Seth Junior was in the other group. Seth Junior was like, "Oh, look at all the shiny things! I'll take that part," instead of really understanding, because everyone got stuff for their play. They got all those coffins with gold and shiny things. But my group here, they only got the green hat. So, he said, "Oh, I'll go over there."

D. Oh, so you let them chose?

B. A little bit, but what I didn't say was that I was gonna dim the ones who got all the shiny stuff, and I'm gonna light up the inside in the ones who only chose the green hat. So that's even a trick for you humans, like if someone says, "Look what a big house, that's really nice and shiny. What a nice car! What a nice wife, look how nice and young and shiny." Huhuh, like that! But it might not be as nice and shiny when it comes to the end of it. Inside, even if they only had this little green hat on, they were the ones actually teaching. The spirit guides, at this point, didn't have that big of a part, more than when it came to the intervention, where they tried to assist their person, the ones who were dimmed. They were trying to make them open up. The ones who were sending light, in the green hats, the spirit guides were trying to make them direct it to the right spot, so they didn't direct it to the belly or the feet. They said, "Send your intention of wellbeing. And, first of all, try to send it to the heart, because the heart area is closer to the mental, so it will rub off on the mental, hopefully. And then they stood behind their person in the green hat, and they said, "I can see now the heart area is lit up a little bit, so try now to split your viewpoint and your energy, and send the same intention of wellbeing and care, but split it up and also include the center-point. The center-point will make the whole being understand more. The heart can simply feel like empathy and compassion and just sort of surrender a little bit, but the whole experience of understanding fully comes when the center point is lit up.

D. Very nice!

B. It's not so strange, really. But that was my play.

D. It's a wonderful play. This one said she saw you in a little green hat yesterday. So we were guessing some medieval character.

B. I wanted to be like somewhat of a rebel. And they said, "Who was like a good rebel in the past?" And I said, "Uhmm, I'm gonna be Robin Hood!" There were other rebels that did good, but it didn't end that well. This was about igniting compassion, and also that surrendering is not defeat. Surrendering, apologizing, and understanding that you might have done something wrong, it actually clears a lot of prior actions, and it clears many, many different knots in your Coat of Karma. Some people are really afraid to apologize and to surrender, but a lot of karma is actually related to that. To apologize and to be in the mindset of leaving an idea or a mindset behind—meaning surrendering (*will clear up certain karma*). Because it's not defeat, it is growth. So, that will be it. Ophelia said, "That will be it." (*He looked to the right for a moment, and then to the left, where she normally positions herself.*)

D. Did she move? Which side is she on?

B. She moves around a little bit. Huh huh. Zachariah also came in, and he was taking notes of this play, so he was there journaling this. He actually really saluted my ways of teaching. He said, "This is really interesting. Did you come up with this all by yourself?" And then he said, "I'm going to be on the sideline of this play and monitor the outcome."

D. That is a brilliant teaching.

B. But also, what do you do if you are by yourself and you don't have anyone, like in your workplace or in your family, or a friend? What if no one comes in and lifts you up? That's the next level (*of his training*), –how do you do this by yourself.

D. That's a bigger challenge.

B. Part two, coming later. How do you do this if someone doesn't come and help you? If the only assistance you might have comes from a spirit helper. Next time I'm doing the play, I'm gonna dim them all, and the spirit guides are gonna be the only link to that light.

D. That's a lot more difficult.

B. Much more difficult. So there are steps here. But that's coming up next. So I'm gonna go now, but la la la la la la la.

D. Thank you for coming. That was a really, really good teaching.

B. Zachariah said it was really good too, and he said, "Who told you to do this?" and I said, "I did it all by myself."

D. Maybe Zachariah will stop lecturing so much and move on to plays?

B. Maybe he comes to me, asking for advice; "What do think, Bob? What do you think we should do with this one?" And then I will say, "Let me see..." (*as he was stroking his chin in contemplation*) That would be a funny outcome or turn of event! Okay, so anyway, I go now, but see you soon.

As Volume 1 draws to a close, we should take a moment and think about the last few teachings Bob gave to us. It is all too easy to get caught up in the dramas of life on Earth, but within all our personal struggles, we should always keep in mind the words that Bob spoke to his students as he sat in all his finery on the back of a mule: "It's worse to be traitor to yourself, than to the incarnation and to the game. The game might not be fully real, it might be staged, like this. You will encounter events that are staged, just to see if you listen to that inner being and your spirit friends and what is ringing true to you."

About the Authors

Christine Kromm Henrie is a spiritual channel, a certified past life and between lives soul regression therapist, psychic, and karmic astrologer. She was born and lived in Stockholm, Sweden until 2014, when she moved to the USA and married David Henrie, with whom she now shares her work.

She had an intense spiritual awakening in 2009, during a past life regression, which became the starting point for her practice with the higher realms. She began to receive messages and visions from her spirit guides about her soul assignment to develop the skills needed for them to speak through her. Accepting their advice, she studied different modalities of mediumship, psychic development and astrology in Sweden and England during the next five years. This intensive training enabled her to perfect the link and the ability to maintain this altered state for extended periods of time.

After moving to the USA, her formal training continued in soul regression and hypnotherapy, becoming a licensed regression therapist. Christine has two offices in Stockholm, Sweden, where she offers private soul regressions and progressions, assisting people to recall lessons from past lifetimes and memories from their spiritual home. Astrological consultations are also available online.

A near–death experience at age eleven, and a transcendental epiphany in his early twenties, led David Henrie to lifelong inquiry into the nature of the spirit. His studies focused on NDE's, reincarnation, spiritualism, and the theological beliefs within Buddhism and other pre–Christian religions. After a lengthy career as a petroleum engineer and executive in the U.S., he now lives in Sweden with his wife, where his time is dedicated to writing and research. David conducts the trance sessions and converses with the spirits whom Christine channels. He transcribes the recorded dialogues and assembles their teachings into their co–authored books.

Christine and David also give lectures about the channeled material and the regression work, helping people to remember their soul mission and purpose. Their practice and publishing imprint is through **Access Soul Knowledge**, a Swedish company.

For further information, please visit:
www.AccesSoulKnowledge.com.

www.ingramcontent.com/pod-product-compliance
Lightning Source LLC
Chambersburg PA
CBHW020415010526
44118CB00010B/259